Know

By the same author:

Know the Bible

A daily guide to searching the scriptures

Michael Eaton

Hodder & Stoughton
LONDON SYDNEY AUCKLAND

British Library Cataloguing in Publication Data
A record for this book is available from the British Library

ISBN 0 340 78728 7

Typeset by Avon Dataset Ltd, Bidford-on-Avon, Warks

Printed and bound in Great Britain by
Clays Ltd, St Ives plc

Hodder & Stoughton
A Division of Hodder Headline Ltd
338 Euston Road
London NW1 3BH
www.madaboutbooks.com

'They . . . searched the Scriptures every day' (Acts 17:11)

CONTENTS

CONTENTS

PREFACE

What are the characteristics of this particular guide to 'searching the scriptures'? Three of them are specially important to me, and I hope to many Bible-readers.

First, it takes into account the work that has been done on the Scriptures in recent years. It is well known among biblical scholars that the old (rather destructive) 'historical-critical' approach to Scripture did not yield much that was of positive value for modern men and women. More recently in biblical studies there has come a much-to-be-welcomed emphasis on the last stage of the production of the biblical writings, and therefore on its message rather than its sources. This has also brought a much greater emphasis on the structure and flow of thought of each of the biblical books. Campbell Morgan of Westminster Chapel once wrote an 'Analysed Bible' in three volumes. He wrote before the rise of 'rhetorical criticism' yet he was quite a good 'analyser'. However, much more sophisticated work has been done on the structure of the Scriptures since Campbell Morgan's days and a little of it is reflected in the pages that are ahead of us. In the case of some books of the Bible (I think especially of Ecclesiastes, Song of Songs, Isaiah, Jeremiah, Ezekiel, Amos, Micah, Revelation) the book comes alive once the reader grasps the structure and flow of thought. Without a good analysis of the larger prophets and some of the poetical books, we tend to lose our way as we read. And think how confused we become reading Ezra 4:6–23 (with its two digressions and a leap from verse 24 to pick up from verse 5) if we lose sight of its structure.

Highly controversial passages like Romans 7:13–25 (not 14–25!) would become clearer if their structure were appreciated. The 'bag-of-bones' approach to Scripture has largely died (although it is not quite buried) and modern Bible-reading has become much more holistic, more sensitive to literary qualities. These are trends – taken into account within these pages – that are positive gain and will help us to get to the Bible's spiritual message.

Second, it makes an effort to point the way to the relevance of the Scriptures. It is not that I plunge into an exposition of the relevance of Scripture, for this book is a guide to the reader's own Bible-reading, not an exposition of Scripture (a task I have attempted elsewhere). There is today a need for a quest for relevance more than at any time in the last half-century. In recent years even the Bible-believing Christian has tended to turn away from Scripture. What has happened is that a vast gap has arisen between the scholars and practically minded Christians out and about in God's world. The scholars do not help the ordinary Christian very much and the ordinary Christian is not very scholarly! I try to bridge the gap – or at least suggest the bridge exists – between modern scholarship and the new 'movements of the Spirit' that are present in many modern lands. The 'charismatic movement' that has dominated the Christian world since the 1960s (whatever weaknesses might have to be confessed) has undoubtedly brought liveliness and lay-involvement in the churches. Yet it has tended to drift away from the Bible and therefore to become somewhat unstable. There is need of a back-to-the-Bible movement. For the Bible is still a highly relevant book. It is relevant to our minds; it will give us an orientation and the beginnings of an understanding of our world and of the human race. More than ever we need to know who we are! The Bible will be relevant to our heart and our feelings, for it is not a book of cold philosophy. It is a book of noise, worship, exuberance, and the mighty works of God. It is more like a football match than a cathedral service!

Most important of all, the Bible is relevant to what we do and the way we live and the stresses we face every day. There is a very great tendency nowadays for scholars and popular writers to leave each other alone. We need something that in a few sentences popularises the information provided by the multi-volume commentaries that continue to flow from the publishers, and nudges us in the direction of discovering for ourselves the amazing relevance of the Christian Scriptures. So the questions I put down here before my Bible-reading friends are ones that nudge us in the direction of a quest for relevance. The words 'modern' and 'today' appear often. What do I need to know? How do I need to respond? What do I need to do? These bottom-line questions are vital as we read the Christian Bible.

When you drive a car you never keep the steering wheel absolutely straight. You pull slightly to this side, slightly to that side. You drift to the left and pull back; you drift to the right and pull back. You make endless minor adjustments to stay on the road. In the 1960s an adjustment was needed to stay on the high road of true Christian faith. The churches needed greater liveliness, greater power. The sermons of the churches were becoming lectures and people were falling asleep or finding TV more interesting. Now after forty years or so, the Christians in the west are fewer, but thousands pour into the churches in other parts of the world. If we take a global viewpoint, we see new waves of liveliness among the Christians – plus plenty of eccentricities – but we need the Bible more than ever! Habits of daily Bible-reading have not disappeared but I think they have become confused. At one point we might have said, 'Our gospel must come to you not in word only, but also in power, and in the Holy Spirit' (to adapt the words of 1 Thessalonians 1:5). But now perhaps it is the other way around, and we need to say, 'Our gospel must come to you not only in the Holy Spirit but also in the Word of the Scriptures.'

Third, it considers the world at large and not simply the world of Christians. Admittedly the Bible is a Christian book. It begins by pointing to a Christ who is yet-to-come. It reaches the point where it describes the coming of Christ. Then it looks back on Christ and what he achieved in his death and resurrection. Yet it is not a book that is only for Christians! For a start we all need to consider the answers the Bible gives to the greatest questions that can ever be asked. These are days of 'comparative religion'. So be it. Let us do some comparing! Numerous religious fundamentalisms are arising in our world (and oppressive secularism is also fundamentalist in its own way!) with misguided violence and intolerance. We all need to listen to what they all have to say. Some things will have to be rejected. Some of our ideas will need to change (what is the point of reading the Bible – or anything! – if we are never to discover anything new?) We need some answers to life's big questions. Post-modernism seems to think there are no answers, only questions. But it is a philosophy that will prove unstable. If we do not give answers there will arise religious tyrannies that will step into the gap. We need a post-post-modernism – fast! According to the one textual tradition of the Bible, God said to his apostles, 'Go into all the world and preach the good news . . .' God says something similar to his Bible, not 'Go into all the church', but 'Go into all the world!' The Bible is a relevant book for the whole world but we shall never know it until we read it for ourselves.

INTRODUCTION

Why should we read the Bible? It is the sourcebook of the world's most popular 'religion', the Christian faith. No one understands the history of the world very much without grasping the influence that the Bible has had in it.

Why should we read the Bible? If for no other reason, it is magnificent literature. What power there is to be found in the great literatures of the world: the *Epic of Gilgamesh* (of Mesopotamian times), *The Iliad* (800 BC), Sophocles' *Antigone* (441 BC), the *Quran* (550 AD), the *Gulistan of Sa'di* (Persian poet, 1184–1291), *The Bloody Tenent Yet More Bloody* (Roger Williams' seventeenth-century defence of religious toleration), Jacob Ludwig Grimm's *Cinderella* (1812), Leo Tolstoy's *Anna Karenina* (1873–1876). We do not have to agree with everything we read to profit from it. We are missing something if we have not discovered that literature stretches the mind and gets us asking the right questions. But the Christian Bible stands high and magnificent among the literatures of the world. No one should miss it. What staggering power there is in the beautiful Hebrew poetry of Isaiah 40:1–31. Was ever there such a mighty intellect at work as the one we see in Paul's letter to the Romans, 9:1–11:36? Who can fail to be moved by the returning prodigal or the good Samaritan?

Of course there are yet greater reasons for reading the Bible. As well as its power to explain history and its magnificent literature, the Christian is conscious that the Bible claims to be an inspired revelation. 'Thus says

1

the Lord', say the prophets – hundreds of times. 'All Scripture is given by inspiration', says the apostle Paul. 'The scriptures cannot be broken', says Jesus. Endlessly Jesus told his disciples to read: 'Have you not read . . . ?' he would say to them. The world needs the Bible. Christians need the Bible. The following pages are intended to be a guide to help you read the Christian Scriptures for yourselves.

The Christian faith has a Person at its heart and centre – the Lord Jesus Christ. Yet our Lord Jesus Christ has also arranged that what he wants us to know about him and his gospel has been put in a book. Jesus was a great believer in reading the Old Testament Scriptures. 'Haven't you read . . . ?', he would say (Matthew 12:3, 5; see also 19:4; 21:16). 'Have you never read in the Scriptures . . . ?' (Matthew 21:42). 'Have you not read what God said to you?' (Matthew 22:31). When Jesus went into a synagogue in his home town, 'he stood up to read' aloud from the Scriptures (Luke 4:16).

Jesus' apostles had the same viewpoint. 'From childhood you have known the sacred writings', said the Christian apostle, Paul, to his younger colleague and friend. He hopes that Timothy will always remember the place that the Scriptures have had in his life. The biblical writers themselves ask us to ponder the written Word of God, in good slabs of time, with unhurried detailed study. The voices of those who wrote long ago need to become living voices in our hearts by the Holy Spirit. What the Spirit said then, ready for them to obey in their days, we pray that he will say to us now, ready for us to obey in our days.

The Scriptures were written for practical purposes. They were not intended simply to be literature to entertain us – although like many books written with a practical purpose the books of the Bible turn out to be great literature. The Scriptures are 'profitable for teaching, for rebuke, for correction, for training in righteousness . . .' 'Teaching' is the positive guidance and instruction we need to grow in righteousness and to serve God. 'Rebuke' is the reprimand we need when we have turned aside from truth and righteousness. 'Correction' is the reform and improvement that is needed when we make mistakes. 'Training' is being made ready to serve God and be useful in his kingdom. The Bible is not to be used as a manual for other kinds of subjects. It is not mainly a history book (although it has lots of history in it). It is not a scientific textbook (although a lot of what it says touches upon matters of interest to scientists). It is a training manual in the life of godliness. In dozens of different ways it coaches us, encourages us, rebukes us, trains us, lifts up our hearts in worship, humbles us in admission of our shame, releases us into joy and satisfaction. We are to read it in company with a Person. We take Jesus with us as we read the Scriptures. And we find that as we seek to serve God in a practical way with the Bible at our fingertips, Jesus himself guides us and shows himself to us in all of the Scriptures. We are taught, rebuked, corrected and trained, in the ways of God.

What kind of procedure do we follow in reading the Bible? Perhaps the answer is different for different people. Some will be called to give the Scriptures more intense study than others. But all of us need to be people of the Scriptures in one way or another.

We need a system to cover the whole Bible. There are plenty of good Bible-reading schemes around. Some take you through the Bible in a year (which means you read about a chapter of the New Testament and about three chapters of the Old Testament daily). The Robert Murray M'Cheyne reading scheme takes you through the Old Testament once and the New Testament twice in a year. You have to read about five chapters a day.

One good method is to read the Bible daily in a mixed-up order, and this is the method followed in this study-guide. My order is: Genesis, Matthew, Joshua, Romans, Isaiah, Proverbs, Hebrews, Psalms 1:1–18:50, Hosea, Psalms 19:1–28:9, Joel, Psalms 29:1–34:22, 1 Corinthians, Jeremiah, James, Psalms 35:1–40:17, Exodus, John's Gospel, Judges, Song of Songs, Psalms 41:1–49:20, Ruth, 1 Peter, Lamentations, Psalms 50:1–55:23, Ecclesiastes, 2 Peter, Psalms 56:1–64:10, 2 Corinthians, Esther, Daniel, Psalms 65:1–73:28, 1 John, Mark, Ezra, 2–3 John, Psalms 74:1–79:13, Leviticus, Jude, Psalms 80:1–88:18, 1 Samuel, Galatians, Nehemiah, Psalms 89:1–102:28, Ephesians, Psalms 103:1–109:31, Luke, Philippians, Ezekiel, 1 Chronicles, Colossians, Psalms 110:1–118:29, Numbers, 2 Samuel, 1 Thessalonians, Job, Amos, Psalm 119:1–176, 2 Thessalonians, Obadiah, 1 Kings, Jonah, Psalms 120:1–131:3, 1 Timothy, Micah, Nahum, Habakkuk, Psalms 132:1–139:24, Deuteronomy, Acts, 2 Kings, 2 Timothy, Zephaniah, Haggai, Titus, Zechariah, Malachi, Philemon, 2 Chronicles, Psalms 140:1–150:6, Revelation.

In this order (which creates maximal variety by making a grid of nine types of Scripture in 5 per cent sections and reading off the results horizontally in complete books of the Bible) the law (Genesis-to-Deuteronomy) is read at intervals but in order. The Gospels are read in the order Matthew-John-Mark-Luke. The history books Joshua-to-2 Kings (putting Ruth elsewhere as in the Hebrew Bible) is followed in sequence. Romans-Philemon is read in the order they are found in the New Testament. Isaiah-Ezekiel is read in sequence (putting Lamentations elsewhere as in the Hebrew Bible). Then there are what the Hebrew Bible calls 'the writings' (Psalms, Proverbs, Song of Songs, Ruth, Lamentations, Ecclesiastes, Esther, Daniel, Ezra, Nehemiah, 1 and 2 Chronicles, Job). There are the twelve minor prophets (followed in the biblical order), and the remainder of the New Testament (Hebrews-to-Revelation). All these are read in an order that gives regular changes of the type of book being read.

It is highly adaptable – in two ways. First, you do not have to follow the speed suggested. If you want to take more time to cover a day's reading you are free to do so and need not feel guilty about going slow. If you want to read the Bible in a year you read two readings daily. Feel free to speed up and slow down as you wish. Be disciplined but don't be imprisoned. Second, it will not be a crime if you wish to work through the different books of the Bible in a different order. However, it will be good if you cover the whole Bible eventually. When you have finished you start again! The mixed-up order gives you variety, but eventually you cover the whole Bible. You go at your own pace. The two-year lay-out is just a suggestion, something to aim at.

We need varied methods of study. Although not everyone is called to be as 'academic' as some are, yet all of us need to use some diligence in becoming equipped with the Scriptures.

1. We need to trace out the themes of the Bible.
2. We need to grasp hold of entire books of the Bible, seeing their sections and divisions. The various books of the Bible each have structure. They are not just a mass of unrelated verses. They have order and framework within them.
3. We need to ponder in detail whole paragraphs of the Bible.
4. We need to consider the characters of the Bible, the good men and the bad men, the good women and the bad women.
5. We need to study the words used in the Bible, especially key terms such as 'forgiveness', 'blood', 'righteousness', 'spirit', and so on. There are dangers in this (since a single word is never a total guide to a certain idea; and words have varied meanings) but it is still worthwhile to ponder words.
6. Then we need to meditate upon the application and relevance of what we have learned. Each time we go through the Bible we can come at it with a slightly different approach. There is room for immense variety.

More than anything else we need to know what it means to be taught by the Holy Spirit as we minutely ponder the words of God. In such a way we get to be 'competent, thoroughly equipped for every good work' in the kingdom of God.

We need good principles of interpretation. The basic rule is the Bible made sense in its original context. What God said to the Bible's original readers is the key to what he is saying to us. Any interpretation that would in no way have made sense to the original readers (for example, the idea that the book of Revelation has predictions of helicopters and modern armaments) is bound to be mistaken. The meaning will be the meaning that was natural at the time the book was written. Admittedly as Scripture is fulfilled we see more clearly what it was saying and we are able to fill out the details (for example, knowing the name of the predicted Saviour – Jesus) but the original readers must have been helped or challenged or rebuked by the writer's words written for his own day.

How much do we need to know to be able to start? How clever do we have to be to read the Bible? Obviously the more we know about the Bible the easier it will be to read it. But anyone may begin! The most brilliant scholar will never exhaust the Bible or fully understand it, yet the ordinary person may understand a lot. The deepest lessons of the Bible are not about brilliant science or mathematics; they are about spiritual lessons. The scholar may be quite blind to what it says while the humblest person may find the Bible speaks to them and becomes quite clear as God gives understanding. Actually many of the original Bible-readers were slaves or children! Note, for example, Ephesians 6:1, 5: 'Children . . . Slaves . . .' Paul expected them to be listening for themselves to his letter as it was read in the congregation. The Bible is not just for intellectuals.

The Bible will come alive if you pick up a little of the geography of Israel, but that will come as you proceed. It is worth remembering the three main provinces of Israel in the time of Jesus, Galilee in the north, Judah in the south, Samaria in-between. It will help us if we can have a picture in our heads of the Sea of Galilee in the north, the River Jordan running southwards from the Sea of Galilee into the Dead Sea. A glance at a map of Israel will tell us a few things that will help us use our imagination as we read the Bible.

It will be good to know the rough outline of the storyline of the Bible. It is easily acquired. Genesis 1:1–11:32 gives the background to the story of salvation, telling of the creation of the world, and the sin of the human race. Then Genesis 12:1–50:26 tells the story of Abraham's family who were given promises that a Saviour was to come to the world. Round about 1300 BC, Abraham's family had become a little nation living within Egypt. God saved them 'by the blood of a lamb' (Exodus 1:1–15:27) and gave them his law (as told in Exodus 16:1-to-the-end-of-Deuteronomy). Forty years later Joshua led Israel into Canaan and the land was allocated to the tribes of Israel (the book of Joshua). After Joshua's death the land fell into chaos (Judges, Ruth) but eventually Israel was given kings to rule the land. First there was Saul, then David (1–2 Samuel). When Solomon took over the kingship, there was spiritual decline at the end of his reign. When he died the land split into two and from that point on there were two kingdoms of Israel, the north (which kept the name Israel) and the south (commonly called Judah). The story is told in 1–2 Kings. The northern kingdom had a succession of dynasties, fell into deep idolatry and was destroyed by the Assyrians in 721 BC. The southern kingdom continued but went the same way as the northern kingdom until it too was exiled, this time to Babylon in a series of deportations between 604 and 586 BC. The books of 1 and 2 Chronicles contain another retelling of the story concentrating on the southern kingdom.

The exile lasted about seventy years. Beginning in the 530s BC, the Jews in Babylon were allowed to come back to Judea. When the Babylonian empire fell and the Persian empire took over, the Jews were allowed to return to Judea if they wished. Ezra-Nehemiah tells the story of their return. Esther tells of an incident among the Jews who did not return.

In the midst of all this history there were three other aspects of Israel's life that shows itself in the biblical books: prophecy, wisdom and psalmody. The first prophet (spokesman for God) was Moses, but from Moses onwards there was a whole line of prophets until about 400 BC. Eventually the preaching of some of the prophets was written and found its way into our Bibles. Obadiah and Joel are difficult to give a date to. The book of Jonah focusses on the prophet himself rather than his preaching. The remaining twelve books of prophetic writing are easier to date. Amos had a brief ministry, probably around 760 BC. Hosea's ministry was probably from about 760–723 BC. Micah was next. He worked during the reigns of Jotham (742–735 BC), Ahaz (735–715 BC) and Hezekiah (715–696 BC). Isaiah, who was called to be a prophet 'in the year that King Uzziah died' (about 740 BC), was Micah's contemporary.

Habakkuk perhaps lived in the days of Manasseh. Zephaniah lived during the days of Josiah, one of the last kings of Judah. At the end of the seventh century BC, Nahum wrote of the fall of Nineveh. Just before the exile, Jeremiah warned of its imminence. In Babylon Ezekiel brought the word of God to the exiles. After the return from exile, Haggai and Zechariah encouraged the people of God around the year 520 BC. A century later Malachi was the last prophet whose writings appear in the Old Testament.

Another aspect of Israel's life was its worship and its lamentation. The books of Psalms and Lamentations are representative of these songs of the people of Israel.

Then there was the wisdom literature. Proverbs was a collection that began in the days of Solomon but received additions in later years. Job considered the experience of suffering. Ecclesiastes considered the apparent futility of life. Song of Songs is a collection of love poetry; arguably it is parabolic of one's relationship to God.

Daniel deserves special mention, since more than any other book of the Old Testament it reaches forward into the times of the New Testament. It predicts the rise of pagan kingdoms, mentioning Babylon, Persia and Greece by name and predicting yet one more empire, which turned out to be that of the Romans. It would be in the time of the fourth empire – said Daniel – that salvation would come to Israel.

After 400 BC there were no biblical writings for four centuries. Then Jesus came and a decade or so after his death and resurrection the leaders of the people of God once again took to writing. Four books record the ministry of Jesus from different perspectives (Matthew, Mark, Luke, John). One tells the story of about thirty years of church history (Acts). Twenty-one letters (Romans-to-Jude) were written to various Christian communities, giving them advice about the different crises they were experiencing. The last book of the Bible, the book of Revelation, is a dramatic, highly symbolic glance into the future history of the Church beginning from the days of John the apostle and ending with visions of final glory as the 'new Jerusalem' comes down upon planet Earth.

We need a flexible procedure to follow. It is good to adopt a rough-and-ready routine. We should find a time during the day when we are able to give ourselves to Bible-reading and prayer. Have a notebook ready. You might keep a 'spiritual journal', or (if you are building Bible-study notes to last a lifetime) you might use loose-leaf paper, but in this case take care always to use the same size paper for different types of Bible-study and note-taking.

It is as important to pray as to read the Bible. We are not purely intellectuals, although we use our minds as much as we can. But we do not only listen to God; we speak to God. Confess your sins. Ask for help. Give thanks. Adore God. Sing songs of praise. Tune your heart to be ready to hear God speak to you.

Then give yourself to studying the Scriptures. It is best to make sure you have at least half an hour of free time. Get used to picking up where you left off. The secret of Bible-study is asking the right questions. What is the teaching here? What example does this give me to follow? What mistakes must I avoid? How does this make me feel? Can I imagine what this was like for those who first read this part of the Bible? Does the Old Testament law form a contrast with the gospel at this point?

The order that we shall follow in this study-guide is the order I have suggested above. It divides into two sets of 365. If you work through one a day you will finish the course of Bible-study in two years.

YEAR ONE		YEAR TWO	
Readings 1–20	Genesis	Readings 1–4	Ezra
Readings 21–68	Matthew	Reading 5	2–3 John
Readings 69–76	Joshua	Readings 6–8	Psalms 74:1–79:13
Readings 77–96	Romans	Readings 9–22	Leviticus
Readings 97–123	Isaiah	Reading 23	Jude
Readings 124–135	Proverbs	Readings 24–27	Psalms 80:1–88:18
Readings 136–150	Hebrews	Readings 28–39	1 Samuel
Readings 151–156	Psalms 1:1–18:50	Readings 40–45	Galatians
Readings 157–160	Hosea	Readings 46–50	Nehemiah
Readings 161–164	Psalms 19:1–28:9	Readings 51–56	Psalms 89:1–102:28
Reading 165	Joel	Readings 57–63	Ephesians
Readings 166–167	Psalms 29:1–34:22	Readings 64–66	Psalms 103:1–109:31
Readings 168–188	1 Corinthians	Readings 67–116	Luke
Readings 189–209	Jeremiah	Readings 117–120	Philippians
Readings 210–214	James	Readings 121–140	Ezekiel
Readings 215–216	Psalms 35:1–40:17	Readings 141–150	1 Chronicles
Readings 217–233	Exodus	Readings 151–154	Colossians
Readings 234–269	John	Readings 155–158	Psalms 110:1–118:29
Readings 270–277	Judges	Readings 159–172	Numbers
Readings 278–280	Song of Songs	Readings 173–182	2 Samuel
Readings 281–283	Psalms 41:1–49:20	Readings 183–187	1 Thessalonians
Reading 284	Ruth	Readings 188–204	Job
Readings 285–289	1 Peter	Readings 205–207	Amos
Readings 290–291	Lamentations	Readings 208–209	Psalm 119:1–176
Readings 292–293	Psalms 50:1–55:23	Readings 210–212	2 Thessalonians
Readings 294–297	Ecclesiastes	Reading 213	Obadiah
Readings 298–300	2 Peter	Readings 214–223	1 Kings
Readings 301–303	Psalms 56:1–64:10	Reading 224	Jonah
Readings 304–317	2 Corinthians	Readings 225–227	Psalms 120:1–131:3
Readings 318–321	Esther	Readings 228–233	1 Timothy
Readings 322–326	Daniel	Readings 234–236	Micah
Readings 327–329	Psalms 65:1–73:28	Readings 237–238	Nahum, Habakkuk
Readings 330–334	1 John	Readings 239–241	Psalms 132:1–139:24
Readings 335–365	Mark	Readings 242–254	Deuteronomy
		Readings 255–299	Acts
		Readings 300–309	2 Kings
		Readings 310–313	2 Timothy
		Reading 314	Zephaniah

YEAR ONE

Genesis

Within the Bible, Genesis-to-Deuteronomy should be considered as a whole. Its central content (Exodus-to-Numbers) is the story of Israel's redemption. It has an introduction (Genesis), setting the scene of Israel in the story of the creation and in the Mesopotamian world. And it has a conclusion, the preaching of Moses found in Deuteronomy.

These five books go back to Moses, the first person in the Bible who is said to have written anything. He started the habit (judging by Exodus 17:14) of keeping records for the sake of posterity. Most of Genesis-to-Deuteronomy must go back to him. But this does not mean he wrote its final form. Obviously he did not write the account of his death in Deuteronomy 32:1–52, and there are hints (such as Genesis 36:31) suggesting our books were edited in the days after kingship arose, perhaps in the time of Solomon. There is nothing in these books that demand a date later than Solomon's time. Its contents may be set out as follows:

- The setting of the plan of salvation (1:1–11:32)
- A pioneer of faith: Abraham (12:1–25:18)
- A pioneer of faith: Isaac (25:19–26:35)
- A pioneer of faith: Jacob (27:1–36:43)
- A pioneer of faith: Joseph (37:1–50:26)

Recommended reading: D. Kidner, *Genesis* (Tyndale Commentary, IVP, 1964); M. A. Eaton, *Genesis 1–11*; *Genesis 12–23*; *Genesis 24–50* (Preaching Through the Bible; Sovereign World, 1997, 1999, 1999).

In the following sections the squares □ can be used and ticked ✓ each time you read through the Bible.

□□□ Reading 1 (Genesis 1:1–3:6)

Genesis 1:1–2:3 tells the story of creation. God is pictured as a workman working for six days and having a seventh day in which to rest. Genesis 2:4–25 retells the story of Genesis 1:26–31 in fuller detail. Genesis 3:1–6 then tells the story of how the human race fell into sin.

1. What picture of God emerges as we read Genesis 1:1–2:3? How would life be different if the world came from a different kind of God?
2. 'Eden' seems to be an old word meaning 'Delightfulness'. What can we discover of God's wishes for the human race from Genesis 2:4–24?
3. Genesis 3:1–6 is a classic description of temptation and fall. What are Satan's methods? What were Eve's mistakes? Do you find the same principles at work today? In yourself? In society?

□□□ Reading 2 (Genesis 3:7–6:8)

1. What are the consequences of sin? Personally (3:7–11)? In marriage and companionship (3:12)? In relation to the earth (3:16–19)? In relationship with God (3:21–24)? In society (4:1–5:32)? In relation to Satan (3:13–15; 6:1–8)?
2. If Genesis 3:15 predicts the reversal of all that Satan did, what picture of salvation may be seen here?

Note Genesis 6:1–8. (i) Some have thought the 'sons of God' means the line of Seth. (ii) Others think of some kind of upper class, perhaps kings, who took large numbers of wives. (iii) A third view is that 'sons of God' refers to angels (as in Job 1:6 and elsewhere). In 1 Peter 3:19–20, 2 Peter 2:4 and Jude 6 it is apparently interpreted as referring to angels. We are dealing with the pre-flood world. Matthew 22:30 is true now, but may not have been true then. The main point is that sin in gigantic proportions came into the Mesopotamian world, leading to the end of the world for Mesopotamia.

□□□ Reading 3 (Genesis 6:9–9:17)

1. Consider Noah. What kind of person is used by God as a saviour of others?
2. Consider God's judgment. What brought it? What warning was given? Was there any escape?
3. Consider God's grace in the midst of judgment. In what way is the ark of Noah like the cross of Christ?

4. Noah's ark of salvation led to a covenant with God. In what ways is 'the new covenant' with God via Jesus illuminated by Noah's covenant here?

Note 'Covenant'. A covenant is a promise that has been made more secure by having an oath added to it. There are three kinds: covenants of obligation to a senior, covenants of generosity towards a junior, and two-way covenants between equals. In the 'covenant of generosity' here (i) a covenant has a promise; (ii) it has an oath added to the promise; (iii) a covenant has a beneficiary, someone who is receiving the blessing of the oath; (iv) a covenant of generosity is unconditional, after it has been given, although (v) it might itself have been given as a reward; (vi) a covenant may take time to take place because it is not settled until the oath is given; (vii) a covenant may have attached to it a sign or symbol of some kind; (viii) a covenant involved the shedding of blood in sacrifice.

☐☐☐ **Reading 4 (Genesis 9:18–11:32)**
Genesis 10:1–32 explains the presence of various nations in the ancient Near East, all of whom descended from Noah. There were plenty of people in other parts of the world. When the ages of the people in 11:10–26 are better understood I suspect it will turn out that more than one factor will be involved in their explanation. For the moment take the ages as they stand and do not worry too much about their strangeness.

1. What were Noah's good points and bad points? Fortunately he 'found grace'. What does this mean?

2. In what ways did God change the world after the flood? In what ways did the world repeat its old mistakes? How does the modern world echo the paganism of the ancient world?

3. Acts 2 is the reversal of Genesis 11:1–9. What hinders international unity? What hope is there for worldwide unity among nations? None at all? Some hope? But if so, how?

Note In the second Messianic prophecy of the Bible (after 3:15), Canaan is cursed. This has been misused to justify racial discrimination but the writer is talking about Canaanites, not everyone from the line of Ham (and in any case the nations of Genesis 10:1–32 are nearby). Out of Shem's line will come great blessing (9:26). The prediction is Messianic. In due course Jesus would be a Jew, a Semite, a descendant in the line of Shem. Japheth is to have extended territory. His line will not lead to the Messiah but there is blessing in store for him. The language is picturesque. One person is pictured as taking shelter with another. In the course of history an abundance of gentiles would come to salvation through a Jewish Saviour.

□□□ Reading 5 (Genesis 12:1–15:1)

Abraham is called to start a new nation and to be the forefather of a 'seed'. The great promises of salvation are found in 12:1–9. Then the story tells of Abraham's various conflicts. He (mistakenly?) goes to Egypt (12:10–20). He has conflicts with Lot (13:1–18). He has battles with local superpowers (14:1–12) but rescues Lot (14:13–16). Melchizedek comes to help him and pray for him (14:17–24) and soon the marvellous promise of 15:1 is given to Abraham.

1. Are the promises to Abraham still continuing today? If so, how?
2. Compare Abraham and Lot. After the decisions of these chapters, what results came in the life of Abraham? What results came in the life of Lot? So what conclusions do we draw for ourselves?
3. What are the parallels between Melchizedek and Jesus?

Note The word 'seed' (12:7 and often) is deliberately ambiguous. It can be taken spiritually and physically, singularly and plurally. The 'seed' can be (i) Isaac, (ii) Israel, (iii) Jesus, and (iv) all believers in God's promise. All four themes are tangled up together.

□□□ Reading 6 (Genesis 15:2–16:16)

Salvation starts when God gives us a gift of righteousness. Righteousness is 'reckoned'. It is not our character either before we are saved or after we are saved, that enables us to stand before God.

1. Can God give anyone promises? In what ways does God 'renew his promises' today?
2. What does 'justification only by faith in God's promises' (15:6) mean to us practically? How does it affect and relate to (i) self-righteousness, (ii) assurance of salvation, (iii) godliness of character, (iv) inheriting the promises of God?
3. What encouragements do we receive from the fact that God is in covenant with us through Jesus?
4. Genesis 16:1–16 tells the story of how Abraham 'ran ahead of God' in trying to get the seed born. How may we make the same mistake? (Note Paul's use of the story in Galatians 4:21–5:1.)

Note Genesis 15:17 is apparently God's way of saying, 'May I be cut to pieces like these animals if I do not keep my promise.'

☐☐☐ **Reading 7 (Genesis 17:1–19:38)**

God's covenants need to be 'established' – turned into a certainty. At present promises have been given but not 'obtained' (see Hebrews 11:33). God gives Abraham an unprecedented call to godliness (17:1) and motivates him by fuller revelations of what is in God's mind for him (17:2–8). Circumcision is added as one of God's demands.

1. Can you think of ten things symbolised by circumcision? Two of them are: circumcision is (i) the sign of God's moving in grace and (ii) a test of obedience. What else?
2. Most of us have been in a situation where everybody else seems to be being blessed by God but not us! How does the story of Sarai help us here?
3. Genesis 18:16–33 is the first lengthy prayer of the Bible. What can we learn from it about 'progressive praying'?
4. In Genesis 19:1–38 the annihilation of Sodom and Gomorrah is another example of the outpoured wrath of God. What do we learn from it about homosexuality (does the Bible need cultural adjustment here or not?)? What do we learn from the calamities falling on Lot? And from his rescue (note 2 Peter 2:9)?

☐☐☐ **Reading 8 (Genesis 20:1–22:24)**

1. How long may we go on making the same mistakes? What weaknesses do we find in Abraham here? What effects does it have: (i) on God's graciousness towards us? (ii) on the security of God's purposes? (iii) on our witness to others?
2. Abraham prayed for the wives of others, fairly soon after his own wife became pregnant, after decades of waiting. What do we learn from this?
3. 'Isaac' means 'he laughs'. Everything connected with Isaac reminds us of the grace of God. Events connected with Ishmael remind us of self-effort and 'the flesh'. Can you find the details in Genesis 21:1–34?
4. In Genesis 22:1–24 the covenant which began in Genesis 15:1–21 is at last fulfilled. What leads to God's giving his oath at this time?
5. Consider Genesis 22:20–24 in the light of Hebrews 11:15.

Note The ages of Abraham and Sarah are apparently spread out to about twice their natural length; Sarah is the equivalent of a 45-year-old mature woman. The best way to understand 'oath' is to ask the question, 'Can God change his mind?' Certainly (using a very human way of thinking) we are allowed to think in this way. After we have come to salvation God gives us promises but they gained by faith and lost by unbelief. God gives us warnings;

they are fulfilled by sin and averted by repentance. But when God 'swears in his anger' or 'swears in his mercy', he 'makes up his mind'. After that, the situation cannot be changed. The judgment falls and nothing can stop it. Or the blessing is gained and nothing can lose it. Why is it that the high priesthood of the Levites ceased but the high priesthood of Jesus does not cease (see Hebrews 7:20–24)?

□□□ Reading 9 (Genesis 23:1–25:18)

Now Abraham has to face the challenge of inheritance beyond the grave. God had given Abraham promises about a land, but he has not received any land. He is just about to die.

1. If the ultimate blessing for the believer is after this life, in 'the world to come', how does this affect the way we live day-by-day? Consider Hebrews 11:8.
2. Is Genesis 24:1–67 a model of God's guidance? What aspects of the chapter are purely cultural? What aspects of (i) the invitation Rebekah receives and (ii) its urgency, illuminate the life of faith?
3. Genesis 25:1–18 is full of the side effects of God's grace. When God blesses, there come other blessings besides the central ones. Can you find some 'side effects of grace' in this section?

□□□ Reading 10 (Genesis 25:19–27:29)

A new section, starting in Genesis 25:19, focusses on Jacob. Although it is the 'account of Isaac' (25:19), the word refers to the 'offspring' of someone or something, and so it deals more with Jacob and Esau than with Isaac himself. Jacob was a man with a difficult personality. His name means 'someone who grasps hold of the heel' or (to put it simply) 'Grabber'.

1. What are Jacob's natural weaknesses? What encouragements are there in this chapter for anyone (most of us!) with a difficult personality?
2. 'In Isaac shall your seed be called into being', said God. But for Isaac there were many conflicts and testings. Can you list them from Genesis 26:1–35? However, there are also the remedies of faith. What are they?
3. A unfair, pleasure-seeking father, a deceitful mother, a carnal-minded Esau and a cheating, conniving, crafty Jacob! If God has promised blessing, how does it work out in the life of weak and sometimes wicked people?

☐☐☐ Reading 11 (Genesis 27:30–29:35)

1. Consider the severity and mercy of God – in Esau and Jacob. How often does it happen that we want blessings from God but lose something because we want them too late? How much did Esau lose?

2. Consider the way God showed mercy to Jacob. On what kind of occasion? With what kind of preparation? What kind of response?

3. In Genesis 29:1–35, the deceiver gets deceived. We see the tough training programme that God had for Jacob. Outline the ways in which both God's mercy and God's discipline are to be found in Jacob's life at this point.

☐☐☐ Reading 12 (Genesis 30:1–31:55)

1. What are the sorrows Jacob's wives experience and the pressures Jacob experiences in Genesis 30:1–24? Is God's grace sufficient really? May we do the best we can in painful circumstances? Given the culture of Jacob's day, what do you think of his four wives?

2. In Genesis 30:25–31:54 Jacob finally overcomes Laban. What are the ingredients of his success? What changes appear in Jacob's life at this point?

Note Jacob's procedure is not following anything scientific. There is no known technique for producing patchy animals by controlling what they are allowed to see. It seems Jacob was representing in symbolic action his prayer concerning what he wanted to happen. And God answered his prayer miraculously.

☐☐☐ Reading 13 (Genesis 32:1–33:20)

Jacob makes preparations for meeting Esau (31:55–32:32). He is scared! But when they meet all is well (33:1–20).

1. Jacob is being his old manipulative self here. Was he wise or misguided in making these complicated plans?

2. Jacob prays because he is in a desperate situation. Esau's last words to him years before were threatening. What are the ingredients in his prayer?

3. A man-like angelic being, representing God, appears to 'fight' with Jacob. He does not use more force than he has to – until the end. When Jacob will not yield, the angel puts forth more energy and injures Jacob. For the rest of his life he must live as a cripple with greater dependence on God. His people must live that way too (which is the point of Genesis 32:32). It is a dramatic representation of the greatest spiritual struggle of Jacob's life. What are the spiritual lessons for the Christian today?

□□□ Reading 14 (Genesis 34:1–35:29)

These chapters tell how Dinah was abused and avenged (34:1–31) and relate the last events of this section of the story (35:1–29).

1. Outrage against Canaanite attempts to swallow up Israel by marriage is understandable, but what are we to think of Simeon and Levi's revenge? What did it lead to (see Genesis 49:5–7)? And what are the modern equivalents of outrageous behaviour prompting unnecessary revenge?
2. Jacob returns to Bethel where his pilgrimage had started. Genesis 35:1–29 records various deaths (35:8, 16–18, 19–20, 28–29). It is clearly another turning-point in Jacob's life. How do we face the future when so many aspects of life are coming to an end? What are Jacob's commitments? How does he fulfil them? What encouragements does God give?

□□□ Reading 15 (Genesis 36:1–38:30)

Genesis 36 is all about Esau: his wives and children in Seir (36:1–8), his sons (36:9–14), Edomite chiefs (36:15–19), Horite chiefs (36:20–30), Edomite kings (36:31–39) – and a geographical classification (36:40–43).

1. It seems that involvement with the people of God brings beneficial side effects (Genesis 36:1–37:1). In some ways the greatness of the Edomites (Esau's descendants) seemed to go ahead faster than the greatness of Israel (as 36:31 suggests). What secular blessings were coming to Esau's people? Do the righteous lag behind in prosperity?
2. A man with a destiny needs some preparation before God is ready to use him. What sort of training or discipline comes upon Joseph? How painful might such training be for us? How does it begin?
3. Why does Genesis 38:1–30 come in this part of the Joseph story? In 37:26–27 Judah is cruel. In 44:18–34 he was a man of compassion. What brought the change? Is there any reason why the tribe of Judah was chosen as Messiah's tribe?

□□□ Reading 16 (Genesis 39:1–40:23)

1. In Genesis 39:1–23 we are back in the Joseph-story. What kind of training is Joseph receiving (i) in facing hardship? (ii) in the matter of sexual temptation? (iii) in facing injustice?
2. Are there any encouragements for us when our 'training' is tough?
3. In going from Potiphar's house to Pharaoh's dungeon, Joseph did the same kind of work at a higher level. Can we see any purpose in this?

☐☐☐ Reading 17 (Genesis 41:1–42:38)

1. God has plans to use food in Egypt to feed his people in Canaan. How does God control nations and rulers?
2. What are the signs that God's timing has come for us to be used by God?
3. Why does Joseph seem to play games with his brothers? What is he trying to do? Is it revenge? Curiosity? What is happening in 42:21–22?

☐☐☐ Reading 18 (Genesis 43:1–45:28)

1. Joseph is still testing his brothers. The question is: have they changed their ways since they had sold Joseph into slavery? Why is Joseph so concerned to find out whether there is jealousy among the brothers as there was many years before? How much of life (personal and international) is motivated by jealousy? How do we handle jealousy? In ourselves? In others?
2. They had abandoned Joseph. Will they abandon Benjamin, Joseph's full brother? What do you think of Judah at this point? In what ways can you see a picture of the Lord Jesus Christ in what Judah says?
3. Why does Joseph send every Egyptian away before he reveals himself to his brothers? What are the signs of true and full forgiveness?

☐☐☐ Reading 19 (Genesis 46:1–48:22)

1. Does God sometimes call us to immense changes in our life? Jacob was called by God to emigrate in his old age. What help does he get from God in making this great change?
2. The text stresses that the entire people of Israel left for Egypt. What was God's purpose in moving his people away from Canaan for centuries? What would come of it?
3. Jacob insists on crossing his hand as he prays for Joseph's children. Why does he insist on it? In what ways must we be ready for God to do the unexpected?

☐☐☐ Reading 20 (Genesis 49:1–50:26)

Jacob gives a farewell prophecy. There are three sons who have ruined their lives (49:3–7), one son with a glorious destiny (49:8–12) and eight sons whose future will be undistinguished (49:13–27).

1. What principles of 'sowing and reaping' are found here?

2. What are the lessons of Judah's life? He was the one who committed the terrible sins of Genesis 38.

3. How does Genesis 50:20 help us in times of injustice and suffering?

Note Genesis 49:10. Judah will retain its sovereignty as the royal tribe until one particular person comes who is called 'Shiloh'. The phrase could mean 'he whose right it is' or – as I prefer – it could be a name, 'the Peaceful One'. 'Shiloh' will be a person of great rule: 'the obedience of the nations comes to him'. He will be a person of great wealth. He lets an ass eat valuable grapes. He washes his clothes in wine (49:11)! The days of 'thorns and thistles' will end and a land of abundant luxuriant vines and abundant wine will come instead! He has so much wine his eyes are red, and so much milk his teeth turn white (49:12). When Jesus was born it looked as if the house of David was totally useless, but Someone came who proved that David's line was alive and well. Shortly after Jesus' coming the tribe of Judah lost its identity.

Matthew's Gospel

Matthew's Gospel has the greatest links to the Old Testament. It was specially written with Israel in mind. Among the four Gospels, Matthew is the one that is least in chronological order. Its material is sometimes presented to us in 'blocks' covering particular topics.

The traditions of the early Church said that this was the first gospel to be written (in Hebrew or Aramaic), and that the apostle Matthew is its author. There must be some truth in this (for there is no other reason to choose Matthew as its author). But if this is the case, then *our* 'Gospel of Matthew' must be a second or third edition. It uses the same *material* that we have in Mark's Gospel (but whether it directly uses Mark's Gospel itself is a matter of debate). It also uses some material which it has in common with Luke's Gospel. Third, Matthew had some information that he alone uses. It is all put together to form the most tidy and orderly of the four Gospels. The date of its first (lost!) Aramaic/Hebrew edition might have been very early (late 30s or in the 40s). The date of our current Greek edition could be any time in the apostolic age up to (but probably not after) AD 70.

Some extra reading may be recommended: R. T. France, *Matthew* (Tyndale Commentary, IVP, 1986); C. L. Blomberg, *Matthew* (New American Commentary, Broadman, 1992); M. A. Eaton, *The Way that Leads to Life* [The Sermon on the Mount] (Christian Focus, 1999).

The first section is arguably Matthew 1:1–4:16. Then Matthew 3:1–4:16 is an expansion of the material we have in Mark 1:2–14a. A turning-point of the gospel comes when we reach the phrase 'From that time on . . .' (4:17):

- Birth stories (1:1–2:25)
  - Title and genealogy(1:1–17)
  - Jesus' birth (1:18–25)
  - The Wise Men (2:1–12)
  - To Egypt and back (2:13–25)
- Beginnings in Galilee (3:1–4:16)
  - John the Baptist (3:1–12)
  - The baptism of Jesus (3:13–17)
  - The temptation of Jesus (4:1–11)
  - Settling in Capernaum (4:12–16)

□□□ Reading 21 (Matthew 1:1–25)

Matthew's Gospel begins by pointing to Jesus' fulfilment of the promises of God to Abraham and to David (1:1). Matthew 1:2–17 points to Jesus' descent from them both.

1. David was famous for being 'a man after God's own heart' (1 Samuel 13:14), a man anointed by the Spirit, a righteous king (that is, a king free from idolatry) ruling over a united Israel. What then is the significance of Jesus' being a 'son of David'?

2. What are the differences between the promises to David and the promises to Abraham? What specially is involved in Jesus' being the 'seed of Abraham'?

3. It was unusual for women to have a place in a first-century genealogy. What are the five women here known for (1:3, 5, 5, 6, 16)? What do we learn from their having a place in Jesus' genealogy?

4. Joseph sought to handle a crisis with both love and righteousness. How do we handle such problems?

5. In what ways can we see an appropriateness in Jesus' having God as the father of his humanity?

Note In Isaiah 7:14 the word does indeed mean 'virgin' (despite what is sometimes said to the contrary). The predicted virgin conception is a sign of the security of God's promise to the house of David. The promise was undated and so the Messiah is referred to as if he were present. But Ahaz's unbelief brought delay.

☐☐☐ Reading 22 (Matthew 2:1–23)

1. What is the possibility today that God may reach people in ways that surprise us?

2. What are the spiritual differences between the 'magi' and everyone else in the chapter? What can we learn from each group about the ways in which people respond to Jesus?

3. The wise men started their journey with help only from God, but they could not end their journey without the help of Micah 5:2. What does this tell us about people seeking God in lands where they get little help?

4. Matthew has surprising ways of reading the Old Testament. What do we learn from this about our own Bible-reading?

Note The 'magi' (philosophers-scientists-astrologers) noticed an unusual phenomenon in the sky and interpreted it as signifying the birth of a Saviour-king in Israel. Presumably they had some knowledge of Daniel (also a 'wise man' from the east and one who made prophecies about a Saviour-king). The 'star' is probably supernatural. The gifts were expensive and unusual. To Joseph and Mary they would have symbolised royalty, priesthood and death – three things that characterised the future of Jesus. The point of the quotation from Hosea 11:1 is not that it *predicts* Jesus but that the principle of Hosea 11:1 (God allowed Israel to grow to full nationhood in Egypt and then brought the nation to Canaan) is *repeated* in Jesus. Bethlehem was near Rachel's tomb. Matthew 2:18 quotes Jeremiah 31:15, where Jeremiah refers to the way in which Rachel in her tomb is symbolically weeping at the sufferings of Judah, as the exiles pass by her tomb on the way to captivity in Babylon. Matthew's point is that Rachel is weeping still. Judah is still suffering at the hands of foreign conquerors. The quotation in Matthew 2:23 is not from any known text. There were no 'quotation marks' in ancient texts and no sharp line between quotations and short *expositions*. Matthew seems to be playing with the Hebrew root *n-z-r*. In the Old Testament the Messiah is a king who wears a crown (*nezer*); he is consecrated to God like a Nazirite (*nazir*). He is also the 'twig' (*nezer*) from the chopped-down tree of David's line (Isaiah 11:1). Jesus' growing up in despised *Nazareth*, in lower Galilee, represents the way Jesus fulfils many strands of Old Testament prophecy.

☐☐☐ Reading 23 (Matthew 3:1–17)

There were four episodes at this time: the ministry of John the Baptist (3:1–12), the baptism of Jesus (3:13–15) and his receiving the Holy Spirit (3:16–17), and then the Satanic temptations (4:1–11).

1. Why was John the Baptist's work a helpful preparation for the ministry of Jesus? Does the preaching of salvation need preparation?

2. John's water-baptism expresses repentance *visibly*. Christian baptism expresses faith *visibly*. It is also a kind of 'prayer' for the gift of the Spirit. What is the value of expressing repentance and faith in so definite and visible a manner? Is there a connection between what happened to Jesus and the 'sealing' of the Holy Spirit (Ephesians 1:13)?

3. What are the central ingredients in John's ministry? How many of them are essential in the life of the churches today?

□□□ **Reading 24 (Matthew 4:1–25)**

Matthew 4:17 ('From that time on . . .') marks a long section of Matthew that runs to Matthew 16:21 where we have the same phrase again. It has the effect of dividing Matthew's story into time-sections. *Within* the larger time frame, chronology is not very important to Matthew, although he preserves a few time-links in the story that tie *some* stories together in sequence. The large section is divided clearly into some smaller units, one of which is Matthew 4:17–9:35. It unfolds as follows:

- A summary-statement: the message (4:17), the disciples (4:18–22), the work (4:23–25)
- A sample sermon (5:1–8:1)
- A sample of Jesus' miracles – and the nature of Jesus' ministry (8:2–9:34)
- A summary-statement (9:35)

1. God the Father cannot be tempted but the man Jesus was tempted (4:1–11). What does this mean to us?

2. Consider the nature and the method of Satan's temptations in this story. What are the resemblances to the story of Genesis 3:1–6?

3. If Matthew 4:17–25 summarises Jesus' ministry, how much should modern Christian ministry follow the same pattern? What changes would this involve in what we know of church life?

□□□ **Reading 25 (Matthew 5:1–16)**

The famous 'Sermon on the Mount' is Jesus' description of the spirit and attitudes he wants from his disciples. Its sections are as follows:

- A Basic Description (5:3–16)
- Fulfilling the Mosaic Law (5:17–48)
- Living in the Sight of God (6:1–34)
- Facing God's Judgment (7:1–29)

1. Jesus begins not with anything we *do*, but with a basic description of attitudes (5:3–9), the treatment we might receive (5:10–12) and the way we function in the world (5:13–16). What are the basic Christian attitudes towards others?

2. Why do people who are described in verses 3–10 get the treatment described in verses 10–12?

3. How should the Christian function in society, negatively (verse 13) and positively (verses 15–16)?

Note Salt was a preservative rubbed into meat to prevent putrefaction.

☐☐☐ Reading 26 (Matthew 5:17–48)

Jesus makes the point that he and his disciples 'fulfil' the law and the prophets (5:17–20). Jesus gives six examples (5:21–26, 27–30, 31–32, 33–37, 38–42, 43–48).

1. What does the word 'fulfil' mean in Matthew 5:17? Can the question be answered by a detailed study of verses 21–48?

2. What parts of the Mosaic law are cancelled, extended or somewhat altered when we live directly under Jesus? Verses 21–48 should give us some answers.

3. Does 'enter the kingdom of heaven' mean 'become a Christian' or 'experience the powers of God's kingdom in your daily life'? Does the difference in interpretation have any practical implications?

☐☐☐ Reading 27 (Matthew 6:1–18)

Jesus moves to the theme of living before God. Self-advertisement is unnecessary in the kingdom of God (6:1–18). Neither greed (6:19–24) nor anxiety over money and possessions (6:25–34) is necessary. Matthew 6:1 states a principle (no 'showing off'!) and applies it with reference to giving (relating to others), praying (relating to God) and fasting (self-discipline) – verses 2–4, 5–15, 16–18.

1. What causes religious 'showing off' or self-advertisement? What is Jesus' way of discouraging it?

2. If the Lord's Prayer is a kind of 'prayer list' for us, how should our prayers change?

3. What do you think of fasting? Can it be done for foolish reasons? Can it be taken too far? What is Jesus' recommendation? Complete the following sentence: 'The majority of references to fasting show us that normally fasting is for . . . day/days.'

□□□ Reading 28 (Matthew 6:19–34)

1. Is it the case that Matthew 6:19–24 is addressed to the rich and 6:25–34 to the poor? Or could it be the other way round? Do the rich worry about money? And do the poor want treasures on earth?
2. List the arguments that Jesus gives against greed.
3. What is Jesus' 'deliverance ministry'? When seeking to 'deliver' his disciples from anxiety, how does he set about it?

□□□ Reading 29 (Matthew 7:1–8:1)

1. How far should we take Matthew 7:1–6? Are we allowed to judge at all?
2. How can Matthew 7:12 give us guidance in complicated situations? Think of some examples.
3. Is Matthew 7:21–23 addressed to the disciples or is it considering false prophets? Assuming the latter is true ('I will say to *them* . . .') what difference does it make to us?

Note Verse 6 either (i) balances verses 1–5 and suggests we should not be too undiscriminating, or (ii) is the reaction of the godless person when we judge them hypocritically.

□□□ Reading 30 (Matthew 8:2–17)

In 8:2–9:35, Matthew gives sample miracles, nine of them (three sets of three) interwoven with some connected stories. First there is a trio of miracle stories, which concern leprosy (8:2–4), paralysis (8:5–13) and a fever (8:14–15). Matthew 8:16–17 adds a conclusion.

1. Three miracles reveal the way Jesus has power over sickness and shows mercy to the downtrodden. If Jesus touches the leper (illegally – Leviticus 5:3!), receives the gentile representative of the hated Roman armies, and has mercy on a woman, how should we relate to today's despised and downtrodden peoples? Who are today's untouchables and rejected peoples?
2. It is easy to see how blindness and deafness might have spiritual equivalents (see 2 Corinthians 4:4; Matthew 11:15) but are there spiritual equivalents to leprosy, paralysis and fever?
3. Does Matthew 8:17 imply that there is guaranteed and immediate physical healing in the cross of Christ? Or is it only that *when* there is healing it flows from Christ's cross?

Note Miracle-stories may be read by the modern reader in at least five ways. (i) They are historical events that demonstrate that God is in immediate contact with his universe and may act 'irregularly' at any moment. God is not forbidden from acting in the same way today. On the other hand we must acknowledge the sovereignty of God. No one can 'claim' or switch on a miracle at will. (ii) Miracles are acted parables. This is specially clear in John's Gospel (where for example the healing of a blind man illustrates the fact that Jesus is the light of the world), but it is clear in the other Gospels also. Note for example the connection between Mark 8:21 and the details of the miracle in 8:22–26. (iii) They are signs of Jesus' perfect faith and therefore signs of Jesus' Messiahship (see Matthew 11:2–5). Note that Mark 11:22 replies to the surprise expressed in 11:21. (iv) They are foretastes of the resurrection body and of final earthly glory. (v) They are encouragements to prayer, for they invite us to say to ourselves, 'If God can do that great thing, then he can handle this small thing.'

□□□ Reading 31 (Matthew 8:18–34)

Three approaches to following Jesus (8:18–20, 21–22, 23) end up with miraculous protection of those who follow Jesus (8:24–27). Then two more miracle stories are added (8:28–34; 9:1–8) to make another trio of miracles. The two incidents following show that the one who has supreme authority comes as a Saviour (9:8–13) and the initiator of a new movement among God's people (9:14–17).

1. What three kinds of 'follower' are to be found in 8:18–20, 21–22, 23? What is the point of what Jesus says to two of them (8:18–20, 21–22)? What does he do and say with the third group (8:23–27)? So what are the challenges and encouragements to 'following Jesus' today?

2. Matthew 8:28–34 is a full description of a case of demon possession. What are the characteristics of this man's condition? In what ways might this story be relevant today?

3. What causes people to want Jesus to leave them alone?

□□□ Reading 32 (Matthew 9:1–17)

1. How is the grace of God seen in Matthew's story? Why do the Pharisees not like such sudden conversion?

2. The question about fasting (9:14) is answered by Jesus (9:15), but it leads to some remarks about 'new wine and new wineskins' (9:16–17). Jesus' people are obviously a different group of people from John's disciples and they are doing things differently. What 'new wine of the kingdom' might we expect to find today – and how will it require 'new wineskins'?

☐☐☐ Reading 33 (Matthew 9:18–35)

Next there are three more miracle stories (concerning an official's daughter and a needy woman, two blind men, and a dumb demoniac). A summary ends this section and starts another (9:35).

1. The first miracle story has intertwined the troubles of two people. In what ways were their situations extremely desperate? What encouragement is to be found here for people in desperate trouble?
2. Consider the behaviour and experience of the noisy crowd. What blessing did they get, if any?
3. The blind men come with great faith in Jesus' power, and experience an amazing healing. Since not *every* blind Christian has this experience, how are we meant to apply to ourselves stories like this?
4. What are the marks of prejudice in this passage? Why are the leaders more prejudiced than the people?

☐☐☐ Reading 34 (Matthew 9:36–10:25)

A new sub-section begins at Matthew 9:35 or 36. Jesus sees the needs of the people (9:36–38), sends out his twelve senior disciples (10:1–4), gives them detailed instruction (10:5–42), and Jesus' entire team begins ministering in the towns of Galilee (11:1).

1. What is the connection between praying and going into God's work (ignore the chapter division between 9:36–38 and 10:1–4)?
2. What principles concerning serving God are of permanent value in this chapter? What parts might be purely for the first century (e.g. 10:5)?
3. Does anyone obey the command to 'raise the dead'? (10:8) – even among those of us who believe most in miracles? So was it temporary? Unique to the apostles? Or what? In taking the biblical teaching to ourselves, how do we use commands like these?

Note The first word in verse 9 (*Do not acquire . . .*) does not mean that no provisions should be taken; it means that they should be provided by others ('for labourers deserve their food'). The word in Mark 6:8 is different.

☐☐☐ Reading 35 (Matthew 10:26–11:1)

1. What reasons does Jesus give to persuade us to be free from fear while serving him?
2. How do the warnings of Matthew 10:34 relate to the promises of John 14:27 (both given to Jesus' disciples)?

3. What does it mean to 'take up Jesus' cross and follow him'? What are the rewards of acting upon his command?

□□□ Reading 36 (Matthew 11:2–28)

In the following chapters, each section tells us of the ever-increasing opposition that came against Jesus. Matthew 11:1–30 tells of the sufferings and perplexities of John the Baptist (11:2–19), then of the town that rejected Jesus (11:20–25) and of Jesus' invitation to the weary (11:26–28).

1. What was the cause of John the Baptist's doubts? What does he do about them and how may we follow his example?
2. In what ways does Jesus commend John the Baptist? What was his position in the history of salvation?
3. How does Jesus' prayer and invitation connect (11:26–28) with the previous parts of the chapter? What kind of 'rest' does Jesus offer us and how may we experience it?

Note Verse 12 is difficult. 'The kingdom of heaven suffers-violence/ progresses-forcefully (which?) and forceful people (in a good sense or bad sense?) take it by force'. The majority view takes it to mean 'The kingdom of heaven progresses powerfully and aggressive people (in a good sense) take it' – an interpretation that is supported by Luke 16:16.

□□□ Reading 37 (Matthew 12:1–21)

1. Was there actually any regulation about the Sabbath, in the Mosaic law, which Jesus broke? What are the characteristics of religious legalism? How does Jesus reply to it?
2. Jesus defended David for doing something illegal (12:3–4). What are the implications of this? Were there levels of importance in the law?
3. The Pharisees wish to kill Jesus. Matthew finds a true description of his work in Isaiah 42:1–4. How does the description in Isaiah help us to understand what Jesus was really doing?

□□□ Reading 38 (Matthew 12:22–50)

Opposition to Jesus continued in a slander concerning Jesus' character and work (12:22–37), an unbelieving demand for signs (12:38–45), and hostility and misunderstanding from his family (12:46–50).

1. In what ways is opposition to Jesus unreasonable? What then is the motivation behind it? How does Jesus reply to it?

2. Careless words will be recalled as evidence on judgment day. How are they a sufficient indicator of character?

3. How did Jesus relate to his family? How did his family relate to him? Were there any changes along the way? What does this tell us about our own families?

Note The unforgivable sin is refusing faith in Jesus despite powerful evidence of his Messiahship. No Christian ever commits it. The only reason why it is unforgivable is that it is sinning against the *means* of forgiveness, the message concerning Jesus himself, coming in the power of the Holy Spirit. The first part of the saying must also be emphasised ('People can be forgiven for every sin . . .').

☐☐☐ Reading 39 (Matthew 13:1–23)

1. There is a connection between the rising opposition against Jesus and his beginning to make greater use of parables. What is the connection according to 13:10–17? Are the parables a punishment?

2. The kingdom of heaven was given to Jesus' disciples already but to fully experience it they still have to have 'ears to hear – and hear'! What is God's kingdom, and how do we fully experience it?

3. In what way do 'worries . . . and the deceitfulness of wealth' affect our experience of the kingdom of God?

Note The 'kingdom' has stages. It is in this world already, but its final stage will be when it is made gloriously visible.

☐☐☐ Reading 40 (Matthew 13:24–58)

1. What are the implications of verse 30 for today's Christians? Remember verse 38 ('the field is the world' – not 'the field is the Church').

2. The parables of the mustard seed and the yeast seem to deal with the progress of the kingdom. How successful may we expect the kingdom of God to be in this gospel-age?

3. What are the main points of the parables of the hidden treasure and the pearl? And of the parable of the net?

4. What is the real answer to the question, 'Where then did this man get all these things?'

☐☐☐ Reading 41 (Matthew 14:1–36)

In the section of Matthew's Gospel between 4:17 ('From that time on . . .') and 16:21 ('From that time on . . .'), it seems that after the outline of the main aspects of Jesus' ministry (4:17 to 9:35), we are told how the disciples were sent out to extend that ministry (9:36–11:1). Then we have stories that show at the same time the greatness of Jesus and yet the rising opposition against him. This leads to a change in Jesus' way of teaching (the parables of Matthew 13:1–22). Then the stories of conflict and opposition continue until eventually Jesus repudiates the Pharisees and Sadducees, takes care to know that the disciples realise who he is and then 'From that time on . . .' goes into another stage of his work.

1. What do we learn about conscience from the story of Herod?
2. Jesus expected the disciples to feed the five thousand (note verse 16). He performed the miracle instead of them. What do we learn from this?
3. What are the practical lessons that arise if we take the two miracles (of provision and of walking on stormy seas) as parables?

☐☐☐ Reading 42 (Matthew 15:1–20)

1. Consider (in the light of Matthew 15) the dangers of following traditional 'rules' rather than the godliness that comes from knowing God himself.
2. Can you think of other clever ways (like those mentioned here) of arguing around plain and obvious commands of God?
3. Sin comes from the heart, not from errors of ritual. What are modern equivalents of this principle mentioned here?

☐☐☐ Reading 43 (Matthew 15:21–39)

1. There are different levels of faith. What are the characteristics of the woman's faith (in 15:21–28) that make Jesus call it 'great'?
2. If the miracles are 'acted parables' what is represented by 'the lame, the blind, the crippled, those who could not speak' (15:30) and how does our Lord Jesus Christ feel about different kinds of impediment? What encouragement does this give for our own weaknesses of various kinds?
3. Jesus fed thousands of people twice. All four Gospels report at least one miracle of this kind. What is so important about these miracles (note Matthew 16:8–10)? What is represented by hunger, the gift of food, satisfaction, abundance?

☐☐☐ Reading 44 (Matthew 16:1–18)

1. Jesus refused to give signs to sign-seekers (16:1–4) yet elsewhere signs are offered (Isaiah 7:11) or are promised (Exodus 3:12). What is the sign of Jonah? Why is it the only sign offered to the sign-seekers?

2. The Pharisees were conservative and traditional; the Sadducees were sceptical and politically minded. What does it mean today to 'beware of the yeast of the Pharisees and the Sadducees'?

3. Matthew 16:13 is a turning-point in Jesus' ministry. He starts talking about his Church, his death on the cross and the future of his kingdom. What is the foundation of everything Jesus plans to do?

Note (i) What is the 'rock'? Peter the first pope? Jesus himself? The faith of the disciples? If everything in the passage is taken into account, the answer would seem to be: apostolic revelation concerning the Lord Jesus Christ – such as was first preached by Peter on the day of Pentecost. Note that 'you' in verse 15 is plural, and so Peter represents all the apostles. (ii) 'Gates' were the places where law-courts were held. It speaks of authority.

□□□ Reading 45 (Matthew 16:19–28)

1. If 'binding' and 'loosing' refers to the authority of the Church in withstanding evil and getting God's will done – then how does the Church exercise this authority? Or should these phrases be taken differently?

2. What might be Jesus' reason for not wanting his Messiahship to be prematurely announced?

3. From a revelation of his person (16:16), Jesus turns to speak of his cross (16:22–24). What does Jesus' cross mean (i) for Jesus himself? (ii) for Peter at this time? (iii) for disciples in general?

□□□ Reading 46 (Matthew 17:1–27)

1. The transfiguration was a confirmation that Jesus is God's divine Son (following 16:16), and a foretaste of the glory of Jesus' second coming (see 2 Peter 1:16). Why was this an appropriate time for such an event? Why does Jesus give no signs to his enemies but this sign to his friends?

2. Moses and Elijah (the lawgiver and the greatest prophet) talk to Jesus, an indication that the law and the prophets testify to the death of Christ. What mistakes does Peter make at this time, and how may we learn from his mistakes?

3. Seeing Elijah reminded the disciples of the Jewish belief that the Saviour would have a forerunner. The new Elijah was John the Baptist. What did the ministries of Elijah and John have in common? What are the marks of a 'restoring' ministry?

□□□ Reading 47 (Matthew 18:1–20)

1. What is the difference between 'church' in 16:18 and 'church' in 18:17?
2. What aspect of childlikeness is indispensable for entering the kingdom, and what exactly is 'entering the kingdom' in this passage?
3. The passage moves from childlikeness in ourselves to how we view childlikeness in others. What should we think of the modern pre-occupation with status and privilege?
4. The 'little ones' of Jesus are his childlike disciples. What is the picture of church life in what Jesus has to say in this section of Matthew?

□□□ Reading 48 (Matthew 18:21–35)

1. Consider the question of verse 21. What is Peter's attitude to forgiving other people?
2. How important is it to forgive those who have hurt us? What do we gain if we do? What do we lose if we don't? What are the signs that we have truly forgiven those who have hurt us?
3. Is there a reason why Jesus concentrates on forgiving brothers and sisters (verses 35) rather than on forgiving strangers and enemies?

□□□ Reading 49 (Matthew 19:1–30)

1. What was the teaching of the law (Deuteronomy 24:1–4) about divorce? How were the Pharisees using it? Why does Jesus go to Genesis rather than Deuteronomy?
2. Passages in the Bible about divorce (i) sometimes condemn divorce and make no exceptions (Mark 10:2–12; Luke 16:18); (ii) sometimes mention an exception (Matthew 5:31–32; 19:9); and (iii) on one occasion mention another exception (1 Corinthians 7:10–16). Is there any way all of this can be harmonised? Might there be further exceptions (on grounds of violence, insanity, HIV-positivity)? Does the word 'divorce' in itself imply freedom to remarry?
3. Is Matthew saying children *themselves* are members of the kingdom? Or is it that childlike people experience God's kingdom? If it is the latter, what does this imply?
4. What is the difference between the question of Acts 16:30 and the question of Matthew 19:16? Why are the answers so different?

□□□ Reading 50 (Matthew 20:1–19)

1. What is the point of the parable of Matthew 20:1–16? Is it: everyone will get the same reward in heaven? Surely not (see 1 Corinthians

3:15). Then what is its point? That God's grace is given surprisingly? That those who come into the kingdom late (gentiles?) might achieve more than those who have been in God's kingdom for a long time (the Israel of Jesus' day?)? What other possibilities are there? What are its implications today?

2. What is the significance of the fact that Jesus tells his disciples *privately* what is about to happen? How much may we know ahead of time what God is planning to do?

3. Jesus had a rather detailed foreknowledge of the cross. What does this tell us about the place and purpose of Jesus' death?

□□□ Reading 51 (Matthew 20:20–34)

1. Is it right to be ambitious? How does Jesus reply to the two men who are ambitious to have power in Jesus' coming kingdom? So what do we learn about our own motivations?

2. What is the difference between authority in the world and authority in the kingdom of God? What might this mean practically?

3. The two men of 20:29–34 were also ambitious in their own way! What was it that led Jesus to hear their request?

□□□ Reading 52 (Matthew 21:1–22)

1. Zechariah 9:10–11 predicted that God would come as king of his people to Jerusalem. What kind of 'kingdom' did Jesus reveal in the events of Matthew 21:1–11? Is Jesus' kingdom still 'coming' in the world today? If so, what kind of kingdom is it?

2. How may religion become corrupted into worldly business?

3. What two things did the temple authorities not like about Jesus? How does Jesus reply to them? What might Jesus say to religious leaders (of all kinds) today?

4. A miracle leads Jesus to make some remarks about faith. How may we actually practise verse 21? Is it a matter of persuading ourselves that something we want will in fact happen? If not, what in fact is involved in praying with faith?

□□□ Reading 53 (Matthew 21:23–46)

1. What kind of authority did both John the Baptist and Jesus have? Why does Jesus answer a question in a slightly evasive way? What kind of authority should Christian leaders have? Are they 'managing directors'? Are they simply people whose prayers are answered? Or what?

2. The parable of Matthew 21:28–32 is a classic description of repentance. What are the ingredients of repentance? Some surprising people repent, and some surprising people remain unrepentant (21:31b). How was this so in Jesus' day? And what about today?

3. Considering 21:33–46, what form did 'impenitence' take among the religious leaders of first-century Israel? What is its modern equivalent – or is today's impenitence identical?

□□□ **Reading 54 (Matthew 22:1–22)**

1. What are the significant points of the parable of the wedding banquet? Who are the people who had no prior invitation? What are the qualifications for entering God's kingdom?

2. In the second part of the parable (22:11–14) what might the wedding clothes represent? The true gospel? Good works? True faith? Repentance?

3. The question addressed to Jesus in 22:15–22 is only difficult if religion and state are totally unified, such that honouring Caesar involves honouring Caesar's god, and honouring God involves defying Caesar and his entire system of government (including his coins). What does Jesus say about the matter and what are the implications for a pluralist society?

□□□ **Reading 55 (Matthew 22:23–46)**

1. How does verse 32 'prove' the fact of resurrection? Is God faithful to us if we are unredeemed from death, and if our bodies are not glorified? What are the two causes of scepticism about resurrection? Where is resurrection in the Old Testament Scriptures?

2. Jesus says Leviticus 19:18 and Deuteronomy 6:5 are the law's greatest commands. God's demand can be stated in two parts (love for God and love for people). Or it can be stated in one command (love for people – Romans 13:8–10), but it is never stated as simply love for God. What is the significance of this?

3. When Pharisees and Sadducees ask questions, they set traps and ask about law. But what sort of question does Jesus ask – and why (Matthew 22:41–46)?

□□□ **Reading 56 (Matthew 23:1–22)**

1. Are we really to keep everything in the Mosaic law (23:3a)? If not, how do we interpret 23:3a? Is it dispensational (the law is to be kept until Jesus' death and resurrection)? Is it sarcasm? Is it an *ad hominem* argument (try and keep it if you can – but that will prove you can't!)?

2. What are the marks of legalism-mixed-with-hypocrisy that we find in decayed religion? How may we avoid it? What is its opposite?

3. Do modern religious leaders lock people out (23:13) of God's kingdom?

☐☐☐ Reading 57 (Matthew 23:23–39)

1. Matthew 23:23 is the only verse in the New Testament that seems to demand that disciples tithe. Are we really to tithe mint, dill and cummin? Is the statement (like references to the temple altar and sacrifices in 23:16–22 and 5:23–24) only relevant before Pentecost? What is the Christian approach to proportional giving? Is it greater or smaller than tithing?

2. Can we find modern examples of legalism in details but weakness in the big principles of godliness?

3. How might we admire yesterday's prophets but kill today's prophets (23:29–31)?

4. Does one generation inherit the judgment of the sins of previous generations?

☐☐☐ Reading 58 (Matthew 24:1–28)

1. Is Jesus giving us 'signs of the end'? Or is he telling us what are *not* signs of the end? Note verse 6 ('the end is not yet').

2. Verses 15–28 deal with the events just before the fall of Jerusalem when Roman soldiers destroyed the temple and Christians ran to escape the tragedies that would occur. What can we learn from the destruction of so great an institution as the temple? Is there safety in any religious institution? In any holy building?

3. What are the dangers facing believers in days of religious decline, according to this passage?

☐☐☐ Reading 59 (Matthew 24:29–51)

1. Are there 'signs' of the nearness of the second coming of Jesus? None? One? Many? (note Romans 12:11–14).

2. What are the main characteristics of the second coming as we see them in 24:36–51?

3. What does being 'ready' for the second coming mean, as we see the theme developed in 24:45–51?

Note Everything in 24:4–28 seems to refer exclusively to the fall of Jerusalem, but everything in verses 36–51 refers to the second coming of Christ. The difficult verses in this chapter are 24:29–35. Verses 29–34 are said to predict things that are 'immediately after' the pre-AD 70 tribulation. The events are to take place within one generation (24:34). 'This generation shall not pass away, till all *these things* be accomplished . . . But of *that* day and hour no one knows . . .' Does the pre-AD 70 tribulation in verse 28 somehow jump to a latter-day tribulation and so does 'immediately after' refer to some end-time events? Or do these verses refer to the fall of Jerusalem seen as a *foretaste* of the second coming of Jesus?

☐☐☐ Reading 60 (Matthew 25:1–30)

When an Israelite couple married, the bridegroom would stay at one house with his friends and the recently married bride would be at her father's house with her bridesmaids. At some point in the evening, the bridegroom would set out to collect his bride from her father's house. The bridesmaids would go out from the bride's house to meet him and escort him on the last bit of the journey to his bride. Then the entire company would go in procession to the bridegroom's house where the wedding feast was to be held.

The bridesmaids would be waiting at the bride's house. They might sleep for a while but they were meant to have their oil-soaked burning torches ready all the time. When the bridegroom came near to the bride's house, an announcement would be made and the girls would go out with their burning-oil torches to escort the bridegroom. If when the bridegroom came the bridesmaids were not ready with their torches burning brightly it would be a serious insult to the couple, and such girls were likely to be excluded from further involvement in the festivities.

The parable makes three points: (i) the need of readiness, (ii) the impossibility of last-minute preparation when the Lord 'comes', and (iii) punishment by exclusion.

1. What kinds of 'coming' of Jesus are there, other than the final 'second coming'?

2. What preparations are needed for us to be ready for the arrivals of Jesus in our life in various ways?

3. In what ways may we be excluded from the blessings of God's kingdom by our unpreparedness?

4. The second parable (25:14–30) deals with our 'investing' what God has given us and then giving an account of how we have done so. What then is the readiness that Jesus wants in any time that he might come to us?

5. Does verse 30 deal with eternal punishment of someone who turns out to be a false disciple? Or 'salvation through fiery punishment' (see

1 Corinthians 3:15) for a neglectful Christian? Or could both points (and others) be involved?

Note It is likely that Jesus is dealing with many topics at the same time in the various sections of this chapter. (i) The 'coming' of the Lord may be anticipated (as Matthew 24 has made clear in treating the fall of Jerusalem as a shadow of the end). 'Readiness' is needed for the 'coming' of Jesus in *any* sense. (ii) Jesus addresses both disciples and non-disciples.

□□□ Reading 61 (Matthew 25:31–46)

1. Do warnings of possible judgment undermine assurance of salvation? If not, why not?
2. If Christ's 'brothers' are Christian witnesses, what will this involve for us today, in a world where persecution of Christians is as great as ever?
3. Matthew 25:46 is often cited as a proof text of the traditional doctrine of hell (which was first given full exposition by Augustine of Hippo). Is 'eternal punishment' totally parallel to 'eternal life' (so that one means eternally living and the other eternally suffering)? Or is it likely there is contrast as well as parallelism (life grows; death shrivels – see Romans 5:15, 'the gift is not like the trespass'). What practical difference will the different approaches to 'eternal punishment' make to us? Which is able to be preached?

Note All peoples are gathered before Jesus (including Israel; it is not a judgment only of gentiles). This judgment is not deciding who was 'saved' ('justified' in Paul's vocabulary) but is rather allocating final reward. 'Inheritance' and 'initial-salvation' are different and the theme here is inheritance. The *grounds* of judgment is the good or bad treatment (mentioning food, shelter, clothing) given to Christ's 'brothers'. The question is: who are Christ's brothers (people everywhere? needy people? Christian workers?)? While there are plenty of places in the Bible where we are called to show mercy to the poor, yet this is not the sense here. 'Brothers' in Matthew's Gospel always refers to spiritual relatives, never to men and women in general. The judgment depends on practical response (or lack of it) to Christian witnesses to the gospel. It will have an eternal result.

□□□ Reading 62 (Matthew 26:1–30)

Matthew 26:1–28:20 is the last block of material in Matthew's Gospel. Pharisees avoid his death at Passover time; a woman honours his sacrifice; Judas assists God's plan unwittingly; the Lord's Supper commemorates his death at Passover time.

1. The Pharisees were determined that Jesus should not be crucified at Passover time. In the end, however, it seems this is what happened. The reluctance of Pilate to crucify Jesus slowed down the speed of events. In what ways does Jesus fulfil the symbolism of the Passover-sacrifice of Exodus 12?

2. It seems the only person who truly believed Jesus was about to die was the woman of Matthew 26:6–13. She believed he was to be crucified and spent a year's savings (myrrh was a form of savings) in honouring him *before* his death in the only way she could. In what way is this woman a model of Christian devotion? She showed discernment . . . and what else?

3. It seems Judas was always a fake disciple, pretending to be a genuine member of the apostolic team, for reasons of eventual profit (plus some dipping into the money bag along the way). What reasons do people have for pretending to be loyal Christians or loyal church workers? Do such people – like Judas – have a place in God's plan unknown even to themselves?

4. What are the main ingredients of the symbolism in the Lord's Supper? The bread? The wine? The breaking of bread? The one loaf? The eating and drinking?

☐☐☐ Reading 63 (Matthew 26:31–56)

1. Why is Peter so self-confident (26:31–35), yet so prayerless (26:36–43)? What are his strengths and weaknesses at this point in his life? How may we learn from him?

2. What are the contrasts here between faithless Peter and the ever-faithful Lord Jesus Christ?

3. How does Jesus behave at this moment where he is approaching his supreme self-sacrifice?

☐☐☐ Reading 64 (Matthew 26:57–75)

1. Legal procedure was used to bring about a murder. What must it have been like to face these various injustices in this 'trial' (27:57–61), especially at the hands of religious leaders? How are we to face such injustices ourselves? How did Jesus cope?

2. Jesus is asked to admit under oath to a crime that carried the death sentence (26:63). Caiaphas must have been delighted when Jesus claimed not only to be the Messiah but also to be the one who very soon ('From now on', verse 64) will be exalted as God's right-hand Man, the king of the universe. The false witnesses were unnecessary.

Jesus the faithful witness has given them all they need. What are the contrasts between Jesus the faithful witness and Peter who denies the truth he once confessed (16:16)? What gave Jesus the strength to be faithful? How did Peter become so unfaithful to what he knew?
3. Jesus was calm and passive. His attackers were cruel and violent (26:67–68). What do we learn of human nature from the treatment Jesus is given? Is there any remedy? How does anyone ever get to be like Jesus?

□□□ Reading 65 (Matthew 27:1–26)

1. How may we learn to avoid religious hypocrisy? How does it happen that such 'religious' men can be guilty of deceitful planning ('counsel', verse 1), murderous intentions, cruelty? Are we likely to be led into such things ourselves?
2. 'When he was accused . . . he answered not a word' (27:13). Why does Jesus sometimes (but not always) stay silent before his accusers? Should we always follow his example?
3. Pilate is a man who knows what is right, struggles to do what is right, but fails. What are the steps and stages in his struggle?

Note Matthew 27:9 quotes Zechariah 11:13 but attributes the citation to 'Jeremiah'. Perhaps as the books of the third part of the Old Testament can be called 'Psalms' after the longest book, so the section of sixteen prophets (including Zechariah) can be called 'Jeremiah' after its longest book. In Zechariah 11:4–17, the prophet acts the part of God himself as the Shepherd of Israel. He then asks for a payment for his prophetic performance. The watching crowd collect thirty silver shekels for the payment of Zechariah's performance (11:12). Then the Lord said to the prophet, 'Throw the money to the potter.' 'So I took the thirty shekels of silver and threw them to the potter in the house of the LORD' (11:13). The majority of the people watching Zechariah do not appreciate his message at all. Zechariah despises their payment. He throws it to a poor labouring man, a potter who works at a potter's workshop near to the temple. Matthew's quoting Zechariah 11:13 seems to say: 'Just as Zechariah's throwing away thirty pieces of silver showed the people had no appreciation of God's word, so the leaders of Israel showed they had no self-respect in what they had done to manipulate the death of Jesus. The unworthy shepherds of Jesus' day (predicted by Zechariah) showed no understanding of the cross of the Lord Jesus Christ, in which they played a part.'

☐☐☐ Reading 66 (Matthew 27:27–44)

1. Jesus suffers ridicule and mockery (among other things). Are we sensitive to ridicule? What aspects of Jesus' life and ministry are being scorned in these events?

2. Can the 'man of Cyrene, Simon by name' be taken as an illustration of what it means to 'carry the cross' spiritually? If so, how? (Presumably Simon's name was recalled because he became a Christian. The 'Rufus' of Romans 16:13 seems to have been his son.)

3. The by-passers ridicule the powerlessness of Jesus. 'Save yourself . . . Come down from the cross . . . He cannot save himself . . . Let him now come down from the cross, and we will believe in him' (27:40–42). Could Jesus have saved himself? Why did he make no attempt to do so? What is the significance of his refusal (or his inability)?

☐☐☐ Reading 67 (Matthew 27:45–66)

1. Jesus expected and predicted his crucifixion, so why was he asking a *question* (27:46) as he was being crucified?

2. What is the significance of the tearing of the veil of the temple? Why did Jesus' death cause immediate resurrections? What is the significance of the fact that the earth shook at what was happening?

3. At the end of the chapter, Jesus is dead. Is anyone expecting a resurrection? How safe and secure was the tomb of Jesus?

☐☐☐ Reading 68 (Matthew 28:1–20)

1. The priests had a *message* about resurrection (28:11) but did not *see* the resurrection. Why does Jesus reveal his resurrection only to disciples? Should he have gone back to Pilate?

2. Some disciples 'saw him . . . but . . . doubted'. What is faith? How can one doubt what one sees? Modern people doubt the resurrection. What is the best way of discussing the matter?

3. In the 'great commission' of 28:18–20, what are the promises? What are the commands? Is there any significance in the order of commands? Jesus says, 'Make disciples of all the nations', not 'Make some disciples in all nations'. Is there a difference? Is it important?

Joshua

Just as Genesis-to-Deuteronomy may be considered as a distinct section of the Bible, so may Deuteronomy-Joshua-Judges-Samuel-Kings, with the book of Deuteronomy forming a link belonging to both sections. (The book of Ruth was placed later on in the Hebrew Old Testament.) Moses' review of Israel's history led later writers to continue the process. So at some stage Deuteronomy became Deuteronomy-Joshua. Then it became Deuteronomy-Joshua-Judges, and so on. Eventually Deuteronomy-to-Kings came into being. The entire history makes the point that idolatry is fatal. Israel rises and falls according to the purity of its worship.

Joshua tells of the time when Israel was united, free from idolatry, successful in conquering enemies, and able to inherit what God wanted to give them. Although God was promising to give the land of Israel to the descendants of Jacob, the people had to put forth great efforts to lay hold of it. The modern reader takes Joshua 'spiritually'. Although we know that it refers to historical events and must be read quite literally, we also know that it gives us parallels for modern readers to apply to themselves.

Recommended reading: M. A. Eaton, *Joshua* (Preaching Through the Bible, Sovereign World, 2000); B. K. Waltke, 'Joshua', in *New Bible Commentary* (IVP, 1994).

☐☐☐ Reading 69 (Joshua 1:1–3:17)

1. In what ways must (i) Joshua and (ii) the people prepare for a new stage of success in their lives? Every Christian has an 'inheritance'. What do we do to get it?

2. The first major task was the conquest of Jericho. God had tolerated its sin for centuries but now required its extermination. What is the modern equivalent of 'exterminating Canaanites' (something that was never commanded again)?

3. How is Rahab an example of what James called 'justification by works'? Note James 2:25.

☐☐☐ Reading 70 (Joshua 4:1–6:27)

1. Joshua puts a monument of twelve stones halfway across the dry river-bed (4:9). On the west bank of the river a monument will be built, which will be a replica of the underwater monument in the centre of the river. How should modern Christians recall their spiritual history, remembering that 'the hand of the LORD is mighty' (4:24)?

2. What is the symbolism of circumcision (for ever to be associated with Gilgal) in Joshua 5:1–8? How does the Christian have the promises of circumcision in 'the circumcision of Christ' (Colossians 2:11, 13)?

3. The manna stopped! Israel could not live on miracles all the time! What is the significance of this?

4. In the life of faith, we encounter strongholds that at first seem beyond the possibility of being overcome, but they may be conquered. What lessons do we learn from the fall of Jericho?

Note The slaughter of the Canaanites. Four things should be remembered. (i) The wickedness of the Canaanites had gone on for centuries. Depravity had increased. Sexual perversion, child sacrifice, snake worship and demonisation were commonplace. (ii) The Israelites could fall easily into sin themselves, as the story of Numbers 25:1–18 shows. The people of God themselves would be made extinct shortly if severe action was not taken to preserve them from paganism. (iii) The idea of there being 'war crimes' is taught in the Bible (see Amos 1:1–2:16) but at this stage of world history there was no way of keeping the Canaanites alive while forcing them to reform their ways. (iv) The extermination of the Canaanites is a foretaste of final judgment day. Just as God cleared away wickedness from the land of Canaan, so one day he will wipe planet Earth clean of all sin.

☐☐☐ Reading 71 (Joshua 7:1–9:27)

1. Israel experienced its first defeat at Achan. Why did it happen? What had to be done? The modern Christian does not execute the sinner, so what is the modern equivalent?

2. The town of Ai was taken by clever strategy, not by miracle. The defeat of Jericho and the defeat of Ai are very different. What do we learn from both cases?

3. The kings in the region of the River Jordan hear about the conquering Israelites (9:1). They can see that their wicked ways are about to come to an end. Which of their different options were followed in these chapters (include the story of Rahab!)? What options are open to us when we see we have acted wrongly?

☐☐☐ Reading 72 (Joshua 10:1–12:24)

1. How may God overrule our mistakes? How did God turn around the covenant with Gibeon for good?

2. Joshua needed a long day to be able to overtake the fleeing Canaanites. He spoke a word of faith to the sun and moon! It was undoubtedly a miracle; perhaps one involving the refraction of light rather than a miracle that involved an interference in the astronomical laws of the universe. Yet most of the time the people were fighting battles without having miraculous help. So how and when may we expect miraculous help from God? What do we say to people (ourselves?) when we want a miracle but cannot get one?

3. When Joshua's southern campaign was finished, Joshua and his soldiers returned to Gilgal. What is the significance of this – in their lives and ours?

4. In Joshua 11:1–11, a king of Hazor in the far north gathers a gigantic army against Joshua, a greater number than Israel had faced before. How do we face immense opposition against the kingdom of God?

☐☐☐ Reading 73 (Joshua 13:1–15:63)

Joshua 13:1–22:34 have lengthy lists and geographical details in them, which might seem uninteresting. Yet topics such as inheritance, covenant, oath and 'entering into rest' are major themes of the Bible.

1. Joshua is elderly in these chapters. How do life's responsibilities change as we get older?

2. Joshua 13:13–14 has two extra comments. (i) Israel actually failed to drive out the last remains of paganism and some of the pagan people were still present in the days when the book of Joshua was put together

(13:13). (ii) The Levites had to be content with God alone as inherit-ance (13:14). What is the significance for us of these two points? Are the Levites a key to the nature of the Christian's inheritance?

3. Inheritance is the reward God wants to give us. It is the result of persistent faith and it invariably involves conflict of some kind. How do we see this illustrated in these chapters?

4. What are we to learn from Caleb? He was delighted to have the mountain-area of Hebron. Why?

5. There was great variety in the situations of the different tribes. How much variety may we expect among the people of God, and what do our varied situations imply?

☐☐☐ Reading 74 (Joshua 16:1–18:28)

1. What is it that leads to greatness and eminence? Joshua 16:1–17:18 deals with the two tribes descending from the two sons of Joseph (16:1–4). This leaves seven remaining tribes (as 18:1–2 will note). There seems to be significance in the fact that Judah is dealt with first, and then the sons of Joseph, Ephraim and Manasseh.

2. Those who grasped at easy but premature inheritance did not get the best. Two and a half tribes had asked for land on the other side of the Jordan and had been given what they asked. Was it worth having? What do we learn from this about patience, about ambition, about love of ease? Anything else?

3. The people of Ephraim did not even attempt to displace the pagans of Gezer (16:10). What do we learn from this?

4. The mass of geographical detail in these chapters is hard to follow and one needs a good Bible atlas to follow the information properly. It obviously was vitally important that the twelve tribes knew exactly where their borders were located. What is the spiritual equivalent?

5. In Joshua 18, we discover the readiness of God to lead his people into inheritance. What are the principles we find here?

☐☐☐ Reading 75 (Joshua 19:1–21:45)

1. What exactly is the Christian's inheritance? Is it ever territorial? Is it in this life or beyond the grave? Or both? In these chapters the tribes of Simeon, Zebulun, Issachar, Asher, Naphtali and Dan are given well-defined territories. The author-editor puts Caleb (14:6–15) and Joshua (19:49–50) at either side of the story of the tribes being given their allocations of land. Now the survey comes to a close and there

is a section mentioning Joshua himself (19:49–50). What can the Christian learn from these catalogues of land?

2. God instructs Joshua to set aside six 'cities of refuge' (20:1–2). They seem to be remarkable illustrations of what it means to 'run for refuge' to the Lord Jesus Christ. Can we work this out in detail?

3. In Joshua 21:1–45, provision was made for the Levites whose calling was more spiritual than agricultural. What do we learn from these 'full-time workers'?

☐☐☐ Reading 76 (Joshua 22:1–24:33)

1. In these chapters the people of God spread out to fill the land. How are they to stay together and yet spread out to their different callings? Can Christians learn anything about their unity and variety from these chapters?

2. When Joshua was old, he wanted to give two last farewell addresses, one to the officials of the land and one to the whole people. What are the main points he wants them to remember?

3. Joshua's last word is to appeal for determined decision (24:15). What does God call us to? What is to be our response?

Romans

Paul wrote his letter to the Romans from Corinth in about AD 57. His main purposes were: (i) to establish the Christians at Rome so that they could become a base for his further travels, (ii) to explain his basic message of justification for gentiles without the Mosaic law, and (iii) to give them a sample of his ministry as apostle to the gentiles. Romans 1:1–17 is his introduction (1:1–15) plus his basic statement of his theme (1:16–17). Romans 1:18–3:20 shows why the gospel is needed. Romans 3:21–4:25 is Paul's basic statement of his message of justification by faith in Jesus. Romans 5:1–8:39 deals with the new position of the Christian 'having been justified by faith'. Romans 9:1–11:36 explains how the nation of Israel fits in to God's plan of reaching the world. Romans 12:1–15:13 calls the Christians to live out the gospel in a practical manner in their daily living. Then Romans 15:14–16:25 are his concluding remarks and greetings.

Recommended reading: F. F. Bruce, *Romans* (Tyndale Commentary, IVP, 1985); C. Hodge, *Romans* (1886, often reprinted).

□□□ **Reading 77 (Romans 1:1–32)**
1. What do we learn from the character of Paul seen in these verses?
2. The quotation in Romans 1:17 can be translated in many ways. It could be taken to mean (i) that the Righteous One, Jesus, lived (that is,

was raised from the dead) because of his faith, or because of his faithfulness. (ii) It could be that Jesus lived a godly life because of his faith, or (iii) that the believer lives because of Jesus' faith (or faithfulness). (iv) Then it is possible to take the phrasing differently and take it to mean 'He-who-is-righteous-by-faith shall live'. Is Paul's ambiguity deliberate? What points might he *specially* want us to see in Habakkuk's words?

3. 'The anger of God is (now!) being revealed . . .' In what ways was God's anger being revealed against sin in the Roman empire? And in our world? 'God *is* love; God *becomes* angry.' What causes God's anger? What causes God's love?

☐☐☐ Reading 78 (Romans 2:1–29)

In Romans 2:1–29, Paul moves from shocking paganism (1:18–32) to respectable morality and Jewish pride in the Mosaic law.

1. The shocking sinner is described in 1:18–32, but what are the characteristics of the 'nice' sinner, the seemingly upright person?

2. What was the purpose of circumcision? What was the role of the Mosaic law?

3. What is Paul's view of the law of God in this chapter? Do you agree with the note on 2:14 below?

Note (i) A phrase in verse 13 could be translated, 'The doers of the law shall be vindicated'. It refers to what happens in the judgment day. A debatable question: does Paul refer to 'natural law' in 2:14? The placing of the phrase 'by birth' is debatable. It is doubtful whether it speaks of times when 'gentiles who do not have the law, by nature do things that the law requires . . .' This would imply there is an unwritten law identical to the Mosaic law – an idea never found in Paul's writings. More likely Paul speaks of times when 'gentiles who *do not have the law by birth*, do things that the law requires . . .' The phrase joins on to what precedes, not to what follows. It is identical to the phrase 'by birth' in Ephesians 2:3 and Galatians 2:15. This would imply that Paul is speaking of gentile Christians (as both Augustine of Hippo and Karl Barth believed). Do gentiles have the law at all? Paul (who generally means the Mosaic system when he uses the word 'law') would have said 'No'. Gentiles have 'conscience' but Paul never calls conscience 'law'.

☐☐☐ Reading 79 (Romans 3:1–20)

In verses 1–20 Paul wants (i) to answer some questions – he has several of them in 3:1–2, 3–4, 5–6, 7–8, 9; (ii) to show that Old Testament

Scriptures accused Israel of the sins he has mentioned (3:10–18), and
(iii) to come to a conclusion (3:19–20).

1. Was there any value being Jewish, if it did not automatically bring
   salvation? Is there any advantage in growing up in a Christian home?
2. 'Some slanderously charge us with saying, "Let us do evil things in
   order that good things may come."' Why should Paul ever be accused
   of wickedness? If his gospel was accused of wickedness, should our
   gospel face the same accusation?
3. Verses 10–18 are quotations from *Jewish* Scriptures. So what does that
   imply (see Romans 3:19–20)? What were the charges?

☐☐☐ **Reading 80 (Romans 3:21–31)**
In Romans 3:21–4:25 Paul lays out his basic message of atonement and
justification. He begins: 'But now, without the law, a righteousness from
God has been manifested, being witnessed by the law and the prophets'
(Romans 3:21). 'It is the righteousness of God through the faithfulness of
Jesus Christ to all who believe' (Romans 3:22b). There are eight things
involved in this. Then in Romans 3:22b he begins to develop this theme.
He explains why everyone needs salvation (3:22b–23), how it is entirely
free (3:24a), how it comes to us through what Jesus has done. This is
described as redemption (3:24), propitiation (3:25), and as providing
justification (3:26). This way of salvation has three consequences, he says.
It excludes boasting (3:27–28), is appropriate for everyone (3:29–30) and
fulfils the law (3:21).

1. What are the eight basic things Paul says in Romans 3:21–22a?
2. What are the meanings of the key words here: redemption, propitiation
   (a sacrifice of atonement, *New International Version*, verse 25), justification?
3. How does the cross vindicate God?
4. How does the gospel 'fulfil' or 'establish' the law (3:21, 31)?

☐☐☐ **Reading 81 (Romans 4:1–25)**
The way of salvation is shown in the case of Abraham and David (4:1–8).
In Romans 4:9–12 Paul explains how this gospel relates to the law that
was given to Israel. Paul argues that the goal of our salvation ('inheritance') is not reached through law-keeping but is reached through this
'righteousness of faith' (4:13–17a). From the middle of verse 17 Paul
begins to describe what this faith was actually like as it worked out in
Abraham's life and how Abraham laid hold of the inheritance that God

promised. The faith that inherits blessing is the very same faith that brought Abraham's justification in the first place (4:22–25).

1. Abraham is the model of salvation. What was involved (see Genesis 15:6)? What was not involved? Circumcision, Mosaic law-keeping . . . what else?
2. In what way does the law of God 'work wrath'? Is this true in several ways? If so, in what possible ways is it true?
3. Inheritance comes 'through' justification by faith. What does this involve?
4. What are the characteristics of Abraham's persistent faith?

□□□ **Reading 82 (Romans 5:1–21)**

1. Romans 5:1–11 lists some results of justification in 5:1, 2a, 2b, 3–5, 11 (with deductions in 5:6–10). 'Having been justified by faith we have . . .' What are the results Paul mentions?
2. The main point of 5:12–21 is that life in Adam and life in Christ are in some ways parallel. The Christian is no longer in Adam; they are in Christ. But what is the big difference between the two positions?
3. When there was no Mosaic law (note 5:20) how did believers live godly lives? Why was the law 'added'?

Note Verse 12 is an unfinished comparison. 'Therefore, just as . . .' Verses 13–14 are a digression to explain how death reigned. Verses 15–17 are another digression to explain that 'the gift is not like the trespass'. Then in verses 18–19, the comparison is restarted and completed.

□□□ **Reading 83 (Romans 6:1–23)**

The basic line of thought in this chapter is as follows. If we are under grace, does this encourage sin (6:1–2a)? Paul says, 'No!' because we have 'died' to sin. That is to say, our placement 'in Christ' has finished for ever our *position* under the domineering power of sin.

1. What is the place of 'baptism' (whatever the word might mean in 6:3) in our break with sin's domineering power? (i) Does Paul use the word metaphorically and refer only to a work of the Holy Spirit (as in 1 Corinthians 12:13)? (ii) Is the word referring to water-baptism as a way of expressing faith – and so faith puts us 'in Christ'? (iii) Or does a ceremony with water itself achieve something?
2. Romans 6:11 contains the first command in the letter. What does it mean to 'reckon' ourselves to have died (not 'to be dead') to sin?

3. How does Paul prepare in the early part of the letter for what he says in Romans 6:12–14? Note the word 'therefore'.

4. Romans 6:15–23 is the practical follow-up of what Paul has said in 6:1–14. What are the practical steps that have to be taken in order to follow through with the doctrine of 6:1–10? How does the doctrine of the first half of the chapter relate to the way we live?

☐☐☐ **Reading 84 (Romans 7:1–25)**

In Romans 7:1–4 Paul makes a basic statement. We have died to the law in order to be fruitful towards God. Any law rules over that person only while they are alive. The law can never die, but we can and do die to the law through Jesus. This is precisely what happened. We have died to the law. By 'law' or 'the law', Paul normally means the entire Mosaic system. In this case he specially has in mind the tenth commandment, which is the most demanding sentence in the law.

Romans 7:5–6 is perhaps the key to the rest of the chapter. He compares what it is like to be 'in the flesh' and 'under the law' (on the one side) with being 'in the Spirit' (on the other side). The result of being under law (verse 5) is agony and spiritual death. In verse 6 he puts the other side of the comparison and tells us what it is like to be in the Spirit and 'married' to Jesus.

1. What is it like to be 'married' to the Mosaic law? What is it like to be 'married' to our Lord Jesus Christ?

2. What is it like seriously to try to keep the law of God? For a non-Christian? For a Christian? What kind of 'law' should the Christian be wanting to keep? Surely not the whole 2,000 or more regulations in the Mosaic law? The Ten Commandments (but is the Sabbath literally kept?)? What 'law' are we under? How do the New Testament exhortations handle the matter?

3. On any view of Romans 7:1–25, verse 25a is something of an intrusion into the flow of thought. Paul cannot be thanking God for his bondage! What is in Paul's mind in this intrusive interjection?

Note Interpretations of Romans 7:1–25. The structure of Romans 7:7–25 should be noted (see table on next page):

(i) Is the 'wretched man' a reference to Adam? This does not seem to fit with the flow or argument. Adam was never under the Mosaic law. (ii) Is the 'I' corporate (Israel?)? This seems over-subtle. (iii) Is it the *normal* Christian? But is the normal Christian so defeated and asking 'who' should save them? (iv) Is it the typical average unbeliever? But the average believer does not

	Section 1	Section 2
A question	Is the law sin? (7:7a)	'Did this good thing become death . . . ?' (7:13a)
An answer	No! (7:7b)	No! (13b)
A counter-proposal	'I would not have experienced sin except through the law' (7:7c)	'On the contrary, it was sin working death . . .' (7:13c)
A thought developed	'For . . .' (7:7d–11)	'For . . .' (7:14–25a) ('For' is wrongly omitted by *New International Version*)
A conclusion	'So then . . .' (7:12)	'So then . . .' (7:25b)

delight in the law! (v) Is it some kind of defective Christian? Perhaps it is the Christian trying to live on their own efforts? (vi) Is it an unbeliever or a seeker who has not yet discovered Christ, but is still under the law? The last seems to be right for the following reasons. The theme is the law, especially the tenth commandment. Paul says we have died to the law, and the law 'when we were in the flesh' could only bring despair and death. Verses 7–25 surely expound and develop verse 5. Everything in verse 5 is mentioned again in verses 7–25. The 'wretched man' is explicitly (in verse 5) 'in the flesh' and is asking, 'Who?' He has not found a Saviour. It is likely that the 'wretched man' of Romans 7:13–25 is a description of the maximum the holy law of God can do in the unconverted person. It is an exposition of verse 5. The thrust of the whole chapter is to get us to abandon for ever the attempt to live 'under' the Mosaic law. The tenth commandment intensifies the knowledge of sin but does nothing more.

□□□ **Reading 85 (Romans 8:1–17)**
Romans 8:1–39 is like a sermon with a text (8:1), an exposition (8:2–30) and a powerful appeal (8:31–39). The Christian is released from condemnation objectively (as a matter of fact) and subjectively (as a matter of feeling).

1. What are the reasons Paul gives (8:2–4, 5–17) to show that the Christian is released from condemnation? How much do modern Christians suffer from guilt feelings and condemnation? Is it only westerners who have an introspective conscience?
2. What is the connection between assurance of salvation and godliness (in these verses)?
3. Most of this chapter gives unconditional assurance, but there is an 'if' in verse 17. What is lost or gained according to whether we suffer with Christ?

☐☐☐ Reading 86 (Romans 8:18–39)

1. What are the reasons Paul gives (8:18–25, 26–27, 28–30) to show that the Christian is released from condemnation?
2. Paul refers to predestination rather late in the argument of Romans 1:1–8:39. Could there be a reason for this? Why is Romans 8:29–30 the last argument in 8:2–30, before the question ('What . . . ?') and conclusion in 8:31–39?
3. What fears are being addressed in Romans 8:31–34?

☐☐☐ Reading 87 (Romans 9:1–18)

Paul takes up a question about the nation of Israel. The flow of thought moves as follows. Paul argues that the purpose of God cannot be broken (8:28–39). Yet Israel had so many privileges but seems to have fallen out of the purpose of God. Has the purpose of God failed (9:1–6a)? Paul's answer is: 'No.' The purpose of God has not failed – for four reasons. (i) God's elect was never the whole nation but always a people within the nation (9:6b–30). (ii) Israel failed because of unbelief. (iii) The fall of Israel is not total; there has always been a remnant (11:1–10). (iv) The story is not finished! Israel will be restored to a place within the true and faithful people of God (11:11–33). Paul ends with a burst of praise (11:33–36).

1. Can faith and salvation be inherited by physical birth? If not, what leads one child to be a believer but not another?
2. What Paul has said in Romans 9:6–13 leads him to ask, 'Is God unjust?' (verse 14). What makes him ask this question? Does *your* understanding of Romans 9:6–13 lead to the same question?
3. Does God create hardness of heart? If not, what happens when God 'hardens' someone?

☐☐☐ Reading 88 (Romans 9:19–33)

1. Note the differences between the vessels fitted for destruction and the vessels of mercy ('endured . . . prepared'; 'fit in themselves (Greek middle voice) . . . prepared'; 'prepared *beforehand*' – in one case only). What is the significance of these differences?
2. What new thought comes in at verse 24?
3. Verses 30–33 summarise the situation and prepare for Romans 10:1–21. What was it in Jesus that made Israel 'stumble' over him?

☐☐☐ Reading 89 (Romans 10:1–21)

1. The heart of the chapter seems to be Romans 10:3. What is 'Israel's own righteousness'? Why did it lead to tragedy for the nation?

2. What is necessary for salvation (Romans 10:9–10)? Is there anything else that is needed? Is the gospel too good to be true?

3. What is God's way of getting his good news out to men and women in this world? What are its steps and stages?

▢▢▢ Reading 90 (Romans 11:1–15)

1. How was the first-century Jewish rejection of Jesus like what happened in the days of Elijah? What encouragements does Paul take from the experiences of Elijah in Romans 11:1–10?

2. If a tragedy leads to blessing, surely a blessing will lead to even greater blessing! What is Paul's point in Romans 11:12, 15? What does it lead us to expect in the future preaching of the gospel?

3. Paul's ministry to gentiles could easily give the impression that he had renounced any interest in Israel. 'Paul is not a Jew any more', people might say. How does Paul answer this question? What are the equivalent situations today?

▢▢▢ Reading 91 (Romans 11:16–36)

1. A careful study of Romans 11:11–27 shows that Paul's argument steadily intensifies. He moves from possibility to probability, and then comes to direct prediction. Can you pick out the steps and stages of his argument?

2. In the illustration of 'the olive tree', what do the different parts represent? What is the trunk (not the natural nation since gentiles do not become Jews)? Who are the natural branches? What is the falling out? Who are the unnatural branches? What is the grafting in? What is the root? (Abraham?)

3. Paul's closing verses express sheer astonishment (11:33–36). Does your understanding of Romans 11:1–36 lead to wonder and worship? If not, is there more to Romans 11:1–36 than you realised?

▢▢▢ Reading 92 (Romans 12)

Paul comes now to an appeal for Christian practical godliness. He begins generally (12:1–2), then comes to the use of our gifts within the Christian fellowship (12:3–8), then gives exhortations for a great variety of different circumstances (12:9–21).

1. What is the distinctive Christian approach to the body? And what is the distinctive Christian approach to the mind?

2. What is Paul's definition of a 'spiritual gift' implicit in these verses? What are the principles he puts before us about the use of such gifts?

3. Can you list the different circumstances Paul is considering in 12:9–21? What is his exhortation in each situation?

☐☐☐ Reading 93 (Romans 13)

1. Is the state 'God's minister for good' always? What does Paul mean here? Is it a rough generalisation? Is it something that is true in the long run? Or what?

2. Why is the *one* command on which we concentrate love of neighbour and not love of God? What are the practical implications for the priorities of our life?

3. 'Salvation is nearer to us than when we first believed' (13:11). What could Paul see that made him know Jesus' coming was getting nearer (compare Hebrews 10:25)?

☐☐☐ Reading 94 (Romans 14:1–17)

1. Christians in Rome were divided into the 'strong' (i.e. the bold and liberated) and the weak (i.e. those who were timid about minor matters of behaviour, the over-conscientious). What does Paul ask of the weak? What does he ask of the strong? What arguments does he use? Would the 'weak' admit that they are weak?

2. In verses 1–13 Paul deals with attitudes. From verse 14 onwards he deals more with major principles. What does he mean when he says, 'Nothing is unclean in itself'? How widely may the principle be applied?

3. The kingdom of God consists not of small things ('meat and drink'), but of major experiences of God ('righteousness . . . peace . . . joy). How may the principle ('big things matter not small things') be re-applied in modern life? What are the 'small things' that are secondary?

☐☐☐ Reading 95 (Romans 14:18–15:13)

1. To what extent should we be concerned to please other people, in the way we live?

2. Romans 14:21 explicitly puts wine-drinking forward as one of the examples of these 'matters of opinion'. The drinking of wine was generally widely accepted among Christians until the nineteenth century. Then in Britain in the 1830s, pleas for what was called 'temperance' were put forward by nineteenth-century Methodists (but it soon became a matter of abstinence) and various denominations made 'abstinence' a condition of membership. Similar trends were followed in other countries. In the light of Romans 14:1–23, what must we say in this connection?

3. Actually Romans 15:7–13 is widening what has been said in 14:1–15:6. In 14:1–15:6 he was dealing with the weak and the strong. In 15:7–13 he is dealing with the Jews and the gentiles. What two purposes did Christ have when he came to Israel (15:8, 9a)? How are Jews and gentile Christians (or any groups of Christians from different cultures) to relate to each other?

☐☐☐ **Reading 96 (Romans 15:14–16:27)**

The main message of Paul's letter to the Romans finished at Romans 15:13. Now he has a number of smaller matters to deal with. We could lay them out in nine small units: Paul's purpose (15:14–16), Paul's ministry (15:17–21), Paul's plans (15:22–29), Paul's request (15:30–33), Paul's commendation (16:1–2), Paul's greetings (16:3–16), a warning (16:17–20), more greetings (16:21–23), doxology (16:25–27).

1. What is Paul's view of a pioneering Christian ministry (15:17–18)?

2. Jerusalem never asked for a cent from Paul. It was entirely Paul's idea to help the church there, which was the 'mother church' of all gentile believers. It was not an older church helping a younger church. It was daughter-churches helping their mother. What can we learn about 'money and mission' from Romans 16:1–27?

3. Romans 16:1–27 gives us a glimpse of the way in which New Testament Christians stayed in touch with each other and knew each other. In what way should we stay in touch with the wider Christian world?

4. Where is the dividing line between perversions of the gospel (Romans 16:17–20) and areas where Christians may 'agree to differ'?

Isaiah

The themes of Isaiah seem all to abound with the letter 's': sin, the suffering that arises because of sin, salvation in its several stages, the Servant of God who is the Saviour of the world. King Uzziah of Judah took the throne as sole ruler in 767 BC and died in 739 BC. His days were days of easy prosperity, formal inherited religion, negligence of God's ways, and small achievement for God. In the year that King Uzziah died, Isaiah was called to prophetic ministry. Uzziah's reign had been the most prosperous that Judah had known since the days of David, but then Tiglath-Pileser III of Assyria (745–727 BC) rose to power and began to impose his yoke on the lands near to Judah. Judah was being threatened by Assyria, 'the rod of God's anger'. As the threat from Assyria grew worse, Pekah of northern Israel and Rezin of Damascus formed an anti-Assyrian coalition and tried to compel Ahaz of Judah to join them. When Ahaz refused, they threatened to depose him and put their own choice on his throne. Ahaz – who did not believe that the God who had redeemed Israel by the blood of the lamb could give any help – asked the Assyrian king for help, and Judah became a satellite state of Assyria. Throughout these years Isaiah constantly preached the folly of trusting in any pagan. Neither Assyria nor Egypt could help the people of God. After Sargon's death Sennacherib (705–681 BC) ruled in Assyria. Judah tried to rebel against Assyrian domination, and this resulted in Sennacherib's expedition of 701 BC, during which he overran Judah and besieged Jerusalem. Isaiah 36:1–37:38 records Sennacherib's threat to Jerusalem.

The book of Isaiah is the record of Isaiah's preaching during these years from 739 to about 701 BC. So far as one can tell Isaiah 1:1–35:10 was put together from the many bits and pieces of Isaiah's preaching, plus a few bits of narrative (as in 7:1–17). Then Isaiah 36:1–39:8 gives extracts from historical records. Isaiah 40:1–66:24 must have been preached at some stage but it is difficult to say how or when. Perhaps it was an inspired written meditation about the future of Israel, which Isaiah used as the basis of his preaching in his later years. What is certain is that the whole sixty-six chapters are all brilliantly and marvellously edited into a unified work about the sin of Israel and its future redemption by a coming King, Servant and Conqueror. Generally speaking it is no longer possible to give the exact dates and circumstances in which the various bits and pieces of Isaiah were originally preached or written. What we have to handle is the edited whole. The editing has been done so brilliantly that it must come from the hand of the master himself – Isaiah. The different parts of the book need each other. Certainly one mind put it together, for the massively interwoven 'book of Isaiah' could never have been written by a 'committee' from different centuries! One of its main themes is how the God of the Bible is able to predict the future – something the idols cannot do. Unless there is miraculous prediction in Isaiah the argument of the book falls aside. This amazing note of prediction is only to be found if Isaiah himself wrote the predictions concerning Babylon, a century or so ahead of his own time.

Recommended reading: J. A. Motyer, *Isaiah* (Tyndale Commentary, IVP, 1999); D. Kidner, 'Isaiah', in *New Bible Commentary* (IVP, 1994).

□□□ Reading 97 (Isaiah 1:1–2:22)

Isaiah 1:1–5:30 gives a general survey of the calamity that Israel brought upon itself by its own sin and wickedness, without mentioning any of the kings, places and times that Isaiah knew so well. The five chapters break down into three sub-sections. After the title (1:1), Isaiah 1:1–31 deals with the general condition of Israel. Isaiah 2:1–4:6 deals with the way in which Israel relates to her destiny. Ideal Israel is first described, but then the actual condition of the Israel of the eighth century BC is far different (2:6–4:1). Yet Isaiah 4:2–6 comes back to the assurance that the ideal will one day be fulfilled. The third section of these chapters speaks of Israel's ingratitude. Despite all that God has done for his 'vineyard', the vineyard has produced no fruit. The five chapters hold together as a general description of Isaiah's times.

1. How does Isaiah describe his times (1:2–31)? In what ways does his description resemble our own land or the world in general? What hints of any change come in Isaiah 1:1–31?
2. If the 'temple mountain' is a prophetic symbol of the people of God, what hope does Isaiah 2:1–4 hold out for the future of the Christian faith? What is the point of verse 5?
3. Isaiah 2:6 moves from the ideal to the actual. What is the religious condition of Israel and what will happen to such religion in a day of judgment?

☐☐☐ **Reading 98 (Isaiah 3:1–5:30)**
1. What happens in the leadership of a land when there is social decay (3:1–7)? What causes the decay (3:8–9)?
2. What happens to the relationship between the sexes in a day of judgment (Isaiah 3:1–26)?
3. Isaiah 4:2–6 gives us a picture of future salvation. What is involved in the picture-language here?
4. God did everything he could to provide for Israel's fruitfulness (Isaiah 5:1–30). What is the Christian equivalent? What has God done to enable our fruitfulness? What is the result if Christians are unfruitful?

☐☐☐ **Reading 99 (Isaiah 6:1–8:8)**
A second major section of Isaiah is found in Isaiah 6:1–12:6. It begins with the call of an individual (6:1–13), goes on to speak of a hope for Judah despite a day of great crisis (7:1–9:7) and then makes the same point in connection with northern Israel (9:8–11:16). Isaiah 12:1–6 balances Isaiah 6:1–13. A saved individual is found at the beginning of the section. A saved community is found at the end of the section.

Isaiah 7:1–11:16 goes over the same ground twice, focussing on the south and the north: (i) a crisis of faith (7:1–17), (ii) the judgment of God against unbelief (7:18–8:8), (iii) the reality of the remnant (8:9–22), (iv) the hope for the future (9:1–7). Then again: (i) a crisis of faith (9:8–10:4), (ii) the judgment of God against unbelief (10:5–15), (iii) the reality of the remnant (10:16–34), (iv) the hope for the future (11:1–16).

1. What are the ingredients of salvation and calling, found here in Isaiah 6:1–13?
2. How does Ahaz show himself to be a man gripped by unbelief?
3. How does a 'virgin birth' come to be a sign of the stability of hope to the house of David?
4. What is the nature of God's judgment against unbelief?

Note The flow of thought in Isaiah 7:1–17 seems to be as follows. Ahaz is trembling with fear (7:1–2) but Isaiah gives him great hope, invites him to faith, and offers him any kind of sign he may wish to ask for (7:3–11). Ahaz responds with unbelief (7:12). As a result God will in due course give the 'house of David' a sign of his own: a virgin birth of a divine child (7:14). The sign is *now* undated (Ahaz does not believe in it so it will be delayed by unbelief) but is spoken *as if* it were present (since it was originally offered to Ahaz for his own time). Within a few years the threat to Judah will pass away (7:16), but a worse judgment will come: the king of Assyria (7:17).

Contrary to common opinion there is good reason from context and linguistic-study to believe that 'virgin' in Isaiah 7:14 does indeed mean 'virgin'. It is hardly a 'a sign in the deepest depths or in the highest heights' for an ordinary woman to have a baby in the ordinary manner! The context requires a staggering miracle.

☐☐☐ Reading 100 (Isaiah 8:9–9:7)

Despite the certainty of judgment, Israel will not be exterminated, for there will a 'remnant' of believers.

1. What are the characteristics of the 'the remnant' (8:9–22)? What is the difference between the believing remnant and the spiritists?
2. Is it surprising that Judah's hope (9:1–7) should come not in Judah itself, but in areas to the north, where there would soon be large numbers of Assyrians? Is it significant that Jesus ministered more in Galilee than in Jerusalem?
3. In the day of victory over Midian, it was Gideon who was used by God, but in the day of Judah's salvation it will be the birth of a child that introduces the victory. What are the fourfold characteristics of the coming Saviour revealed in his fourfold name?

☐☐☐ Reading 101 (Isaiah 9:8–10:4)

Isaiah moves from prophecies about Judah to prophecies about Israel. Again the same sequence is followed: (i) a crisis of faith (9:8–10:4), (ii) the judgment of God against unbelief (10:5–15), (iii) the reality of the remnant (10:16–34), (iv) the hope for the future (11:1–16).

1. 'The Sovereign Lord has sent a word against Jacob; it keeps falling on Israel . . . But the people have not returned to him who struck them, nor have they sought Yahweh Almighty' (9:8, 13). What are the similarities between Judah's crisis (7:1–17) and Israel's crisis (9:8–10:4)?
2. How does unbelief refuse to learn?

3. How does unbelief lead to social anarchy, in this section of Isaiah?

☐☐☐ **Reading 102 (Isaiah 10:5–12:6)**

1. How does God use human wickedness for his own purposes? Can we see any 'rod of God's anger' among the nations today?

2. If God uses sinners, how can he punish them? What does Isaiah say about the matter?

3. What do we learn about the coming Saviour from Isaiah 11:1–16?

4. What is the cause of the joy in Isaiah 12:1–6? In what way do the people express their joy?

☐☐☐ **Reading 103 (Isaiah 13:1–16:14)**

We reach the third major section of the book of Isaiah (13:1–27:13). Isaiah has spent twelve chapters showing in general (1:1–5:30) and in detail (6:1–12:6) that Israel desperately needs a Saviour. Now he will spend fifteen chapters (in our Bibles) showing that the gentiles are equally under the judgment of God, but they too will experience the coming of a Saviour. First Isaiah goes round a 'circle' of songs about nations: Isaiah 13:1–14:27 (Babylon and Assyria); 14:28–32 (Philistia); 15:1–16:14 (Moab); 17:1–18:7 (Damascus and Ephraim); 19:1–20:6 (Egypt).

Then he does the same thing again; he goes around a circle of songs about nations, again beginning with Babylon: Isaiah 21:1–10 (Babylon); 21:11–12 (Edom); 21:13–17 (Arabia); 22:1–25 (Jerusalem); 23:1–18 (Tyre).

Then once again Isaiah has a cycle of five songs. Only now what he says is not so tied to particular nations. He is extending the principles he has established and applying them to the whole world. His five songs are as follows: Isaiah 24:1–20 (the world in chaos); 24:21–23 (the conquering King); 25:1–12 (the world comes to Zion); 26:1–20 (secure salvation); 27:1–13 (worldwide victory). The basic point of this entire section (13:1–27:13) is that the nations need a Saviour as much as Israel does.

1. Babylon (Isaiah 13:1–14:23) was a historical reality, but it was also used as representative of what is at enmity towards God. What are the characteristics of Babylon that are noted here (and elsewhere)? What and where is 'Babylon' today? What does God feel about it? What will he do about it?

2. Philistia (14:28–32) apparently wanted Judah to join them in an alliance in order to agitate against the Assyrians. What was Isaiah's answer? Can we really find refuge in God in the midst of political conflict?

3. What were the sins of Moab (15:1–16:14)? What hope of salvation does Isaiah offer the Moabites? What will they – and we – have to do to find rescue?

Note The problem in Isaiah's own day was not Babylon but the closely related kingdom of Assyria. It seems that the promise of Assyria's fall (14:24–27) is intended as a foretaste of Babylon's fall.

□□□ **Reading 104 (Isaiah 17:1–20:6)**

1. The background to 17:1–18:7 (Damascus and Ephraim) is an alliance between them that had failed. God's people must put their trust elsewhere. Does God use failed alliances to force us to put our trust in him? Personally? Nationally? Where is power to be found in world affairs?

2. Israel was often tempted to look to Egypt for help (19:1–20:6). Why is Egypt (or any other worldly resource) unable to help God's people?

3. Isaiah 19:5–10 describes economic collapse. What place might economic collapse have in the purpose of God?

4. In the midst of threats against Egypt there is a promise that Egypt could be healed (19:16–25). What hope does Isaiah hold out for a great pagan nation of the ancient world? What does it imply for the nations of today?

□□□ **Reading 105 (Isaiah 21:1–23:18)**

Isaiah goes around a second cycle of songs: Isaiah 21:1–10 (Babylon); 21:11–12 (Edom); 21:13–17 (Arabia); 22:1–25 (Jerusalem); 23:1–18 (Tyre).

1. What is each *distinctive* problem that each of these five nations face? Babylon suffers from the failure of its gods. And the others?

2. In what way did the past choices made by Jerusalem (22:1–25) affect what was currently happening? What had they failed to do?

3. Compare and contrast Shebna and Eliakim (22:15–25). What were their failures? What were their successes?

□□□ **Reading 106 (Isaiah 24:1–25:12)**

There are five pictures in the visions of Isaiah 24:1–27:13: a devastated city, a divine King, a banquet, a strong city and a renewed Israel.

1. The very environment of the earth is polluted (24:1–3). In what way is the entire planet like a devastated city? What are the causes of worldwide disaster upon the planet? What hope does Isaiah give in 24:13–16b, 21–23?

2. Isaiah 25:1–12 tells of a day when there is great joy for the people of God, because God has delivered them from their many distresses. What distresses are they rescued from in verses 1–5? And in verses 6–8?

3. When God replaces enemies and distresses with his blessings, what actually does he give (25:9–12)?

☐☐☐ Reading 107 (Isaiah 26:1–27:13)

In Isaiah 24:1–23 there was a devastated city, the world of the wicked. In Isaiah 26:1–21 there is another city, a strong city, the people of God. Isaiah 27:1–13 again comes back to the vineyard-picture (compare Isaiah 5:1–30).

1. What are the characteristics of 'Zion, city of our God'?
2. What are the entrance qualifications?
3. What are its privileges?
4. What is its future, near and far?
5. What will God do for his vineyard-people?

☐☐☐ Reading 108 (Isaiah 28:1–30:33)

If the salvation Isaiah has described is actually to come, God has to be the Lord of history. This is the theme of Isaiah 28:1–35:10 (the fourth main section, with Isaiah 36:1–37:38 giving an illustration of the principles). There are six oracles in 28:1–29; 29:1–14; 29:15–24; 30:1–33; 31:1–32:20; 33:1–35:10. God is the King of the nations. Ephraim is drunk (28) but God will act against it (29:1–14) and transform it (29:15–24). Egypt and Assyria are irrelevant (30). The One who brings change is God (31–32), who will graciously create a new Zion and a new world (33:1–35:10).

1. How is drunkenness a good illustration of the general condition of the world?
2. In Isaiah 29:1–24, how will God act in judgment? How will he act in restoration?
3. Israel was constantly tempted to turn to false solutions to solve its problems. How do we do the same thing? And what does God say about the 'Egypts' and 'Assyrias' to which we turn?

☐☐☐ **Reading 109 (Isaiah 31:1–32:20)**
1. What is true leadership, according to these chapters?
2. How do people change under the grace of God, according to these chapters?
3. What new values are found in a godly society?
4. How does the Spirit of God work in transforming society?

☐☐☐ **Reading 110 (Isaiah 33:1–35:10)**
1. Assyria is in view in 33:1–12. How are God's people to face treachery?
2. In what stages does God bring his new Zion (33:13–24) into being?
3. Isaiah 34:1–17 predicts an overthrow of wickedness in the nations. When and how might we expect it?
4. Finally God's people 'come home to Zion' (35:1–10). What is the new world and the new life like? What happens along the road?

☐☐☐ **Reading 111 (Isaiah 36:1–37:38)**
Isaiah 36:1–37:38 is best regarded as the end of the section (28:1–37:38), part of a bridge to 40:1–55:13, and shows how everything that Isaiah has said is working out in history in the case of Assyria and Israel.

1. Rabshakeh insists there is no salvation in faith (36:1–21). How is he like many who oppose God?
2. Hezekiah is slow to come to trust in God at this point. How does he reach faith eventually?
3. What do we learn about prayer in Hezekiah, and about faithfulness to God's word in Isaiah himself?

☐☐☐ **Reading 112 (Isaiah 38:1–39:8)**
Isaiah 38:1–39:8 can be seen as an introduction to Isaiah 40:1–55:13, and are also (like 36:1–37:38) part of a bridge to 40:1–55:13. These verses show how everything that Isaiah will predict about Babylon begins with something that happened back in the days of Hezekiah.

1. Hezekiah seems to get God to change his mind. Is this the ultimate truth about God? Or is it just the way it seems as we relate to him?
2. What is the place of illness in the life of faith?
3. What mistakes does Hezekiah make in these chapters? Why are they so serious?

□□□ Reading 113 (Isaiah 40:1–42:17)

In four more sections Isaiah now will give a general message of comfort (40:1–42:17) and will give a promise that redemption is coming to Israel (42:18–44:23). Cyrus will come as a *political* saviour (44:24–48:22) and a Suffering Servant will come as a *spiritual* Saviour (49:1–55:13).

1. God is a God of comfort (40:1–2). He promises healing after chastening. In what ways is this message reinforced in 40:3–5, 6–8, 9–11?
2. If God is to achieve the salvation he promises, he needs to be the all-powerful Creator. What kind of character does God the Creator have according to 40:12–26? How should we apply it to ourselves (note 40:27–31)?
3. In 41:1–7, God is portrayed as world-ruler. The 'one from the east' turned out to be Cyrus the Persian, the conqueror of the Babylonians. What pictures of God as comforter do we have in 41:8–20?
4. What is the difference between God and the idols (41:21–29)?
5. The 'Servant' of God is the answer to the needs of the gentiles (42:1–9). What can we learn from this 'Servant' here?

□□□ Reading 114 (Isaiah 42:18–44:23)

1. Is the 'servant' of 42:1–9 the same as the 'servant' of 42:18? If not, what is the difference between them? What are Israel's problems in this section?
2. *National* liberation is promised in 42:18–43:21. What does the fact that God acts in history mean to us today? Is God acting in the history of our world?
3. *Spiritual* liberation is promised in 43:22–44:23. What are the differences between national liberation and spiritual liberation in this section?
4. Can the Messianic 'Servant of God' be Israel the nation? If not, why not?

□□□ Reading 115 (Isaiah 44:24–46:13)

1. Isaiah 44:24–45:8 refers to Cyrus the Persian, the conqueror of the Babylonians. Does God raise up secular 'messiahs'? What is their purpose and place in God's rule of the world? Are there some modern examples?
2. Isaiah 45:9–46:13 expects that Israel will protest at such a 'messiah' as Cyrus. What is God's answer?
3. 'You are a God who hides yourself' (45:15). What does Isaiah mean? What other examples are there of the hiddenness of God?

Note It is unusual for a name to be given in prophetic prediction, but not unique. 1 Kings 13:2 is another example. One's faith in such predictions depends on one's general attitude to the miraculous.

□□□ **Reading 116 (Isaiah 47:1–48:22)**
Isaiah 47:1–15 describes Babylon's fall. Isaiah 48:1–22 records an invitation to captives to return home.

1. What reasons does Isaiah give for Babylon's fall (47:1–7, 8–11, 12–15)?
2. Why did God release the Israelites from Babylon? Were they worthy (48:1–2, 4)? What is the point of 48:9–11?
3. What is the significance of Isaiah 48:22? Will the exiles go home from Babylon but still be wicked? What is the weakness of Cyrus' secular messiahship, of political deliverance?

□□□ **Reading 117 (Isaiah 49:1–50:11)**
Isaiah 49:1–6 brings us to the second 'Servant song' (after the first in 42:1–4). Isaiah 49:1–55:13 comes now to deal with Israel's spiritual deliverance, which was not achieved by Cyrus.

1. Are we any closer (from Isaiah's perspective) at identifying the 'Servant'? Could he be the remnant? If not, why not?
2. A third Servant Song is found in 50:4–10. What do we learn here of the calling and task of the 'Servant of God', the Messiah?
3. In 49:14–50:11 what are the contrasts between the nation of Israel and the Servant of God?
4. Every human opponent of the 'Servant of the Lord' will 'wear out like a garment', while God remains forever the same. What can we learn about facing opposition and slander from the 'Servant'?

Note Many find the term 'Israel' difficult here (since the Servant ministers to Israel). The answer to the difficulty seems to be that 'Israel' is here a name for the Messiah, given to him because he does all that Israel failed to do. He is the 'remnant' of Israel reduced to one.

□□□ **Reading 118 (Isaiah 51:1–52:12)**
Isaiah predicts that a Suffering Servant will come as a *spiritual* Saviour of the world (49:1–55:13). In 51:1–52:12 there are encouragements (51:1–8), appeals (51:9–16) and commands (51:17–52:12)

1. Isaiah invites his believing readers to 'Look to the rock from which you were cut'. What lessons do we learn about salvation by considering the case of Abraham? How does Isaiah develop the point? What other events of the past does Isaiah want us to consider?
2. In Isaiah 51:9–16, the prophet appeals to God to do what he has promised to do. What do we learn from these verses considered as a model of prayer?
3. How does 51:17–52:12 help us to enter into what God has promised us?

☐☐☐ Reading 119 (Isaiah 52:13–55:13)

1. What are the contrasts in this section between human spiritual blindness and the faithfulness of the Messiah?
2. What are the themes in this section that are picked up in the New Testament teaching concerning salvation?
3. What is the reward of the Servant, after he has poured out his soul unto death?

Note Isaiah 53:12 is best translated: 'Therefore I will allocate to him the many, and the strong he will allocate as spoil.'

☐☐☐ Reading 120 (Isaiah 56:1–57:21)

A slight change of perspective comes into Isaiah at Isaiah 56:1. Isaiah 40:1–55:13 viewed salvation as a 'home-coming' politically and spiritually. Isaiah 56:1–66:24 focusses more on the people who, after they have arrived home, are still not all they should be. Its three main sub-sections are as follows:

* The needs and sins of the people (56:1–59:13)
* The coming of one who conquers sin (59:14–63:6)
* A prayer and some answers (63:7–66:24)

1. What is the lifestyle for which Isaiah appeals in 56:1–8? Why is Sabbath-keeping important to Isaiah?
2. In 56:9–57:21 the godly and the ungodly may be seen. What are the habits and hopes of each group?
3. Dumb dogs, sleeping dogs and greedy dogs all appear here! They are illustrations of the 'shepherds'. What are the points of these illustrations?

Note Sabbath. The Sabbath was first of all an event in the life of God, who did the work of creating the universe in six 'days', and then on a seventh 'day' (which has still not ended) rested. God's Sabbath is his enjoyment of what he had done. It included God's desire to involve human beings in his enjoyment. This threefold pattern is the way in which God wants to work in his world. It is the way in which we are to live. (i) Life must be led and governed by God. (ii) Eventually God achieves his purpose. (iii) 'Entering into rest' is the occasion when we reap the benefits of what God has done. 'Entering into rest' is the final consummation of God's covenant. It is when he swears the oath of the covenant and says – on oath – 'I will indeed bless you.'

☐☐☐ Reading 121 (Isaiah 58:1–60:22)

1. What is Isaiah's criticism of one kind of religion (58:1–59:13)?

2. What is the significance of the picture of God's salvation as a 'light'?

3. God sends Someone as a rescuer (59:14–20), a mediator (59:21), a shining light to be a guide to the nations (60:1–22). What new things happen to Zion as a result? What is the equivalent for Christians today?

☐☐☐ Reading 122 (Isaiah 61:1–63:6)

1. In many ways Isaiah 61:1–3 is another 'Servant Song'. In these verses what are Messiah's (i) endowments and (ii) work? What are the implications for the life and work of the Christian churches? What does 'favour . . . vengeance' imply concerning the Messiah's work (note Luke 4:19 where the book is closed mid-sentence).

2. In 61:10–62:7 the Messiah is rejoicing in what he will do. What is his work? And what is the significance of the oath in 62:8–12?

3. In 63:1–7 the Messiah comes from a great battle with Edom (the traditional enemy of God's people). What is the state of his clothing? What is represented by the imagery?

☐☐☐ Reading 123 (Isaiah 63:7–66:24)

1. Isaiah 63:7–64:12 shows us a prophetic vision of the praying Church. What are the two ingredients of prayer in Isaiah 63:7–14 and 63:15–64:12?

2. What can we see of the 'spirit' of prayer in these prayers? What is the significance of the prophets crying, 'Oh that . . . !' in such an emotional manner?

3. Isaiah 65:1–66:24 are full of judgments and promises. What are the Lord's judgments upon the impenitent? What are the Lord's promises for people, weak though they are?

Proverbs

Proverbs is a collection of wisdom-sayings, ranging in length from a couple of lines to paragraphs roughly the same length as a chapter in a modern Bible. The collection was gathered over several centuries, from the days of Solomon (tenth century BC) to at least the days of Hezekiah (around 715–686 BC). It has at least three authors (Solomon, Agur, Lemuel are explicitly mentioned) and probably many more (since the proverbs were *collected* from various sources).

What is wisdom? It is the task of putting what we know into practice. It is not the same as knowledge (as we generally use the term). One can know a lot but be unwise. One can be ill-educated and untaught and yet be wise. The two things are quite different. Wisdom *aims* to know a lot but the essence of wisdom is skill in using what we know. It is godliness turned into practical reality. It begins with the fear of God. No one is wise who does not have a reverence for the power and greatness of God.

Our book of Proverbs has eight sections in it:
- The importance of wisdom (1:1–9:18)
- The proverbs of Solomon (10:1–22:16)
- The words of the wise (22:17–24:22)
- Additional sayings of the wise (24:23–34)
- Additional proverbs of Solomon (25:1–29:27)
- The words of Agur (30:1–33)
- The words of Lemuel (31:1–9)
- A song in praise of a virtuous wife (31:10–31)

Recommended reading: D. Kidner, *Proverbs* (Tyndale Commentary, IVP, 1964); K. T. Aitken, *Proverbs* (Daily Study Bible; St Andrews/Westminster, 1986).

□□□ Reading 124 (Proverbs 1:1–2:22)

Proverbs begins with a introduction (1:1–6), a theme statement (1:7) and a massive exposition of the value of wisdom (1:8–9:18). It seems that the call to 'My son' or 'My sons' is often (but not always) the marker of a new section, with a new turn of thought. It is apparently used this way in 1:8, 2:1; 3:1, 11, 21; 4:1, 10, 20; 5:1; 6:1, 20; 7:1; 8:32). Then there are also sharp and obvious changes in the line-of-thought in 1:20 and 8:1). If these observations are valid then there are fifteen sections in the lengthy discourse of 1:8–9:18. In Proverbs 1:1–2:22: (i) The young person is to heed parents (1:8–9) and refuse the deceptions of those who want gain by violence (1:10–19). (ii) Wisdom is like a businesswoman in a market appealing for attention (1:20–33). (iii) Men and women must seek it (2:1–5); God gives it (2:6–8). It delivers us from bad men (2:9–15) and bad women (2:16–20). The unit closes with a promise and a threat (2:21–22).

1. What is the purpose of the book of Proverbs according to 1:1–6 (with verse 7 as a basic motto)?
2. What are the invitations given by dangerous friends (1:10–19)? What are the alternative offers of 'Lady Wisdom'?
3. How do we become wise according to 2:1–11? What will be the results of such wisdom (2:12–22)?

□□□ Reading 125 (Proverbs 3:1–5:23)

In Proverbs 3:1–4:27: (i) loyalty is needed (3:1–4) and humble trust (3:5–10). (ii) The disciple must be willing to be disciplined (3:11–12). Wisdom will bring great blessing (3:13–18) and has marvellous credentials (3:19–20). (iii) Wisdom involves confidence and persistence (3:21–26) and it will lead us into neighbourliness (3:27–35). (iv) Wisdom must be passed on by parents (4:1–9). (v) There are two pathways through life (4:10–19). (vi) Attentiveness and purposefulness are needed (4:20–27). (vii) The loose woman is a special danger (5:1–14). The wife of one's youth is a better companion (5:15–23).

1. Are wisdom and self-confidence opposites? And what is the relationship between wisdom and physical health (3:1–10)?
2. How does God rebuke and discipline us (3:11–12)?
3. How important is neighbourliness? What are its characteristics?

☐☐☐ Reading 126 (Proverbs 6:1–7:27)

In Proverbs 6:1–7:27: (i) entanglements in false commitments (6:1–5), laziness (6:6–10) and trouble-making (6:12–19) will ruin life. (ii) Adultery is folly (6:20–35). (iii) Womanly unfaithfulness is lethal (7:1–27).

1. What makes people lazy? How does this part of Proverbs encourage diligence?
2. What are the ingredients of mischief-making mentioned here?
3. Wisdom literature uses a lot of space persuading us away from immorality. What kind of arguments does it use to convince us?

☐☐☐ Reading 127 (Proverbs 8:1–9:18)

(i) 'Lady Wisdom' preaches a sermon again in the city streets (8:1–31); and (ii) two women offer two invitations (8:32–9:18).

1. What is the significance that it is in public places that 'Lady Wisdom' calls out to people? When wisdom comes what comes with her (8:12–36)? What are her achievements?
2. Wisdom is building a house (8:23–9:1) and invites her guests (9:2–4). Who is invited? What is provided as food at the feast?
3. Why is Jesus called 'the wisdom of God'? What does the description of wisdom have in common with the New Testament picture of Jesus?

☐☐☐ Reading 128 (Proverbs 10:1–12:28)

In Proverbs 10:1–29:27 we have 594 verses with a similar number of individual proverbial sayings. Occasionally it is possible to see a string of connected proverbs but most of the time no special sequence can be detected. There is a lot to be said for studying Proverbs in the higgledy-piggledy way in which it comes to us. It makes the point that every aspect of life is intertwined with every other aspect of life. Proverbs 10:1–29:27 is unstructured because a lot of life is unstructured. On the other hand it is worthwhile to trace themes in the proverbs. The next seven days' readings invite us to look at the proverbs just as they come to us, but at the same time some twenty-one themes are suggested for further explorations.

1. *Laziness and diligence* (mentioned in 10:4) are themes of the book of Proverbs. Can you trace this theme elsewhere? What are the excuses lazy people give? What are its results?
2. What are the punishments and rewards of *pride and humility* respectively? They are mentioned in 11:2. And where else?
3. What are the results of accepting *discipline*? What are the results of

rejecting it? See 12:1 (and about twenty-four proverbs elsewhere in the book).

□□□ Reading 129 (Proverbs 13:1–15:33)

1. Proverbs has much to say about *family life*, especially the attention of children to their parents (13:1), the impact we may have on future generations (13:22) and the need of discipline (13:24). What are the marks of a good parent? How might this question be answered by the parents of young children? How might it be answered by parents of children in their late teens?

2. *Our talk, our discretion and our silence* is another theme of wisdom literature (see 14:3, 5). Even proverbs referring to other topics still relate to the way we speak (see 14:7, 23, 25). What is the advice given by the sayings in Proverbs on the subject? You will need to explore the wide range of epigrams all over the book.

3. *Emotions and feelings* receive comment in the wisdom writings (as in 15:13). Yet the proverbs about emotions tend only to make observations rather than give advice (as in 15:13). What is the point of observations without advice? Why do the wise men include them?

□□□ Reading 130 (Proverbs 16:1–18:24)

1. Proverbs has a lot to say about different aspects of society. Wisdom is *the special need of kings* (see 16:10, 12–15 for a cluster of proverbs concerning the king; see also 14:28, 35; 17:7; 20:26, 28; 22:11; 29:14). What view of power is implied in these epigrams? How much of it can be applied to power structures in the modern world?

2. The *immense value of wisdom and the great danger of folly* are constantly impressed upon us. 'Better to meet a bear robbed of her cubs than a fool in his folly' (17:12; see also 17:21) but 'a discerning man keeps wisdom in view' (17:24). Have wisdom and proverbial lore fallen out of modern life, especially in the west? If so what has caused the change? Is it loss or gain?

3. Proverbs 18:1–24 makes mention of the 'spirit' ('The human spirit will endure sickness, but a crushed spirit who can bear?') and the 'heart' ('The heart of the discerning acquires knowledge') – 18:14, 15. These words are very common in these chapters (about 100 references). What is the teaching of Proverbs about *the inner life* of men and women?

☐☐☐ **Reading 131 (Proverbs 19:1–21:31)**

1. *Plans and purposes* are of great interest to wise people. 'Many are the plans in a man's heart, but it is the LORD's purpose that prevails' (19:21; see also 12:5, 20; 15:26; 16:3; 20:5, 18; 21:2; 27:1). What recommendation should we make to ourselves concerning our plans for the future?

2. It was not only Hebrew wisdom that has much to say about *business methods* and the widespread habit of using corrupt weights and measures (see 20:10, 23); it was a common theme throughout ancient wisdom. Proverbs 20:14 also tells us something about our pretences in doing business. What other advice can be found that is relevant to modern business? What can be found in Proverbs about harnessing resources, about oppressive business practices, about God as the defender of the oppressed?

3. *Self-deception* is a concern of wisdom. No person is wise who has not learned to observe his own self-deceit! 'A person's entire ways may seem right to him, but the LORD weighs the heart' (21:2; compare 26:12; 28:11 and many other sayings). How can we learn not to hide ourselves even from ourselves?

☐☐☐ **Reading 132 (Proverbs 22:1–24:34)**

1. It is not only kings that are the concern of wisdom; *the treatment of the poor* receives frequent mention. 'Do not exploit the poor because they are poor', says 22:22. Many other sayings pursue the same theme. In what ways do we tend to misunderstand or ill-treat poorer people? How can we correct our tendencies in this respect (note 22:2, and within this chapter 22:7, 9, 16).

2. *Envy* (23:17), *jealousy, vengeance* are the concerns of wisdom. Why is it that these are sins we scarcely can see in ourselves? How does Proverbs help us?

3. Wisdom sayings give warnings about *retribution*. 'Will God not repay each person according to what he has done?' asks 24:12 (note also 24:14, 16, 19–20). What does Proverbs say about rewards and retribution? What are we to say about times when its principles do not seem to be true?

☐☐☐ **Reading 133 (Proverbs 25:1–26:28)**

1. *Patience and gentleness* are frequently commended to wise people. 'Through patience a ruler can be persuaded, and a gentle tongue can break a bone' (25:15). What other advantages does Proverbs see in a cool and calm spirit towards others?

2. *Thoughtfulness* is the theme that underlies wisdom. Take Proverbs 25:17: 'Seldom set foot in your neighbour's house – too much of you, and he will hate you.' Thoughtful people could have devised this proverb for themselves. How much wisdom is obvious? Then why do we need Proverbs? And what are we to think of 26:9?

3. *Gossip and tale-bearing* are viewed in the wisdom writings as highly destructive activities. Note 26:20, 22. And are 26:17 and 26:23–26, 28 related to the same theme? What rules should we make for ourselves concerning (i) spreading gossip and (ii) hearing gossip? Does it make any difference if the gossip is true?

□□□ Reading 134 (Proverbs 27:1–29:27)

1. *Husbands and wives* are a major concern in our lives. Proverbs might seem at times a bit cynical ('A quarrelsome wife is like a constant dripping on a rainy day; restraining her is like restraining the wind or grasping oil with the hand', says 27:15–16). It does not flatter men either (note 20:6!). Is the cynicism (if that is what it is) of Proverbs justified?

2. *Guilt, conscience, integrity* receive mention here. 'The wicked man flees though no one pursues' (27:1). 'He who hardens his heart falls into trouble' is a saying that may be put alongside it (27:14). What does Proverbs say about integrity and conscience and its results in our peace and security?

3. *Trust in God* is a theme that must not be overlooked. 'Whoever trusts in the LORD is kept safe' (29:25).

□□□ Reading 135 (Proverbs 30:1–31:31)

Further collections of proverbs come in Proverbs 30:1–33 (The words of Agur) and 31:1–31 (The words of Lemuel; the Good Wife).

1. What kind of changes will take place in our lives if we take Proverbs seriously? Take Proverbs 30:1–33 as an example.

2. Women (31:1–3), wine (31:4–7) and weakness (31:8–9) are the concerns of Lemuel. How would life change if society were 'wise' in these matters? How can changes come about? Legislation? Harsh punishments? Or what?

3. What is surprising to us about the model wife of Proverbs 31:1–31? What is the significance of our surprise?

Hebrews

No one knows who wrote Hebrews but it was obviously one of Paul's friends (but probably not Paul himself) because of the reference to Timothy in Hebrews 13:23. It was clearly written to Jewish Christians, perhaps in Rome, perhaps in the AD 60s. They were discouraged and tempted to redefine their faith to make it more in line with their Jewish persecutors (with Jesus as only a glorious angel). The writer appeals to them to hold on to true and bold Christian faith and so achieve something for God by persistent faith.

Recommended reading: Z. C. Hodges, 'Hebrews', in *The Bible Knowledge Commentary* (J. F. Walwoord and R. B. Zuck, eds., Victor Books, 1983).

□□□ Reading 136 (Hebrews 1:1–2:4)

1. Hebrews 1:1–4 says eight things about the Son of God. Can you list what they are?
2. Hebrews 1:5–13 has seven quotations from the Old Testament. What is the main point that is made by the string of quotations? How does verse 14 fit in?
3. Hebrews 2:3 is rightly translated 'How can *we* escape if we *neglect* so great a salvation?' (NRSV). It does not say 'How can *you* escape if you *reject* so great a salvation?' Does it make a difference?

□□□ Reading 137 (Hebrews 2:5–18)

The writer refuses to allow his readers to think angels are greater than they really are. The future glory is not for angels. It is for human beings (2:5). Psalm 8 speaks of the human race being eventually crowned with glory (2:6–8a). The writer makes two comments. (i) We do not see this happening (2:8b) in men and women. (ii) We do see it happening in Jesus (2:9). So Jesus is fulfilling human destiny. The only way for humans to reach their destiny is to be taken there by Jesus. Jesus pioneers the way to glory (2:10). Jesus and his people have one human nature (2:11, confirmed by Old Testament citations in 2:12–13). He became human to destroy Satan (2:14–15) for those who have the same faith as Abraham (2:16). It involved making atonement for sin (2:17) and being a perfect sympathiser (2:18).

1. What was God's plan for the human race? How was it lost? How is it regained?
2. How is Jesus' faith (Hebrews 2:13a) a proof of his humanity? How is Jesus a model believer?
3. What were the sufferings and temptations of Jesus that enable his ministry to us as a sympathetic Saviour?

Note Both in the Hebrew of Psalm 8:1–9 and the Greek of Hebrews 2:9 'a little' may mean 'for a little while'.

□□□ Reading 138 (Hebrews 3:1–19)

A second major section begins at 3:1. Jesus is like Moses (as leader of a covenant) yet much greater than Moses (3:1–6). Verse 6b is a turning-point. We *experience* the privilege of being a house-of-testimony (like the tabernacle) *only* if we persist in faith. So just as it was vital to persistently obey Moses, so it is vital for Christian Jews to persistently obey Jesus (3:7–4:13). The sections are as follows:

• Two captains of salvation: Moses and Christ (3:1–6)
• Citation of the Scripture (3:7–11)
• Exposition of the Scripture (3:12–4:11)
• The failure of the wilderness generation (3:12–19)
• The nature of the 'rest' (4:1–5)
• Appeal: enter rest today (4:6–11)
• Final warning: God's penetrating word (4:12–13)

1. In what ways was Moses faithful? In what ways was Jesus faithful? How is Jesus greater than Moses?

2. What is 'entering into rest'? Which of the options do you find convincing? Or do you have another approach?

3. What is needed for us to 'enter into rest'?

Note 'Entering into Rest'. This has been taken to refer to heaven (as R. C. H. Lenski and the Puritan Richard Baxter thought), or the millennium (as G. H. Lang thought), or the new heavens and new earth (as was the opinion of P. E. Hughes), or the victorious Christian life (as Andrew Murray thought), or assurance of salvation (as John Brown of Haddington said). Nor is it simply the 'rest' that comes to a Christian when he first comes to Jesus. So what is it? There are three ways of getting to see what it means. (i) One is to consider the illustration that the writer himself gave us in the story of the Israelites crossing the Red Sea. (ii) Another is to consider the equivalent terms that are used in the letter to the Hebrews. (iii) A third is to consider the significance of God's Sabbath in Genesis 2:1–3. From studies along these lines, it seems that 'entering into rest' is the reward that comes to the Christian in this life as a result of their diligent faith. It is the joy of inheriting promises. It is experiencing the oath of God's mercy. It is when after years, maybe, of persistent faith, we come to have an assurance that we have obtained that which we have been looking for and which God has promised us. See also note on 'oath' (Reading 8).

☐☐☐ Reading 139 (Hebrews 4:1–13)

It might be thought that since Canaan can be entered only once in the story of the Israel the chance for them to be in a similar position has gone for ever because of the progress of salvation-history (4:1). But in fact there is still the 'good news' of God's promises, still a 'land of Canaan' to be inherited. It will require persistent faith. Hebrews 4:3 perhaps means: 'For we who have made a firm commitment to continue in faith are expecting that we shall sooner or later enter into God's rest'. Hebrews 4:4–9 argues the same point from the Sabbath of Genesis 2:1–25. Hebrews 4:10 tells us what the 'rest' feels like. Verse 11 calls us to pursue it! And verses 12–13 warn us that sooner or later God's decision about us will come upon us and we shall either 'enter rest' or lose the privilege.

1. Do you agree with the suggested 'flow of argument' above? If not, what is your understanding of the flow of thought here?

2. Verse 11 calls upon us to pursue this 'rest'. How do we obey the writer's appeal?

3. What is the point of Hebrews 4:12–13 here?

☐☐☐ **Reading 140 (Hebrews 4:14–6:12)**

A third major section in Hebrews (4:14–7:28) considers the priesthood of Jesus. It begins with a general call to trust in Jesus as our high priest (4:14–16). Hebrews 5:1–10 outlines the Old Testament priesthood (5:1–4) and how Jesus fulfils it (5:5–10). Then Hebrews 5:14–6:20 is a lengthy passage of warning. Hebrews 7:1 picks up from 5:10 and continues the exposition of the priesthood after the order of Melchizedek.

1. In what ways does the Old Testament priesthood picture what Jesus would do? In what ways were the Old Testament priests *not* like Jesus?
2. How did Jesus learn obedience? What extra qualification in the life of Jesus was brought to him by his sufferings? How did it work out in practice?
3. How does Hebrews 6:7–12 follow up Hebrews 6:1–6?

Note The Warning Passages in Hebrews. The six warning passages in Hebrews (2:1–4; 3:7–4:13; 6:3–8; 10:26–31; 12:14–17; 12:25) speak of a sin after which there is no recovery, and only a fearful expectation of judgment. There are three possible lines of interpretation. (i) Is it that there is a sin that is so serious that salvation is lost and no recovery is possible? The difficulty of this is that even those who believe that salvation may be lost tend to shy away from saying repentance is impossible, and yet the impossibility of restoration is certainly involved in what our writer says. (ii) Is it about imitation Christians? Is it that there may be a spiritual illumination that falls short of true salvation and once the spiritual illumination is refused salvation then becomes impossible? There are problems in this. It is hard to believe that the various phrases used do not refer to true Christians. Our writer says, 'How shall *we* escape . . . ?' And no one has ever found a way of telling the difference between non-saving 'illumination' and true faith. People who hold such a view tend to live with needless fears. A third approach seems preferable. (iii) Our writer is speaking of loss of inheritance, loss of reward, loss of what we are meant to achieve for God. The evidence for this is as follows. (a) It fits the story behind Hebrews 3:1–4:16. The Israelites in the wilderness were true Israelites. They never were taken back to Egypt. But nor did they get to Canaan. They did not lose their *status*; they lost their *reward*. (b) It fits Hebrews 10:1–40. There is a fearful judgment but if the readers will hold to their faith they will be richly *rewarded*. The warning is not about loss of salvation; it is about loss of reward. It is exactly parallel to 1 Corinthians 3:15. Hebrews 6:10 can hardly be saying, 'God in his justice will save you because of your good works' – which is not a biblical idea at all. Rather Hebrews 6:10 is saying, 'God in his justice will *reward* you because of your good works'. If progress is impossible, reward is lost. (c) It fits the theme of 'oath' that we have in Hebrews. If God 'swears in his wrath' something is lost, and nothing can get back what has been lost. Moses was forbidden to enter Canaan and God would not change his mind. But Moses did not lose his status as a child of God. By faith and patience (says

Hebrews) we inherit promises. By unbelief and impatience we lose promises, and (if God takes an oath) lose them for ever. Esau lost inheritance (because Jacob had taken a death-bed oath) but his status as Jacob's child was unchanged.

☐☐☐ Reading 141 (Hebrews 6:13–20)

The digression (5:11–6:20) continues. The writer urges them to press on to inherit the promises (6:9–12). He now uses Abraham as an example of what this 'inheriting the promises' actually involves. Hebrews 6:13–15 uses Abraham as an example of how *we* are to inherit promises. Verses 16–20 deal with the promises *already* obtained. God has *already* sworn that Jesus is unshakeably available as the seed of Abraham, and the 'anchor' of all believers. The promise concerning Jesus is already 'obtained'; but the Hebrews must press on to inherit their own promises.

1. What are the differences between God's promise-without-an-oath and God's oath? Can the promise be lost? Can the oath be lost?
2. Are there any differences between 'inheriting', 'obtaining', 'receiving an oath' and 'entering into rest'? Are they all the same thing? If not, what are the differences?
3. What was required for Abraham to receive God's oath (Genesis 22:1–24)?
4. In what way is Jesus' being in heaven like an anchor tied to the sea-bed?

☐☐☐ Reading 142 (Hebrews 7:1–28)

1. The writer now comes back to where he left off at Hebrews 5:10. What are the six points he mentions concerning Melchizedek in 7:1–3? How does the chapter apply the same points to Jesus?
2. The Levites' priesthood came to an end. Will Jesus' priesthood come to an end? If not, why not?
3. The heavenly ministry of Jesus has a 'better hope' than anything promised in the Mosaic law. What are the expectations that Christians have as they trust the high-priestly work of Jesus?

☐☐☐ Reading 143 (Hebrews 8:1–13)

Our writer has considered the priesthood of Jesus (4:14–7:28). Now he focusses on the offering that is offered by our great high priest (8:1–10:18). He thinks of two sanctuaries (8:1–6), two covenants (8:7–13), the ritual of the tabernacle (9:1–10), and the taking of Jesus' blood to heaven (9:11–28). Hebrews 10:1–18 argues the effectiveness of Jesus' sacrifice.

1. In what ways is the new covenant *not* like the covenant made in the days of Moses?
2. What is involved in the covenant promises of 8:10–12?
3. Is the new covenant fulfilled totally in every Christian? Is it *progressively* fulfilled? How is Jesus administering the new covenant *now*?

□□□ Reading 144 (Hebrews 9:1–28)

1. What three things are achieved by the blood of Christ (Hebrews 9:11–15)? What is the significance in the changes of tense ('having secured . . . shall . . . cleanse . . . may obtain')?
2. In what way was the blood used in Old Testament ritual? What is the fulfilment of this in the new covenant?
3. According to Hebrews, why is it important to know that Jesus only had to die for our sins once?

□□□ Reading 145 (Hebrews 10:1–18)

1. What are the spiritual blessings that cannot (according to our author) be given through the Mosaic law?
2. God never wanted animal sacrifice to be a permanent way of worshipping God. What did God want instead? What is it in the cross of Christ that satisfies God?
3. What are the enemies (Hebrews 10:13) that Jesus plans to conquer before his second coming?

□□□ Reading 146 (Hebrews 10:19–39)

Hebrews 10:19 is the great turning-point of the letter to the Hebrews. It resembles Romans 12:1 in being the point where argument changes to exhortation.

1. What are the encouragements to faith that our writer gives us in 11:18–19?
2. What does he ask of us in 10:22–25?
3. What is the nature of the warning here? Is it addressed to Christians? Is there a clue in the word 'rewarded' (10:35)?

Note 'Boldness' (10:19) is something objective here. We could translate it, 'since we have grounds for boldness . . .'

☐☐☐ Reading 147 (Hebrews 11:1–22)

1. What kind of faith is being exhibited in Hebrews 11:1–40? Is he telling us how Old Testament saints became believers? Or is he telling us how they achieved something for God? Is Hebrews 11:6 addressed to those who have already believed?
2. Why does creation get a mention (11:3) before he goes on to speak of the great deeds of faith in the Old Testament?
3. What were the achievements of faith in the characters mentioned in Hebrews 11:4–22?

☐☐☐ Reading 148 (Hebrews 11:23–40)

1. Faith has to show a lot of endurance (Hebrews 11:35–38). Does this apply to Christians who live in parts of the world where there is little persecution?
2. How do we fit together the idea that believers 'obtain promises' (11:33) with 11:40? What is it that they obtained? What was it that they did not obtain? What does this imply about the future orientation of their faith? And what might it imply for us?
3. Can faith be increased? If so, how? What is the writer's purpose in Hebrews 11:1–40?

☐☐☐ Reading 149 (Hebrews 12:1–29)

1. Does Hebrews 12:1–2 fit with Hebrews 11:1–40? In what ways is Christ also a model believer (compare 2:13)?
2. What forms might God's chastisement take? How do we cope if we have reason to think that we are being chastised by God?
3. Hebrews 12:12–24 contrasts two mountains, Sinai and Zion. What are the points of contrast?

☐☐☐ Reading 150 (Hebrews 13:1–25)

1. What practical matters are of special concern to our writer in Hebrews 13:1–6?
2. It seems someone was accusing the readers of this letter of having no altar, no sacrifice, no priest – now that they had left Judaism. What is our writer's reply?
3. What is the 'perfection' for which our writer prays (13:21)?

Psalms 1:1–18:50

Music and worship and poetry go back a long way in Israel's story. There are great songs in the Old Testament that go back to days before any of our psalms were written (Exodus 15:1–27, Judges 5:1–31 and others). But singing songs of praise and prayer obviously received a great boost through David, around 1000 BC. He himself was obviously a gifted musician and poet.

As we read the praises and pleas of Israel we shall do well to note the different types of psalm. They are not always psalms of worship, and sometimes (e.g. Psalm 1:1–6) they are not directly addressed to God at all. We should pick up a few ideas about parallelism. The psalms are written in Hebrew poetry whose outstanding mark is stating things in two or three parallel lines. In the first verse of the Psalter we notice the three parallel phrases:

• Blessed is the man
  1. who does not walk in the counsel of the wicked
  2. or stand in the way of sinners
  3. or sit in the seat of mockers.

There are fourteen psalms (3:1–8; 7:1–17; 18:1–50; 30:1–12; 34:1–22; 51:1–19; 52:1–9; 54:1–7; 56:1–13; 57:1–11; 59:1–17; 60:1–12; 63:1–11; 142:1–7) that are linked to incidents in David's life. Though the psalm titles have often been questioned they are part of the text that has come to us as the word of God; Jesus took them seriously (as in Mark

12:35–37, for example). To read the psalm in the light of the titles (which is what their original editors are asking us to do) often throws light on the psalms themselves.

Recommended reading: J. A. Motyer, 'Psalms', in *New Bible Commentary* (IVP, 1994); D. Kidner, *Psalms* (Tyndale Commentary, IVP, 1973, 1975).

□□□ Reading 151 (Psalms 1:1–4:8)

Psalms 1:1–2:12 seem to be an introduction to the whole collection. The first psalm speaks of the individual's blessedness; the second speaks of the worldwide conflict that is behind it. Then Psalms 3:1–41:13 seem to be a collection of 'Davidic' psalms (that is, written by him, or taken by him into his repertoire). Only Psalm 33:1–22 is without mention of David. (Psalms 9:1–10:18 should be treated as one psalm).

1. What is the secret of happiness (Psalm 1:1–6)? Can happiness be obtained by seeking it?
2. God speaks with anger in Psalm 2:1–12. How do we fit this into our picture of what God is like?
3. Psalm 3:1–8 is David's prayer at a time when he was in great distress. Does this psalm help us in facing criticism and enemies?
4. The fourth psalm is similar to the third in its background; it could have also been written with David's conflict with Absalom in mind. They are two of about fifty-six psalms written by someone who is in bad trouble but is looking to God for help. Both refer to finding such peace as to be able to sleep (3:5; 4:8). How do we find such peace that we can sleep easily?

Note In Psalm 2:1–12 we hear the voice of those who rebel against God (2:1–3) and how God himself replies (2:4–6). The Lord's anointed speaks in 2:7–9, and the psalmist himself draws fiery conclusions in 2:10–12. Psalm 2:1–12 is one of about nine psalms that specially focus on Israel's king (Psalms 2:1–12; 18:1–50; 20:1–9; 21:1–13; 45:1–17; 72:1–20; 89:1–52; 110:1–7; 132:1–18).

□□□ Reading 152 (Psalms 5:1–7:17)

Psalm 5:1–12 could still have the same setting in the life of David as Psalm 3:1–8. It has similar themes. The temple had not been built. God's 'house' is the tabernacle (as in 1 Samuel 1:24; see 1 Samuel 2:22). Psalm 6:1–10 is the first of seven psalms known traditionally in the churches as 'penitential psalms' (the others are 32:1–11; 38:1–22; 51:1–19; 102:1–28; 130:1–8; 143:1–12).

1. What does it mean to 'wait' on God (Psalm 5:3)?
2. In Psalm 6:1–10, David is dangerously sick. Is sickness always the result of sin? Is sickness ever the result of sin? How does he reach such confidence in 6:9–10?
3. 'Cush' in the title of Psalm 7:1–17 was presumably one of Saul's friends and an enemy of David (see 1 Samuel 22:7). What can we learn from this psalm about the value of a clear conscience?

Note In Psalm 6:1–10 it should not be thought that David has a low view of life after death. It must be remembered (i) he is speaking as one who feels himself under God's anger, and (ii) 'remembering' God is what one does among people who are alive on earth. David's point is that *earthly* opportunities are lost after death. It is a common Old Testament viewpoint.

□□□ Reading 153 (Psalms 8:1–10:18)
Psalm 8:1–10 is the first of about forty-two psalms that are full of praise and thanksgiving. Psalms 9:1–10:18 belong together. They are an imperfect 'acrostic' psalm (where each verse begins with a different letter, following the sequence of the Hebrew alphabet). The two psalms together fall into three sections. Psalm 9:1–12 makes the point that God is sovereign despite human wickedness. Psalm 9:13–10:6 tells us that despite the certainty of evil's defeat it causes much suffering for the moment! Psalm 10:7–18 is the third section.

1. What is the psalmist's view of the dignity of the human race in Psalm 8:1–10? How does it contrast with modern views of the nature of men and women?
2. What enables us to have confident faith in the midst of injustice? How does David have such confident faith in Psalm 9:1–12?
3. What are the characteristics of prayer in Psalm 10:7–18?

□□□ Reading 154 (Psalms 11:1–14:7)
Like many of the psalms at this point in the Psalter, one can see how Psalm 11:1–7 would fit into the life of David (for instance, at 1 Samuel 18:8–19:7). It points us to the Lord's protection (11:1–3), his sovereign control (11:4–6), his willingness to give us himself so that we 'see his face' (11:7–8). Again Psalm 12:1–8 is the song of a man who is in bad trouble. This time David's problems specially involve flattery and deceit. In Psalm 13:1–6, David's problem seems to be with God himself. He begins with five questions about God.

1. In Psalm 11:1–7, what does it mean to see God's face? How does 'seeing God's face' help us when people 'set their arrows' against us?
2. In Psalm 12:1–8, how does David contrast the words of his enemies with the words of God (12:6)? How is God's word a strength to us amid the deceitfulness that often troubles us?
3. Trouble tends to make us question God himself. In Psalm 13:1–6, how did David cope when he had such questions?
4. Psalm 14:1 makes a very blunt assertion. What does the psalmist think is so foolish about unbelief?

□□□ **Reading 155 (Psalms 15:1–17:15)**

Psalm 15:1–5 tells us the conditions of entering God's sanctuary. Psalm 16:1–11 testifies to God's goodness in giving David total security in the face of great danger.

1. In Psalm 15:1–5, what is the Christian equivalent to 'your sanctuary' and 'your holy hill'? What are the qualifications for dwelling there? And what is its advantage?
2. Despite all of his faults and failures, David was a man who found security and joy in God. How is this seen in the sixteenth psalm? How may we, like David, become a person after God's own heart?
3. How is the New Testament able to apply this psalm to Jesus (Acts 2:24–32)?
4. In Psalm 17:1–15 we notice the threefold 'Hear . . . give . . . rise' (17:1, 6, 13). Upon what basis does David put his prayer to God?

□□□ **Reading 156 (Psalm 18:1–50)**

David begins in Psalm 18:1–3 with a summary of his love of God, and then describes his experience. He was like a drowning man who was rescued (18:4–6), like a man in an earthquake and volcanic eruption combined (18:7–8). God came to his rescue upon the wings of angels with abundance of thunder and lightning (18:9–15). So David was drawn out of the waters (18:16), delivered from enemies (18:17), rescued from disasters (18:18) and given spacious liberty (18:19). Psalm 18:46–50 is David's conclusion, in which he again is praising God.

1. David's deliverance in the account of 1 Samuel is not described so graphically as in Psalm 18:1–19. What is David's view of the matter? How can he use such dramatic language?
2. Psalm 18:20–27 explores the reasons for God's deliverance. What are they, one in David (18:20–23) and one in God (18:24–27)?

3. Psalm 18:28–45 looks at principles involved in David's rescue. What are they? On David's side (18:28–29, 32–34, 36–38, 40–42)? On God's side (18:30–31, 35, 39, 43–45)?

Hosea

Hosea's message was influenced by his difficult marriage. He preached in northern Israel from about 760 to 723 BC, at the end of the reign of Jeroboam II and, after him, during a period where there were six kings in a period of thirty years. Shallum murdered Zechariah (753 BC), the last of the line of Jeroboam. He then reigned for one month and was himself murdered by Menahem (752 BC). Menahem passed the throne to his son Pekahiah (742 BC). Pekahiah was murdered by Pekah (740 BC). In due course Pekah was murdered by Hoshea (not Hosea the prophet!) in 732/1 and the kingdom came to an end altogether in 723 BC. There were thirty years of political assassinations and intrigues of one kind or another. Society was decadent. Religion was corrupt and infiltrated with sexual perversion.

The most convincing view of Hosea's marriage is that he was asked to marry a woman who was immoral, and already had children as the result of her immoralities. This interpretation also fits the precise situation in Israel, for Israel had tendencies to spiritual unfaithfulness from the very earliest days. At some time in the reign of Jeroboam II, maybe about 760 BC, and maybe when he was about twenty-five years old, Hosea met and fell in love with a girl named Gomer who was known for her immoral ways, and had several children already. His call to be a prophet came at this time and at God's instruction he married Gomer and adopted her children. They then began to have children of their own. Later his wife fell back into her old ways and she deserted Hosea.

A similar story comes in Hosea 3:1–5. It again refers to Gomer but the occasion is a later occasion. Gomer fell into slavery, and God called Hosea to go to the rescue of his estranged wife. Hosea does as he is instructed, buys his wife out of slavery, insists on a period of deprivation for a lengthy time, and then takes her back. Nothing more is told us, but the story only makes sense on the assumption that from that point on they lived together happily!

One special difficulty in the Book of Hosea is the places where the Hebrew text is difficult to translate. Some notes on this matter are found in the Appendix (pp. 457–60).

Recommended reading: M. A. Eaton, *Hosea* (Bible in Focus, Christian Focus, 1980); D. Kidner, *Love to the Loveless: The Message of Hosea* (IVP, 1981).

□□□ Reading 157 (Hosea 1:1–3:5)

1. Does our personal experience (such as a difficult marriage) affect our ministry?
2. What aspects of life are equivalent to 'Baal' – the pagan god – today?
3. What is the equivalent of Hosea 3:1–5 in Christian experience? Does God ever hold back his love in order to bless us eventually?

□□□ Reading 158 (Hosea 4:1–7:16)

1. In what aspects of our society is there special need of a restoration of 'faithfulness . . . mercy . . . knowledge of God' (4:1)?
2. Does God withdraw from people (see 5:6)? If so, how and why, and what can be done about it?
3. How may we warn our world without seeming needlessly harsh (see 5:8–12)?
4. What is the teaching about repentance in 6:1–3?
5. 'They are like a burning oven' (7:4; see also 7:6). How may men and women become like an out-of-control fire?

□□□ Reading 159 (Hosea 8:1–11:12)

1. 'They have gone to Assyria'. May nations keep bad company? If so, what are the results of their doing so?
2. Hosea points to the consequences of events in Israel's *past* decisions. How long do a nation's decisions affect it, for good and for bad?
3. How did Israel despise the goodness of God? Does our nation do the same?

4. God powerfully drew Israel out of the land of bondage. How does God 'draw' us today?

□□□ **Reading 160 (Hosea 12:1–14:9)**
1. What lessons does Hosea draw from the life of Jacob (12:1–14)?
2. How is God like a lion, a leopard, a bear (12:14–13:11)?
3. How is God's call to us like a lover's plea (14:1–9)?

Psalms 19:1–28:9

1. God reveals himself in creation (19:1–6) and in his word (19:7–10). What are the differences between the two ways God has of speaking, and how does the double revelation impact the psalmist's life – and ours (19:11–14)?
2. Psalm 20:1–9 is a prayer written for use before a battle. How might we use it ourselves? Assuming that our Lord Jesus Christ is our King, how do we pray for his victory?
3. Psalm 21:1–13 is closely related to Psalm 20:1–9. One is a prayer before battle. The other is a prayer after battle. In 21:1–7 the people review their victory, giving thanks to God for assisting their king. What is the explanation of the extravagant language often used of Israel's king (as in verse 4)? In 21:8–12 they look to the future. How do past victories help us to face the future?

□□□ **Reading 162 (Psalm 22:1–31)**

Psalm 22:1–31 describes an execution.

1. How can 'all the ends of the earth' be affected by the suffering of one individual in Israel?
2. Is it significant that there is no self-pity and no confession of sin in this psalm?

3. What are the perplexities – anticipated here – that came upon Jesus while he was being crucified (22:1–5, 6–9)?

4. The sufferer appeals for help (22:10–11), laying the details of his suffering before God (22:12–18). How does the knowledge of the details of Jesus' suffering bring blessing to us?

5. The sufferer asks for life even in the face of execution (22:19–21), and then he confidently speaks out his expectation that global praise, festivity and victory will come from his suffering (22:22–31). If the modern believer is to 'take up his cross', how much of Psalm 22:1–31 is a faint shadow of what we might have to endure? Does this explain why Christ had to suffer so much?

□□□ **Reading 163 (Psalms 23:1–25:22)**

1. Psalm 23:1–6 is one of the psalms (see earlier on Psalms 9:1–20; 16:1–11) that specially testify to God's goodness. In what ways are believers like sheep (23:1–3a), travellers (23:3b–4) and guests at a meal (23:5)? What is the psalmist's final assurance (23:6)?

2. Psalm 24:1–10 (like Psalm 15:1–5) tells us the conditions of entering God's sanctuary. What are they? And what qualifies him to come into our presence (24:7–10)?

3. Psalm 25:1–22, like Psalms 9:1–10:18, is an imperfect 'acrostic' psalm. David is in trouble and takes his trouble to God (25:1–5). He has to confess his sins at the same time (25:6–7) – unlike the sufferer of Psalm 22:1–31. He knows God will guide even sinners into ways of righteousness (25:8–10), and so he can confess his sins confidently (25:11). How does this psalm give help to us when we discover we are more sinful than we ever realised? What blessings is David hoping for in the remainder of the psalm?

□□□ **Reading 164 (Psalms 26:1–28:9)**

1. Psalm 26:1–12 continues the theme of the believer's godliness that we have had in Psalms 1:1–6, 15:1–5 and 19:1–14. The psalmist seems very confident about himself. What enables him to speak in this way? May we be the same?

2. Psalm 27:1–14 again specially testifies to God's goodness. The psalmist is in trouble, faced with enemies, critics and misunderstanding. In 27:1–6 he expresses his confidence. In 27:7–12 he puts his request to God. Is it important that he looks at God before he looks at his situation? What does it tell us about the 'psychology' of facing trouble?

3. Psalm 28:1–9 seems to be part of a series (26:1–28:9) in which David was in a situation that threatened his life. The 'holy place' in the tabernacle clearly meant a lot to David (28:2; see also 26:6–8; 27:4, 5). It was not a very attractive tent looked at from the outside. Why did David love it so much – and what is the Christian equivalent?

Joel

Recommended reading: M. A. Eaton, *Joel and Amos* (Preaching Through the Bible, Sovereign World, 1998).

□□□ **Reading 165 (Joel 1:1–3:21)**
Joel lived at a time (at a date which is much disputed, maybe around 835 BC) when there was an unprecedented locust plague (note Joel 1:2). The prophet calls the people to repentance (1:2–14), and tells them how to pray (1:15–20). Then (2:1–17) he uses the locusts as a picture of the 'day of the Lord' – the occasion when God will judge sin and save his people. The people heeded Joel (2:18 is a narrative of something that happened) and the prophet promised physical restoration immediately (2:18–27) and spiritual blessings eventually (2:28–32). Among the coming spiritual blessings would be the final conquest of all sin (3:1–21).

1. What do unprecedented calamities say to the nations of the world (Joel 1:1–20)?
2. What is God's programme of salvation in Joel 2:28–32? How does it come to pass (so far as we can say)?
3. What kinds of sin specially attract God's attention and bring down his anger (Joel 3:1–21)?

Note Prophetic predictions are often 'panoramic'. That is, they come as a total picture, but the vision unfolds in stages. The 'valley of Jehoshaphat' ['the Lord judges'] is symbolic. There was no place by that name.

Psalms 29:1–34:22

□□□ **Reading 166 (Psalms 29:1–31:24)**
Psalm 29:1–11 is a song of praise. David calls on the angels to praise God
(29:1–2). His glory is reflected in a mighty storm (29:3–9b). It all led the
worshippers in Jerusalem to admire God's glory (29:9c). Psalm 31:1–24
is a psalm of David when he was (as so often) in trouble. He tells us how
he prayed. 'Free me from the trap' (31:1–8). 'My times are in your hands'
(31:9–18). In verses 22b–24 he had reached a position of confidence.

1. What deduction does David draw (29:10–11) from his meditation on
   the angels' worship of the Creator-God?
2. David evidently had many ups and downs in his life and could be almost
   killed at the very time he felt so secure (as Psalm 30:1–12 reveals).
   What are the lessons we learn from sudden rebukes from God? What
   hope is there for our future?
3. Psalm 31:15: 'My *times* are in your hands.' Are there seasons and
   epochs in our lives? How does God use them?

□□□ **Reading 167 (Psalms 32:1–34:22)**
Psalm 32:1–11 is called a *maskil* ('a wisdom-song'); see also Psalms 42:1–
11; 44:1–26; 45:1–17; 52:1–9; 53:1–6; 54:1–7; 55:1–23; 74:1–23;
78:1–72; 88:1–18; 89:1–52; 142:1–7). It begins with an announcement
(32:1–2) and tells of the time when David's conscience was distressed

(32:3–5). From this he announces something he had learned: everyone ought to pray (32:6–9). Psalm 33:1–22 is a song of praise. The writer calls upon the people to worship God with many instruments (33:1–3). God's word and his ever-watchful purposes are a cause of great praise (33:4–7, 8–11, 12–15, 16–19). Psalm 33:20–22 (matching verses 1–3) ends with words of confidence.

1. In Psalm 32:10–11, David tells the secrets of an on-going sense of security. What are they?
2. What does 'Sing unto him a new song' (33:3) mean for us?
3. Psalm 34:1–22 has 1 Samuel 21:10–14 as its background. It is again an imperfect 'acrostic'. In 1 Samuel 21:1–15, we are impressed by David's cleverness, but Psalm 34:1–22 lets us know he was praying hard! Psalm 34:1–10 tells us some lessons he learned. (i) He is committed to worship (34:1–2). What other lessons did he learn?

1 Corinthians

Acts 17:1–34 tells us how Paul left Thessalonica and went on to Beroea and Athens (Acts 17:10, 15). Then he went on to Corinth, where he stayed during the time from the autumn of AD 50 to the spring of AD 52. He spent much of his time preaching in the synagogue (Acts18:4), but there was so much opposition from Jews in Corinth (Acts 18:5–6) that Paul went to another house, next door to the synagogue.

In the spring of AD 52 Paul left Corinth where he had spent the previous two winters, travelled through Ephesus (Acts 18:19), briefly visited Jerusalem ('the church') and returned to Antioch, which he had left over two years previously (Acts 18:22). After this brief visit (April 52?) Paul went back to Ephesus as he had promised and spent nearly three years there (Autumn 52–Summer 55). It was while he was in Ephesus that Paul heard some sad news about the church in Corinth and wrote them a letter, which we may call his 'previous letter' (see 1 Corinthians 5:1–11). Then he had more news from them via 'Chloe's people' (1 Corinthians 1:11). The Corinthians also wrote Paul a letter (1 Corinthians 7:1). So Paul wrote another letter, which we call 1 Corinthians. It was completed just before Pentecost (1 Corinthians 16:8; AD 55). The chronology is as follows:

Time spent in Antioch	AD 49 (winter months)
Paul in Asia Minor and Macedonia	AD 50 (spring, summer)
Paul in Corinth	autumn 50–spring 52
Paul's fourth visit to Jerusalem	April 52?
Paul in Ephesus	autumn 52–summer 55
The 'painful' letter	AD 54?
1 Corinthians written	early AD 55

The church at Corinth had many problems, including divisiveness; dubious morality; legal conflicts among church members; confusion about marriage in days of crisis; quarrels about whether it was right to eat idol-meats in the temple, or at all; women who valued their liberty too much; chaos in the Lord's Supper; rivalry and confusion in the use of spiritual gifts; and even doubts about the nature of life after death. Paul writes to help them.

Recommended reading: M. A. Eaton, *1 Corinthians 1–9, 1 Corinthians 10–16* (Preaching Through the Bible, Sovereign World, 1998, 1999).

□□□ Reading 168 (1 Corinthians 1:1–31)
After an introduction (1:1–9), Paul tackles the problem of disunity in the Corinthian congregation.

1. What are the signs of God's faithfulness in 1:1–9?
2. Is it ever right to have a division within a congregation? What might be a justifiable division? What is not justifiable? How does Paul argue against disunity in 1:10–31?
3. The Greeks admired Greek 'wisdom'. What is the modern equivalent? How does Paul rebuke intellectual snobbishness?

□□□ Reading 169 (1 Corinthians 2:1–16)
1. How did Paul's own ministry in Corinth prove the points he was making (2:1–5)?
2. What are the characteristics of true wisdom (2:6–16)?
3. What are the differences between the 'natural' person and the 'spiritual' person (the reference is to the Holy Spirit) – in 1 Corinthians 2:1–16?

☐☐☐ Reading 170 (1 Corinthians 3:1–23)

1. Is there such a thing as a 'carnal Christian' (see 1 Corinthians 3:1–5)? If so, what exactly is the spiritual state of such a person?

2. The Corinthians' divisiveness clearly involved a wrong view of Christian ministers. How does Paul correct this in 3:1–23?

3. What are the implications of Paul's pictures of the Church as a building, and as a field (3:6–11)?

☐☐☐ Reading 171 (1 Corinthians 4:1–21)

1. How should we view Christian preachers (see 4:1–5)?

2. What were the mistakes that the Corinthians were making (4:6–21)? Can you find the same mistakes in modern churches? What are Paul's instructions?

3. 'Shall I come to you with a whip, or in love and with a gentle spirit?' (4:21). What did Paul do when his people were wandering from his gospel? What is the 'whip'?

☐☐☐ Reading 172 (1 Corinthians 5:1–13)

Paul moves to a new topic.

1. How should a pastor keep a church clean and consistent in godliness, without introducing heavy legalism?

2. What is the misunderstanding that Paul clears up in 5:11? What is true and right 'separation' from the world?

3. How does Paul use the Passover story in speaking to the Corinthians?

☐☐☐ Reading 173 (1 Corinthians 6:1–20)

The disputes among Christians in Corinth were so severe that they were taking each other to court.

1. Who is responsible for maintaining Christian godliness in a congregation? The pastor? The elders? The congregation? Or who? How does Paul handle the matter? What is the nature of his encouragements?

2. Paul says the Corinthians were 'washed . . . sanctified . . . justified'. What do these terms refer to? A ceremony? Spiritual experiences? What sort of 'sanctification' does he have in mind? Why does he put it before justification?

3. What is the Christian view of the body?

4. Why should a Christian be moral?

☐☐☐ **Reading 174 (1 Corinthians 7:1–24)**

Interpretation of 1 Corinthians 7:1–40 must take into account two facts. (i) Verse 26 speaks of a 'present distress'. Clearly there was some crisis taking place in Corinth, perhaps persecution, perhaps a famine. It is not the 'crisis' of the second coming of Jesus that was in mind, for that would be true at *all* times and would not account for Paul's unusual instructions here. Paul's main point here is: a time of acute distress is not the time to be getting married. One must notice the difference between 1 Corinthians 7:1–40 (on the one hand) and Ephesians 5:22–33; 1 Timothy 4:3; 5:14 (on the other hand). Among the various things Paul has to say about marriage, 1 Corinthians 7:1–40 is *unusual*; the instructions in Ephesians and 1 Timothy are the more normal. It would be a mistake to take 1 Corinthians 7:1–40 as 'normal' and Ephesians-and-1 Timothy as unusual. It is the other way around. (ii) The background in Corinth must be noted. The Corinthians were saying something like this. 'Paul, you have forbidden us to engage in what you call "immorality". Perhaps it is best (since we are people of the Holy Spirit) for us to have no sexual relationships at all – not even husbands with wives. The body counts for nothing. Physical needs can be met with the prostitutes in the pagan worship-centres.' Paul is replying to this. He says that (a) Immorality is to be shunned and forbidden. (b) It is all right to be single, and it is for the best at the moment if one can accept this singleness. (c) Within marriage, sexual relationships are obligatory. 'Spiritual' marriages are not to be attempted. (d) Physical needs cannot be met with the prostitutes in the pagan worship-centres.

1. What are four general principles that come at the beginning of Paul's advice – in 7:1a, 7:1b–2, 7:3–6, 7:7?
2. In 7:8–13 Paul has a word for widows and widowers (7:8–9), a word to married Christian couples (7:10–11) and a word to Christians with unbelieving spouses (7:12–13). What does he say to each group?
3. How far should we take Paul's 'stay as you are' principle (7:17–24)? In what situations might it apply today? Is it affected by what he says in verse 26?

☐☐☐ **Reading 175 (1 Corinthians 7:25–40)**

1. Paul distinguishes in this chapter between command and advice (e.g. 7:25). What is the difference between law and wisdom? What happens if we break the law? What happens if we ignore wisdom?
2. Under what situations should we postpone our desire to marry (see 7:26–35)? Why?

3. Christians are to marry 'in the Lord'. What does this mean? If a mistake has been made, what should be done about it? Should the marriage be ended? Does Romans 8:28 apply? Or what?

Note Verses 36–38 have been interpreted to refer to (i) a fiancée, (ii) a wife in a non-sexual marriage or (iii) a father and his daughter. The second is certainly wrong (Paul would denounce it!). The first is more likely than the third.

□□□ Reading 176 (1 Corinthians 8:1–13)

1 Corinthians 8:1–11:1 deals with 'idol-meats'. When a Christian woman in Corinth bought meat at the local market-place, the meat had previously been offered to an idol in a pagan temple. It raised questions in their minds about whether a Christian should eat meat that had been used in this way. There were other problems associated with eating and drinking in Corinth. The city was a place of feasting and partying. Many social gatherings took place at the local pagan temples. If a Christian wanted any kind of 'social life' with his neighbours, the pagan temples were the place to go. But at the same time those places were full of idolatry and immorality. It raised many questions: How can I mix with worldly people? Can I go to the temple with my neighbours when I know there is likely to be much sin and wickedness there? Would it be all right for me to eat this meat, which has been used in idolatry? Is there maybe a curse on it? Could it be that there is some kind of demon hanging around this meat because the meat has been offered to an idol? Paul urges the Christians not to get involved with idolatry. But he says that where no idolatry is involved they may eat meat previously offered to idols without asking questions for conscience' sake.

Another difficulty for Paul was that some Corinthians were attacking Paul himself. He was willing to leave aside certain foods when eating with Jews. At other times he seemed very liberated. He refused to accept financial support from the Corinthians.

1. What are the similar questions that modern Christians, especially young people, ask? Can I go to a meal with my friends? What will I do if they invite me to a place of non-Christian 'worship'? What others?

2. What word should be given to those who feel they are 'liberated'?

3. 'If what I eat causes my brother to fall into sin, I will never eat meat again.' Really? Never? How long do these rulings last for?

□□□ Reading 177 (1 Corinthians 9:1–27)

1. What were Paul's 'rights' as a preacher? How and why did he forgo them? Under what situations should we forgo our rights?

2. What is the teaching here about reward? Is it possible to be an unrewarded Christian? In this life? Eternally? What is the motivation for godliness?

3. 'I am not a lawless person in relation to God but rather have a law within me from Christ.' (The Greek has no word for 'under' here. It does have a prefix meaning 'in'). Paul is not under the Mosaic law, but he is not entirely lawless. So what is the 'law within me from Christ'?

□□□ Reading 178 (1 Corinthians 10:1–22)

1. How do the believers of the wilderness period of Israel illustrate what Paul wants to say here? What five sins does he specially warn against (in 10:6–10)?

2. What are the two principles in 10:13 that should help us in time of temptation?

3. How do Paul's warnings in 10:16–22 relate to the subject of eating 'idol-meats'? What might be the equivalent of idol-meats today? How should Paul's advice be reapplied?

4. How can Paul use the Lord's Supper to illustrate what happens in a pagan temple? What are the parallels? Why is one right and the other wrong?

□□□ Reading 179 (1 Corinthians 10:23–11:1)

1. What is Christian freedom? Is there anything that cancels it? Is there anything that balances it?

2. 'Do not ask questions on account of conscience.' In what situations does this advice apply today?

3. In one way Paul allows freedom to eat idol-meats. In another way he forbids it. What is the crucial principle that makes the difference? What affect will it have in a multicultural society – such as Corinth or many places today?

□□□ Reading 180 (1 Corinthians 11:2–22)

1 Corinthians 11:2–22 could be about veils or about hairstyle (note New International Version margin, which is quite a likely translation). In applying such a passage we have to distinguish between permanent principles and *expression* of those principles in local and culture-bound ways.

1. What are the permanent principles argued from creation in 1 Corinthians 11:2–16?
2. What are the culture-bound ways of *expressing* God's will that maybe will have to be adapted in different times and cultures? So how do we *express* Paul's principles in this matter? Or is the entire subject culture-bound? Can this be demonstrated?
3. What is the point of 1 Corinthians 11:19? Is it sarcasm? Does it mean disunity tests character? Or what?

☐☐☐ Reading 181 (1 Corinthians 11:23–34)

1. At the Lord's Supper we look *back* (11:24, 25). What are we doing as we look back in remembrance? What is the point of the remembering?
2. At the Lord's Supper we look *forward* (11:26). What are we looking forward to?
3. We look *within* (11:28). What are we looking for? What is it to partake 'worthily'? With total godliness? With faith? Or what?
4. We look *around* at brothers and sisters who form 'the body' of Christ (11:29). Again: what are we looking for? And of course we look *up* in thanksgiving!

☐☐☐ Reading 182 (1 Corinthians 12:1–31a)

The Corinthians were rich in gifts of utterance and knowledge (as 1 Corinthians 1:5 has said), but they were making at least the following four mistakes. (i) They were admiring wildness and noise for its own sake. The more they felt they were being led into excitement, the more they thought this was the work of the Holy Spirit. (ii) They said that – or were behaving as if – some gifts had to be experienced by everyone. (iii) They valued the unintelligible gifts more than intelligible gifts. (iv) An atmosphere of rivalry and superiority was coming into the congregation.

1. What are the principles Paul gives them? Feeling 'led' proves nothing (12:2). What else in 12:3, 4–10?
2. How does the phrase 'as he wills' address the Corinthian situation? And what is its relevance today?
3. In 12:11–14 Paul brings in his 'body' illustration. How does he work this out in 12:15–16? In 12:17? In 12:18? In 12:19–20? In 12:21–24a? In 12:24b–31a?

□□□ Reading 183 (1 Corinthians 12:31b–13:13)

1. Four times Paul uses the word 'if'. Love is greater than what four things?
2. What are the characteristics of love? When are they needed? For example, when we confront the bad and the weak, 'Love is patient'. When we confront what others have of value, 'Love is not jealous'. In what setting is each characteristic needed?
3. In 1 Corinthians 13:8–13, what is partial? What is perfect?

□□□ Reading 184 (1 Corinthians 14:1–25)

Paul now wants to raise the Corinthians' estimate of prophecy and slightly restrain their immense love of tongues.

1. Prophecy is speaking with God-given words. Tongues is non-rational prayer. What other differences are there between them (14:1–5)?
2. What is the main point of 14:6–19? Does it have other applications besides Paul's immediate purpose?
3. In modern charismatic churches, how should use be made of Paul's point in 14:20–25?

Note 1 Corinthians 14:20–23. In Isaiah 28:11–12, the prophet says that if the Israelites will not listen to intelligible prophecies, God will speak to them in an unintelligible manner. God will send foreign invaders and the Israelites will be forced to listen to the unintelligible chatter of the Assyrians or (later) the Babylonians. Paul's point seems to be that in the way in which the Corinthians are using the gift they are turning tongues (which ought to be a means of blessing) into a means of judgment towards outsiders. They are turning a gift to God's people (tongues rightly used) into something resembling God's judgment upon unbelieving Israelites. They are giving a sign to non-Christian visitors that is entirely wrong and that drives the visitors away. Tongues *wrongly used* becomes comparable to the unintelligible talk the Israelites were forced to hear when invaded by the Assyrians. 1 Corinthians 14:22 is a result clause. 'Tongues, then, are a sign, not . . .' He is dealing with the result of the Corinthians' poor and immature use of the gift of tongues.

□□□ Reading 185 (1 Corinthians 14:26–40)

1. What are the practical rules Paul draws up in 14:26–32?
2. Should there be different kinds of worship meetings in the churches? Where might be the best occasion for the instructions of 14:26 to be followed?
3. 'If you stamp out the false, you will stamp out the true.' Imagine that

the instructions of 14:26–32 are not being followed. What should be done?

Note In 14:33b–35, Paul has a word for the women of the fellowship. The demand for silent women (i) cannot be absolute and all-inclusive for there is plenty of evidence that women were allowed to speak in Christian meetings (even in 1 Corinthians – see 11:2–16). (ii) The text is authentic. They appear in all known Greek New Testament manuscripts (although some manuscripts alter their position). Verses 39–40 show that Paul is still dealing with the theme of prophecies and how they are handled. The women are asked not to act authoritatively in the matter of having authority over what prophecies are accepted and what are to be questioned. 'The law' that Paul mentions does not mean the Mosaic legislation. It means 'the Old Testament' (as in 14:21 where he referred to Isaiah). He is thinking of Genesis 2:18–25 (which he has already commented on in 11:8–9).

☐☐☐ Reading 186 (1 Corinthians 15:1–28)

The Corinthians believed in life after death but seem not to have expected any resurrection further than the spiritual resurrection they already had in Christ. Paul begins by establishing that they believe in Christ's resurrection (15:1–11), and then points to some implications (15:12–23).

1. What is the significance of Christ's resurrection according to 15:1–23?

2. What are the items Paul mentions that come at or near 'the end'?

3. What impact do these final events have upon us *now*?

☐☐☐ Reading 187 (1 Corinthians 15:29–58)

Paul must help the Corinthians to recapture their hope of their own resurrection to physical glory. First he puts to them some arguments in favour of resurrection (15:29–34). He has three ways of urging them to return to clear resurrection-faith. And then in 15:35 he will begin to answer some of their questions.

Note Baptism for the dead (15:29). One interpretation takes the verse to mean that some people had come to salvation but had not had opportunity to be baptised before they died. So others got baptised 'for the benefit of' the Christians who had died. Paul points out that it is a strange thing to practise this sort of weird baptism for dead people – but not to believe in the resurrection. If this is a correct interpretation it must be remembered it was only a peculiar practice of some Corinthians and Paul does not approve of it.

There is another interpretation, which might be right. Sometimes a person would become a Christian and live for Jesus. Then the Christian would die –

perhaps even dying for his faith in Christ. People who watched them would be so impressed that they would come to faith in Christ and would express their faith in baptism. They would be baptised for the sake of – out of regard for – what they had seen happen in the life of their friend who had died. Paul's point is: What would be the point of that if a Christian is never raised from the dead?

Either way, Paul is arguing that the Corinthians' custom implies a hope in final resurrection.

1. What other arguments for resurrection does Paul use in 15:30–33a, 33b–34?
2. How does Paul handle the question: 'How are the dead raised? With what sort of body do they come?' (15:35). In 15:36a? In his illustration (15:36b–38)? In 15:39?
3. 'For one star differs from another star in glory' (15:41). 'This is the way it is in the resurrection of the dead' (15:42a). Is there variation in glory in heaven? Does verse 58 help us to answer this question?
4. What precisely are the contrasts in 15:42b–44b?

☐☐☐ Reading 188 (1 Corinthians 16:1–24)

1. What is the connection between money and the unity of the churches (16:1–4)? What practical action does Paul take in this matter? If we read 1 Corinthians 15:58 and 16:1 without a chapter division, what effect would it have on us?
2. 1 Corinthians 16:5–12 provides us with a useful glimpse of Paul's plans, the opposition he faced and his work of supervising his churches in a loving gracious manner. What can we learn about large-scale church work from these verses?
3. Is there a logical order in the fivefold appeal of 16:13–14? What is the flow of thought?

Jeremiah

Jeremiah lived and worked in the period from about 627 to the fall of Jerusalem in 587 BC. It was his task to speak of Israel's sin and of the inevitable chastening of God that would come upon the nation through the Babylonians. At the beginning of this time Assyria and Egypt were two great powers but after 612 BC, Babylon became the dominant power of the ancient Near East. Jeremiah constantly insisted that, no matter what false prophets might say, the hope of Israel was to be found in the purification of the people in exile. Only after the exile would there be hope of restoration and the continuing moving of the nation towards the coming of worldwide salvation.

In Jeremiah's book there are indications of deliberate arrangement within the text. There are about thirty-five points at which major dividers are found in the book, and there is evidence that the thirty-five sections fall into seven blocks. It is immensely valuable to follow Jeremiah's own hints concerning the thread of thought in his work.

Recommended reading: D. Kidner, *The Message of Jeremiah* (The Bible Speaks Today, IVP, 1984); R. K. Harrison, *Jeremiah and Lamentations* (Tyndale Commentary, IVP, 1973).

□□□ **Reading 189 (Jeremiah 1:1–3:5)**
Jeremiah 1:1–20:18 are entirely general, and have only one date (3:6), with few names or details until the last chapter. The subject matter is laid out thematically rather than chronologically.

- Section 1: God's love, man's sin, God's threat (1:1–20:18)
  A. Title, call and early message (1:1–3:5)
  B. God ready to reject Judah (3:6–6:30)
  C. Useless religion (7:1–10:25)
  D. Disloyalty to the Covenant (11:1–13:27)
  E. Unavoidable judgment (14:1–17:27)
  F. The sovereignty of God (18:1–20:18)

Jeremiah 1:1–3:5 has a title (1:1), Jeremiah's call (1:1–10), and then three initial prophetic messages (1:11–12, 13–19; 2:1–3:6). Since there is no heading at 2:1 we should take it that 2:1–3:6 was a message given to Jeremiah at the time of his call, and closely connected with it.

1. What are the ingredients of a call to serve God? Although no one is called to be precisely the same as Jeremiah, do all believers have a 'call' of some kind?
2. There is a lot of sadness in God's complaint against Jerusalem (2:1–37). What were the main elements in Judah's departing from God? How does God react to our waywardness?
3. How does Jeremiah 3:1–5 use the law of Deuteronomy 24:1–4?

□□□ **Reading 190 (Jeremiah 3:6–6:30)**
The second unit of the section is marked by a date (3:6) and the new heading in 7:1. It makes the point that 'Faithless Israel is more righteous than unfaithful Judah' (3:11). The north was famous for idolatry but Judah in the south had become even worse! So God offers the north a chance to return to him (3:12–4:2). Judah had best break up its hard ground (4:3–4). An undefined disaster is coming from the north (4:5–31). Judah has become so accustomed to sin that no one is upright (5:1–31). Jerusalem will be besieged by a ruthless enemy (6:1–15). The city must go back to its 'ancient paths' (6:16). But they had become totally careless (6:17–30).

1. What does it mean to 'break up hard ground', when we are far from God?
2. Does a nation always deteriorate from generation to generation? What

does it mean to look for 'ancient paths' (6:16)? What did Jeremiah have in mind?

3. What are the particular sins and their consequences mentioned by Jeremiah in 6:17–30?

□□□ **Reading 191 (Jeremiah 7:1–8:22)**

The third unit of the section is marked by the new heading in 7:1, and a further heading in 11:1 ('This is the word that came to Jeremiah . . .'). The third section makes the point that Israel's religiosity is entirely useless. Jeremiah was told to preach on the subject in the gate of the temple (7:1–7). Otherwise it will be destroyed like Shiloh (7:8–20). The ceremonies of the law are not as important as the demand for obedience (7:21–28). Jerusalem will soon be destroyed if no change takes place (7:29–34). The leaders will be specially degraded (8:1–3). Jerusalem could possibly have recovered but is persistent in sin (8:4–17). Jeremiah is distressed about the matter (8:18–22; 9:1–9). Great calamity is to come (9:10–22). What is needed is the knowledge of God (9:23–26). Idolatry is fatal (10:1–16). God's wrath is about to fall (10:17–25).

1. If centres of religion (Shiloh, Jerusalem) become centres of wickedness, what are the dangers today of 'religious capital cities' (Rome, Canterbury, Mecca . . . where else?)?

2. If the *ceremonies* of the law are not as important as the demand for obedience (7:21–28), what religious requirements today are perhaps not as important as we might think?

3. What does Jeremiah have to say about *recovery* from our religious hypocrisy?

□□□ **Reading 192 (Jeremiah 9:1–10:25)**

Jeremiah shows great love for his people and his grief that they should be under judgment. On the other hand he hates their sin so much he wishes he could escape. They will experience the Lord's judgment (9:2b–9). Jerusalem will be ruined (9:10–16). The prophet sings a funeral song over them (9:17–22). Their only hope is that they should become 'wise unto salvation', and 9:23–10:25 takes up the matter of wisdom.

1. How much is it right to use sarcasm and scorn in speaking of pagan gods ('Their idols are like scarecrows in a cucumber field')? How can one combine respect for other people with concern for the truth?

2. How much are we to identify with the sins and pains of others ('Woe is me because of my hurt! My wound is severe')?

3. When should exile (or its spiritual equivalent) be accepted as inevitable?

□□□ **Reading 193 (Jeremiah 11:1–13:27)**
A fourth unit within Jeremiah 1:1–20:18 might be entitled 'Disloyalty to the Covenant' (11:1–13:27). The people had rebelled against the law of Moses. Josiah's reform could not stamp out idolatry (11:9–17) and Jeremiah's preaching about the subject endangered his life (11:18–23).

1. Jeremiah was like Jesus ('I was like a gentle lamb, led to the slaughter'). How far should we go in taking no action against our enemies? How easy did Jeremiah find it (see 12:1–4)? What is God's reply to his complaint?
2. What is the main point of the incident of the spoilt waistcoat (13:1–11)?
3. 'Every wine jar should be filled with wine' was obviously a common saying. Jeremiah twists it to mean the people are filled with confusion and imagines the day when jars of wine are smashing one another into destruction. How is it a picture that fits today's world?

□□□ **Reading 194 (Jeremiah 14:1–17:27)**
A fifth unit ('Unavoidable Judgment') is found in 14:1–17:27. The situation in Judah is so bad that Jeremiah is forbidden to intercede for the nation (14:1–15:9). God tells the prophet that judgment is unavoidable (15:1–4) and that Jerusalem's fate is settled (15:5–9). The prophet is distressed and God answers his complaint (15:10–21). Jeremiah is asked to take his own part in bearing the anger of God against Judah's sin (16:1–9). The people are entirely insensitive to idolatry and must be purified before God will bless them (16:10–18). Only then will blessing come to them (16:19–21). Their sin is indelible (17:1–4).

1. There is obviously a difference between what Jeremiah wanted and what he told the people of Judah. What light does this throw on the work of a prophet?
2. According to Jeremiah 17:5–13, what is the root of Judah's sin and what change needs to take place in their lives?
3. Jeremiah once again shows how costly it was for him to be a prophet (17:14–18). What kind of person was he? Are we to be as sensitive as he was?
4. The 'Sabbath' (17:19–27) was a test case for showing how obedient Judah was to God. What is the modern equivalent? Is it another holy day (Sunday)? Or is it something deeper?

☐☐☐ **Reading 195 (Jeremiah 18:1–20:18)**

A sixth unit within Jeremiah 1:1–20:18 is to be found in 18:1–20:18, which might be called 'the Sovereignty of God'. Jeremiah 20:1–6 introduces the priest Passhur.

1. What is the main point of the 'parable of the potter' (18:1–23)? In Jeremiah 18:1–10 it is a threatening parable, but does 18:11 imply that we could turn it around to become an encouraging parable?
2. Why do we take our obstinacy to absurd lengths (18:13–17)?
3. What is the point of the 'parable of the broken bottle' (19:1–15)?
4. In Jeremiah 20:1–6 the priest Passhur is angry with the prophet. What is the difference between these two men (officially and personally) and which do modern people (including ourselves) resemble?

☐☐☐ **Reading 196 (Jeremiah 21:1–23:40)**

A change of style comes in Jeremiah 21:1–18 with specific characters now introduced into the Book of Jeremiah: King Zedekiah, Pashhur son of Malchiah, the priest Zephaniah son of Maaseiah, and King Nebuchadnezzar of Babylon. Another sharp change of direction will come in Jeremiah 30:1, and this makes it likely that Jeremiah 21:1–29:32 is a distinct unit. Although they could be one section, they are generally thought of as two. We may lay out the material as follows.

- Section 2: Certain judgment; Certain captivity; Certain restoration (Jeremiah 21:1–25:38)
  A. Zedekiah's enquiry; The failure of kings and prophets (21:1–23:40)
  B. Two baskets of figs (24:1–10)
  C. Universal judgment (25:1–38)
- Section 3: Jeremiah's conflict with the false prophets (26:1–29:32)
  A. Temple sermon (26:1–24)
  B. The bonds and yokes (27:1–22)
  C. Hananiah's falsehood and doom (28:1–17)
  D. Jeremiah's letter (29:1–32)

1. Why is it that people want the help of religious leaders, but will not heed what God's messengers say?
2. Jeremiah 22:1–30 moves from Zedekiah to consider the other kings of Jeremiah's times. What are the characteristics of *political* leaders and how is God's Messiah different?
3. Next Jeremiah moves from kings to prophets (23:10–40). What are the characteristics of *religious* leaders and how is God's Messiah different?

□□□ Reading 197 (Jeremiah 24:1–25:38)

1. In Jeremiah's parable who are the good figs and who are the bad figs? Why did the future lie with those exiled?

2. Jeremiah 25:1–38 is Jeremiah's definitive statement that exile to Babylon is inevitable, and will last for seventy years (a round number). If God's long-suffering may tolerate sin for decades and if it takes further decades for God to purify his people, how do we interpret recent decades in the story of our own nation or section of the Church?

3. It seems that eventually the punisher gets punished (24:12). Does this principle apply today? Can recent examples be found?

□□□ Reading 198 (Jeremiah 26:1–27:22)

Jeremiah 26:1–29:32 focusses upon Jeremiah's conflict with false prophets. First we have another report (compare Jeremiah 7:1–34) of the temple sermon. The result of the sermon is more fully reported in 26:7–19).

1. Why do religious officials get so angry about any true message from God? What then are the marks of true and false prophecy (or preaching)?

2. Can we give any reason why Jeremiah was rescued but not Uriah (26:20–24)?

3. How can 'King Nebuchadnezzar of Babylon' be called 'my servant'? Is this true of all kings and authorities? Can there be unchristian 'secular' messiahs? If so, where are they today?

□□□ Reading 199 (Jeremiah 28:1–29:32)

Hananiah opposes Jeremiah (28:1–4) and Jeremiah replies (28:5–11) and has a message for Hananiah himself (28:12–17).

1. What are the similarities between the *style* of Jeremiah's preaching and Hananiah's preaching? How would anyone know who to believe? How can one tell who to believe and who not to believe among modern preachers?

2. How does Jeremiah's advice to the exiles of Babylon (29:5–7) apply to the modern Christian in 'exile' in this world?

3. Jeremiah 29:11 is a favourite verse for many people. What did it mean in its original context? How do we apply it to ourselves today? What sort of person does it fit? What good news can we give to any people who are conscious that God is chastening them?

☐☐☐ Reading 200 (Jeremiah 30:1–31:40)

A sharp change comes in Jeremiah 30:1, after the previous material. There is a dividing line at Jeremiah 37:1. This makes it likely that Jeremiah 30:1–36:32 are one or more major divisions.

- Section 4: Covenant and the hope of restoration (30:1–36:32)
  A. Hope of restoration (30:1–31:39)
  B. Assurance of the people's return (32:1–44)
  C. Restoration of Judah and Jerusalem (33:1–25)
  D. Message to Zedekiah (34:1–7)
  E. Treachery against a Covenant (34:8–22)
  F. The Rechabites (35:1–19)
  G. Scroll destroyed (36:1–32)

In Jeremiah 30:1–24, Jeremiah predicts that the exile will be followed by a return to Judah, but before that return the sufferings of Judah will be great. Yet the Babylonian power will come to an end and the Messiah will come. The people of Judah will be *corrected* but not destroyed, just as those who were persecuted by Pharaoh (in Moses' days) were protected from God when they were taken across the Red Sea into the wilderness. Jeremiah expects the same thing to happen again. The exiles will be the ones whom God eventually uses (31:2).

1. Are the promises of Judah's return to their land a shadow of the gospel? A shadow of modern political events? A shadow of a future spiritual revival? Or are they not a shadow of anything? Should we relate Jeremiah 32:1–33:26 to Romans 11:26?

2. In patriarchal times, Joseph and Benjamin were Rachel's children. They were the ancestors of northern tribes, taken off in exile in 722 BC. In Jeremiah 31:15–17 Rachel is envisaged as weeping for them as they pass her tomb. Now the Lord promises comfort to Rachel. Israel's northern exiles come home. But Ramah near Bethlehem was also the assembly point of Judean exiles (40:1). What is the point of Jeremiah 31:15–17? How does Matthew make use of the passage in Matthew 2:18?

3. What was good about the Old Covenant? What was defective in the Old Covenant? What is new in the New Covenant?

☐☐☐ Reading 201 (Jeremiah 32:1–33:26)

1. Jeremiah was told to buy a field that was in the midst of territory occupied by the Babylonians, at a time when he was himself in prison.

What was the point of this? What did Jeremiah feel about it? What encouragements did God give him?

2. Jeremiah 32:40 seems a very unbreakable promise. Is it too good to be true? Are there any conditions unmentioned which have to be met?

3. In 33:2–3 what are the encouragements to be found in God himself? In his promises? What is needed for us to gain the promise?

□□□ Reading 202 (Jeremiah 34:1–36:32)

Jeremiah 34:1–22 contains much that is of interest in connection with covenants. The 'covenant of generosity' in Jeremiah 34:8–11 is actually the only 'covenant of generosity' in Scripture where people take the covenant-oath – but then they broke the covenant-promise. In a 'covenant of law' the juniors have to promise obedience.

1. In what way is God a covenant-keeper? In what ways are men and women covenant-breakers?

2. What do you think of the Rechabites? Is there any place for communities that are stricter than what God requires? Did God approve of the Rechabites totally? Partially? Not at all?

3. Jeremiah 36:1–32 is full of interesting information. What can we learn here about the prophets' methods of producing their prophetic books?

□□□ Reading 203 (Jeremiah 37:1–39:18)

The events of Jeremiah 37:1–45:5 are in chronological order, which sets the section aside as a major unit.

- Section 5: Incidents in crucial years (37:1–45:5)
  A. Zedekiah consults Jeremiah (37:1–38:28)
  B. The fall of Jerusalem (39:1–18)
  C. Offer of release (40:1–43:13)
  D. Jeremiah in Egypt (44:1–30)
  E. Message for Baruch (45:1–5)

1. Why are people happy to have preachers pray for them, even while they do not receive the preacher's message? The Babylonians temporarily withdrew from Jerusalem. What effect did this have on Zedekiah? What affect did it have on Jeremiah? What can we learn from Zedekiah's character? What can we learn from Jeremiah's character?

2. Did Zedekiah take any notice of what Jeremiah said to him? If not, why was he so eager to hear a word from God, through Jeremiah? What kind of person does this illustrate? Are we similar or are we different?

3. In the events of 587 BC (recorded in Jeremiah 39:1–18) what Jeremiah had preached for many years was proved to be right. It was a day of judgment after years of preaching. What happens to Zedekiah? What happens to Jeremiah? What happens to Jeremiah's supporter (Ebed-Melech)? What will our response to God's word do for our destiny?

☐☐☐ Reading 204 (Jeremiah 40:1–43:13)

1. Jeremiah is offered freedom and a new life in Babylon. What would you have done if you had been Jeremiah? What choice did Jeremiah make and what does this show us about his character?

2. Gedeliah was made governor of Judah. A lot of Jews were asking his advice (40:1–12). He would not believe a warning that his life was in danger and refused to believe anything bad about Ishmael (40:13–16). Why was Gedeliah insensitive to danger? How can we find a middle way between gullibility and suspicion?

3. The army officers said, 'We will obey the Lord' (42:5), yet they insisted on going to Egypt – against God's wishes. Why were they so unwilling to hear Jeremiah's word (43:2)? What can we learn about ourselves from this story? Our prejudices? Our fears? Our inconsistency?

☐☐☐ Reading 205 (Jeremiah 44:1–45:5)

1. 'We will do whatever we want' (Jeremiah 44:17). What are the characteristics of human sinfulness that are obvious in Jeremiah 44:15–18?

2. 'Go ahead then!' says God (Jeremiah 44:24–25). Does God ever encourage us to do that which is not his will? If so, when and why?

3. Is it good to be ambitious (see Jeremiah 45:1–5). 'No, never'? 'Yes, if the ambition is good'? 'For some people, yes; for some people no'?

☐☐☐ Reading 206 (Jeremiah 46:1–47:7)

The most obviously marked major section in Jeremiah is Jeremiah 46:1–51:64; and this leaves Jeremiah 52:1–34 on its own as a distinct section.

- Section 6: Oracles to the nations (46:1–51:64)
  A. Egypt (46:1–28)
  B. Philistines (47:1–7)
  C. Moab (48:1–47)
  D. Ammon (49:1–6)
  E. Edom (49:7–22)
  F. Damascus (49:23–27)
  G. Kedar and Hazor (49:28–33)

H. Elam (49:34–39)
I. Babylon (50:1–51:64)
• Section 7: The fall of Jerusalem (52:1–34)

The point of the 'oracles to the nations' (in Jeremiah and in other prophetic books) is to show that the whole world needs God's salvation. Israel
might be wicked but we are not allowed to think the gentile nations are
any better!

1. Egypt (Jeremiah 46:1–28) was totally defeated at the battle of
   Carchemesh in 604 BC. 'The swift cannot flee nor the strong escape'
   (46:6). What do we learn here about God as the Lord of the nations?
   How then should we view modern wars and conflicts?
2. Jeremiah 46:27–28 brings a message of comfort, but what exactly is
   the comfort? Who today may take this comfort to themselves? All
   nations? Some nations – but which ones, if any? Or is it to be taken to
   heart by the Church? How do we apply this Scripture to our own
   situation?
3. One nation (Babylon) was used to punish another nation (the
   Philistines). Does this still happen? How should we view the many wars
   taking place today?

▢▢▢ Reading 207 (Jeremiah 48:1–49:39)
Smaller nations are considered in Jeremiah 48:1–49:39: Moab, Ammon,
Edom, Damascus, Kedar, Hazor and Elam.

1. What were the special sins of Moab (48:7, 11, 27, 29)? Can they be
   found in our nation?
2. An unexpected change comes in 48:47; 49:6, 39. Of what significance
   is this?
3. What were the special sins of Amman (49:2, 4, 5)?
4. 'A nation that has neither gates nor bars; its people live alone' (49:31).
   What national dangers are being described here?

▢▢▢ Reading 208 (Jeremiah 50:1–51:64)
At the beginning and end of the oracles of Jeremiah (46:1–51:64) are
to be found Egypt and now Babylon (50:1–51:64). Is there any reason
why these two great nations should be at the beginning and end of the
series?

1. Jeremiah had preached that the Babylonian exile was God's will. How can Babylon be condemned in Jeremiah 50:1–51:34, if the nation had been doing God's will?
2. What caused the disaster of the Babylonian exile (50:4–7)? What function did the exile have in their history? How may the people of God find their way back to him? And in our own country?
3. The Lord had a plan against Babylon (51:1–2, and elsewhere). Babylon had been the Lord's hammer (51:20) but now faces judgment itself. Does this principle still operate in our world (a 'hammer' is used and then judged)?
4. What is the point of the incident in 51:59–64? Jeremiah had said the return to Israel was decades ahead (Jeremiah 26:1–24) so what was the purpose of the instruction to Seraiah? Should we have plans for our nation or our churches that run decades ahead into the future?

□□□ **Reading 209 (Jeremiah 52:1–34)**

1. The events of Jeremiah 52:1–34 confirmed the genuineness of everything Jeremiah had said for forty years. The future will always show that God's word proves true. But what does that mean for the present moment?
2. God planned for the destruction of the temple (52:13). What does God think of holy buildings?
3. How does the book of Jeremiah end? A Davidic king is still alive. He is being treated well. What does this imply?

James

The letter to James could be called a guide to spiritual recovery. It was written at a fairly early time in the apostolic age, by James the Lord's brother, senior pastor of the church of Jerusalem for many years. It seems that it was addressed to Jewish Christians. Apparently they had become proud and critical people. They discriminated against the poor. They did not control their tongues. They were arrogant towards their employees. They were also facing many trials and troubles. God was not answering their prayers. Success was not coming their way. James writes to help them.

Recommended reading: J. A. Motyer, *The Message of James* (IVP, 1985); D. J. Moo, *The Letter of James* (Tyndale Commentary, IVP, 1985).

□□□ **Reading 210 (James 1:1–27)**
1. If the letter of James is a guide to spiritual recovery, is it significant that James begins with the trials that they are experiencing? What is the way of spiritual recovery that he suggests at this point?
2. What is 'the high position' (1:9) of the poor person? What is the 'humiliation' of the rich person? How should rich and poor Christians think of themselves? How should we view the rich and the poor?
3. What is James' teaching about temptation? Does it ever come from God?

Where does it come from? Does God give us anything that helps? If so, what, and how does it work?

☐☐☐ Reading 211 (James 2:1–26)

James 2:1–26 develops the point concerning our approach to the under-privileged. James 3:1–18 develops his teaching concerning the tongue, and much of James 4:1–5:20 will take up different ways in which we should resist being stained by the world. So James 1:26–27 is the hinge around which much of the letter turns.

1. List the ways (suggested by James 2:1–5) in which the poor are ill-treated.
2. What are the arguments against discrimination that James uses?
3. In our society, what changes would come into the land if we took James' teaching seriously?
4. What is the main thrust of the argument in 2:14–26? Does it continue the paragraph in 2:1–13? What are the practical implications of James 2:14?
5. If the word 'him' in James 2:14 (compare 'him' in 5:20) refers to the poor person, how would it change our reading of the letter?

☐☐☐ Reading 212 (James 3:1–18)

1. The tongue is like a horse (3:3). The tongue is like a rudder (3:4–5). These are positive illustrations. We can go places and achieve things for God – if we can use the tongue skilfully. What is the intended character of Christian talk?
2. The tongue is like a fire (3:6). The tongue is like a wild animal (3:7). The tongue is like poison (3:8). What is the point of each of these illustrations?
3. James does not go into any details here. He does not tell us how to control the tongue. Why is this? What is the implication?

☐☐☐ Reading 213 (James 4:1–17)

1. Where do different types of war and conflict come from? There are wars outside because there is a war inside. What does this mean for our attempts to handle conflict near and far?
2. What is James' teaching about prayer in 4:3? What is the secret of having our prayers answered?
3. What is 'adultery'? So what is spiritual adultery?
4. James 4:7–10 has four or five instructions to help us return to God.

What are they? Is there any reason for the order in which they are put to us?

5. What exactly does James mean by 'the law'? He cannot be speaking of the law simply and straightforwardly, because he shows no interest in the hundreds of regulations that were in the Mosaic covenant. Is it the principles that the law was pointing to, transformed and coming to us via the Lord Jesus Christ. Or what?

Note Verse 5 begins: 'Or do you think that it is for nothing that the scripture says . . . ?' After that the translations differ widely. Probably it should be: '. . . that the Spirit which God made to live in us jealously longs for us' (4:5). It is not referring to any particular text of Scripture but is a summary of the common Old Testament teaching that God is a jealous God and hates unfaithfulness.

□□□ Reading 214 (James 5:1–20)

1. What are the wrong attitudes towards wealth mentioned in James 5:1–20?

2. Is James being too political? What do you think of his getting involved in class-conflict and telling people what salaries to pay their workers? How much should preachers deal with these things? How can they do it in a practical and well-informed manner?

3. What should we do about social injustices if we are ourselves rich? What should we do about social injustices if we are poor and powerless?

Psalms 35:1–40:17

Psalm 35:1–28 is a song in three sections (1–10, 11–18, 19–28), written when David was specially vexed with injustice. In his pleas for vengeance (35:4–6, 8, 24b–26) there is no personal vindictiveness (for David was a forgiving person), but a realistic plea for justice as God's king, God's representative on earth. Psalm 36:1–12 considers human and divine character, first looking at the wicked person (36:1–4), then at the contrasting goodness of God (36:5–8). Upon this basis the psalm considers the future experiences awaiting the righteous (36:9–11) and the wicked (36:12). Psalm 37:1–40 is a song about the prosperity of the wicked. Its sections (1–11, 12–20, 21–31, 32–40) each begin with a statement of the problem (1, 12, 21, 32).

1. In what ways might we use such 'curses' as we find here? Might the words 'Let destruction come upon him' be used when praying against our own weaknesses and sinful habits?
2. What is the 'life' and 'light' promised to the righteous?
3. What are the three characteristics of the wicked according to 37:12, 21, 32? How do we cope with such wickedness when it is nearby? Is David's expectation only a long-term hope, or may we expect his promises to come to pass speedily?

☐☐☐ **Reading 216 (Psalms 38:1–40:17)**

Psalm 39:1–13 is a companion to Psalm 38:1–22. Again David was being disciplined for his sins (as 39:11 shows). So severe was the discipline that David was struggling not to protest even in the presence of wicked people (39:1–3). He felt he was about to die and the possible brevity of his life was an agony to him, although he was forcing himself to face the facts (39:4–6). A string of questions and comments come in 39:7–11. All he can do is pray (39:12–13), pleading for help (12a), grieving over the alienation between himself and God (12b), asking for restoration (13). In Psalm 40:1–17 David or one of his descendants has been through an experience from which he hopes many will learn (40:1–3). Presumably one of the lessons learned is the theme of 40:4–5. God's help is superior to human help. If God is willing to help his people we must relate to him rightly – and this is the theme of 40:6–8. Psalm 40:9–11 continues to develop the topic of verses 1–3. He used his experience to tell of God's righteousness. Verse 11 is a statement: 'You will not withhold your mercy . . .' Next, Psalm 40:12–15 takes a look at the enemies that are still nearby. Troubles are around him, some of them David's own fault (12). He prays for rescue for himself (13), confusion for his enemies (14–15), joy for God's people (16), rescue for himself (17).

1. In Psalm 38:1–22, David knows God is angry with him (38:1–12). We might want to ask: Is not God 'propitiated' (no longer angry) after we have come to faith in his promises? What sort of anger is this? What do we do about it (following the hints of 38:13–22)?
2. What do we know about 'watching our ways' for the sake of others?
3. These psalms (note 40:3b especially) prompt us to ask: Do others learn from what they see has been our experience of God? Do we learn from what we can see others have experienced of God?

Exodus

Exodus to Numbers tells the story of the creation of Israel and its establishment as the people of God. In Exodus 1:1–15:21 we have the story of how the people of God came to be in need of deliverance by the blood of a lamb. The people were experiencing persecution and slavery (1:1–22). God prepared a deliverer, Moses (2:1–4:31). After an initial period of conflict with Pharaoh (5:1–7:7) there came a time when Pharaoh was confronted by nine powerful judgments from God (7:8–10:29), but it was a tenth judgment, the battle over the 'firstborn son', that led to the redemption of Israel by the blood of a lamb (11:1–14:31). They march out of Egypt singing a song of triumph (15:1–21).

The rest of Exodus tells the story of the establishment of the people of God. They journey to Sinai (15:22–17:7), facing two different reactions to their redemption (17:8–18:27). Then they arrive at Sinai and the 'books of the law' record no further travelling until Numbers 10:11. The whole of Exodus 19:1 to Numbers 10:10 finds its setting at Mount Sinai.

Recommended reading: M. A. Eaton, *Exodus 1–20, Exodus 21–40* (Preaching Through the Bible, Sovereign World, 2002, 2003); R. A. Cole, *Exodus* (Tyndale Commentary, IVP, 1973).

☐☐☐ Reading 217 (Exodus 1:1–3:10)

1. How do we face change? At the point where 'Exodus' begins, the people of God go through a time of many changes and great difficulty. What were the sudden changes? What was God planning?
2. By faith Moses' parents rescued him from death. What were the characteristics of their faith? May we look for events that are 'natural' to rouse faith? What happened to their faith after three months? Does faith lead us into civil disobedience?
3. What are the characteristics of Moses' call to serve God?

☐☐☐ Reading 218 (Exodus 3:11–6:30)

1. Moses has five objections to serving God. (i) He thinks he is inadequate. 'Who am I that I should go . . . ?' (3:11). (ii) He believes that he does not know enough. 'Suppose I go . . . and they ask me "What does his name mean?" What shall I tell them?' (3:13). What are the others? How does God answer him?
2. Moses eventually became famous for his faithfulness. Are there indications in this part of Exodus of the way in which he came to learn to be faithful even in small details?
3. How does God encourage Moses after some discouraging experiences?

Note 'Yahweh' is linked with the verb 'to be' and almost certainly has the meaning 'he is'. It is generally translated LORD (with capital letters). God says, 'I am that I am.' This is the fullest form of the name of God. Then God says: 'This is what you are to say . . . "I am" has sent me to you' (3:14). The name has been shortened to 'I am'. Then God says: 'Say to the Israelites, "Yahweh . . . has sent me." ' 'Yahweh' is the name 'I am that I am' shortened to one word. In effect, God says to Moses, 'Watch and see what is about to happen right now and that is exactly what I am and what my name means.' Many have read ideas of 'eternity' or 'absoluteness' into God's name, but 'philosophical' approaches miss the point. What we have here is a reference not to philosophy but to history! God says, 'I am that I am' in what is about to happen right now! God's name refers to his redeeming his people by the blood of a lamb. What God was about to do would be a revelation of his name and his nature.

☐☐☐ Reading 219 (Exodus 7:1–8:32)

1. Moses had advance knowledge of what would happen in his interviews with Pharaoh. How much is the giving of 'advance knowledge' part of God's way of revealing himself?
2. What were the functions of the various plagues that come upon

Pharaoh? Does God still send warnings upon powerful people who resist his will?

3. Do miracles soften Pharaoh's heart? If not, what is their purpose?

□□□ **Reading 220 (Exodus 9:1–11:10)**

1. Is there any progress in the different judgments? Are there any changes in Pharaoh as the events proceed? What effect does a series of judgments have upon anyone determined to resist God?

2. In Romans 9:17 how does Paul apply this story to unbelieving people in his own day? How should we apply it in our world?

3. The tenth judgment was different from the previous nine. What new ingredients can be found at this point? God says, 'I will bring one more plague . . . About midnight I will go throughout Egypt' (11:4). Why is God more directly involved at this point?

□□□ **Reading 221 (Exodus 12:1–13:22)**

1. The Passover was to be forever remembered (12:1–6). In what ways does the Passover foreshadow the death of Christ as a sacrifice for sin?

2. After the great deliverance, God required that his people dedicate themselves to him. There were two feasts and one ceremony that were specially laid upon Israel at this time: the Passover, the feast of unleavened bread and the dedication of the firstborn. What is the symbolism of the feast of unleavened bread and what is the point of the dedication of the firstborn?

3. What are the characteristics of the leading of God? Does God follow quick routes? The safest? The easiest?

□□□ **Reading 222 (Exodus 14:1–15:27)**

1. The faith of the Israelites (see Hebrews 11:29) soon received a challenge. The people are alarmed when they see Pharaoh's armies in the distance. They are fearful (14:10) and complain against Moses (14:11) and have regrets about their leaving Egypt (14:12). Is there a difference between first faith and persistent faith? What light does the letter to the Hebrews throw on this (see Hebrews 3:14; 6:11)?

2. God showed the people of Israel that he is the God who rescues us when we are in extreme distress. They saw the great power of Yahweh and they had seen that his power had come to their aid when they needed him (14:31). What does 'knowing his ways' mean in Hebrews 3:10?

3. Once they are redeemed and rescued, the Israelites have something to sing about. What are the themes of their worship in Exodus 15:1–27?

□□□ **Reading 223 (Exodus16:1–18:27)**

1. The Hebrew word *manna* seems to be a very old word meaning 'what is it?' They called the food the 'what-is-it', the 'what's-its-name', the 'manna' (16:31). Later a pot of it was kept 'before the LORD' (that is, in the tabernacle when it was built) to remind them of how God provided for them (16:32–34). What other lessons do we gather from the incident of the manna?

2. How do 'unbelieving believers' handle troubles? How do they view their leaders? What does God think of their grumbling?

3. What is the response of the Amalekites to Israel's redemption, and how does Israel handle it? What is the response of Jethro, and what part does he play in his newly appreciated Israel?

□□□ **Reading 224 (Exodus 19:1–20:26)**

1. Salvation by the blood of the lamb is a step towards God's getting our lives to be under his guidance. In fifty days God took Israel from Passover to Sinai. In fifty days God took the Church from the shedding of Jesus' blood to the outpouring of the Holy Spirit. God put Israel under his law. How does God get us to 'fulfil' the Mosaic law?

2. What was the *original* purpose of the Ten Commandments? How many of them could incur penalties from a magistrate or law-court? For how many of them was disobedience punished by the death penalty? What is the Christian equivalent of the Sabbath? What is special about the tenth commandment?

3. Exodus 20:18–21 receives comment in Hebrews 12:18–21. What is the difference between coming to Sinai and coming to Zion?

□□□ **Reading 225 (Exodus 21:1–22:31)**

Exodus 19:1–24:11 deals with the forming of a covenant between God and Israel. But is the Christian under the Mosaic law? If you use that phrase to mean 'principles of righteousness', then a Christian most certainly keeps principles of righteousness! But actually this is not the meaning of the phrase 'the law' in the majority of times when it is used in the Bible. 'The law of God' is everything that God gave to the nation of Israel at the time of Moses. In that sense of the term, the Christian is not under the law. They walk in the Spirit and by walking in the Spirit they fulfil the Mosaic law, indirectly. The Christian even goes beyond and higher than the Ten Commandments, by walking in the Spirit under the explicit instruction of Jesus and his apostles, whose teachings we find in the New Testament.

Exodus 21:1–11 concerns slavery. Then four rulings deal with killing (21:12–14), violence to a parent (21:15), kidnapping (21:16) and verbal abuse of a parent (21:17). In Exodus 21:18–22:17 there are fourteen commands. The first four in 21:18–27 deal with injuries. Next we have three rulings in 21:28–36, which concern animals. In Exodus 22:1–15 we have six rulings, which concern various types of theft or neglect. One more regulation comes here. If a man has a sexual relationship with a single girl, he must pay a bride-price to the father. He may have to marry her as well, but that will be decided by the father (22:16–17). The rulings in Exodus 22:18–31 deal with different members of society, the worst (18–20), the weakest (21–27) and the wisest (28–31).

1. How do we read the law? Try reading this legislation asking the question: Should my country have a comparable – but perhaps higher – legislation in this matter?
2. Then try reading the legislation asking the question: Will the Holy Spirit be asking me to go *higher* than what I am being told here?
3. The Christian must want to go forward from the law, not backward. So how can I go higher than these regulations?

☐☐☐ Reading 226 (Exodus 23:1–24:18)

Next come nine rulings that show compassion towards people who are unprotected (23:1–9). A further six rulings have to do with worship and sacred festivals (23:10–19b). Then the 'Book of the Covenant' ends with a section preparing for the invasion of Canaan, and underlining the Lord's exclusive claim on his people (23:20–30). In Exodus 24:1–18, seventy elders, Aaron, two sons of Aaron, Joshua (see 24:13) and Moses himself – seventy-five in all – are invited to ascend Sinai.

1. The Christian is not under the Mosaic law, but the movement from law to grace is not a movement backward; it is a movement forward. So how can I *outstrip* these regulations about justice (23:1–3)? What would have happened at Jesus' trial if this legislation had been kept? How can I show compassion in an even greater way than the law of Moses? Can I go higher than the law in impartiality?
2. What are the contrasts to all of this in the Christian life? What matters are parallel and similar? For example we obey the Holy Spirit, not the details of Mosaic legislation. What other contrasts are to be found?
3. Why did God need the blood? Why do the people need the blood? Why does God require the death of Jesus? What does it mean for the blood of Jesus to be sprinkled on us (Hebrews 9:14)?

□□□ Reading 227 (Exodus 25:1–26:37)

The tabernacle was a tent, a temporary and transportable place for the priests of Israel to conduct daily symbolic worship. No one went inside it except the priests. No one ever went inside the Holy of Holies except the high priest. It was the place where God was specially and visibly present in Israel (although it was not possible for anyone to see his radiating glory). It has now been abolished. The Christian is not under it; but he fulfils it. (i) The tabernacle was the earthly dwelling-place of God. (ii) It was to be a shadow of the gospel. (iii) It was to be a model of heaven and earth, and a symbol of the Old Covenant and the New Covenant. (iv) It represents levels of spiritual experience. Outside in the courtyard there is, symbolically speaking, no fellowship with God. Yet the great altar was visible and so was the laver for washing. In the first compartment were three items of furniture, all symbols of fellowship. Yet Jesus opened up a new and living way. On the cross a way was made open to a deeper level of fellowship than had been known before.

1. What do we learn about giving from Exodus 25:1–40? How can the passage be Christianised?
2. If the ark (25:10–22) represents God's presence, the table (25:23–30) represents table fellowship, and the lampstand (25:31–40) represents the light of the Lord, what do these items tell us about the nature of the Christian life?
3. Exodus 26:1–37 proceeds to describe the coverings (26:1–14), the wooden frame (26:15–30), the veil and the screen (26:31–37). Although the structure was not a solid building, yet it was well protected and secure in its own way. It was humble and unostentatious from the outside but colourful when viewed from the inside. Are there spiritual lessons to be learned here?

□□□ Reading 228 (Exodus 27:1–28:43)

1. If the altar represents sin-bearing atonement (27:1–8) and the outer courtyard (27:9–19) represents this world, what do we learn about the death of our Lord Jesus Christ?
2. If the lampstand represents God's gospel as the 'light of the world', what does it mean to have the light of God in our lives?
3. In Exodus 28:1–43 the instructions of God to Moses move to deal with the priests who are to minister in the tabernacle. Very beautiful clothing will be specially made for them. The priest will have (i) a breastpiece, (ii) an ephod, (iii) a blue robe, (iv) a tunic worn over linen undergarments, (v) a turban and (vi) a sash, all mentioned in 28:4. Two

items are not yet mentioned: the gold plate on the turban, and the linen undergarments. Can we find any symbolism in these items of clothing? Verse 12 explains some of it.

☐☐☐ Reading 229 (Exodus 29:1–30:38)

1. The servants of God must be consecrated to him. The high priest must be washed (29:4b), clothed (29:5–6) and anointed with oil (29:7). What is the symbolism here?

2. The servants of God need themselves to be appointed by God to all the aspects of their ministry. The sin offering makes symbolic atonement for the sins of Aaron and his sons. There was to be a whole burnt offering, symbolising utter consecration. The other ram is a peace offering. This blood would be applied to the right ears, the right thumbs, the right toes of Aaron and his sons (29:19–20), and would also be sprinkled on the garments (29:21). What is the symbolism here?

3. In Exodus 30:1–38 we have a description of the altar of incense (30:1–10). In the laws of Moses it represents the intercessions of the whole sacrificial system. What does it represent for us? And the census tax (30:11–16)? The bronze laver (30:17–21)?

☐☐☐ Reading 230 (Exodus 31:1–33:23)

1. God wants his work to be done under the gifting of the Holy Spirit. Should our reading here lead us to have wider ideas about the 'gifts of the Holy Spirit'?

2. In Exodus 32:1–35 the story switches to what is happening at the bottom of Mount Sinai. What are the sins the people are falling into? Impatience. What else?

3. How inconsistent can the true people of God be, and yet still be God's people?

4. God puts the situation to Moses. What is his purpose? In what way do we see the greatness of Moses at this point? What do we learn from the way he prayed?

☐☐☐ Reading 231 (Exodus 34:1–35:35)

Moses has asked to know more of God; and God is promising to answer his prayer. Now (in Exodus 34:1–7) what God promised begins to happen.

1. God's name is his character. What do we learn of God's character in these chapters? How will this affect the way we live?

2. Moses' praying in Exodus 32:1–34:35 has distinct parts to it. How should prayer grow and develop?

3. What are the three requests in Exodus 34:8–9? Should we want the same things?

4. In Exodus 34:1–35 we have another section of legislation. What is the relevance of all of this for the Christian? When the Christian reads the Mosaic law – and he should do, for not a jot or tittle will be unfulfilled – how does he read it?

5. How does talking with God transform us without our being very conscious of it?

☐☐☐ Reading 232 (Exodus 36:1–38:31)

1. If the tabernacle represents levels of fellowship, what is symbolised by (i) the courtyard, (ii) the holy place and (iii) the Holy of Holies?

2. Can you detect progress in the three stages of the tabernacle (outside, holy place, holiest of all)?

3. Why did God tear down the veil at the time of Jesus' death on the cross?

☐☐☐ Reading 233 (Exodus 39:1–40:38)

1. We have mention here of the ephod (39:2–7), the breastpiece (39:8–21), the robe (39:22–26), the tunics (39:27), the turban (39:28a), the linen undergarments (39:28b), the sash (39:29), and the gold plate (39:30–31). All eight items of the priests' clothing are mentioned. Seven times it is emphasised that these garments were made exactly as the Lord commanded Moses. (i) The ephod represents intercessory prayer. (ii) The breastpiece speaks of sympathy. And the others?

2. Eventually it was time for the worship-system to be put into operation. On the Israelite New Year's Day (what is the symbolism?) the tabernacle is to be set up and put into position (40:1). It is all anointed with the sacred anointing oil (40:9–11). Everything was being done by Moses, God's prophet, priest and king. Then the visible presence of God comes down upon the tabernacle. What is the equivalent of this in Christian faith?

3. The great lesson of the tabernacle is *not* that the Church is meant to be inflexible and under minute rules and regulations. Far from it! What in fact are the major lessons to be learned from the entire tabernacle system of worship?

John's Gospel

John's Gospel was the last of the four Gospels to be written. It was written by the apostle John, probably with the help of some friends. It supplements what we know about Jesus from the other three Gospels. John's main theme is to point us to the life and light that is to be received by faith in the Lord Jesus Christ, the Word of the Father who became flesh.

Recommended reading: W. Hendriksen, *John's Gospel* (Baker/Banner of Truth, 1953, 1954); J. C. Ryle, *Expository Thoughts on the Gospels: John* (often reprinted).

☐☐☐ **Reading 234 (John 1:1–18)**
The Gospel begins with an introduction in 1:1–18 in which are outlined the main themes to be found in the story that starts in John 1:19. Almost every line in John 1:1–18 has its equivalent in John 1:19–22:25. John is telling us what to look for in the story that is ahead of us. The steps in the preface move towards the thought of becoming a son of God:
- The Word (1:1–2)
    - Creation (1:3)
        - Life and life (1:4–5)
            - John the Baptist (1:6–8)
                - Light coming into the world (1:9–10)

- Rejection (1:11)
  - Receiving sonship (1:12)

Now he seems to work backwards to the same point as we had when we started:

- Becoming a son (1:13)
- Coming into the world (1:14)
- John the Baptist (1:15)
- Grace received from him (1:16)
- Grace coming through him (1:17)
- The ultimate revelation (1:18)

1. In what way may the 'Son of God' be described as 'the Word'? What are the ideas that are involved?
2. John 1:1–18 seems to be aiming to convince us of the divine glory of the Son of God. How is the greatness of God's Son, 'the Word', to be seen in these verses?
3. What is the 'life' that is given to believers by the Son of God?

□□□ Reading 235 (John 1:19–51)
1. What did John the Baptist think of himself? What did he think of Jesus?
2. John 1:19–58 gives small glimpses of people who met Jesus (John the Baptist, Peter, Andrew, Philip, Nathaniel). What do we learn from each of them?
3. Jesus is the 'staircase' of Genesis 28:12. Do we use him to climb up to God? Or is it that God uses him to send blessings down to us?

□□□ Reading 236 (John 2:1–25)
1. What do we learn about Mary from this passage? Could she ever make mistakes? What was her advice to the servants (2:5)?
2. What is the symbolism of the 'new wine'? And what does the water represent? Does 2:6 give us a clue?
3. In what way may the cleansing of the temple be applied to our own lives? To churches and religious organisations? To buildings? Why does religion tend to become commercial?

□□□ Reading 237 (John 3:1–15)
1. List the good characteristics of Nicodemus. But what do all 'good' people need, according to Jesus?

2. What is the 'new birth'? What does John 3:1–36 say?

3. After Nicodemus has been shown his need of new birth, Jesus turns to speak of his cross. Is there any significance in the change of subject?

Note 'Water and the Spirit' is probably not a reference to Christian water-baptism, for two reasons. (i) Christian baptism did not exist. It was inaugurated at the end of Jesus' ministry, after his resurrection. (ii) Nicodemus could not be expected to know about it. What he could be expected to know were the promises of Ezekiel 36:25–26, which promise a new covenant with spiritual cleansing and newness of spiritual life.

☐☐☐ Reading 238 (John 3:16–36)

1. How much does God love us? How can we tell?

2. What do we do to get God to love us? What do we do that gets God to be angry with us (John 3:16, 36)?

3. What do we learn from John the Baptist and his disciples about (i) rivalry and (ii) humility?

☐☐☐ Reading 239 (John 4:1–26)

1. What were the problems of the woman of Samaria? What does Jesus put to her as the answer to her need?

2. Was Jesus taking a risk in speaking to such a woman? If so, how did he handle the 'risk'?

3. Jesus asks about the woman's husband. He is forcing her to face one aspect of her sinful life. After she has admitted her need Jesus never mentions it again. Do sinners need reminding of their sins? Do we? What is Jesus doing?

☐☐☐ Reading 240 (John 4:27–54)

1. What changes took place in the woman's life? What happened to the water-pot? The man in her house? The people in the town? What brought about such change?

2. Jesus was more 'successful' in Samaria than in Judea or Galilee (note verse 44). The opportunities there were great (4:34–38). Why was Jesus more welcome in Samaria than elsewhere?

3. How does 4:58 affect us today in a world greatly interested in miracles?

☐☐☐ Reading 241 (John 5:1–15)

At a pool known as Bethesda, a paralysed man is among a multitude of sick people (5:2–3a; John 5:3b–4 is not in the best manuscripts). The pool is thought to be able from time to time to give miraculous healing, and for thirty-eight years this man has been visiting it in the hope of miraculous healing (5:5). Jesus comes by, asks him a question (5:6), listens to his answer (5:7) and heals him (5:8).

1. What are the characteristics of the man? The help that he looks for has been long delayed. What else?
2. So what does Jesus do? Jesus cuts across everything the man has said. Jesus acts sovereignly. He chooses one man out of dozens and displays his mercy in that one person. What are the other characteristics of Jesus' way of working?
3. What do verses 13–14 imply about sin, sickness, conversion and healing? Did the man come to salvation before he was healed or vice versa? Is sickness always the result of sin? Was it the result of sin in this case?

☐☐☐ Reading 242 (John 5:16–47)

1. Who does Jesus claim to be? How does he present his claim?
2. In John 5:19–23, Jesus explains more fully his relationship to the Father. What in fact is his relationship to God? What is the difference between the claims of Jesus and the claims of other religious figures?
3. What spiritual experiences come to the person who hears the voice of the Son of God?

☐☐☐ Reading 243 (John 6:1–24)

1. John is interested in different levels of faith. What are the differences between the 'believers' of John 6:2, 26 and 68? What kind of faith do you have?
2. What kind of Messiah do worldly people want (6:14–15)? What kind of Messiah does Jesus wish to be?
3. Feeding people using almost nothing, and walking on stormy water, are two ways in which Jesus demonstrates his great power and great faith. What do these two miracles tell about Jesus? What sort of people ought we to be if we have faith in such a Saviour?

☐☐☐ Reading 244 (John 6:25–51)

1. The Jews ask for a sign just after the feeding of five thousand people. What does this tell us about sign-seekers?
2. Jesus says that he himself is the sign from God. Remembering the story of the manna falling in the days of Moses, what does the story in John 6:25–51 say to us about Jesus?

3. What does it mean to us in practice that Jesus is 'bread of life' for us? How do we get to experience him in this way?

☐☐☐ Reading 245 (John 6:52–71)

1. What was specially offensive among Jesus' sayings at this time (6:60)? Why was it so offensive?

2. Why does Jesus tell people that it takes a special work of God in their hearts for them to believe (6:65)? How will it help them to be told this?

3. Why did Jesus choose as an apostle someone he knew had no faith and would betray him?

☐☐☐ Reading 246 (John 7:1–24)

1. Jesus' brothers badly misunderstood Jesus' method of ministry. What are worldly methods of self-promotion? What is Jesus' way as we see it in this chapter?

2. When Jesus began to teach the people (7:14), it was obvious to everyone that he had great spiritual understanding. So where did this profound knowledge of his come from? How can anyone come to spiritual knowledge? What are the answers Jesus gives?

3. What do you think of Jesus? In John 7:1–24, why were people afraid to talk of Jesus? Why are they afraid to talk of Jesus today?

☐☐☐ Reading 247 (John 7:25–52)

1. The people in Jerusalem at this time of the Festival of Tabernacles were all very confused. Jesus claims to be both ordinary and extraordinary, known and unknown. What is 'ordinary' about him? What is extraordinary?

2. What were the different reactions to Jesus at this Feast of Tabernacles? Why are the different reactions so intense or even violent?

3. At this point he makes two great claims for himself (7:33–34, 37–38). What are they? What does it mean to 'drink' from Jesus?

4. Men and women are looking for answers and are dissatisfied with the biggest questions we can ever answer. Can God be known? Is there a way of arriving at certainty concerning what is true and what is false? The temple guards say 'The words he says are greater than the words of any other person who has ever spoken!' (7:46). What is the difference between listening to Jesus and listening to power-hungry religious leaders?

☐☐☐ Reading 248 (John 7:53–8:30)

1. What is the difference (in John 7:53–8:11) between the 'holiness' of the Pharisees and the holiness of Jesus?
2. After a pause Jesus (still at the Feast of Tabernacles) makes another great announcement. 'I am the light of the world', he says. What does Jesus mean when he speaks of himself as light?
3. 'Who are you?', they ask Jesus (8:25). How does Jesus answer?

Note John 7:53–8:11 is not found in the early Greek manuscripts of the New Testament. It was added much later. Some scribes put it in Luke's Gospel. It has no connection with John 1:1–7:52 or with John 8:12 and the rest of the Gospel. We must follow the flow of John's Gospel from John 7:52 to John 8:12, ignoring the verses in-between. John 7:53–8:11 is probably historically authentic, but it is not part of John's Gospel and must be considered separately.

☐☐☐ Reading 249 (John 8:31–59)

1. What does Jesus say about continuing faith in John 8:30–32? What is the secret of fruitfulness?
2. What is Jesus' teaching about 'freedom' in this chapter? Freedom from what? What is it like to be 'free'?
3. Jesus is genuinely seeking to help these Jewish leaders. He offers them freedom; they are in bondage (8:33–36). True believers are Abraham's children; Jesus' enemies are at the moment Satan's children (8:37–47). Now Jesus presses upon them a third point – in 8:48–59. What is his argument here?

Note John 8:31–32 is a parenthesis – remarks in brackets. Throughout John 8:12–29, 'they' refers to unbelieving Jewish people, the Pharisees and their supporters. The same people are obviously speaking throughout 8:33–58. Throughout 8:12–29, 33–58, Jesus is speaking to the Pharisees and their supporters, but this means that verses 30–32 are an aside. At this point the text makes it clear that Jesus is speaking only to the recent believers. Verse 33 goes back to the original listeners.

☐☐☐ Reading 250 (John 9:1–23)

In John 7:1–53 most of the characters are very confused. In John 8:1–59 Jesus claims to be the light of the world. In John 9:1–12 Jesus heals a blind man. It is obvious that the blind man is (among other things) an illustration of the blindness of the world and the way in which Jesus is able to dramatically cure anyone's spiritual blindness.

1. What is the connection between sin and suffering? What two theories are the Jews considering in John 9:1–23? What does Jesus say?

2. The man is blind from birth. Jesus uses an offensive way of giving eyesight. The change is obvious. How does the miracle illustrate the need of the world – and its only hope?

3. The blind man's story is a model of what it means to bear witness to the Lord Jesus Christ. How does he share to others what has happened to him?

☐☐☐ Reading 251 (John 9:24–39)

1. How is the newly healed man a model of a new believer?

2. How are the Pharisees a model of the new believer's enemies?

3. What help does Jesus give to the newly healed man?

☐☐☐ Reading 252 (John 9:40–10:18)

Notice the flow of thought here. As John 10:1 begins John does not say, 'After these things . . .' or anything like that. There is no change of location in John 10:1. Much confusion is to be found among the people of Jerusalem (John 7:1–53) but Jesus is the light of the world (John 8:1–59) and cures blindness of every kind (John 9:1–41). His enemies confuse people and are themselves confused. They slander his followers and want to kill Jesus himself. John 10:1–42 continues the themes of these previous chapters.

Jesus uses a picture taken from the life of sheep and shepherds. In the countryside there would be some kind of enclosure in which the sheep would be kept. At night-time there would be many flocks of different shepherds. There would be a gate and a gate-keeper watching to see that no thief entered into the enclosure. In the morning the shepherd would come and call for his sheep. He would have names for each one. There would be many shepherds, but the voice of each shepherd would be known and recognised only by his own sheep. As he called them, often using their names, they would come out of the enclosure, and the shepherd would walk away with the sheep following him. The Pharisees did not understand the meaning of Jesus' parable (10:6). So Jesus tells a second similar parable. The details and the point of this parable are somewhat different from what we had in 10:1–5. Now the 'sheepfold' is a circle of large and heavy rocks. The sheep all belong to one flock. There is an opening in this sheepfold but there is no door or gate in this type of enclosure. Instead the shepherd sleeps at the opening. He himself is the door. The sheep cannot get out and no one can come in without coming to where he is at the opening or doorway in the circle of rocks. Outside the sheepfold are thieves and robbers of various kinds.

1. In John 10:1–5, how does Jesus use his picture? What is the 'enclosure'? Who is the shepherd? And so on. What are the points being made?

2. In John 10:6–13, how does Jesus use his illustration? What new points are being made?

3. Very few people really understand themselves. Some overvalue themselves. Others undervalue themselves. Many misinterpret themselves in one way or another. But here in John's Gospel we see how much Jesus had a true knowledge of himself. What does he say about himself, and his place in the purpose of God?

□□□ Reading 253 (John 10:19–42)

1. Jesus' claims caused division (10:19). What are the two ways of reacting to Jesus? How do you respond to Jesus?

2. It is now the Festival of the Dedication of the Temple – and once again Jesus is there to take part in the celebrations. It was winter (John 10:22). Jesus is walking in a covered section of the temple courts (10:23). While he is walking along he is approached by some of those who are hostile to him. They are trying – as they have tried before – to get him to say something that they can use to bring trouble upon him. Jesus makes statements (i) about his Messiahship (10:25–26), (ii) about their sinfulness (10:27), (iii) about the success of his mission from God (10:28–29), and (iv) about his relationship to God the Father (10:30–33). What does he say under each heading?

3. Jesus explains his Sonship in two ways. Jesus has been attacked for claiming equality with God. But if they will think a little, they might remember that in the Psalms earthly judges are given the title 'gods'. How does the argument proceed?

□□□ Reading 254 (John 11:1–27)

1. It might be disappointing to us if the Lord Jesus Christ allowed us to become ill. In what other ways was Jesus rather disappointing to his friends in this story? What was Jesus' purpose in his being so 'disappointing'?

2. What does Martha think about what has happened? How does she take the words of Jesus (11:21–24)? In what way is her viewpoint defective or limited?

3. What does Jesus mean when he says he is himself the resurrection and the life? Could any other religious leader say the same thing?

☐☐☐ Reading 255 (John 11:28–57)

1. What were the differences in character between Martha and Mary? What did they both need to know?
2. Jesus was just about to raise Lazarus from the dead. So why was he weeping (11:35)?
3. How certain was it that Jesus actually had raised Lazarus from the dead? Could there have been any real doubts? How do the Pharisees react to what seems an obvious miracle?
4. The Jews want to put to death a person who has just claimed to be the resurrection and the life! What does this tell us about unbelieving people?

☐☐☐ Reading 256 (John 12:1–36)

1. Consider the three characters in the first half of this chapter: Mary, Judas and Jesus. What was Mary like? In what way was Judas the total opposite? What special character do we see in the way Jesus relates to both of them?
2. Kings who enter cities in triumph generally come as conquerors. For this reason their coming causes much fear. But how is Jesus different?
3. A corn of wheat has to 'die'. It has to go into the ground, it has to dissolve and break up into pieces. Only then will something spring up as a harvest. How does Jesus use this as an illustration of his own work?

☐☐☐ Reading 257 (John 12:37–50)

1. The result of unbelief was abandonment to deeper unbelief. God punishes sin by abandoning the sinner to his sin. How is this illustrated in this chapter? Is it illustrated in our own society?
2. John is interested in unbelief in Israel; he is also interested in dubious 'faith' that might sometimes turn out not to be faith at all. There were 'believers' who did not have the courage to speak out their faith. John is severely critical of them, but he does not tell us whether they were truly Christian or not. What do you think? Remember Nicodemus became a true believer (John 7:50–52) and Joseph of Arimathea publicly honoured Jesus by giving Jesus an honourable tomb.
3. Jesus ends his public ministry with a final appeal to Israel (12:44–50). What is the essence of his last words to them?

☐☐☐ Reading 258 (John 13:1–17)

1. Is there anything we can do to promote humility in our own lives? How does John 13:1–17 help us here?

2. What is Peter's attitude to having his feet washed? Is it humbling to receive as well as humbling to serve?

3. Jesus uses washing the body and washing the feet as a parable. What is the point of 13:10?

☐☐☐ Reading 259 (John 13:18–38)

1. Consider the character of Jesus in 13:21. Why was Jesus upset? What did he feel like? Why did he not mention Judas' name? Does God allow 'Judases' in our lives? How should we handle them?

2. We have read Jesus' last words to the Pharisees (John 12:44–49). Now we have the last words of Jesus' three-year ministry. What would be on your mind if you were to be crucified tomorrow? What is on Jesus' mind?

3. Is it really true that love has evangelistic power (13:35)? How does it work?

☐☐☐ Reading 260 (John 14:1–31)

1. Jesus clearly wants to encourage and strengthen the disciples. How does he do it? What kind of encouragement does he give?

2. What do we do that is greater than even what Jesus did? Has anyone ever worked greater miracles than Jesus (including taking up his own life in resurrection)? Did Jesus in his earthly ministry ever do anything as great as what happened on the Day of Pentecost? So how do we understand John 14:12?

3. What is the ministry of the Holy Spirit to the disciples? And to us?

☐☐☐ Reading 261 (John 15:1–27)

1. How does Jesus work out his vine-tree illustration? The branches draw their energy from their being in the tree. What other aspects of the illustration are used by Jesus? Who is the gardener and what does he do? What happens to dead branches?

2. What is the difference between a servant and a friend? How does Jesus use the difference to explain what he wants to be to us?

3. In view of John 15:18–26 what will be the character of friendship between Christians and others?

☐☐☐ **Reading 262 (John 16:1–33)**

1. The disciples are about to face some immense changes in their lives. What were the changes that were ahead of them? In John 16:1–33, how does Jesus help us to face change?

2. What does it feel like when the Holy Spirit is at work in our hearts?

3. What are the indications of the Holy Spirit's coming in power? According to Jesus, what happens when the Spirit comes?

Note 'And when he comes he will convince the world about sin and about righteousness and about judgment' (16:8). Expositors discuss the exact meaning of the word used here, but it must include the idea of 'convincing'. In every reference to 'convicting' in the New Testament (see Matthew18:15; Luke 3:19; John 3:2; 8:46; 1 Corinthians 14:2 and elsewhere) the idea of being convinced of one's guilt is involved. 'He will convince people about righteousness' perhaps means that the Holy Spirit will convince us of a new approach to righteousness altogether. We shall see that our own righteousness is useless and is disguised wickedness. We see that Jesus was 'the Righteous One' and committed no crime. We shall see that God gives us a gift of righteousness in our Lord Jesus Christ – the result of the death, resurrection and ascension of the Lord Jesus Christ.

☐☐☐ **Reading 263 (John 17:1–26)**

After Jesus preaches, he prays. It is a good combination. The prayer has three sections in it (17:1–5, 6–19, 20–26). John 17:1–26 at first gives the impression of being a rather repetitive chapter, going round and round a few points. But close study will show that there is scarcely any repetition in it at all. John's thought moves very rapidly from one point to the next, often mentioning a number of strikingly different ideas side-by-side. The thought is very simple yet immensely profound.

1. Make a list of the topics for which Jesus prays. How does it compare with the things for which we pray?

2. As we study John 17:1–26 we notice that there is much more in it than praying. Jesus is also assessing the work that he has done. What are the things that Jesus had already achieved at this stage of his work?

3. If Jesus gets his prayers answered (note John 11:41–42), what things are bound to happen because Jesus prayed? What would it mean to us if we were to live daily on the intercession of Jesus?

Note A Greek two-word phrase in John 17:12 has a variety of different meanings. (i) Sometimes it means 'unless'. 'You would have no power over me *unless* it had been given you from above' (John 19:15). (ii) Sometimes it means 'if . . . not'. 'If this man were not an evildoer, we would not have handed him over' (John 18:30). (iii) Sometimes it means 'other than'. 'We have no king other than Caesar'. (iv) Sometimes the two words refer not to an exception but to something that is altogether a total contrast. It is difficult to translate adequately and we have to use words like 'But on the contrary there was . . .' or 'However there is . . .' or 'But altogether different is the case of . . .' Matthew 12:4 is to be translated: 'David entered the house of God, and ate the showbread, which it was not lawful for him to eat, neither for them that were with him. However it was lawful for the priests.' (The word does not mean 'except'. The priests were not with David.) Other examples are in Luke 4:25–26; Galatians 1:6–7; 2:16; Revelation 21:27. And John 17:12 has the same kind of usage. 'I kept them in your name . . . I guarded them . . . Not one of them has perished. However the son of perdition has perished' (17:12). Judas is not an exception (as if to say Jesus failed in the case of Judas!). Rather Judas is a total contrast. He was not 'clean'. He had no faith. He was never given by the Father to the Son. He was a pretender through-and-through.

☐☐☐ Reading 264 (John 18:1–23)

1. How voluntary was Jesus' sufferings? Could Jesus have escaped them? If so, why did Jesus choose not to resist his crucifixion?
2. Should we take Jesus' promise that we shall never be lost to include even physical protection? What is the point of John 18:7–9?
3. Judas obviously expects a fight; he brings weapons. What does this tell us about Judas? Peter is ready to fight. What does this tell us about Peter? Jesus refuses to fight. What does this tell us about Jesus?

☐☐☐ Reading 265 (John 18:24–40)

1. How sincere is Jesus' trial? What does this tell us about religious leaders? What does it tell us about law and legality?
2. What is the relationship between Jesus' kingdom and this world? What does Jesus mean when he says his kingdom is not *from* this world?
3. Two questions are being raised: Is Jesus an evil-doer? What sort of king is he? Two different conclusions are being sought: The Jews are trying to pervert the truth and kill Jesus. Pilate is trying to avoid a decision and release Jesus. The big question is: Who is this Jesus? How does Jesus himself help us to answer the question?

☐☐☐ Reading 266 (John 19:1–27)

1. In Pontius Pilate we see a man struggling to avoid doing what is wrong. Have you ever been in a situation where you are about to do something that is wrong but you are struggling not to do it? First he says: take

Jesus yourself (18:31; he wants to pass the responsibility to someone else). Second he says: I find no guilt in him (18:38; he wants to do what is right). Third he says: let me release Jesus and punish Barabbas (18:39; he thinks he has found a way to do what is right). What are the next stages of his struggle – in John 19:1–27?

2. Jesus suffers terribly. There is physical violence (19:1), mockery (19:2–3), disgrace (19:5), blind hostility (19:6), misuse of the law of Moses (19:7), and the total injustice of a man being declared innocent and then being sentenced to death (19:8–16a)! What is God's purpose in the sufferings of Jesus?

3. How does the death of Jesus fulfil the Old Testament Scriptures? Why is this important to John?

□□□ Reading 267 (John 19:28–42)

1. 'It is finished', said Jesus. What was it that Jesus knew had been accomplished on the cross?

2. John obviously sees some symbolism in the blood and water that came from the wounded body of Jesus. What do the blood and water represent? What is it that Jesus offers us as the result of his cross?

3. 'Not a bone of him shall be broken.' The quotation is from Psalm 34:20. The idea is from Exodus 12:46; Numbers 9:12. What is the significance of the unbroken body of Jesus?

□□□ Reading 268 (John 20:1–31)

1. John 20:1–31 records some of the first witnesses to the resurrection of Jesus. What is the significance of the fact that a woman is the first eye-witness of Jesus' resurrection? Would this be very acceptable in the first century? If not, why did John record it in this way?

2. Why would Jesus not let Mary cling to him? What mistake was she making? What is to be the nature of our post-resurrection fellowship with Jesus?

3. What are the results of Jesus' resurrection according to this chapter? Because Jesus is raised from the dead, the people of God may have peace. What else?

Note John 20:22. What exactly was this gift of the Holy Spirit? (i) It was not a purely symbolical act, predicting the Day of Pentecost. The word 'Receive!' is an 'aorist imperative' (as the Greek scholars call it) and an aorist imperative cannot refer to something in the future! (ii) It is not a gift enabling 'priests' to forgive sins. This is not a natural reading of the text. And verses 19–20 speak of 'disciples'. Many disciples were there including some of the women! This gift is for all disciples, not merely for 'the priests' (and in any case, the New Testament never calls Christian preachers 'priests'!). (iii) Was it the giving of the Spirit to create the Church? The Church was functioning even before the Day of Pentecost (read Acts 1:1–26!). The Day of Pentecost was a 'baptism of power' (as Acts 1:8 predicted) upon a Church which was already functioning. The Church with the resurrection-power of Jesus came into being on the day of the resurrection. (iv) Was it the day when resurrection-power was given to the disciples? Christians are 'raised with Christ' and are to reckon themselves alive to God (as Romans 6:1–14 puts it in detail). This verse echoes Genesis 2:7. In Genesis 2:7 God created a human being by breathing life into him. In John 20:22 Jesus created the Church – the 'new humanity' – by breathing resurrection-power into his people. John 20:23: 'If you forgive the sins of anyone, they are forgiven them. If you retain anyone's sins, the sins are still unforgiven'. Strictly speaking only God can forgive sins (a point that is made in Mark 2:7). This verse cannot mean that 'priests' or Christian ministers have the right in themselves to forgive sins. Surely what we have here is that Christians have the power to say what the gospel is and therefore who is forgiven and who is not forgiven. If someone convinces me they have believed in Jesus, I might say to them, 'Your sins are forgiven.' It is not that I personally am doing the forgiving. I am simply saying, 'Because I know what the gospel is I can tell you your sins are forgiven.' Similarly if someone tells me they have no faith in Jesus I might say to them, 'You still are in your sins. You are not yet forgiven.' This is what the preachers of the New Testament often do (see Acts 2:38; 3:19; 13:26–38). And they can tell someone that they are not forgiven (as in Acts 8:23). The resurrection of Jesus and the power of the Holy Spirit give us an understanding of the gospel, and we can apply it in our own lives and in the lives of others.

□□□ Reading 269 (John 21:1–25)

John 20:31 sounds like the end of John's Gospel and yet there is another chapter! John 21:1–25 is written in the same style as the rest of the Gospel. It may be (but we cannot be dogmatic about it) that John the apostle provided the material for his Gospel, the material we find in John 1:19–20:31, and a group of his friends (the 'we' in 21:24) put it all together, with an extra chapter at the end and John 1:1–18 as a beginning. Perhaps it was his friends (rather than John himself) who called John 'the disciple that Jesus loved'.

1. Obviously the disciples were somewhat discouraged; they had all badly disowned Jesus at the time of his arrest. He discouraged their return to fishing. Without him they could catch nothing, not a single fish! Then Jesus suddenly appears. How does Jesus encourage them?
2. Jesus recommissions Peter – three times after three denials of Jesus. What do we learn of the generosity of Jesus here? How long did

Peter have to wait? What did he have to do? How did God overrule what had happened?

3. John and Peter had different ministries. Peter died at an early stage in the persecutions of the emperor Nero. John lived to an old age. What are the practical implications of Jesus' word: 'You follow me!' (21:22)?

Judges

The book of Judges tells what happened from the third generation onwards, after Israel's deliverance from bondage in Egypt, in a period of Israel's history that runs from about 1195 to 1050 BC. God saved Israel by the blood of a lamb. Pharaoh had been punished by ten mighty judgments. The Sea of Reeds (as we should call it) had been dramatically divided and the people had walked across dry land before the sea came flooding back again. The generation who experienced those events could never completely forget what had happened.

Then there was the persistent disobedience of Israel while they were in the wilderness between Egypt and Canaan. Eventually God left that generation in the wilderness for forty years. The time came when all the adults who had experienced the crossing of the Sea of Reeds had died. Only a few who had been children or teenagers at the time were alive to remember what had happened.

Then during another forty-year generation, Joshua and his soldiers conquered the main highways of Israel and devastated the greatest of the Canaanite cities. When Joshua died it was eighty years after Israel's salvation through the blood of the lamb. There was no one alive who remembered that time. Judges tells us of what happened next.

Recommended reading: M. A. Eaton, *Judges and Ruth* (Preaching Through the Bible, Sovereign World, 2000); H. Wolf, 'Judges' in *The Expositor's Bible Commentary*, vol. 3 (Zondervan, 1992).

☐☐☐ **Reading 270 (Judges 1:1–3:6)**

In Judges 1:1–3:6 (which itself divides into two, 1:1–2:5; 2:6–3:6), we are told of the decline of Israel.

1. What were the victories of Israel during this period and how did they come about? What were Israel's failures at this time?
2. What is the point in Judges 2:1–5? Is it that repentance is ineffective or that tears may be insincere? If not, then what is the teaching and does it apply to us?
3. What are the stages of spiritual decline that we see in 2:6–3:6? May we see the same stages in our own nation? Is there anything that can be done about it?

☐☐☐ **Reading 271 (Judges 3:7–5:31)**

In Judges 3:7–16:31 we have the story of various judges plus the story of Abimelech's experiment with kingship. There are fourteen main characters: Othniel (3:7–11), Ehud (3:12–30), Shamgar (3:31), Deborah and Barak (4:1–5:31), Gideon (6:1–8:32), Abimelech (8:33–9:57), Tola (10:1–2), Jair (10:3–5), Jephthah (10:6–12:7), Ibzan (12:8–10), Elon (12:11–12), Abdon (12:13–15), and Samson (13:1–16:31).

1. Othniel is a somewhat colourless rescuer for Israel; we know nothing about his personal character. Is there a reason why the story of this first judge is told without any personal detail?
2. Ehud was a man with a personal defect in his life. Shamgar was a man with inadequate equipment (3:31). What are we meant to learn from these men about the life of faith?
3. Ehud made a dagger for himself (see 3:15–21). Shamgar used an ox-goad (see 3:31), but what did Deborah use? She used a man – Barak! What is the relationship between Deborah and Barak? In what ways do they both know their limitations? In what ways are they both people of faith? What lessons can we ourselves learn from them concerning the life of faith?

☐☐☐ **Reading 272 (Judges 6:1–8:32)**

1. What are the marks of a call to serve God, in the life of Gideon? What did God teach him – and us – in his early steps of faith?
2. From Judges 7:1–8, what kind of people does it seem God likes to use?
3. How does God prepare Gideon to achieve something for the kingdom of God?
4. Sometimes Gideon is a wise leader; sometimes he is a man of obvious

weakness and inclined to make precisely the kind of mistakes we might ourselves have made. How may we learn from his strengths? How may we learn from his weaknesses?

☐☐☐ Reading 273 (Judges 8:33–10:5)

1. What happened in the days after Gideon? What could he have done, and what should he have done, at the time he was offered the kingship of Israel?
2. What can we learn about leadership from these chapters? How should we face invitations to responsibility? What will happen if we neglect true leadership?
3. Despite the terrible chaos brought into Israel by Abimelech, God still did not abandon them. Tola was raised up to deliver the nation (10:1–2). Jair came a little later (10:3–5). His riding on an ass is a picture of peace and humility. His family's doing the same thing suggests that he mobilised them in the interests of supervising the nation in the ways of peace and prosperity. Abimelech was not the last word in the story of Israel. What do we do at the end of a disastrous period of poor leadership?

☐☐☐ Reading 274 (Judges 10:6–12:15)

1. What should we do when we have committed ourselves to something that is entirely foolish? What should Jephthah have done when he found out how foolish he had been?
2. Why is Jephthah mentioned as a hero of faith in Hebrews 11:32? What were his gifts? How did he use them?
3. What are the lessons of faith that are visible in the stories of Ibzan (12:8–10), Elon (12:11–12), Abdon (12:13–15)? Ibzan was a multi-tribalist; he was concerned with national unity. What about the others?

☐☐☐ Reading 275 (Judges 13:1–15:20)

Samson's story is found in 13:1–16:31. There are two stories about Samson: (i) the story of his marriage to a Philistine woman and the various events that resulted from it (14:1–15:20). It ends by noting how Samson came to lead Israel for twenty years (15:20). Then (ii) there is the story of the events that led up to Samson's great victory at the time of his death (16:1–31).

1. Manoah and his wife are treated rather differently by the angel, yet they both treat each other rather well. What can we learn here about two people who are close but who are dealt with differently by the Lord?
2. Judges 14:4 says, 'His father and mother did not know that this was from Yahweh, for *he sought an opportunity against the Philistines.*' But who is this 'he'? A study of Judges shows, I believe, that it refers to Samson. Samson was seeking an opportunity against the Philistines. He was mixing business and pleasure in befriending the woman of Timnah! What are the sincere characteristics and the foolish characteristics of Samson?

□□□ Reading 276 (Judges 16:1–18:31)

The story moves forward about twenty years. It is hard to imagine that Samson's purpose in what happens here is purely wicked immorality. He goes to Gath, a Philistine town a long way from his home. Yet he must have known that his visit could not be kept secret. There was only one way into the town – through the town gates. Samson surely knew that it would hardly be possible for such a famous person as he was to enter the town unnoticed. Ancient towns were only small villages. Strangers could not enter them without being noticed. One remembers also Samson's long hair, which must have made him conspicuous. It seems he was looking out for a way to provoke the Philistines once again and was walking deliberately into a dangerous situation – something he had done before. 'He saw there a prostitute' (16:1). Once again Samson decides to use a woman as a mean of provoking the Philistines. In Judges 17:1–21:25 we have (again in two units, 17:1–18:31; 19:1–21:25) a description of the chaos in Israel at the end of this period.

1. What is happening here? Is Samson as foolish as he seems? Is he being clever? Or is it a case of a risky way of doing God's work?
2. What happens eventually in Samson's life that ruins his happiness? How did it happen? But why is Samson a man of faith according to Hebrews 11:32? How might we be vulnerable to the same mistakes?
3. Despite the judges who rescued Israel, the situation is steadily deteriorating, until there is finally terrible chaos. What are the marks of chaos in Judges 17:1–18:31, and what does our author think is the remedy?

☐☐☐ **Reading 277 (Judges 19:1–21:25)**

Judges 19:1–30 is surely the ugliest story to be found anywhere in the Bible!

1. The point of this ugly story seems to be presented in the opening line of the chapter. What sort of king does Israel need? How does kingship (a Davidic king? King Jesus?) give hope of changing the kind of things we read of in the previous chapters of Judges?
2. Was Israel's solution to the wickedness of Judges 19:1–30 any real help? What happens to a nation when God is angry with it?
3. Jesus comes to call not the righteous but the kind of people we find in Judges 20:1–21:25. So what is the bottom line of the book of Judges? The people need a righteous shepherd-king to bring them back into the ways of God. Is this the purpose of Judges? The worst story in the Bible points us to . . . what? The worst sins need . . . what?

Song of Songs

Song of Songs is a collection of love poems. It seems Solomon wrote them or took them into his collection of poems (see 1:1), yet there is also evidence that the songs have been updated in a later vocabulary. Some think the poems are intended as allegory (words that are a code for something altogether different), speaking of the love of God. Others think that they are simply love poetry, which should be used by the Christian to encourage a high view of courtship or of marriage. But there is another approach, which is perhaps more satisfactory.

In a number of cultures in ancient times, love poetry was used to write about spiritual ideas. There are ancient love poems that may be read from ancient Egypt, from Sumeria, even from Tamil-speaking South India. They contain spiritual ideas intertwined with love poetry. Religious thinking and sexual thinking seem to have been closely allied! In the Bible marriage is *par excellence* the greatest illustration of a spiritual relationship with God. The natural and spiritual interpretations of sexual love are intertwined. The Bible widely and explicitly uses marriage as the highest and greatest illustration of the relationship between God and the believer or (in the New Testament) Jesus and the believer. The spiritual relationship tells us how to be married; the marriage relationship tells us how to relate to Jesus. The two topics are mutually explanatory. This surely gives us the key to the Song of Songs. They are songs about marriage. But in the providence of God (and perhaps also in the mind of the collector) they mirror a spiritual relationship with God. This approach takes seriously the tradition of the Church. The greatest saints have always expressed their love of Jesus in terms of the Songs of Songs (Bernard of Clairvaux; Hudson Taylor; Charles Spurgeon; Watchman Nee). Surely the instinct of the greatest of Christians cannot be completely despised. The greatest expositions have always done the same (George Burrowes; James Durham). This 'perfect illustration' approach (as I call it) is worth exploring.

One task in reading the Song is to work out who the different speakers are. (i) The viewpoint of what is said often makes it quite clear who is the speaker. (ii) The words 'you' or 'your', in Hebrew, are identifiable as masculine or feminine and so help us identify who is speaking to whom. (iii) Shifts of pronouns are *not* specially significant. This point solves many problems. (iv) Observation of the key terms ('beloved', and others) often clearly marks who is speaking or who is being addressed.

Is the lover of the song really a king? Both of the couple seem at times to be a humble pair who spend their time with shepherds and can be alone in a village without gathering attention. Then in the next moment they seem to be a king and a queen who could hardly go anywhere without drawing attention. There are several suggested interpretations, but the one that fits best is that the king/queen language is only part of the marriage-culture (just as a man today might call his wife 'my princess').

Recommended reading: George Burrowes, *The Song of Solomon* (Banner of Truth, 1958); Hudson Taylor, *Union and Communion* (OMF; often reprinted).

□□□ Reading 278 (Song of Songs 1:1–3:5)

In the first poem, a girl has been making love with a shepherd-king. She wants his passionate love to be even greater (1:2–3a). Lots of others would like his love as well but unlike them she has been in the king's bedroom (1:3b–4). She is shy and has suffered from a tough family life, but she is conscious of her beauty (1:5–6). She wants a closer relationship than ever with her lover (1:7–8). Then a man speaks, telling her where to find him (1:8) and describing how he sees her beauty (1:9–11). The girl (1:12–14, 16–17; 2:1, 3–6) and the man (1:15; 2:2) sing their appreciation of each other. Song of Songs 2:7 is the closing refrain. In the second poem (2:8–3:5) the lover approaches (2:8–9) and invites his much-loved friend to come for lovemaking (2:10–15). He gets a warm response from the girl (2:16–17). This passage is then followed by one that is totally opposite. There comes a unit that speaks of being deprived of one's lover (3:1–3) and then clinging to him when he is found (3:4–5). So the different units of Song of Songs 2:8–3:5 form a poem about the woman yielding to her lover, losing him and finding him again.

1. Without trying to make this song a detailed allegory, is it possible to see here a rough similarity between the-girl-and-the-shepherd-king and the-believer-and-God (a New Testament Christian would say 'Jesus')?
2. What is the Christian equivalent of Song of Songs 1:8?
3. There is often an up-and-down relationship in marriage. How much is it an illustration of an up-and-down relationship to God (the variations being our fault not God's fault!)?

□□□ Reading 279 (Song of Songs 3:6–6:3)

The third poem (3:6–5:1) is about a marriage. First there is a procession in Song of Songs 3:6–11, then a description by the man of his bride (4:1–14, with the appeal of verse 8 in the middle), then the words of the woman (4:15), the man (5:1a) and the narrator (5:1b) concerning the climax of the marriage. The procession is bringing the bride, not the bridegroom. Verse 6 asks: 'Who is this lady coming up from the wilderness?' The word 'this' is feminine; it refers to a woman. (In Isaiah 63:1, the word 'this' is masculine.) So in this picture the bride herself is coming. The fourth poem is about a broken relationship. The woman's disinterest when her lover was knocking at the door produced a broken relationship between the two of them (5:2–6). Then the woman went through many painful experiences when she sought to get her lover back (5:7–8). Yet she could still tell others of her lover's great beauty (5:9–16), and she knew where she would eventually find him (6:1–3).

1. How may the poetry here illuminate our understanding of the Church as the bride of Christ?
2. How may we understand the descriptions in these chapters? What are the spiritual equivalents of the beauty and purity that is being described?
3. May we read this poem in the light of Revelation 3:20? How does Jesus knock at the door of our heart? How are we to respond?

□□□ Reading 280 (Song of Songs 6:4–8:14)

In the fifth song we find first a tender song of admiration for the girl's beauty and uniqueness (6:4–7, 8–10), followed by the girl's desire for solitude and privacy (6:11–13). Her modesty does not prevent her being admired again (7:1–5, 6–9). She responds to her lover's appeals and invites him to join her in the privacy of the countryside (7:10–13). She would like him as a brother as well as a lover (8:1–4). The sixth poem is found in 8:5–14. It is like a bunch of photographs, a series of pictures that do not seem to have much connection with each other except that they are all about a lover and his beloved. Here is a lover leaning for rest on her lover (8:5a). Then here is another picture: a lover waking up his love when she is asleep under a tree. Then comes another picture: a girl who wants her lover always to wear her 'seal' on his heart and on his arm. Now there comes a comparison of two pictures. It is a comparison between a young girl and a mature bride. First comes the young girl. It is an old picture, a recollection of something that happened when she was young. One day her brothers were talking about her (8:8–9). Next comes a statement by the mature girl, many years later (8:10). Finally comes a picture of some friends in a vineyard-garden (8:11–14).

1. If the Song is parabolic of a love relationship with God, then much of these chapters is God's admiration of his people. 'The LORD, your God . . . will rejoice over you with gladness . . . he will exult over you with loud singing' says Zephaniah 3:17. How might Jesus admire his Church? Does he see what she will one day become?
2. It is easy to find a spiritual equivalent of the bride leaning on her beloved (8:5a), but how might the other 'photographs' find a spiritual equivalent? What is the spiritual equivalent of older brothers showing fear for their younger sister?
3. In 8:11–14 the bride expresses her sense of the value of her love, and the beloved wants more than anything to hear her voice. What are the spiritual equivalents?

Psalms 41:1–49:20

Psalm 41:1–13 is the last of the first collection of David's psalms (3:1–41:13). It speaks of David's distress in sickness (41:1–3) and in sin (41:4), but worse still were the 'friends' who visited the sick king but were hoping the worst for him (41:5–9)! King David is a picture (or 'type') of Jesus, not in his sin and suffering (unless they foreshadow Jesus bearing our sins and diseases upon the cross) but in his kingship and his experience of ill-treatment. Psalms 42:1–43:5 is a single psalm with three sections (42:1–5, 6–11; 43:1–5). It might be specially appreciated by someone whose troubles have taken them far from home (geographically or spiritually). The psalmist was in the far north (42:6) and was homesick for Jerusalem. He is spiritually thirsty (42:1–5), drowning in an ocean of depression (42:6–11), discouraged by numerous enemies (43:1–5).

1. Why does God allow traitors and betrayers even among our friends (41:9) and visitors (41:6)? Is there any purpose in it?
2. How do we handle depression and come 'home' to God?
3. How in practice might God send 'life' and 'light' to the lonely and depressed?

☐☐☐ **Reading 282 (Psalms 44:1–46:11)**

Psalm 44:1–8 celebrates Israel's glorious past, and the 'but' in verse 9 comes as a surprise. Israel has suffered great reversal (44:9–16) despite the nation's obedience (44:17–22). Psalm 45:1–17 was perhaps composed for the wedding of one of the kings of Judah, but it certainly looks forward to a greater David and a greater queen:

- The king inspires the poet (45:1)
  - The king is highly honoured (45:2)
    - This king is to be a warrior (45:3–5)
      - This divine king has a wife (45:6–9)
    - The queen is to be a wife (45:10–11)
  - The queen is highly honoured (45:12–14)
- The queen inspires the poet (45:15–17)

Psalm 46:1–11 is a song about Jerusalem, but the Christian has good reason to take Jerusalem as a foretaste of the fellowship of the people of God.

1. What might be some reasons for unexplained defeat after a time of obedience (we remember Job)? What do we do when life is unfair and God is asleep?
2. What are the characteristics of the king in Psalm 45:1–17? How do they fit Jesus? What are the characteristics of the queen? How do they fit God's people?
3. Heavenly bliss is both a garden-paradise and a cubical city (Revelation 21:16). In what ways are the people of God like a city?
4. How does the promise of the abolition of war relate to today's militaristic world? Is the promise wholly future? Wholly 'spiritual'? Is it fulfilled in stages? Or fulfilled only as the gospel is successful? Or what?

☐☐☐ **Reading 283 (Psalms 47:1–49:20)**

In Psalm 47:1–9, hope for worldwide unity is found in worldwide acknowledgment of the God of the Bible (47:1). Verses 2–5 (beginning 'For' in the Hebrew) explains. Verse 6 starts again ('Sing praises') and explains again ('For . . .') in verses 7–11. Psalm 48:1–14 is a another Jerusalem-psalm from the Korahites. A sequence can be seen in Psalms 46:1–11 (where the city was fearfully threatened), 47:1–9 (where God is on his throne in Jerusalem) and 48:1–14 (where we are called to rejoice in the security of the city). The beginning and end of the latter psalm tell us Jerusalem is a great city with a great God (48:1–2, 11–14). The central sections tell us of great deliverances (48:3–7), great sights and songs

(48:8–10). Psalm 49:1–20 (best read in a literalistic translation such as the NASV or ESV) has two sections (verses 1–12, 13–20). In the fact that death is inevitable, all people are 'like the beasts that perish'. But *after* death it is only those who are 'without understanding' who are 'like the beasts that perish' (verses 12 and 20 are not identical). 'Take' in 49:15 is the verb used of Enoch (Genesis 5:24) and of Elijah's being 'taken' to heaven (2 Kings 2:1).

1. Some places of the world are oppressively state-controlled. Others are (oppressively?) pluralist and postmodern. No ideology is certain except that no ideology is certain. How do we apply Psalm 47:1–9 in such a world?

2. Has Jerusalem in the twenty-first century even vaguely resembled Psalm 48:1–11? What does this tell us about the interpretation of 'Jerusalem' in the Bible?

3. What is the teaching here about (i) money, (ii) death *without* spiritual understanding and (iii) death *with* spiritual understanding?

Ruth

The story of the book of Ruth must have been written down in the days of David (as 4:17–22 shows). It would have been valued because of its connection with David. It explained how he came to be descended from a Moabitess. It also shows how God has purposes of incorporating gentiles into his people, and it shows us too how redemption works. A redeemer has to have at least three qualifications. (i) He must have the power to redeem. (ii) He must have the legal right to redeem. And (iii) he must have the desire to redeem. Boaz illustrates the three points perfectly.

Recommended reading: A. Cundall and L. Morris, *Judges, Ruth* (IVP, 1968); M. A. Eaton, *Judges and Ruth* (Preaching Through the Bible, Sovereign World, 2000); G. J. Keddie, *Even in Darkness: Judges and Ruth . . .* (Evangelical Press, 1985).

☐☐☐ Reading 284 (Ruth 1:1–4:22)

1. How does Ruth 1:1–22 show us God has mysterious purposes even in the greatest of troubles?
2. What are the marks of Boaz as a redeemer? He is near at hand. He is gracious, concerned. What else? How does this help us to understand what our redemption means?
3. What are the blessings of redemption? 'Rest' (3:1). What else? In what ways is the Christian's relationship to Jesus like the marriage relationship?

4. 'Redeemers' had (i) to redeem a family member who had fallen into slavery; (ii) to redeem a family member from landlessness; (iii) to redeem a family member from childlessness if her husband died prematurely, (iv) to redeem a family member from loss of life if his life could be rescued by the payment of a price (see Exodus 13:13b). How can God be called Israel's 'Redeemer'?

1 Peter

1 Peter is a letter written by the apostle Peter, probably in the AD 60s. Its purpose was to encourage Christians in Roman Asia to live a godly life despite the sufferings and trials they were experiencing. Peter introduces himself (1:1–2) and gives a word of praise (1:3–12), and then proceeds to give his readers reasons why they ought to live godly lives (1:13–2:12). In 1 Peter 2:13–4:11 he comes to details. Then in 4:12–5:11 he specially takes up the matter of the sufferings that they are having to endure. A conclusion comes in 5:12–14.

Recommended reading: M. A. Eaton, *1 Peter* (Preaching Through the Bible, Sovereign World, 1999); W. Grudem, *First Epistle of Peter* (Tyndale Commentary, IVP, 1988).

□□□ **Reading 285 (1 Peter 1:1–25)**
1. The first twelve verses of the letter give (amid a burst of praise) a description of the basic spiritual blessings of the Christians that make it possible for them to live godly lives. How do these verses prepare the way for the call to godliness that is about to come? What are the basic experiences of the Christian?
2. Why does Peter begin his appeal in verse 13 with a call to use the mind?
3. What are the encouragements to godly living in 1:13–25?

□□□ **Reading 286 (1 Peter 2:1–25)**

1. What are the five ingredients of Christian love in 2:1?
2. Peter uses a temple as a picture of the Church. What do the details of his illustration represent? The cornerstone? The other stones? The priests in the temple?
3. What do you think of 'submission' in these days where equality is admired more than submission? Does 1 Peter 2:13–17 still have relevance in today's world?
4. Peter's teaching concerning slavery leads into wonderful teaching about the cross of Christ (2:18–25). What are the main points that he has to say abut Jesus' atoning death?

□□□ **Reading 287 (1 Peter 3:1–22)**

1. Peter has instructions for Christian wives (3:1–7) and Christian husbands (3:8), but 3:9–12 is relevant to both husbands and wives. How does what he says in 3:9–12 also have importance in Christian families?
2. Again Peter relates a practical situation (injustice) to the death of Christ. How does Christ's cross help us to face injustice?
3. 1 Peter 3:19 is a much disputed verse. One possible interpretation, which commends itself, runs as follows: 'In the power of the Holy Spirit Jesus went [after his resurrection] and proclaimed his victory to the evil spirits who were famous in connection with the sin leading to the flood, and who are now confined awaiting final punishment'. If this is a correct reading, how does it help people facing injustice?

Note Peter explicitly denies that salvation is by baptism in any superstitious manner, for baptism does not 'cleanse the flesh' – the sinful nature. It can only save as the occasion of and the expression of faith in Christ (which seems to be the point of 3:21).

□□□ **Reading 288 (1 Peter 4:1–19)**

1. Is it possible for us to have the same hatred of sin that Jesus had while he was suffering upon the cross? If we are 'armed with the same mentality', what does Peter promise it will do for us?
2. What is the place of 'vindication' in the Christian life?
3. What difference does it make to us to feel that we are living in the end-times? But is this realistic?

☐☐☐ **Reading 289 (1 Peter 5:1–14)**

1. What does Peter have to say about Christian pastors?

2. What are the enemies of Christians? How – according to Peter – do we withstand them?

3. 1 Peter 5:12–14 seems quite unexciting. But what does it tell us of the nature of the Christian Church and of Christian ministry?

Lamentations

No one knows who wrote the book of Lamentations. Possibly it was Jeremiah, but we cannot be 100 per cent certain. From the first line to the last line it is a book that is full of grief over the destruction of Jerusalem. Why was Lamentations written? On the whole, the Bible is a book full of rejoicing. So why should there be a book of the Bible that is so fully given over to lamenting and sorrowing? After centuries of idolatry, God warned Judah that 'From the north disaster will be poured out on all who live in the land' (Jeremiah 1:14). He would send them something that would forcibly correct them. So it turned out. Judah was exiled; Jerusalem was destroyed. The pathway to restoration was to face what had happened and come to full repentance. Lamentations are songs of repentance. Sometimes sorrow is the pathway to joy. Weeping lasts for a night-time but joy comes in the morning (Psalm 30:5).

Recommended reading: R. Brooks, *Great is Your Faithfulness* (Evangelical Press, 1989).

☐☐☐ **Reading 290 (Lamentations 1:1–2:22)**
1. What were the ingredients that came upon Judah in the fall of Jerusalem? For example, the people became isolated (1:1). What else?
2. Why should focussing on the terrible events in the fall of Jerusalem be of any help to the people of Judah?

3. Sometimes in these poems (e.g. 1:12) you have words that could have been spoken by Jesus on the cross. Is there any significance in this?

□□□ **Reading 291 (Lamentations 3:1–5:22)**

1. Is there any progression of thought as we move from poem to poem? What new elements are found in Lamentations 3:1–66? Does the poet answer his own problem? How can the people recover from the fall of Jerusalem?

2. Lamentations 4:1–22 dwells upon the horrors of the siege of Jerusalem in 587–586 BC. Is there any good reason why the poet should dwell upon these events in such detail? Is he looking at the character of God? The seriousness of sin? What is his purpose?

3. Lamentations 5:1–22 turns to prayer. Why was prayer not in the first chapter? In what way have the first four chapters prepared for the fifth chapter?

4. Did Judah ever turn to idolatry after 586 BC? Was any Jew worshipping another god when Jesus came? What function did the horrors of the exile have in the story of Judah? Are there any parallels in modern countries?

Psalms 50:1–55:23

☐☐☐ **Reading 292 (Psalms 50:1–52:9)**
Asaph was another choir-director, and Psalm 50:1–23 is the first of the
twelve Asaph-psalms (50:1–23, 73:1–83:18). The psalm records a court
case. The court gathers (50:1–6); the charge is presented (50:7–21). A
warning (but not a final sentence) is issued (50:22–23).

1. Is God really so disinterested in religion (50:8–13)? What things would
   be mentioned if there were a modern up-date of these words referring
   to modern religions?
2. Psalm 51:1–19 (another one of the 'penitential' psalms) is famous as
   the greatest expression of repentance ever written. How do David's
   words in verses 18–19 fit into the psalm? What would be the effect
   that the sin of David the king might have, even upon the capital city?
   How much do our sins have repercussions?
3. Are there people in our society who carve out their career by slander
   and deceit (see Psalm 52:1–9)? Is there anything of this in our own
   lives? How are such destined to be like an uprooted tree? And in what
   way are the righteous like olive trees?

☐☐☐ **Reading 293 (Psalms 53:1–55:23)**
1. Psalm 53:1–6 is almost identical to Psalm 14:1–7, but Psalm 14:5
   refers to the fears of the wicked whereas Psalm 53:5 speaks of the

needless fears of God's people. How often do our fears turn out to be entirely needless? Why is fear always groundless according to Psalm 53:5?

2. The title of Psalm 54:1–7 links it with the occasion when David's own people (the Ziphites in David's Judean home territory) had betrayed him (see 1 Samuel 23:1–29). How does David respond in Psalm 54:1–2? Is Psalm 54:7 an Old Testament illustration of Mark 11:24? Is it a statement of faith in what is about to happen?

3. In Psalm 55:1–23, David is again in trouble (55:1–3). His enemy's voice (verse 3a), their stares (verse 3b), their ill-will (verse 3c) and their specific words (verse 3d) all cause David suffering. He would like to run away (55:4–8) but turns instead to prayer (55:9–21), where he lets out all of his bitterness. One person who had previously been a friend especially grieves him (55:3). He commends prayer to everyone (55:22–23). Is 55:17 an ideal pattern for personal prayer? How are we to understand verse 23d? Is it really true? In what way?

Ecclesiastes

Ecclesiastes is a piece of wisdom-writing, in the tradition of Solomon. It is the story of what Solomon could have learned, and it could have been written by Solomon himself (but the name is not mentioned and the Hebrew seems post-Solomonic). Two reasons may be given as to why it was written. (i) Most philosophers of the ancient world were pessimists. 'The Preacher' is saying, 'View life without faith in God and your pessimism is right.' Much of the time he is a pessimist but then he brings in the viewpoint of faith. (ii) 'The Preacher' also warns us that too rosy-coloured a view of *this* life is likely to meet up with some disillusionment. Holding on to God in faith is the remedy.

Recommended reading: M. A. Eaton, 'Ecclesiastes', in *New Bible Commentary* (IVP, 1994); D. Kidner, *The Message of Ecclesiastes* (IVP, 1976).

□□□ Reading 294 (Ecclesiastes 1:1–3:22)

1. Some basic facts of life are put to us (1:1–11). Neither wisdom (1:12–18) nor pleasure-seeking give any answer (2:1–11). Is there then no difference between them (see 2:12–23)?
2. A turning-point seems to come in 2:24. What answers are there in 2:24–3:22 to the problems outlined in 1:1–2:23?

3. 'The Preacher' seems specially troubled by injustice. What does the fact of injustice show about life? Is there a practical remedy?

☐☐☐ **Reading 295 (Ecclesiastes 4:1–6:12)**

1. Ecclesiastes 4:1–16 deals with companionship and isolation. What are the hard facts the Preacher puts to us? Does he have any remedy?

2. May God be the required companion? How do we approach him according to 5:1–7?

3. Ecclesiastes 5:8–6:12 deals with poverty and wealth. GNB is good in 5:8 ('Every official is protected by the one over him'). Ecclesiastes 5:9 either means 'Despite bureaucratic delays a stable land is worth having' (see NIV), or it might be translated '. . . but an advantage to a land for everyone is: a king over cultivated land'. What are the many weaknesses of wealth according to the Preacher? Does he have any practical advice?

☐☐☐ **Reading 296 (Ecclesiastes 7:1–9:10)**

1. Ecclesiastes 7:1–8:1 is concerned with suffering and sin. Is suffering ever instructive (7:1–6)? What are its dangers (7:7–14)? How easy is it to be wise? Does the Preacher say anything positive here?

2. Authority and injustice are dealt with in 8:2–9:10. What answer does our wise man give (in 8:12–13) to the misuse of authority and the injustice mentioned in 8:1–11?

3. Ecclesiastes 9:7–10 is marvellously positive. Are we to take it seriously?

Note 'The dead know nothing' means only that the dead know nothing of this world. It is similar to statements in Job 14:21–22 and 2 Kings 22:20. The point is: by faith our life has to be victorious in *this* world.

☐☐☐ **Reading 297 (Ecclesiastes 9:11–12:14)**

1. Ecclesiastes 9:11–10:20 deals with wisdom and folly. Apparently not even Solomon's wisdom is the answer to every problem. What are the limitations of wisdom?

2. What is the connection between wisdom and words (10:12–15)?

3. A change in the direction of thought comes in 11:1 where for the first time sustained exhortation comes into the book (11:1–12:8, with an epilogue in 12:9–14). A lot of agricultural and economic imagery is used. Ecclesiastes 12:1–7 is one of the Bible's few undisputed allegories. The writer's 'before . . . before . . . before' (12:1, 2, 6) is an urgent call to act fast. Why is the urgency so great?

4. Ecclesiastes 12:9–14 is the editor's commendation of the wise man whose material he has been giving us. The editor or 'presenter' uses his own words for only one style is found throughout the book. What does the book of Ecclesiastes claim for itself here?

2 Peter

2 Peter was the second letter sent by Peter to the Christians of Roman Asia Minor. 'This is now . . . the second letter . . .' he says (2 Peter 3:1). Although scholars have questioned whether Peter really wrote 2 Peter, there seems no doubt that this is what the letter itself claims. If this is so, Peter wrote this letter while he was in Rome, and he wrote it to the Christians of the Roman province of Asia Minor (see 1 Peter 1:1).

Like the first letter, it was designed to encourage the Christians to live a godly life, but 2 Peter has certain other characteristics in addition. Peter knew he would not live long, and his letter is a farewell letter (like 2 Timothy). Unlike 1 Peter, our letter here is also concerned especially with false teaching regarding godliness and the coming judgment of God.

After introducing himself and his readers (1:1–2), Peter calls his disciples to live on God's grace and take responsibility for their zeal in godly living (1:3–11). He explains why he has been specially concerned to write his letter (1:12–15) and reminds them of the hope of the second coming of Jesus (1:16–21). Then he warns them against false prophets (2:1–22) and reasserts the promise of Jesus' coming (3:1–10), plus its practical implications (3:11–18).

Recommended reading: M. A. Eaton, *2 Peter* (Preaching Through the Bible, Sovereign World, 2002); D. M. Lloyd-Jones, *2 Peter* (Banner of Truth, 1983).

□□□ **Reading 298 (2 Peter 1:1–21)**

1. First (in 1:1–4) there is mention of what God has given to us. What matters does he mention? Then (in 1:5–11) he focusses on the ways in which we should respond to what God has done for us. What should we add to our first faith?

2. What are the connections according to Peter between the transfiguration of Jesus and the second coming of Jesus? In what two ways does Peter assure us of the truth concerning the second coming?

3. Scripture did not come because someone decided to write about some religious ideas (1:21). How in fact did it come into existence, and what should be our attitude to the Christian Scriptures?

□□□ **Reading 299 (2 Peter 2:1–22)**

1. If it is true that 'there *will* be false teachers' (2:1a), what is the 'false teaching' that is around right now? Or isn't there any?

2. In Peter's long sentence in 2:4–10a, he first gives three examples of God's judgment: 'For if God did not spare angels . . .' (2:4); 'if he did not spare the ancient world . . .' (2:5); 'and if he condemned the cities of Sodom and Gomorrah . . .' (2:6). Then he gives one example of God's rescue: 'And if he rescued Lot . . .' (2:7–8). Then he comes to a conclusion: 'then the Lord knows . . .' (2:9–10a). What is the point of his three examples? The first is: supernatural eminence cannot withstand judgment. What of the other two?

3. The situation in the last verses of the chapter – if we may put it diagrammatically – looks like this.

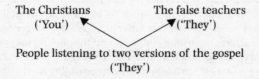

The Christians   The false teachers
('You')   ('They')

People listening to two versions of the gospel
('They')

The word 'they' does not refer to the Christians. It refers either to the false teachers or to their potential converts. A little study in 2 Peter will reveal that 'you' is the word Peter uses to refer to the Christians. Again and again he calls the Christians 'you' (1:2, 4–8, 11, 12, 13, 15, 19, 20; 2:1). Then in 2 Peter 2:1 he says, 'But false prophets also came in among the people just as there will be false teachers among *you*' and he goes on to say *'They* quietly bring in destructive heresies'. It is quite clear that there is a difference between 'you', the Christians, and 'they', the false teachers. So is there such a thing as 'reformation without conversion to Christ'

(2 Peter 2:20–22)? What are we to say about such people? Is there anything we can do to help them? What makes a true Christian if it is not self-reformation?

☐☐☐ **Reading 300 (2 Peter 3:1–18)**

1. According to Peter, critics of the second coming of Jesus generally have two main objections that they express to us. Their first is this. 'This idea that Jesus might come at any moment seems to have been mistaken and disappointing. "The fathers" – the first generation of Christians – "hoped that they might see the coming of Jesus in glory and judgment, but they have died." Every generation of believers hopes that Jesus will come in their day but each generation seems to be disappointed. We should abandon the idea altogether!' What is the second objection?
2. What answers to the scoffers does Peter give in 2 Peter 3:5–10?
3. Since all these things are in this way to be dissolved, what sort of people ought you to be? What is the answer to Peter's question?

Psalms 56:1–64:10

Reading 301 (Psalms 56:1–58:11)

1. Psalm 56:1–13 arose from David's house-arrest recorded in 1 Samuel 21:10–15. There is no 'taking of vows' in the New Testament, so what is the equivalent of Psalm 56:12 for the Christian?

2. The title of Psalm 57:1–11 links it with the event of 1 Samuel 21:1–42. The structure follows the same route backwards and forwards:
   - A cry of prayer (57:1)
     - Confidence in prayer (57:2–3)
       - Threatening enemies (57:4)
         - Longing for God's honour (57:5)
       - Defeated enemies (57:6)
     - Confidence in praise (57:7–8)
   - A cry of praise (57:9–10)

   Then the writer adds the central thought again (57:11)!
   Is it possible to be 'in the shadow of God's wings' (57:1) while in great danger (such as hiding from Saul in a cave)? How can we keep God's glory central in whatever conflicts we experience?

3. Psalm 58:1–11 contains some vicious words (in 58:6–9), yet the psalm complains about men whose 'venom is like the venom of a snake'

(58:4). Is he contradicting himself, or does 'venom' have to be rightly directed? But this is the psalm with a 'social conscience' (58:1). Does this throw light on the 'cursing' psalms? Is it relevant to remember the 'curse of the law' against evil-doers?

☐☐☐ Reading 302 (Psalms 59:1–61:8)

1. Saul's attempts to kill David (see 1 Samuel 19:10–12) form the background to Psalm 59:1–17. It has two sections in parallelism.
   - Prayer, 59:1–5   Prayer, 59:11–13
   - Dogs, 59:6–7   Dogs, 59:14–15
   - But you . . . 59:8–10   But I . . . 59:16–17

   David does not want his enemies to be *immediately* destroyed. Rather he wants Israel to see God's purposes taking place over a longer time, so that Israel will learn that God protects his people (59:11–13). Meanwhile the 'dogs' – Saul and his friends – are still prowling (59:14–15), but David is confident (59:16–17). What might be God's purposes when enemies of God's kingdom do not immediately disappear?

2. Psalm 60:1–12. Something in the event of 2 Samuel 8:3 made God angry (as is clear from the title of the psalm, combined with 60:1). Behind Edom's invasion was the anger of God. So David turns to prayer. 'You have rejected us . . .' (60:1). He lays the situation before God (60:1–3). But God has a banner – a rallying-point – in time of trouble (60:4). David asks for help (60:5). God answers. The central (60:6) and northern (60:7a) areas of the land belong to him. The parts to which great promises have been made (Ephraim, Judah) are his weapons (60:7b–c). Nearby enemies he will treat with scorn (60:8). David turns to prayer again but with greater confidence than ever (60:9–11). What is the rallying-point in time of trouble?

3. In Psalm 61:1–8, David is away from home and exhausted, so he looks for a high refuge (61:2), a strong tower (61:3) and (most of all) a peaceful tent-home where he may be with God (61:4). A change comes in 61:5 where David becomes convinced that his vows of commitment to God have been heard and he is able to ask for length of life (60:6) and safety on his throne (60:7). His prayer ends in greater praise and commitment than ever (60:8). How is prayer for length of life and safety on the throne fulfilled in Jesus even more than it was fulfilled in David?

☐☐☐ **Reading 303 (Psalms 62:1–64:10)**

1. Psalm 62:1–12 was written at a time when there was immense pressure on David (62:3). Someone was trying to remove him from his position as king (62:4). A key word is 'alone'. David speaks of rest in God alone (62:1). 'He *alone* is my Rock' (62:2, 6). Has anyone tried to remove you from some position you hold? What taught David to trust God alone?

2. Psalm 63:1–11 comes from a time of discomfort (in the heat of the Judean desert) and loneliness. David longs for God himself. Only towards the end of the psalm are enemies mentioned (63:9–10) and David becomes confident that his kingship (although threatened by Absalom) would continue. Saul's kingship came to an end even while he was alive. David was confident this would not happen to him. How could he be so confident?

3. David's enemies are specially frightening in Psalm 64:1–6. Verses 7–10 make the point that those who shoot arrows have God's arrows fired at them. Does God delight to recompense sins with 'poetic justice' so that 'the measure we give is the measure we get' – very exactly? Are there examples of this that can be quoted?

2 Corinthians

Paul sent 1 Corinthians with Timothy (see 1 Corinthians 16:10–11; Acts 19:22), but Timothy found the Corinthian church in turmoil, and so went back to Paul with bad news. The apostle also had to change his plans several times. Plan number one was to travel from Ephesus to   Corinth by land, going there and back through Macedonia; this is the plan he mentions in 1 Corinthians 4:19 and 16:5–8. Plan number two was to go to Corinth by sea and then on to Macedonia by land. Then he would travel back the same way. This meant he would have seen them twice (see 2 Corinthians 1:15–16).

But Paul had to follow a plan number three! 'Deadly peril' faced Paul in Ephesus (2 Corinthians 1:8–10), and his enemies were causing him so much trouble in Corinth that he felt he should go there for a short visit. Some self-appointed Christian teachers had arrived in Corinth and were causing Paul even more problems (2 Corinthians 11:13–15). They came with letters of recommendation from Jerusalem (see 2 Corinthians 3:1–3), called themselves 'apostles' and wanted to be rivals to the apostle Paul. Paul had been attacked by one particular man in Corinth (see 2 Corinthians 2:5–8, 10; 7:12).

This visit was a very painful time for Paul (see 2:1; 13:2). He was humiliated (12:21) and withdrew. For a while he felt he could not go to Corinth (1:23). He then sent them a very severe and tearful letter (see 2:3–4), taken by Titus. Back in Ephesus Paul was very anxious about how this 'severe letter' would be received. He was so anxious that he left Ephesus to travel in the direction of Corinth. He stopped at Troas, hoping to meet Titus. He had many fears for his work (7:5). He eventually left Troas but somewhere along the way he met Titus and found that all was well. The 'severe letter' had been successful. Paul now writes 2 Corinthians – the fourth of his letters to the Corinthians. The 'calendar of events' must have been roughly as follows.

1 Corinthians written	early AD 55
Paul second (painful) visit to Corinth	mid-AD 55
The tearful and sorrowful letter	late AD 55?
Paul travels to Troas	autumn AD 55
Paul meets Titus	autumn AD 55
2 Corinthians is written	late AD 55
Paul visits Corinth	spring AD 56
Romans is written	early AD 57
Paul's last visit to Jerusalem	May AD 57

□□□ Reading 304 (2 Corinthians 1:1–24)

1. There were a lot of conflicts in Corinth, but everything Paul says here is encouraging. What are the grounds of encouragement for the Christian?
2. Paul had been through a great time of crisis. What do we learn in troublesome times and how do we learn it?
3. Paul's enemies in Corinth had accused him of instability, but Paul has an answer. How is the Christian brought to stability and faithfulness?

□□□ Reading 305 (2 Corinthians 2:1–17)

In 2 Corinthians 2:14–7:4 we have a major exposition of Paul's adequacy in ministry (2:14–3:6a), and its origin in the Holy Spirit as the supreme gift of the new covenant (3:6b–4:6). The Holy Spirit, Paul says, gives him strength amid physical weakness and the hope of a glorified resurrection body (4:7–5:10). He preaches a message of reconciliation through the cross of our Lord Jesus Christ (5:11–6:2) and explains how he takes the trouble to avoid stumbling blocks in the way of ministry (6:3–10). If they see all of this, the Corinthians will be ready to respond to him as he appeals for warm, open-hearted and close relationships between himself and them (6:11–7:4).

1. Paul feels that his task is to keep his people rejoicing. How does this affect our view of Christian ministry? How does Paul fulfil this part of his calling in 2 Corinthians 2:1–17?

2. One person had insultingly and arrogantly rejected the apostle's authority. That man had since repented and should now be forgiven (2:5–11). How should a Christian leader handle a wicked opponent in the church? Should it ever happen today?

3. How does Paul use his illustration in 2:14–16a? What kind of person, he asks, is adequate for such a ministry (2:16b)? What is Paul's answer (2:17)?

□□□ Reading 306 (2 Corinthians 3:1–18)

1. How does Paul use his illustration of a letter? What is the parchment? Who are the readers? Who is the scribe? Who is the author? Who is the ink?

2. According to Paul, to look to the Mosaic covenant today is deadening. What does he have in mind? Can we find this happening in our churches? Can the letter of the New Testament also be killing?

3. According to Paul, to gaze in the face of Jesus Christ is a transforming experience. How might this work out in our own lives?

Note The translation of 2 Corinthians 3:2 should probably be: 'You are our letter, written on *your* hearts . . .' (see RSV).

□□□ Reading 307 (2 Corinthians 4:1–18)

1. 2 Corinthians 4:1–6 brings a unit of thought to a conclusion. Paul has an encouraging ministry (4:1). He has an open method (4:2). He has to fight an obscure mentality (4:3–4). He serves an enlightening Maker (4:5–6). How do each of these matters affect Christian witness?

2. In 4:7 Paul takes up another aspect of this matter. Paul is being criticised for his physical weaknesses. Paul was getting older by the day! How does physical deterioration affect Christian ministry?

3. Our bodies are weak, clay pots, but they are destined for resurrection glory. What is the Christian view of the body? Do we despise it? Admire it? Or what? How will this affect us day-by-day?

□□□ Reading 308 (2 Corinthians 5:1–6:2)

1. In what way is death like moving from one house to another? What is the difference between the two homes?

2. When is the judgment day (note 5:10)? At death? At the end of the

world? Both? Does this help us to answer the questions: When do we get our resurrection body? At death? At the end of the world? Both? What do you think Paul says?

3. What motivated Paul? Fear? Love? Both fear and love? What is to motivate you and me?

Note What is the home in the heavens? Is it (i) heaven or some kind of heavenly temple for my bodiless personality to live in? (ii) The Church? (iii) A new body? The tent is the temporary body; so 'the house' must surely be a new body.

□□□ Reading 309 (2 Corinthians 6:3–7:1)

1. 'We put no obstacle in anyone's path . . .' In the midst of slander and suffering, what steps did Paul take to protect his preaching of his message? In what modern ways do we have to do the same? But how do we at the same time remain free (see 1 Corinthians 9:1)?

2. There are nineteen phrases in 6:4b–7. Can you divide them in groups, perhaps about seven? How much should the Christian try to avoid or expect to avoid sufferings?

3. 2 Corinthians 6:11–13 is a moving plea to be talked to, to be given affection and open-hearted warmth of love. Do you identify with this? How much do people need affection?

□□□ Reading 310 (2 Corinthians 7:2–16)

1. What does Paul do when he is criticised? Keep quiet? Open up his heart? Go elsewhere? Or what? What would it do for our relationships if we followed Paul?

2. In 7:5 Paul now is ready to continue the explanation that he started giving to the Corinthians back in 2 Corinthians 1:12–2:13. He was saying, 'I said goodbye to them and went on to Macedonia' (2:13). Now he continues: 'For when we came into Macedonia . . .' Even someone as great and as clear-minded as Paul could become overwhelmed with distress – and he is quite ready to admit it. How did he cope – and how do we?

3. What does Paul tell us about repentance? Its origin? Its nature? Its results?

Note We would do well to keep in mind some Greek words: *Metameleia* ('regret') or *metamelomai* ('to regret') refer mainly to feelings. The root is sometimes translated 'repent' (as in Matthew 21:32), but it means 'regret'. (ii) The Greek words *metanoia* ('change of mind') or *metanoieo* ('to change one's mind') refer to the change of mind that is ready to change direction in one's life. (iii) The Greek words *epistrophe* ('a turn-around') or *epistrepho* (to turn around') refer to a change of direction, amendment of life. There are similar words in biblical Hebrew. Often many different ideas concerning turning from sin are lumped together in English under the heading of 'repentance', but it would make for clear thinking if the different emphases of the different New Testament Greek words were remembered.

□□□ Reading 311 (2 Corinthians 8:1–24)

Paul requests that the Christians at Corinth should resume their intention to help the Christians in Jerusalem.

1. How were the Macedonians model givers? Their generosity was not hindered by their poverty. What else?
2. How much should we give to God's work? Are we allowed to spend anything on ourselves (say, on a holiday) when there are so many in the world who scarcely get any sort of holiday? How can one answer such complicated questions? Did the Macedonians have the answer? 'First they gave away themselves to the Lord.' How does this principle help us?
3. 'By his poverty we become rich.' What kind of wealth is this? Is the Christian gospel a prosperity movement? Or does this only refer to the riches of God's grace? Or does the truth lie somewhere in between the two extremes?

□□□ Reading 312 (2 Corinthians 9:1–15)

1. What is Paul's style of fund-raising? Why does he give the Corinthians plenty of advance notice concerning the financial need?
2. There is a 'sowing and reaping' principle in Christian giving (9:6). Is the Christian allowed to be motivated by the thought of reward?
3. 2 Corinthians 9:8–9 contains vast promises. How would it affect us if we took them seriously?

□□□ Reading 313 (2 Corinthians 10:1–18)

2 Corinthians 1:1–9:15 is addressed to the vast majority of the church, but it seems that 2 Corinthians 10:1–13:14 is addressed to a much smaller group who were still hostile to Paul. Paul speaks of 'some people' (10:2), and says, 'We will be ready to punish every act of disobedience once *your* obedience is complete' (10:6). The bulk of the congregation have submitted to Paul but a few are still in danger of admiring the Jerusalem intruders. Paul is writing to the congregation as a whole, but at this point specially rebukes those who are still supporting people preaching 'another

Jesus'. It is quite clear that what he is saying now refers to the intruders. Paul refers to them as 'some people'. He does not refer to them as 'some of you'. The intruders will not even be reading 2 Corinthians, but they are a powerful group, always trying to get the Corinthians' attention. A few of the congregation are likely to be still listening to them and taking notice of them.

1. Paul is deliberately speaking with 'the meekness and gentleness of Christ'. What does this tell us about the nature of Christian ministry? What weapons should be called 'worldly weapons'? What is wrong with them?

2. There is a style of ministry that Paul calls 'building up'. The intruders at Corinth have a ministry of breaking down (10:8). What does Paul have in mind?

3. What does Paul teach here about having 'areas of ministry'?

□□□ Reading 314 (2 Corinthians 11:1–15)

1. Any cult-leader can use the *word* 'Jesus'! But the Jesus of the Bible is unique. What is unique about him? Can it be said that some modern 'Jesuses' are not the genuine Saviour?

2. Why is Paul 'boastful' here (or is he?)? Are there times when we should do the same thing as he is doing?

3. How often do we find ourselves in situations that resemble the situation in the garden of Eden (Genesis 2:1–3:24), when Satan said, 'Has God *really* said . . .'?

□□□ Reading 315 (2 Corinthians 11:16–33)

1. Is it foolish to parade before other people the secrets of one's inner struggles? What does Paul mean when he says, 'I am not speaking as the Lord would speak'? So why does he do it?

2. False teachers (and politicians? and who else?) generally ill-treat their congregations. Why do people endure such treatment?

3. In Corinth, Paul was resisting a take-over. How often does something unchristian seek to take over the Church? Does it happen in our circle? What should be done about it? If it never happens to us, why not?

□□□ Reading 316 (2 Corinthians 12:1–19)

1. Paul comes to revelations, visions, dreams and 'what the Lord told me'. Are such dramatic spiritual experiences possible? Why does Paul give no details of what happened to him? Why keep it secret for fourteen

years?

2. Paul's 'thorn in the flesh' was something evil, a 'messenger of Satan'. Yet it was permitted by God. What was its purpose? Is God likely to bring something to us that is immensely humbling?

3. There are four ways God can answer prayer. He can say 'Yes'. What else? What happened to Paul and what did it do for him?

Note The 'thorn in the flesh'. (i) Was it some physical difficulty? Malaria? Poor eyesight? Severe headaches? Epilepsy? (ii) Was it his enemies, possibly one special enemy? Was it persecution? Or a heretic constantly troubling the church? (iii) Was it some temptation that Paul found very powerful? Sexual temptation? Homosexual inclinations? (iv) Could it have been his agony over Israel, the nation that he loved so much? (v) Could it be rejection by those he loved? (vi) Was it a speech impediment? (vii) Could it have been a psychological trauma, which had damaged him mentally? Bouts of depression? Suicidal impulses? Grief over his involvement in Stephen's death? (viii) Slanders to which he could not reply? (ix) Was it the pain of disgrace? (x) Could it have been an unconverted wife who had left him? Did Paul have a broken marriage? (xi) Or – an opposite possibility – was he immensely troubled by his being called to remain single? Not all of these are equally convincing but any of them might be our 'thorn in the flesh'.

□□□ Reading 317 (2 Corinthians 12:20–13:13)

1. 'I fear that when I come, I may perhaps not find you as I want you to be'. What does he have in mind? What are the things we really look for in a Christian congregation?

2. 'We are weak in him, but we shall live with him by the power of God in our relationship to you' (13:4). In what way is the Christian a mixture of weakness and power?

3. Paul says (in effect): 'Test yourselves to see if right now you are holding to this trust in God that you have shown in days gone by. Are you applying your faith at this moment?' Do we need to test whether we have faith? When and why?

Esther

The book of Esther is a single lengthy story of a genocidal plot against Jews in the Persian empire. It is set in the days of Ahasuerus (or Xerxes the Great as the Greeks called him) around the 470s BC of his reign. The great theme of the book is the amazing providence of God even though he seems to be absent. Nowhere does the word 'God' appear in the book, yet his involvement in events can be seen in every chapter.

☐☐☐ Reading 318 (Esther 1:1–3:15)

1. What do we see of the folly of paganism (ancient and modern) in Esther 1:1–22? We can see its pride (1:4), its drunkenness (1:8). What else?

2. What must it have been like for Esther to be forced into a king's harem of wives? What does the writer of Esther want us to see here? Could Esther make any sense of her sufferings?

3. Why does Haman hate Mordecai so much? How do we handle injustice that comes against us because of our nationality or our distinctiveness? Why was Mordecai so unyielding? Should we be the same?

☐☐☐ Reading 319 (Esther 4:1–5:14)

1. How does Mordecai put to Esther the dangerous necessity of going to see the king to get Haman's plan overthrown (4:8–9)? What arguments does he use and how do they apply to us?

2. What are we like when we suddenly face the prospect of all of our

expectations coming to disaster? How does Esther react to the challenge of the day?

3. How easy is it to 'read providence'? What happens that encourages Esther? Do we have to 'cooperate' with providence? Why is Esther so slow to bring her request to the king?

☐☐☐ Reading 320 (Esther 6:1–7:10)

1. What striking 'coincidences' can be found in these chapters? What will it do for us if we have a confident trust in the sovereignty of God? Can we in fact have such confidence?

2. Mordecai might have felt somewhat hurt that his previous loyalty to the king had done him no good. He had discovered a plot (see 2:21–22a) and Esther had told the king (2:22b). But now his life was in danger. What can we learn here about delayed reward? Should we live for God's rewards?

3. One gets a strong sense in the book of Esther that events move at a slow and leisurely pace. It all seems so unhurried. And yet Haman comes to a very abrupt end. Is the providence of God slow or swift? Or what?

☐☐☐ Reading 321 (Esther 8:1–10:3)

The enemies of God may leave an after-effect even when they have been vanquished. Haman's orders concerning the extermination of the Jews scattered throughout the Persian empire still stand.

1. We note, first, that the possessions of God's enemies eventually come to the righteous. How does the principle work that 'The sinner's wealth is laid up for the righteous' (Proverbs 13:22) and 'The meek inherit the earth' (Matthew 5:5)?

2. The best way to defeat Haman's instructions without cancelling them was to give the Jews permission to defend themselves (8:9–11) and the right to plunder the property of those who attacked them. On the thirteenth day of the twelfth month, the same day chosen by Haman (see 3:13), the Jews were permitted to avenge themselves (8:12–13). The permission of violence within the nation was given for purely defensive reasons, and it was a temporary measure. The phrase 'including the children and women' refers to the Jewish people (as 3:13 makes clear). The Jews themselves only attacked any armies of aggression. The purpose of the story is to show how Haman's vindictiveness was turned around for good. How is Romans 8:28 illustrated here? Are we able to believe God works all things together for good – really?

3. What is the Christian application of all of this? How do we revise the teaching to take into account the different situation of modern times?

4. 'Purim' was a Jewish festival that came into being at this time. The word means 'lots' and celebrates the casting of lots to choose the day for the Jews' slaughter. If the date had not been so far ahead there would have been no time for organising Jewish self-defence. How much should we remember the history of God's dealings with us?

Daniel

The theme of the book of Daniel is the kingdom of God in its relationship to the kingdoms of this world. It shows us how God rules over pagan empires with the intention of bringing in his own kingdom. All other kingdoms of this world arise from human sinfulness, and will inevitably be crushed and defeated by the kingdom of God. The kingdom of God is a kingdom of spiritual power.

The precise date at which Daniel was written is uncertain but it presents itself as a record of what happened in the sixth century BC. Yet there are predictions that run forward into the Greek and Roman empires, and even further, and they do so with great accuracy.

Recommended reading: S. Ferguson, *Daniel* (Communicators Commentary, Word, 1988); M. A. Eaton, *Daniel* (Preaching Through the Bible, Sovereign World, forthcoming).

☐☐☐ Reading 322 (Daniel 1:1–3:30)
1. Is it possible for a man of God to stand in the midst of pagan authority (or today we might say oppressively secular authority) that is likely to want to crush the believer? How is it to be done?
2. God seems to want to speak to people – even a pagan king. And God's people like to speak to him. What do we learn about fellowship with God from this chapter?

3. What is it like to have a state-enforced religion? How is Matthew 22:21 a comment on Daniel 3:1–30?

☐☐☐ **Reading 323 (Daniel 4:1–6:28)**

1. Daniel 4:1–37 tells us how God is able to bring a pagan king to a realisation of the reality of God. What are the ingredients in Nebuchadnezzar's conversion?

2. Our story leaps forward more than twenty years, to the days of Belshazzar. If Daniel 4:1–37 was about a king coming to salvation, Daniel 5:1–31 is about a king confirming his ruination. What are the ingredients in Belshazzar's ruining his own life?

3. 'Daniel prospered during the reign of Darius, that is, during the reign of Cyrus the Persian' (6:28). One might think this would be entirely impossible. How can a believer survive and even prosper in such adverse circumstances?

Note 'Darius the Mede' could be Ugbaru, governor of Gutium, or Gubaru an appointee of Cyrus, or Cambyses, Cyrus's son. But most likely Darius the Mede and Cyrus the Persian are the same person. Daniel 6:28 should be translated as above.

☐☐☐ **Reading 324 (Daniel 7:1–8:27)**

1. Daniel 2:1–49 told of four empires; Daniel 7:1–28 will do the same. Why are worldly kingdoms viewed as coming 'from the sea'? Why are they beastly and animal-like?

2. Does the world still experience figures who rise up against the kingdom of God? Are there 'little horns' in our world just as there was Antiochus who rose up against Israel? What is their significance?

3. These chapters are about great movements among the nations of the world. Are Christians too individualistic and self-centred in their reading of the Bible? How much should we take note of the movements among the nations of the world?

☐☐☐ **Reading 325 (Daniel 9:1–10:21)**

1. What do we learn from Daniel's example (9:1–19) of prayer and the study of the Scriptures?

2. What are the six aspects of the work of the Saviour in Daniel 9:24. What are the six things God is willing to do for us in Christ?

3. Daniel 10:1–12:13 is the longest of the five prophetic visions of the book of Daniel. It has a section dealing with the preliminary preparation of the prophet (10:1–11:1). Then comes the prophetic vision (11:2–12:3), and then there is a conclusion (12:4–13). Might we receive a clearer knowledge of God's will if we did more self-preparation?

☐☐☐ Reading 326 (Daniel 11:1–12:13)

1. Does the mass of detail in Daniel 11:1–45 suggest that we ought to know more history than we do? Of what relevance are pagan aggressors, political agitators, marriages and murders, to the kingdom of God?

2. A lot of modern civilisation owes some of its blessings to Greeks and Romans, yet both of these cultures produced persecutors of the people of God. What does it mean that such blessings and such wickedness emerge from the same people? What does it tell us about the culture in which we live? How should we relate to it?

3. What are the final destinies that Daniel envisages for the people of the world? How many destinies are there? Are there variations within each destiny? How should this affect the way we live from day to day?

Psalms 65:1–73:28

Reading 327 (Psalms 65:1–67:7)
Psalm 65:1–13 is the first of a group of four. They focus on great deliverances (65:1–13; 66:1–20) and a harvest of worldwide blessing (67:1–7; 68:1–35). The first words of Psalm 65:1 could be literally translated: 'For you is submission and praise, O God, in Zion . . .' It is the end of the Jewish year (see 65:11), and there is thanksgiving at the tabernacle in Zion. The three paragraphs focus on: privileged access (65:1–4), protection (65:5–8), provision (65:9–13).

1. What might be our greatest causes for thanksgiving at the end of a year?
2. If the 'house' of God today is the spiritual household of all believers, what is the modern equivalent of 'bringing offerings' to God's house (Psalm 66:13)?
3. What does the psalmist want immediately and what does he want eventually (67:1–3)? What is needed for there to be worldwide happiness (67:4)?

□□□ **Reading 328 (Psalms 68:1–70:5)**
Psalm 68:1–35 is a song accompanying a procession. In Psalm 69:1–36 David prays about a crisis involving false accusation. Psalm 70:1–5 resembles Psalm 40:13–17. David has taken some lines of his earlier

psalms to make a short, sharp prayer for a time of trouble. Or maybe Psalm 70:1–5 was written in a time of crisis and later David expanded it.

1. Should we have processions in churches? Or on the streets? Planned or spontaneous? What are their dangers? What is the New Testament equivalent of a 'procession'? Marching to the heavenly Zion?
2. Psalm 69:1–36 is the most frequently quoted psalm in the New Testament. How much may we see the Lord Jesus Christ in these psalms? Not every verse fits Jesus (see 69:5). To what extent may we see Jesus in the troubles of David?
3. Sometimes David must have spent hours composing a song for God (Psalm 69:1–36); sometimes he produces a short extract to use speedily when he was in trouble (Psalm 70:1–5). How much time should we spend in prayer and praise? When might we be leisurely? When might we be short?

□□□ Reading 329 (Psalms 71:1–73:28)

1. What is David's attitude to the prospect of old age (Psalm 71:1–24)? What is ours (if we are getting on in years)? If we are young, what do we expect for the future?
2. Psalm 72:1–20 (like 127:1–5) was, according to its title, written by Solomon. It focusses on kingship and refers to a king who cares, a king who rules, a king who brings worldwide blessings. What is 'kingship'? Since we reign in Christ (Ephesians 2:6 pictures us as enthroned kings and queens) how can we share God's caring kingship in this world?
3. In Psalm 73:1–28, a man testifies to a time when he almost fell badly (73:2). What led to his recovery – and what will lead to our recovery and stability?

1 John

1 John – written by the apostle John in Ephesus in the AD 90s – is often taken as if it is designed for us to discover whether we are truly the children of God. But John is quite dogmatic about the salvation of his readers (1 John 2:12–14). The letter must be read in its historical setting. False teachers were denying that Jesus is the Son of God come in the flesh. Yet the intruders were quite insistent that they were having fellowship with God. John writes to help the churches. Fellowship with God depends on faith in the *incarnate* Son of God. It will be *experienced* as we walk in love towards people and obedience towards the Lord Jesus Christ.

Recommended reading: M. A. Eaton, *1, 2, 3 John* (Focus on the Bible, Christian Focus, 1996); Z. C. Hodges, '1 John', in *The Bible Knowledge Commentary* (Victor, 1983).

☐☐☐ **Reading 330 (1 John 1:1–2:2)**
Several topics are mentioned three times and this suggests the letter goes round the same topics three times.
• First Series of Meditations
  1. The historical basis of the gospel (1:1–4)
  2. The basis of fellowship (1:5–2:2)
  3. Obedience (2:3–6)
  4. Love (2:7–11)

5. Reassurance (2:12–14)
6. Not loving the world (2:15–17)
7. Antichrists and loyalty to the faith (2:18–27)

1. Are the historical facts of the gospel so important (see 1:1–4)? Why?
2. What do we need to know about God if we are seeking fellowship with him?
3. What is the procedure for seeking fellowship with the Father and the Son?

☐☐☐ **Reading 331 (1 John 2:3–27)**
1. 'We know that we have known him' (2:3). How is it possible to know that our fellowship with God is real?
2. What is the connection between knowing God and loving people? Is it possible to love God but not people? Never? Ever? Sometimes?
3. Why is John eager (in 2:12–14) to reassure his readers of their salvation and spiritual strength?

☐☐☐ **Reading 332 (1 John 2:28–4:6)**
• Second Series of Meditations
    1. Assurance at the parousia (2:28–3:3)
    2. Not sinning (3:4–10)
    3. Love (3:11–18)
    4. Reassurance (3:19–24)
    5. Testing the spirits and loyalty to the faith (4:1–6)

1. How does our hope of glory affect us now?
2. How do we help the needy without (i) being deceived when there is no real need, (ii) helping someone continue a bad lifestyle, or (iii) creating dependency, which could later bring problems? 'How does God's love abide in anyone who has the world's goods and *sees a brother or sister* in need and yet refuses help?' What is implied in the words 'see' and 'brother or sister'?
3. If our hearts condemn us, what is the pathway of recovery?
4. How do we test what claims to be revelation from God?

Note 'Everyone who has this hope . . .' is better translated 'Everyone who holds to this hope . . .' 1 John 3:4 is literally translated by the RSV: 'Everyone who commits sin is guilty of lawlessness; sin is lawlessness.' The words 'the law' do not occur in 1 John. 1 John 3:9 says, 'No one born of God commits sin.' A common interpretation emphasises the tense ('will continue to sin'), but this treats the Greek present tense as though it were a *marked* present continuous tense, which it is not. And this interpretation is difficult to live with practically. Another possibility is: the Christian has no *permission* to sin, may not *justify* sin, may not be *casual* about sin. I might say 'No, the Christian does not do that' or 'No, you *cannot* do that.' I mean you ought not to do it and I am not giving you permission to do it.

☐☐☐ Reading 333 (1 John 4:7–21)

- Third Series of Meditations
  1. Love (4:7–12)
  2. God's indwelling (4:13–16)
  3. Love perfected (4:17–21)
  4. Faith, love, obedience and overcoming the world (5:1–5)
  5. The testimony to the gospel (5:6–12)
  6. Knowing eternal life (5:13–17)
  7. Final affirmations (5:18–21)

1. In new birth a *capacity* for love is placed within us. Everyone who loves does so because they are born of God (4:7). The new Christian begins to love everyone. But what is 'perfected love'? How may we know it?

2. Will all Christians have boldness in the day of judgment? Why should there be any differences?

3. 'Perfect love casts out fear.' Whose love? Whose fear? In how many ways may this phrase be taken? Which is right? Does it make any difference?

☐☐☐ Reading 334 (1 John 5:1–21)

1. What does the Holy Spirit witness to and how does he do it?

2. What do we learn about prayer from 1 John 5:15? Do we always know God is hearing us? What if we do not?

3. Does God ever give us permission to sin? Never? Sometimes – but only in judgment? How does 1 John 5 relate to Psalm 106:15? And Numbers 22:34, 35?

Note Jesus 'came' as our Saviour through water (he was baptised) and through blood (he truly died). The false teachers had their theories about Jesus' baptism but did not think he really died on the cross. The AV/KJV of 1 John 5:7 is absent from all Greek New Testament manuscripts except two made in the fifteenth century. No scholarly modern translation includes them. The 'sin unto death' (1 John 5:16) must (in the context of 1 John) be the sin of denying the gospel of the Son of God come in the flesh. The gospel is the *means* of forgiveness. On 1 John 5:18, see note on 1 John 3:9 above.

Mark's Gospel

Mark's Gospel is generally thought to be the earliest Gospel. That is not 100 per cent certain and its relationship to Matthew is difficult to determine and is probably complicated. Mark's Gospel seems to have a less obvious purpose than Matthew's. He has a great interest in sheer facts. What this means – and it is more certain than guesses about dates and sources – is that Mark's material is more 'primitive' than that in the other Gospels. The material is not so slanted to make any special points. Although his Gospel is shorter than the others, his stories are actually told in fuller detail. There is good reason to think it was written by John Mark of Jerusalem, colleague at different times of Peter and Paul. The way in which Mark 1:21–39 carefully records the events of one day suggests that Mark's Gospel is more in chronological order than Matthew's (where some rearranging has obviously taken place).

Mark's Gospel has a very balanced structure, one which puts Mark 8:27–9:1 as the heart of the Gospel:

A. Prologue: The beginning of the Gospel (1:1–13)

    B. Galilee (1:14–8:26)

        C. Jesus, the Son of God (8:27–9:1)

    B. Travelling to Jerusalem (9:2–15:47)

A. Epilogue (16:1–8)

Recommended reading: M. A. Eaton, *Mark* (Preaching Through the Bible,

Sovereign World, 1998); R. T. France, *The Gospel of Mark* (Bible Reading Fellowship, 1996).

□□□ Reading 335 (Mark 1:1–20)
The Galilean section of this Gospel begins with a summary statement (1:14–15). Then 1:16–3:6 records the beginning of Galilean ministry and the rise of opposition against Jesus.

1. Why did Jesus need to receive the Holy Spirit? How much is his receiving the Spirit a pattern of our receiving the Spirit?
2. The Spirit leads Jesus into a place where Jesus experiences a wilderness, is alone with animals and is attacked by Satan. Why did Jesus need to endure such hardships?
3. Training was very high on Jesus' agenda, and the disciples were chosen early in the Galilean ministry (1:16–20). What did their training consist of? How much is Jesus' method of training a model for us? How is God's work like fishing?

□□□ Reading 336 (Mark 1:21–45)
Here we have a day's ministry in Capernaum (1:21–39) and an event that made Jesus famous (1:40–45).

1. If Mark 1:21–39 is a typical day in the ministry of Jesus, then what in fact were the ingredients of his ministry? Should the same ingredients be found in today's Church?
2. The scribes were learned, balanced, cautious, full of quotations from their reading, traditional, predictable. But what was Jesus' ministry like? Whose ministry should we follow? Obviously Jesus'. But what changes would this involve in the Church?
3. What are the advantages of avoiding premature publicity when God is at work?

□□□ Reading 337 (Mark 2:1–17)
1. Jesus healed a man to prove he could forgive sins. How does the healing illustrate the forgiveness?
2. The Roman system of taxation in which Levi was involved was corrupt, oppressive and involved supporting a pagan occupying power for the sake of money-making. Levi went from his sins to being a follower of Jesus in a matter of minutes. So how long does it take to become a disciple of Jesus? Why was Levi able to change so swiftly?

3. What do we see of the graciousness of Jesus at this point of Mark's Gospel?

☐☐☐ **Reading 338 (Mark 2:18–3:6)**

1. Jesus' disciples were a distinct group. The 'Jesus movement' was not just a new patch on the old ministry of John the Baptist. How much should we expect new movements to come into the Church of the Lord Jesus Christ? Should we resist the trend? Should we welcome new 'denominations'?

2. Jesus referred to a story where David did something that was forbidden altogether! David acted illegally when he helped himself to the consecrated bread at Nob (see 1 Samuel 21:1–6). Did Jesus really approve of David's breaking the law? Why did he defend himself in this way? What do we learn about Mosaic law?

3. Legalists do strange things. They take God's law, add to it and then get so strict you cannot even chew a piece of grain! Yet they hate Jesus (3:2) and plot to destroy him (3:6). How can there be godliness without legalism?

☐☐☐ **Reading 339 (Mark 3:7–35)**

1. Jesus now concentrates for the moment on his apostles. How does he train workers for his kingdom? How much does this resemble or not resemble modern ways of training Christian leaders?

2. One might think that learned theologians might be able to appreciate the Son of God standing before their very eyes. But the theological experts from Jerusalem say Jesus is demon-possessed (3:22–30). So what is the way to come to a spiritual understanding of Jesus?

3. A strong and powerful person has a house in which he keeps many prisoners. Rescuers want to attack the house to release the prisoners within it, but the house is like a fortress, and it is guarded by its powerful occupant. So what do they do? They attack the powerful resident first and overcome him. They tie him up so that he is unable to resist what they are doing. Then they break their way into the house and set free the captives. What do the different parts of the parable represent?

☐☐☐ **Reading 340 (Mark 4:1–20)**

Mark 4:1–34 introduces us to the time when Jesus turned to teaching in 'parables'. The word (Greek *parabole*; Hebrew *mashal*) has a wider meaning than the English word might suggest. It includes riddles and proverbs of various kinds. The parables are not simple little stories designed to make Jesus' teaching easily understood. They are rather designed to bring perplexity, to provoke, to shock, to challenge.

1. It seems from what Jesus says (4:9) that some people do not have ears, some have ears but do not hear, some have ears and they do hear. What kind of people are in each category?
2. What are the causes of failure to receive Jesus' word?
3. What sort of 'secret' or 'mystery' is the kingdom of God (4:12)? Something no one ever understands? A secret that is *now* revealed? Or is it like a sealed envelope given to some but still needing to be opened? What does it mean in practice to understand the parables?

☐☐☐ Reading 341 (Mark 4:21–34)

1. Verses 21–22 seem to mean that God has no plans to allow his kingdom to be hidden. What is the point of verses 24–25? Verse 24 is sometimes taken to refer to money but the context is about understanding and entering God's kingdom.
2. In verses 26–29 the point is that the harvest continues to progress even when the farmer is asleep, because God sends rain and sunshine. How does the parable apply to the kingdom of God?
3. In 4:30–32 a tiny seed becomes a great tree. How does the picture apply to the kingdom of God?

☐☐☐ Reading 342 (Mark 4:35–5:20)

We move from parables to miracles. Jesus shows himself to be Lord over creation (4:35–41), over Satan (5:1–20), over death (5:21–24, 35–43) and disease (5:25–34).

1. Jesus could be tired. Jesus could control the weather. What did the disciples learn (and what do we learn) about the person of the Lord Jesus Christ from this story? How fully can we understand him?
2. What are the characteristics of 'demon possession' as we see them here? Do we still find people with the same problem? If so, how may they be distinguished from the mentally ill? Do mentally ill people have supernatural knowledge?
3. What are the reasons – then and now – for the fact that Jesus is sometimes not welcome?

☐☐☐ Reading 343 (Mark 5:21–43)

1. What do Jairus and the sick woman have in common? Their stories are intertwined because they are similar. Both face immense challenges to their faith. What encouragement does Jesus give us when our faith is stretched?

2. 'They laughed him to scorn' says one translation of the parallel verse Matthew 9:24. How does this picture the ignorance of the world in the face of the power of the Lord Jesus Christ?

3. Jesus avoided publicity and did not want even a resurrection to be advertised. What were his reasons and should we act similarly today?

☐☐☐ Reading 344 (Mark 6:1–29)

1. Jesus was rejected in his own town. It is difficult for 'experts' or people who think they know all about something or someone to come to faith. Why is this?

2. When the going gets tough, the tough get going. Mark 6:7 starts a new phase in the work of Jesus. Again rejection (6:1–6) leads Jesus to push forward his work. What are the principles of ministry here? How much of it was restricted to this particular mission to Israel? How much of it is valid for all time?

3. Herod Antipas was a confused man for much of the time. What caused his confusion? What did it lead to? How could he have reached a clear understanding of Jesus? What causes confusion about Jesus today and what is the remedy?

Note 'Jesus could do no miracles there.' Actually Jesus could work miracles by his own faith (as he always did when he raised the dead). 'Could not' does not mean that it was beyond his ability (since he healed 'a few') but that it was not appropriate for him to do much in a place where there was such unbelief. In a similar way one might say 'A Christian cannot steal', meaning that it is inappropriate for a Christian to do so and not that it is impossible.

☐☐☐ Reading 345 (Mark 6:30–56)

1. Jesus' feeding of five thousand people was a historical event but it is obvious that the disciples were to learn many lessons from it (see 8:14–21). What are its lessons? We are in a 'wilderness' but Jesus provides what we need. His provision is abundant. What else?

2. If provision in a wilderness contains much symbolism, so does walking on the waves of a storm. In what way is the believer's life like a storm? How does Jesus relate to the storms of life?

3. Jesus is immensely popular after his two sensational miracles. But he sends the disciples ahead (6:45) while he plans to walk around the lakeside hills, praying (6:46). Why did Jesus need to pray so much? On what occasions does he specially give himself to prayer? Are we to be like him in this?

☐☐☐ Reading 346 (Mark 7:1–23)

1. In Old Testament times, only priests were obliged to ceremonially wash their hands before eating. The Pharisees made the rule more strict and imposed it on everyone who would submit to them. Why is it that religious people tend to become increasingly strict as time goes by?

2. If sin comes from the heart (7:21), can hand-washing rituals (or any other rituals) give power against sin? Can religious severity give power against sin? If not, why not? How then do we evaluate modern religions?

3. Jesus calls these strict people 'hypocrites'. In what way are strict people inclined to be hypocritical? Could strict religion *prevent* godliness?

☐☐☐ Reading 347 (Mark 7:24–37)

1. Does Jesus ever seem unsympathetic to us (as he seemed unsympathetic to the Syro-Phoenician woman)? What was his purpose then and what might his purpose be with us?

2. Deafness and dumbness are mentioned for the first time here in Mark's Gospel. If Jesus has such power over the diseases of the body, are such stories also pictures of his ability to open our ears to his word, and use our tongues to his praise?

3. Why was Jesus so emotional (7:34) in this healing? What was it that was disturbing to him?

☐☐☐ Reading 348 (Mark 8:1–26)

1. The miracle of feeding the five thousand (6:30–44) was obviously of such great importance that Jesus repeats it with something similar. Why was it so important? What were they meant to understand (note 8:18–21)?

2. The Pharisees were traditionalists and legalists; the Herodians were political and sceptical. What is the leaven of the Pharisees and of the Herodians, and how might we take note of Jesus' command (8:15) today?

3. What is the connection between the miracle that seems at first only to half-succeed (8:22–26) and the confusion of the disciples (8:18–21)? When we only half-understand what Jesus is doing, what is our need?

☐☐☐ **Reading 349 (Mark 8:27–9:1)**

This section is the climax and centre-point of the Gospel of Mark. Jesus goes to Caesarea Philippi outside of Galilee and the authority of Herod Antipas, in order to have quality time with his disciples.

1. Four different views of Jesus are mentioned in 26:27–29. Obviously there are different views of Jesus today also. What is the difference between a low view and a high view of Jesus? What evidence has Jesus given for his being the Messiah?

2. What might be the reason for Jesus' wanting people to come to see who he is in a quiet manner? Why may Peter not tell it to everyone (26:30) immediately?

3. The teaching of Jesus now focusses on his approaching death ('He *then* began to teach them that the Son of Man must suffer many things . . .'). Peter has seen who Jesus is but does not like the idea of his dying on the cross. Do we still have admirers of Jesus who dislike the cross? Why does Jesus rebuke Peter so severely?

4. Consider 8:38–9:1. How soon after the death of Jesus is the 'coming of the Son of Man'? See notes on Daniel 7:1–28 (p. 204).

☐☐☐ **Reading 350 (Mark 9:2–32)**

1. The transfiguration came immediately after the predictions of Jesus' death. What was God doing in the life of the disciples, who would one day have to preach about the death and resurrection of Jesus, and his future coming in glory?

2. There are obviously weaknesses and misunderstandings in the disciples. What are they? At such times what might Jesus do to help us?

3. The people of Mark 9:1–32 have in them a mixture of faith and unbelief. What are the signs of their faith? What are the signs of their unbelief? How may we grow in faith?

☐☐☐ **Reading 351 (Mark 9:33–50)**

1. What exactly is greatness? How does our attitude to children reveal whether we are truly great?

2. Should a Christian be motivated by the thought of reward? Was Jesus motivated by the thought of reward?

3. The thread of thought leads Jesus to playfully juggle with the word 'salt'. (i) The salt-like character of the Christian might be lost (9:50a). (ii) In which case the Christian can expect to be 'salted' – purified – by fire. (iii) Yet another use of the word 'salt' is made in verse 50b. Here the word 'salt' is used to refer to good relationship within the fellowship

of the Christian. How much does Jesus demand of us? What is 'saltiness' in Christian relationships?

4. The warnings about 'Gehenna' are not necessarily warnings of eternal punishment in this passage. It was a term that was used in the first century AD of fiery chastening from God as well as eternal punishment. 'Gehenna' can be used of being 'saved through fire' (1 Corinthians 3:15) as well as of a punishment that will never be reversed. A sentence like 'Everyone will be salted with fire' (9:49) has more to do with purification than with irreversible punishment. So how seriously do we take the warnings of Jesus about greatness and smallness?

☐☐☐ Reading 352 (Mark 10:1–31)

Three key matters here are divorce (10:2–12), children (10:13–16) and wealth (10:17–31).

1. Jesus taught that marriage generally should not be brought to an end (see Matthew 5:31–32; 19:3–12; Mark 10:2–12; Luke 16:18). Are there any exceptions to the generalisation? If so, why does Mark not mention them?

2. In some ways children are obviously not models of a member of the kingdom of God. We think of their love of entertainment and toys, their ignorance of what life is like in the wider world. What is it then about children that Jesus recommends as a model for us?

3. What is the meaning of Mark 10:25? What kind of interpretation will it lead to if we take 'entering the kingdom' to mean 'experiencing as a believer the powerful blessings of God's kingdom'? And how will that affect our attitude towards wealth?

☐☐☐ Reading 353 (Mark 10:32–52)

1. Jesus is steadily moving towards Jerusalem. Jesus was going ahead of the disciples (10:32). He was moving forward with determination. Was Jesus ambitious?

2. The disciples were coming behind with less enthusiasm. Jesus predicts his sufferings and death (10:33–34) and continues to teach his disciples what they need to know about his kingdom. When James and John approach Jesus asking for positions of honour in his kingdom (10:35–37), he warns them of what would be involved. Does true greatness always involve suffering?

3. Jesus is about to give himself as a 'ransom' – the payment of a price that releases slaves. He does it for everyone. 'Many' is a Hebrew way of

saying 'everyone'. Why did Jesus need to be a ransom? Is the forgiveness of sin a problem even to God?

☐☐☐ Reading 354 (Mark 11:1–18)

It is now Sunday. Jesus has six more days to live as a man on planet Earth.

1. Why is the story of Jesus in the New Testament so unbalanced with such a concentration on the week of Jesus' death? What does Jesus' death on the cross mean to us?
2. Jesus finds that the temple is still (see John 2:1–25) being used as a commercial centre for small-time religious business. Do religious institutions – even the temple – have a tendency to become commercial? For the moment Jesus did nothing. He observed before he acted. In what ways should we be like Jesus at this point?
3. On the Monday morning, Jesus passes a fig tree that gives the impression that figs will be found on it. But the abundant foliage is misleading. Jesus curses the fig tree. It is a miraculous parable. Israel makes great claims for its religious life. But what do we learn about God's attitude towards religious 'foliage'?

☐☐☐ Reading 355 (Mark 11:19–33)

1. The next day, Tuesday, Jesus uses the withered fig tree to teach some principles about faith. Verse 22 is often translated 'Have faith in God' but another translation is 'Hold on to the faithfulness of God'. When we are praying, what does it mean to have faith?
2. Verse 23 has in it the word 'if'. Half of the Church seems to neglect Mark 11:23, but the other half of the Church seems to treat it as a kind of technique that we can use to get anything from God. The important word is 'if'. Are we always able to pray with an absolute assurance of what is about to happen? Where is the balance to be found?
3. The Tuesday of Jesus' last week on earth is a day of questions. First comes a question concerning Jesus' authority (11:27–33). He says: 'My authority is the same authority as that of John the Baptist!' But what kind of authority is that? What authority may we have?

☐☐☐ Reading 356 (Mark 12:1–17)

1. The parable of Mark 12:1–12 was directed to the religious leader of the land. Most religious movements begin with sincerity. How does it happen that such people as the religious leaders of Jesus' time should

end up rejecting and even killing the Son of God? What are the modern equivalents? Are we in danger of 'stumbling' over Jesus?

2. If we are loyal to a pagan ruler, we tend to be loyal to his religion. If we are loyal to God, we tend to be disloyal towards any pagan leader. What was Jesus' solution to this problem? Does it change if the ruler is a Christian?

3. How do we respond to people who like religious discussion – sometimes (as in 12:13–15a) insincerely?

☐☐☐ Reading 357 (Mark 12:18–36)

1. The resurrection of dead people takes a lot of believing. The Sadducees think the idea worthy of ridicule. Whether we believe in resurrection or not tests our spiritual understanding. Why did the Sadducees deny the possibility? How 'miraculous' is our view of life after death?

2. Are there different levels of authority in the Mosaic law? What are the highest levels? What are the lowest levels? What parts of the law are too low for a Christian? How much can we still regard with great respect?

3. What is it to be 'not far' from the kingdom of God? Were the religious leaders of Israel 'not far' away from God's kingdom?

4. When the religious leaders ask questions, what are their questions about? When Jesus asks a question, what is his question about? What is the difference in their concern?

☐☐☐ Reading 358 (Mark 12:37–13:14)

1. What is the nature of hypocritical religion according to 12:37–40?

2. What is the nature of true love of God according to 12:41–44?

3. What are (i) the similarities and (ii) the differences between the fall of Jerusalem and the second coming of Jesus? The disciples take it for granted that the end of the world and the end of the temple are the same occasion. Jesus does not initially correct them. Why not?

☐☐☐ Reading 359 (Mark 13:15–37)

1. 'Of that day or that hour no one knows, not even the angels in heaven, nor the Son, but only the Father' (12:32). What does the sequence 'no one . . . angels . . . the Son . . .' tell us about Jesus? Why does he not know the date of his own second coming? What are we learning about Jesus?

2. Jesus predicts the future here. When someone makes predictions that we cannot test, what might lead us to accept the predictions? What might cause us to be cautious? What might make us cautious at first but then change our minds? What might make us accept the prediction but then learn to be cautious? How do you view Jesus' predictions? How would you view the predictions of others?

3. What is to be our attitude towards the second coming of Jesus? How can we realistically expect something at any moment and yet make plans that imply it will not happen? Does it help if the second coming may be anticipated (as the fall of Jerusalem anticipated the end of the world)?

☐☐☐ Reading 360 (Mark 14:1–26)

1. The events of the last day of Jesus' life seem the greatest example of God getting his will done while people were trying to get their own way. In what ways were the plans of Jesus' enemies overthrown? What encouragement does this give us today?

2. The actions of Mary and of Judas are placed side-by-side in Mark's story. What are the differences between them? In ambitions? With regard to money? In their understanding of the cross? It is easier to admire Mary than to be like her. Should we seek to develop her kind of recklessness and extravagance?

3. How should we treat our enemies? How did Jesus treat Judas?

☐☐☐ Reading 361 (Mark 14:27–52)

1. Jesus knew he had less that twenty-four hours to live. What would you be doing if you knew you had less than twenty-four hours to live? In what way was Jesus still faithful to the disciples despite the immense burden he was carrying himself?

2. What are the weaknesses of this disciples here? What remedy does Jesus propose to them?

3. The incident of Mark 14:51–52 is to be found only in Mark's Gospel (compare Amos 2:16). An unidentified disciple stayed longer than the others (note 14:50). What do we learn from him?

☐☐☐ Reading 362 (Mark 14:53–72)

1. Jesus' suffering makes him 'able to sympathise' (Hebrews 2:18; 4:15; 5:8). What different kinds of suffering did Jesus endure at this time? Betrayal. What else? How do we learn to lean on the sympathy of Jesus?

2. A heavily armed crowd arrive, sent by senior priests, theologians and the Pharisaic elders. They obviously do not have much spiritual understanding of Jesus. If such capable and highly placed people

misunderstand Jesus so badly, what hope is there that we should come to spiritual understanding?

3. What mistakes does Peter make at this time? Should he have tried to look like a casual bystander, warming himself at the fire (14:54)? Should he have been willing to surrender his life with Jesus? Compare Peter on this day and Peter on the Day of Pentecost. What made the difference?

☐☐☐ Reading 363 (Mark 15:1–20)

1. Controlling the tongue is the most difficult aspect of Christian discipleship (James 3:2) – and total silence is not the answer! Jesus sometimes speaks, sometimes stays silent. What can we learn from him at this point?

2. The innocent died and a guilty man, Barabbas, was released. In what ways is the gospel precisely illustrated here?

3. The priests were believers in the Old Testament. They were looking for a Messiah. But when the Son of God was in front of them they were not capable of realising who he was. How does it happen that religious knowledge can be combined with spiritual blindness?

☐☐☐ Reading 364 (Mark 15:21–47)

1. It was a Roman habit to get the man to be crucified to carry his own cross, but Jesus at this point was so physically weak that someone else was forced to do the work. How is the incident a good illustration of Mark 8:34?

2. There was immense disgrace for Jesus at this time. Why are we so sensitive to disgrace and dishonour? What were the ingredients in the disgracing of Jesus? Does God call upon us to 'despise the shame' when we are doing his will (Hebrews 12:2)? Is faith ever shameful?

3. What is the significance of the three hours of darkness? Note Amos 8:9 and Isaiah 13:10. What do we learn from Jesus at this point?

☐☐☐ Reading 365 (Mark 16:1–20)

Late on Saturday night, after the Sabbath has finished at about 6 p.m. three women go to buy spices to anoint the body of Jesus – Mary Magdalene, Mary the mother of James, and Salome. They agree to anoint Jesus' body early on the following morning (16:1), which will be a Sunday. Early the next day the three women go to the tomb of Jesus but they are wondering how to get the stone rolled away from the tomb entrance (16:2–3). When they get there the stone is already rolled away (16:4). A young man is there, dressed in a way that suggests he is an angel (16:5; Matthew says there were two angels; Mark writes only about the one they spoke to). The angel tells them of the resurrection (16:6). They are invited to see the place where Jesus had been (16:6), but then must go to Galilee where Jesus will appear to them (16:7). Shocked and fearful the women hurry away, saying nothing to anyone because they are fearful (16:8). At this point Mark's Gospel ends. Verses 9–20, which appear in many Bibles, were added later but are not really part of Mark's Gospel. They are not found in the earliest manuscripts of this Gospel.

1. Is it a good idea to retell the story of the Christian faith so that there is nothing miraculous about it? Is it possible to have a Christian faith without believing in the resurrection of Jesus? If not, why not?

2. 'Go tell his disciples and Peter . . .' Why Peter? Had he not ruined his life by denying Jesus?

3. 'He is going ahead of you into Galilee . . .' Why Galilee? Why did Jesus not go back to Pilate and Caiaphas in his resurrection body? How does Jesus prove his resurrection to us?

YEAR TWO

Ezra

Jerusalem was destroyed in 587 BC and most of the population were deported to Babylon. The few left behind were sunk in idolatry. At the point where Ezra-Nehemiah opens, in 538 BC, the people had been in exile for over sixty years, since the first deportations in 604 BC. The exile was a time of purifying punishment, but suddenly the Jews had an opportunity to go back to Israel. The book of Ezra is about cooperating with God in his work of restoration. It is his work to restore, yet God's people must respond to him. Cyrus the Persian took over without even much of a struggle. So as the book of Ezra opens it is 539/8 BC, 'the first year of Cyrus, king of Persia' (Ezra 1:1). Some kings of Persia are the following:

- Cyrus 539–530 BC
- Cambyses 530–521 BC
- Darius I 521–486 BC
- Xerxes I 486–46 BC
- Artaxerxes I 464–424 BC

Recommended reading: M. A. Eaton, *Ezra, Nehemiah, Esther* (Preaching Through the Bible, Sovereign World, 2002), D. Kidner, *Ezra, Nehemiah* (Tyndale Commentary, IVP, 1979).

☐☐☐ Reading 1 (Ezra 1:1–3:13)

1. History is controlled by God, yet the believer is responsible to flow with what God is doing. In Ezra 1:1–11 what events tell us of the activity of God? What challenges come to the Jews in the Babylonian (now become Persian) empire?

2. Ezra 2:1–70 lists the names of those who returned to Jerusalem in 538 BC. To have one's name recorded is a great honour. Can you think of Scriptures that speak of being given a name? How does this link with Jesus being given a name that is above every name?

3. Seven months later the people had settled in their new homes (3:1). It was time to re-establish the worship of the Lord in Judah, and build the temple. There were certain things that came before the laying the foundation. God's work requires unity . . . And what else?

Note 'Sheshbazzar' (Ezra 1:8–11; 5:14–16) was possibly the governor of Judea for a very short time before Zerubbabel became the governor, or more likely the official Babylonian governor while Zerubbabel who descended from Judah's kings was unofficially the leader of the people.

☐☐☐ Reading 2 (Ezra 4:1–6:22)

1. There are three kinds of opposition in this chapter (in 4:1–5, 6, 7–23). What are they?

2. How does Ezra 5:1–6:22 give the people of God a model for relating to civic authorities?

3. From about 535 to about 520 BC the people were discouraged and gave themselves to their own pursuits. What led to their resuming the work again? What does this tell us of the need for modern believers?

Note The editor of Ezra wants the reader to see that this opposition of the 'people of the land' was a very longstanding affair and would continue for years. So he jumps ahead to the days of Ahasuerus (4:6), and then to the days of Artaxerxes (4:7–23) before resuming his narrative:

- Ezra 4:1–5: The days of Cyrus (536/5 BC; the date is that given in 2:8)
- Digression (4:6): The days of Xerxes (486–465 BC)
- Digression (4:7–23): The days of Artaxerxes (464–424 BC)
- Ezra 4:24: The story resumed: The days of Cyrus again (536/5 BC)

The project was eventually successful, as by March 516 BC the temple was completed (6:15). In April the Passover was held (6:19).

□□□ Reading 3 (Ezra 7:1–8:36)

It is now the year 458 BC, the seventh year of Artaxerxes. For more than fifty years the temple has been standing. Yet the building of the city of Jerusalem is still facing much opposition. The incident of 4:7–23 took place in Artaxerxes' reign. What they now need is a teacher. God sends Ezra.

1. What are the *prior* qualifications of a great teacher in Ezra 7:1–28?
2. Ezra was given an opportunity to help God's work (7:11–28); he mobilised a large number of supporters (8:1–20); he proceeded with prayerfulness (8:21–34). So what are the three characteristics of a great leader?
3. Precisely how did Ezra come to be so favoured and appreciated by Artaxerxes? What leads the state to appreciate the churches?

□□□ Reading 4 (Ezra 9:1–10:44)

1. When Israel entered Canaan they were told not to intermarry with the Canaanites. Few Christians would object to multinational marriages but multifaith marriage is more difficult. Why was Ezra troubled? How does he handle the matter?
2. Must families be broken up, and children be made fatherless, in the interests of religious purity (10:2b–4)? Yet it was a case of life or death for the future of Israel. If anyone wanted his pagan wife and children more than the God of Israel, he could start a new life within the Samaritans but his status in Israel would be lost (Ezra 10:7–8). What happens in this chapter is an example of the 'lesser of two evils'. What are modern examples of the same dilemma?
3. Ezra 10:1–44 is a list of those who had the courage to deal radically with sin. Is tough-minded obedience to the written word of God the only way of preserving the Church? Or must we sometimes compromise?

2–3 John

2 John has in view the same kind of situation we had in 1 John. There are people who deny that Jesus is the Son of God in the flesh, and they are trying to infiltrate John's churches. In 3 John the situation is rather different. There the problem is not heresy but needless divisiveness. 'The elder' (2 John 1; 3 John 1) is the apostle John himself, or the leader of the churches in the Ephesus area. The 'elect lady' (2 John 1) seems to be the congregation.

Recommended reading: M. A. Eaton, *1, 2, 3 John* (Focus on the Bible, Christian Focus, 1996).

□□□ Reading 5 (2–3 John)

1. John is the 'apostle of love' and yet says some hard things in 2 John. Is he in fact lacking in love? How can we balance faithfulness to the gospel with graciousness towards people?
2. 2 John 8 mentions the receiving of a reward. What is the reward? Is it 'commercial' to be motivated by reward?
3. Presumably we should not say such things about *every* disagreement about professing Christians (see 2 John 9–11). What aspects of the gospel are so vital that their denial calls for strong words?
4. Is hospitality a spiritual gift? How much should we be concerned about hospitality today?
5. Was Diotrophes a Christian? Did he have a personality disorder?

Psalms 74:1–79:13

☐☐☐ **Reading 6 (Psalms 74:1–75:10)**

1. 'We are given no signs; no prophets are left, and none of us knows how long this will be' (Psalm 74:9). What should be done when we feel like this?

2. In Psalm 74:22 the psalmist wants God to gain honour. Is it possible to readjust our thinking so that we pray for God's concerns more than for our own?

3. In Psalm 75:1, God's people are grateful to God. God is in control of timing, judgment and any stability that there might be in our world (verses 2–3, and onward). Do we believe in the control of God over our world? How will it affect us if we have the same viewpoint as the psalmist?

☐☐☐ **Reading 7 (Psalms 76:1–77:20)**

1. Psalm 76:1–12 begins with the home of God, Jerusalem, which is like a lion's den (the meaning of a word in verse 2) and a warrior's headquarters (76:1–3). Is the modern view of God too soft and flabby? What kind of God has God shown himself to be?

2. How does the wrath of men and women turn to God's praise (76:10)? What examples can be cited?

3. Does God withdraw himself that we might learn more of him? If so, what are we to learn (77:11–20)?

233

□□□ Reading 8 (Psalms 78:1–79:13)

1. Psalm 78:1–72 speaks of the duty each generation has to pass on what it knows to the next. How do we fulfil this duty? And what are we to pass on?

2. The biblical writers often survey the story of Israel. Is it possible to survey the story of the church over the last century or so? What lessons might we draw?

3. Psalm 79:1–13 was obviously written shortly after the destruction of Jerusalem in 586 BC. The writer is distressed about what 'they' – the nations – did to Jerusalem (verses 1–3, 5–7, 10–11). But verses 4, 8–9, 12–13 speak of 'us', the people of God. When we are suffering we tend to blame others but are we ever to think that God is disciplining us through the way others treat us badly? How should we view ourselves at such times?

Leviticus

Leviticus is a direct continuation of Exodus. The scene of action is Mount Sinai. The tabernacle has been constructed. The next matter must be the system of ceremonial holiness in connection with the tabernacle system of worship. Leviticus proceeds to describe the sacrifices (Leviticus 1:1–7:38), the priesthood (8:1–10:20), the rules about various kind of cleanness and uncleanness (Leviticus 11:1–15:33), followed by a section concerning the Day of Atonement (Leviticus 16:1–34). The rest of the book has laws about holiness. It begins with principles about sacrificing animals and eating meat (17:1–16); about forbidden sexual relationships (18:1–30). It gives principles for righteous society within Israel (19:1–37), including honour of parents and of God (19:3–8), good neighbour-liness (19:9–18) and other matters. This is followed by a section on capital crimes (20:1–27), one giving rules for priests, and rules about eating sacrifices (21:1–22:33). Leviticus 23:1–44 covers the festivals of Israel, and Leviticus 24:1–9 gives rules for the oil and the showbread. Leviticus 24:10–23 gives guidance arising from a specific case of blasphemy. Leviticus 25:1–55 deals with the sabbatical and jubilee years. Leviticus 26:1–46 gives an exhortation to obey the law. Leviticus 27:1–34 deals with vows and gifts.

Leviticus might seem to be a wearisome book, but viewed as a step towards the coming of Christ it is in fact exciting. The interpretation of the cross of Christ draws upon ideas that come from Leviticus.

Recommended reading: D. Tidball, *Leviticus*, (Crossway Bible Guide, Crossway, 1996); C. J. H. Wright, 'Leviticus', in *New Bible Commentary, 21st Century Edition* (ed. D. A. Carson et al., IVP, 1994).

☐☐☐ Reading 9 (Leviticus 1:1–2:16)

1. The burnt offering (Leviticus 1:1–17) expresses the worshipper's total consecration. If the sacrifice foreshadows what Jesus did on the cross, what is the symbolism of laying one's hands on the victim's head? Is there more symbolism like this?
2. Animals were expensive but pigeons were cheap. What is the approach to poverty implied in 1:14–17? What should be our attitude towards needy people?
3. The grain offering (Leviticus 2:1–16) expresses the dedication of the worshipper's labours. There was no bloodshed in the grain offering but then it was never offered on its own. Is this significant?

☐☐☐ Reading 10 (Leviticus 3:1–5:13)

1. The fellowship offering (Leviticus 3:1–17) was like a festive party, a meal among friends. Is the kingdom of God to be like a party? In what ways?
2. The first three offerings were positive and joyful – and they were voluntary. The next two are somewhat sad and sorrowful – but they were compulsory. They speak of sin-bearing (see 1 Peter 2:24). The blood of the first and third was offered inside the tabernacle; the blood of the last two (4:1–5:13 and 5:14–6:7) was offered outside the tabernacle. What symbolism can the Christian find here?
3. The sins that could be forgiven by these sacrifices are quite minor. Serious sins (murder, adultery, dishonouring parents) were punishable by the death sentence. What are the differences between the sacrifice of Christ and the Old Testament sacrifices?

☐☐☐ Reading 11 (Leviticus 5:14–7:38)

1. The 'reparation offering' of Leviticus 5:14–6:7 dealt with such things as misuse of holy things, failure to obey minor matters of the law, breaking trust with a neighbour. Should we practise restitution more than we do? Does it affect our sense of forgiveness?
2. Should the idea of restitution be brought into international politics? Or into prison reform? In what ways might Israel's laws be wiser than ours?
3. Leviticus 6:8–7:38 is more for the priests than for the ordinary people.

The priests were allowed to profit from the sacrifices (see 6:17). The New Testament even uses the term 'wages' (1 Timothy 5:18; see also 1 Corinthians 9:13). How much should we profit from spiritual work?

☐☐☐ Reading 12 (Leviticus 8:1–36)

1. The priests required washing, clothing, anointing and so on, to do their work. What aspects of the Christian life are similar?
2. Blood was applied to the ears (for hearing), the feet (for walking), the hands (for daily activities). What might this mean for the Christian?
3. The priests' ordination took seven days. Why so long? To what aspects of the Christian life should we give plenty of time?

☐☐☐ Reading 13 (Leviticus 9:1–10:20)

1. What is 'blessing' the people (9:23)? Can people be 'blessed' without sacrifices for sin? If not, why not?
2. Was it not terrible than Aaron should lose two of his sons so shortly after they were ordained? What is the significance of so swift and terrible a punishment?
3. 'The law is only a shadow . . . not the realities' (Hebrews 10:1). 'Sacrifice and offering you did not desire' (10:5). Should modern Christian worship resemble the tabernacle? If not, what should be the differences?

☐☐☐ Reading 14 (Leviticus 11:1–12:8)

In Leviticus 11:1–15:33, the regulations concerning several kinds of ritual-ceremonial cleanness and uncleanness are *only* a matter of ritual and ceremony. Leviticus 11:1–47 deals with foods. Leviticus 12:1–8 deals with childbirth. We note in Acts 10:1–48 that unclean foods symbolise gentiles, and *eating* unclean foods represents *fellowship* with gentiles.

1. The 'unclean' creatures tend to be birds of prey, creatures that look repulsive, creatures with close contact with the earth, creatures that are inconsistent. How might these represent different kinds of sinfulness that ought to be avoided?
2. What are the different meanings that Leviticus 11:44a has for the Old Testament believer and the modern Christian?
3. Did God accommodate himself to *superstitions* that people tend to have about foods and sexuality and childbirth? If this is so, do the *superstitions* point to something profound? What might be the connection between Leviticus 12:1–8 and Psalm 51:5 or 58:3?

☐☐☐ **Reading 15 (Leviticus 13:1–15:33)**
Leviticus 13:1–14:57 deals with skin diseases and fungal diseases. Leviticus 15:1–33 deals with bodily discharges. In the Old Testament, 'leprosy' is not the modern disease that goes by that name.

1. In what way do the various ailments here (contagion, repulsive sights, isolation, grief, torn clothes and so on) illustrate the chaos caused by sin? Is there a reason why the decisions have to be in the hands of a priest?
2. What symbolism can be seen in hyssop (a bushy plant ideal for making a mop)? In tough resilient cedar wood? In bowls of clean water? How is the Christian cleansed from wicked ways?
3. The purpose of these laws is stated in 15:31. What is the spiritual and Christian equivalent? Does Hebrews 10:22 refer to ritual or to spiritual experience?

☐☐☐ **Reading 16 (Leviticus 16:1–34)**
1. The ritual here was symbolic. Christ was the reality. What are the differences between the symbolic high priest and the ultimate High Priest, Jesus?
2. Why did the sanctuary need atonement (note Hebrews 9:23)? Does heaven need to be 'covered' by the blood of Christ? If so, why?
3. How confident may we be that our sins may be forgiven? (Note Hebrews 9:9, 14.)
4. When the high priest cleansed himself and the holy place, he did not wear his colourful clothes. But he put them on to atone for the sins of the people. Why the difference?

☐☐☐ **Reading 17 (Leviticus 17:1–16)**
Leviticus 17:1–16 is about the sanctity of blood.

1. How does atonement work in Old Testament symbolism (Leviticus 17:11)? How does the blood of Jesus Christ bring forgiveness of sins?
2. Does God really need blood atonement in order to forgive sins?
3. Disregarding the sanctity of blood brought the penalty of being cut off from the people of God (either banished or executed). What is the 'penalty' for disregarding the blood of Christ?

☐☐☐ Reading 18 (Leviticus 18:1–19:37)

Leviticus 18:1–30 forbids incestuous sexual relationships (18:6–18) and other pagan customs (18:19–23).

1. What does Leviticus 18:5 mean? Does it refer to eternal life or civic life? Is it a real offer? Or is it hypothetical? Does Exodus 20:12 give any light on the subject?
2. What are the punishments of sin – looked at in at least three ways – in 18:24–30?
3. What is the unifying thread of this chapter (19:2, 3, 4, 10, 12, etc.)? If some aspects of the law are 'weightier' that others (Matthew 23:23), what are the most weighty parts here?

☐☐☐ Reading 19 (Leviticus 20:1–22:33)

1. Leviticus 20:1–27 focusses on capital crimes, which were liable to the death penalty. Stoning as a method of execution involved the community. Verse 4 warns against ignoring crime in the nation – and so again stresses community responsibility. Although the Christian is under something higher than these Mosaic rulings, yet we may learn from the idea of community responsibility. How much may we learn from the Mosaic law without being directly under it (Romans 6:14)?
2. Leviticus 20:3 speaks of divine enmity against wickedness. What was it then (and what is it now) that arouses divine enmity against us?
3. For the priests there were restrictions on mourning and marriage (Leviticus 21:1–22:33). Why were the priests obliged to hold to higher standards than other people? Why were they not to be so caught up with rituals involving death and bereavement? In what ways do these regulations point to Jesus?

☐☐☐ Reading 20 (Leviticus 23:1–44)

Leviticus 23:1–44 contains instructions about seven festivals. The Sabbath is involved in all of them. Then there were four in spring (Passover, Unleavened Bread, Firstfruits, Pentecost), and three in autumn or fall (Trumpets, the Day of Atonement, and Tabernacles).

1. Christ is our Passover lamb (1 Corinthians 5:7), but what is the symbolism of unleavened bread (note 1 Corinthians 5:8)?
2. Passover and Unleavened Bread could be celebrated in the wilderness. The Firstfruits had to be celebrated when the people entered the land. How does Christ fulfil this festival (see 1 Corinthians 15:20, 23)?

3. What does the Feast of Trumpets symbolise? The preaching of the gospel? The second coming of Jesus?
4. 'Tabernacles' recalled the time when Israel lived in tents. What does it recall for the Christian?

□□□ Reading 21 (Leviticus 24:1–25:55)

1. The 'holy place' of the tabernacle had within it various symbols of fellowship with God. If the lampstand (Exodus 25:31–40) represents the light of the Lord, what does it mean to be keeping the lamps burning continually?
2. Leviticus 24:10–16 records the execution of a blasphemer. Why was there no religious toleration in the time of the Mosaic law? Most Christians today would not support the death penalty for blasphemy. So in what way did God's will for society change as the story of the nations went forward?
3. The rules concerning the Year of Jubilee meant that ideally most families in Israel could own land that could not be taken from them. Land could be leased but not sold. What are the economic and political advantages of protecting land-ownership? Are there spiritual equivalents to the principles of jubilee?

□□□ Reading 22 (Leviticus 26:1–27:34)

1. Leviticus 26:1–46 contains lists of blessings for those who keep the law, and curses for those who do not. God is the one who will carry out the promises and the threats. But how does the Christian apply such Scriptures today? Do they apply to other nations besides Israel? Do anti-Christian countries find that their land suffers from these biblical curses? Or are they to be applied spiritually? Could 27:7 be applied to evangelism, for example?
2. There are references here to fear as a punishment (as in 27:36). Is a fearful spirit ever given as a punishment?
3. Are there vows that should be taken in the New Testament Church? If not, what is the equivalent of a vow when we are living in the Holy Spirit?

Jude

Jude was a brother of the James who led the Jerusalem church, and a half-brother of Jesus. We can only guess when the letter of Jude was written. The readers had heard the preaching of the apostles (see Jude 18). So it could not have been more than a generation after the apostles preached. What is more important was that it was written at a time when the churches were drifting away from authentic faith in the Lord Jesus Christ. There were people trying to change the character of the church. The central theme of Jude is preventing the character of the Christian church from being changed.

☐☐☐ Reading 23 (Jude)

1. Why was Jude wanting his friends to 'contend for faith'? There are always people who want to change the character of the Christian gospel. How does it happen today?

2. Verse 11 mentions Cain, Balaam, Korah. Cain is famous as a worshipper who had no faith in blood atonement. What were the lessons to be learned from the other two?

3. There are four commands in verses 20–21. What are they and how do we obey them?

Psalms 80:1–88:18

☐☐☐ **Reading 24 (Psalms 80:1–81:16)**

1. Psalm 80:1–19 is a prayer for God's favour. What is it like when God's face 'shines' upon us? How do we seek to have him relate to us in this way?

2. The psalmist does not pray 'Turn our circumstances' but 'Turn us' (80:3). What is the difference? Is it important?

3. Psalm 81:1–16 was written for a festival (81:3), probably Tabernacles. It calls for joyful worship (81:1–3). The keeping of the festival is part of God's demand (81:4–5). How do we encourage ourselves to serve God? One way is to call to mind the great things he has done. What was it that the psalmist remembered God did (81:6–7) and said (81:8–10), and how did he apply the lesson (81:11–16)?

☐☐☐ **Reading 25 (Psalms 82:1–83:18)**
Psalm 82:1–8 is a court scene with the assembly (82:1), the accusation (82:2), the commands of the law (82:3–4), the witnesses (82:5), the verdict (82:5) and sentence (82:6–7) and a closing prayer (82:8). The 'gods' are earthly rulers (although some have taken them to be spiritual beings).

1. How did Jesus make use of Psalm 82:1–8? What is one mark of 'deity' which Jesus possessed supremely?

2. God claims sovereignty of the highest administrators of justice. What practical difference will this make to us?

3. Psalm 83:1–18 gives us a picture of the people of God surrounded by immense hostility. What is the position of God's people in the world? How do they cope? What should they wish for and pray for?

□□□ Reading 26 (Psalms 84:1–85:13)

1. In what ways are the people of God like a sparrow or swallow (as in Psalm 84:3) who have found a safe home? Is the 'home' just a building or does the building point to something greater?

2. From Psalm 85:1–13, how should we pray for revival?

3. Psalm 85:1–13 mentions mercy, truth, righteousness and peace. How do these different characteristics of God fit together? Do mercy and peace fit easily with truth and righteousness? And in our own lives?

□□□ Reading 27 (Psalms 86:1–88:18)

1. David wrote Psalm 86:1–17 at a time when arrogant people were threatening his life (86:14). What are the reasons he gives in verses 1–6 for being confident that God will hear him?

2. God's people are like a city (Psalm 87:1–7). To be a citizen requires a certain kind of birth (87:4–5) and a certain kind of registration (87:6–7). What are the joys of the city? And what are the conditions of membership?

3. Psalm 88:1–18 is the psalm of a man who has lost all hope. At the end of the psalm, the man still has found no comfort. So why was the psalm included in the book of Psalms? Is there anything in it that encourages us? What encouragement did the man himself have (note verse 1)?

1 Samuel

The books of 1 and 2 Samuel are actually only one book in the Hebrew original. It was apparently first divided into two books by the Greek translators in the third century BC. 1–2 Samuel tells us of the rise of kingship in Israel. This is important to us because much of the Bible is concerned about kingship or kingdom. If you were to put into one word the message of the Bible, probably the word that summarises the entire message is 'kingdom'. 'The kingdom is at hand', said Jesus.

Recommended reading: M. A. Eaton, *1 Samuel* (Preaching Through the Bible, Sovereign World, 1995); R. F. Youngblood, '1 Samuel' in *The Expositor's Bible*, vol. 3 (Zondervan, 1992).

☐☐☐ Reading 28 (1 Samuel 1:1–3:21)

1. What significance did Hannah have in the kingdom of God? Are there any advantages in having an enemy?
2. Hannah's psalm looks out to wider matters than her own concerns. She glories in God's character, his holiness (2:2a), his uniqueness (2:2b), his reliability (2:2c), his knowledge (2:3c), his justice (2:3d). What other lessons has she learned that she is now singing about?
3. 'Those who honour me I will honour, but those who despise me will be disdained' (2:30). What dishonours God? How does God honour people in this chapter? God honours us by speaking to us. What else?

□□□ Reading 29 (1 Samuel 4:1–6:21)

1. When we experience defeat, do we need to enquire into the cause? Did the Philistines find a true answer?

2. What are the marks of religious superstition we find in these chapters? The ark was used as a kind of 'good luck charm'. How is this done today?

3. What are the differences between the Israelites and the Philistines? Who are the more sensible?

□□□ Reading 30 (1 Samuel 7:1–9:27)

1. After a time of stagnation in the story of Israel, God gave the nation a chance for renewal and restoration. What can we learn from Samuel about rebuilding a nation – or a church?

2. As Samuel got older, the need of a new leadership began to be obvious. Could the blessing be inherited by his sons? Apparently not. Did the people have the answer? If not, how then can good leadership be found?

3. Saul is famous for ruining his life. Yet in 1 Samuel 9:1–27 we discover how well he started out. What are the signs of his sincerity and spirituality at this time? How does God honour us when we are free from manipulation?

□□□ Reading 31 (1 Samuel 10:1–12:25)

1. Three things were on Saul's mind at the time of his being chosen as Israel's king: his need to find the asses, his financial need and the question whether he would have the ability to do the work of a king. How were his need met – and what do we deduce concerning our own needs?

2. The new king immediately shows some signs of God-given maturity and wisdom. He has learned to control his tongue (10:13–16). What else?

3. Have you ever done something that you then bitterly regretted? Israel made a mistake in demanding a king. How did Samuel help them?

□□□ Reading 32 (1 Samuel 13:1–14:52)

1. King Saul began his kingship well, but this changes in 1 Samuel 13:1–23. Apparently there was an arrangement similar to the one mentioned in 1 Samuel 10:8. Samuel had promised to come to consecrate the army to God. But Saul is getting panicky. What led Saul into disobedience? What leads us into disobedience?

2. Jonathan cannot bear the thought of the people of God being in continual defeat. He strikes a blow for freedom. Consider his faith and how it worked out. What made him start? What made him continue? How does faith work out in difficult times?

3. Saul does not appear well in this account. What are the signs that Saul is out of touch with God? What sometimes leads us to lose our clarity of mind?

☐☐☐ Reading 33 (1 Samuel 15:1–16:23)

1. Now comes a further stage in the fall of Saul, one in which he ruined his life. How did it happen? What should we be careful to avoid if we wish to escape Saul's fate?

2. It does not say 'the LORD has rejected you'; it says, 'the LORD has rejected you from being king'. Is the difference important? What could Saul have done?

3. In 1 Samuel 16:1–23, Samuel was depressed. His life's work had been to find a king for Israel, but his life's work had gone wrong. How does God help Samuel? Are things as bad as he thinks? How do we handle depression – especially in old age?

☐☐☐ Reading 34 (1 Samuel 17:1–18:30)

1. David was a nobody – a teenager whom no one thought could be king. But how do nobodies become significant in the kingdom of God? What prepared the way? What training did David get?

2. David was back with the sheep (see 17:15) and still 'only a boy' (17:33). What 'coincidences' took place to change his entire life? How important is timing in our lives? If it is important then how do we live with God's timing?

3. Everyone saw the same giant Goliath, heard the same thundering threats, yet David viewed them differently. In what sense is faith a matter of seeing things differently?

☐☐☐ Reading 35 (1 Samuel 19:1–21:15)

1. David must have felt that he had had more than enough of troubles. Does God sometimes put us through one level of trouble only as the first stage to put us through something more intense? How does this happen with David? What is the purpose of it?

2. A new phase in David's life begins. How did he cope with the changes from his anointing by Samuel, his rise to fame and popularity, and now to be nothing but a fugitive? But are there compensations when God tests us to the limit?

3. In the midst of troubles we are likely to make mistakes. David is going through a bad patch. He has run away. Some readers might be critical of him. He has spent nights out in the open air. He is tired. What else distressed him? What would you have done? Sometimes David lied! When Jesus referred to this time in David's life (Mark 2:25) what did he have to say?

☐☐☐ Reading 36 (1 Samuel 22:1–24:22)

1. God knows how to give us a break when we are desperate. How did he do it for David? In what way does David begin to act like a future king? How does God train us for our future work for him?
2. At about 1 Samuel 23:29, David is getting close – although he did not know it – to the days when he will be the king. Some more aspects of his training stand out. David was given the work of a king before he was given the title of a king. What else?
3. Leaders are inclined to be aggressive, pushy people. They would not be leaders if they were not made that way. But for such people – and all of us – there is a need to develop a more gracious spirit. It was precisely this lesson that David has to learn. How did he learn it?

☐☐☐ Reading 37 (1 Samuel 25:1–26:25)

1. Perhaps David thought that he had learned how to show mercy. But Nabal is deliberately provocative and insulting. What did David still have to learn? Do we ever think we have learned something when we are only halfway to where God wants us?
2. In what ways does Abigail shine out as a truly great person? Like the rudder of a great ship, the tongue can steer us to where we truly ought to go (see James 3:4). How does Abigail illustrate James' point?
3. In what ways did Nabal ('Fool') live up to his name? What leads us (for have we never been like Nabal?) to be so foolish?

☐☐☐ Reading 38 (1 Samuel 27:1–29:11)

1. David is actually at the end of his troubles with Saul, yet he does not know it. He does a foolish thing when he joins the Philistines. Why do we sometimes act foolishly when we are very close to spiritual blessing? What are the ingredients of his foolishness?
2. David was living a double life. What led him into this? How did God get him out of it? David was at his worst just before God gave him the kingdom. Does God ever bless us when we are at our worst? What might be the reason?

3. Saul had been rejected from the kingship. He had lost his usefulness, his joy. What else? What could Saul have done to recover? In despair he tries to get access to Samuel by going to a woman who has given herself over to contact with evil spirits. Samuel says, 'You and your sons will be with me' (28:19). In what ways is this a statement of great mercy? What do we learn about 'being saved through fire'?

□□□ **Reading 39 (1 Samuel 30:1–31:13)**

1. David goes back to the town that was given him by the Philistines, Ziklag, only to find that the Amalekites had invaded the town (30:1–3). The entire army was shattered and grief-stricken (30:4). How does God use calamity in our lives? How did God use this event in the life of David? What were the marks of his recovery?

2. After we recover, how does God encourage us? After David had recovered, how did God encourage him?

3. Is there an illustration of 1 Corinthians 12:25 here?

4. The 'backslider' is sometimes left alone by God. How do we see this illustrated in Saul? The psalmist could say 'I called on the LORD in distress' (Psalm 118:5). Why could Saul not do the same?

Galatians

The first Christians were all Jews. When totally pagan people in Antioch turned in large numbers to the Lord Jesus Christ around AD 45, it caused a whole host of questions for the Jewish Christians. Did gentiles need some kind of preliminary course in which the men would be circumcised and they and their families become Jews – in order to become Christians? Do Christians have to be culturally Jewish?

Barnabas sought the help of Saul of Tarsus (AD 46?), and a year or more later, after a prophetic prediction of famine in Jerusalem, the Antiochene Christians sent a gift to the Jerusalem church, asking Saul and Barnabas to take it (Acts 11:30). It is likely that Galatians 2:1–10 tells of a meeting that Paul had with the Jerusalem leaders at this time (AD 47?). A serious rift could have arisen if their approach to gentile Christians were the subject of disagreement. But Paul's ministry was accepted as genuine. Gentiles were not required to keep the Mosaic requirements that were demanded of Jews.

After Paul's return from his second visit to Jerusalem, the church of Antioch sent out Barnabas and Paul to preach to gentiles in lands to the north. In the spring of AD 47 they went by boat to Cyprus and then on to the cities of (northern) Antioch, Iconium, Lystra and Derbe, preaching and founding new churches. These are cities of south Galatia. Many came to faith in Christ; the Spirit was poured out on them (Galatians 3:3–4). Miracles took place (Galatians 3:5). They were greatly rejoicing in their new salvation and spoke much about their blessedness (Galatians 4:15).

No one said anything about the Mosaic law! Then Paul and Barnabas came back to Antioch and reported what had happened. Their trip must have taken about a year (AD 47–48).

When Paul got back to Antioch, a problem had arisen. 'Judaisers' from Jerusalem were starting to urge gentile Christians to live under the Mosaic law. They did not like Paul and wanted to undermine Paul's influence in Galatia. Then Peter paid a visit to Antioch as recorded in Galatians 2:11–14. For a while he had easy fellowship with the gentile Christians. He was not living according to Jewish food-regulations. However the news of Peter's behaviour was causing a strong reaction from the conservative Christians at Jerusalem. Peter's well-known about-turn took place and Paul had to rebuke Peter in words that are summarised in Galatians 2:11–14.

At about this time (AD 48?) Paul received news that conservative semi-Christians had very swiftly moved into his work at Galatia, and were agitating there more than ever. Paul received news that they had reached southern Galatia and were troubling the churches that had been founded only a year previously. The successes of the gentile mission were scandalising the conservative imitation-Christian Jews, and they were visiting gentile Christians to propagate their teaching, both in Jerusalem and in southern Galatia. The Galatians had become suspicious of Paul, doubting his apostleship and suspecting that he was (as the Judaisers said) a corrupter of the original Jerusalem gospel. The problem was a major one.

This is how it came about that in AD 48 and early 49 Paul did two things to resist the 'Judaisers'. He wrote his letter to the Galatians to the churches of southern Galatia, and he went to Jerusalem for the famous consultation of Acts 15:1–41.

Recommended reading: D. K. Campbell, 'Galatians', in *The Bible Knowledge Commentary* (ed. J. F. Walwoord and R. B. Zuck, Victor Books, 1983).

□□□ **Reading 40 (Galatians 1:1–24)**
Paul introduces himself (1:1–5), denounces false teaching (1:6–10) and moves to the first main section where he outlines the story of his apostolic independence (1:11–2:15).

1. Paul can be very yielding and undogmatic (note Romans 14:1–23, especially verse 5). Why does he not say 'let everyone be convinced in their own mind' in Galatians 1:1–24? May we ever use language like Paul's? If so, in what circumstances?

2. Paul resisted the gospel for some time. What were the human causes of his unbelief (as he describes it)? Why do people reject the gospel?

3. Paul is going to great lengths to show (i) that he truly is an apostle on a level with Peter, James and John and (ii) that his message – while based upon the same facts and being basically the same as the preaching of the other apostles – is somewhat independent of theirs. It goes beyond the preaching of the apostles before about AD 50. So what aspects of Paul's teaching go further than the teaching of the others?

☐☐☐ Reading 41 (Galatians 2:1–21)

Paul tells of another visit to Jerusalem (2:1–10). Everyone agreed that salvation was through faith in Jesus and that the Mosaic system of life was not necessary for gentiles. But during a visit to Antioch, Peter backed away from the agreement (2:11–14). The Judaisers thought that godliness was a matter of holding to their Jewish culture. In Galatians 2:15–5:12, Paul re-states his gospel. After a basic statement (2:15–21) he adds numerous explanations and arguments.

1. How is Peter's mistake made in modern churches? Did Peter change his gospel? Or was he only afraid to live it out in relation to gentiles? Why do some religious people inspire such fear that even an apostle is afraid of them?

2. Are there two types of sinner (2:15–16)? What is the way of salvation, according to 2:16?

3. Galatians 2:17 (however interpreted in detail) asks: Does this gospel lead to sin? What kind of gospel is *vulnerable* to the charge of moral carelessness?

☐☐☐ Reading 42 (Galatians 3:1–29)

Paul develops 2:15–21 with a string of arguments and explanations. There is an argument from experience (Galatians 3:1–5), and from the story of Abraham (3:6–14). What was given through Moses does not cancel what was given through Abraham (3:15–18). The law was only an interim-measure (3:19–22) until Christian faith came in fullness (3:23–25). Now every believer is a son of God through faith (3:26–29). Believers are no longer servile but full adult sons (4:1–7). They should not turn back to old Mosaic ways (4:8–11). Paul appeals to them (4:12–20). The story of Abraham and Hagar illustrates the folly of turning to the flesh (4:21–5:1). They should not abandon their freedom (5:2–12).

1. Is our experience of the Spirit really an *experience* or something we 'take by faith'?
2. How does Abraham's story show what is the gospel?
3. If the gospel could exist without the Mosaic system, why was the Mosaic system added to what believers already had in the days of Abraham?

□□□ Reading 43 (Galatians 4:1–5:1)

1. Old Testament believers (says Paul) were like children in a wealthy home. When they grow up they no longer need to be ordered around by the servants. Are there still Christians who are like 'Old Testament believers' in their timidity? What does it mean to be a 'grown-up' son or daughter of God?
2. How did Jesus redeem believers from being in bondage to the Mosaic system?
3. How does the story of Abraham's relationship with Hagar illustrate the folly of turning back to ways of the Mosaic law?

□□□ Reading 44 (Galatians 5:2–25)

Galatians 5:13 starts a new major section. Paul wants his people to be free from the law, but he has to explain that there is a way of godliness that involves not the law but the Holy Spirit. The new life is a life of love (5:13–15), led by the Holy Spirit (5:16–25). It is bearing the burden not of the Mosaic law but of each other (5:16–6:10). Galatians 6:11–18 brings Paul's letter to a close with a final appeal.

1. Paul urges the Galatians not to abandon their freedom (5:2–12). What kind of freedom is he thinking of? Circumcision only? The Mosaic law as a way of justification and new birth? The Mosaic system as a way of sanctification? The Mosaic law as a culture and way of relating to people? Or does he have all of these on his mind? How does 5:3–4 help us to answer these questions? What are the implications for the way we live day by day?
2. If we are not under Mosaic law, how is love to receive guidance? Can love be described in words? If so, whose words? What words?
3. If we are pulled one way by the flesh and another way by the Spirit, which 'pull' will win and how do we live the Christian life?

□□□ Reading 45 (Galatians 5:26–6:18)

1. In what way (if at all) should the Christian life be burdensome?

2. Does it matter how we live? If we are eternally free from condemnation, what is there to motivate the Christian to godly living?

3. How is our attitude towards the cross the test of our spiritual understanding? Are there versions of the gospel that do not glory in the cross?

Nehemiah

The book of Ezra-Nehemiah is a collection of documents, all of which deal with the way in which many Israelites were called back to the land of Israel to restart the work of God from the 530s BC onwards. The whole book could have been compiled at any point after the last years of Darius II (423–404 BC). There is nothing in it that compels a date after about 400 BC. Nehemiah himself is a model of leadership. More than anyone other than Jesus, he is an example of a man who got things done for God.

In the year 538 BC the new Persian ruler Cyrus allowed the exiles to go back to Israel.

During 538–516 BC the returned people sought to get the temple rebuilt. This is the main subject of Ezra 1:1–6:22 (except for a digression in 4:6–23).

Events in Xerxes' reign, 486–465 BC, are mentioned (in a digression) only in Ezra 4:6.

Events in Artaxerxes' reign, 464–424 BC, are mentioned (in a digression) in Ezra 4:7–23.

The gap between Ezra 6:22 and Ezra 7:1 involves a jump of nearly sixty years. In 458 BC Ezra comes to Jerusalem. This is the main subject of Ezra 7–10.

Then in the book of Nehemiah we read of the conversation of Nehemiah with his king (1:1–4). It took place in about 446 BC, twelve years after Ezra came to Jerusalem. Most of the book of Nehemiah tells of what happened in the months that followed, in 445 BC.

Recommended reading: M. A. Eaton, *Ezra, Nehemiah, Esther* (Preaching Through the Bible, Sovereign World, 2002); D. Kidner, *Ezra and Nehemiah* (Tyndale Commentary, IVP, 1979).

☐☐☐ Reading 46 (Nehemiah 1:1–3:32)

1. In one way or another, every Christian is a 'leader'. Every Christian has some area where God has given them scope for taking initiative. How was Nehemiah being prepared for a call from God? What ways is God likely to use in bringing us into his service?
2. Where does prayer fit in as God is calling us into his service? What are the characteristics of Nehemiah's prayer? Notice the different kind of prayer in 2:4.
3. Prayer is to be combined with programme. What practicalities did Nehemiah follow?

☐☐☐ Reading 47 (Nehemiah 4:1–6:14)

1. God's work is likely to face opposition. What does Nehemiah do to overcome and win through?
2. Many of God's people were facing severe financial stress (5:1–2), and this was leading to exploitation. In what ways was Nehemiah a social reformer? Why are there few Christian social reformers nowadays? Should preachers become social reformers? If not, who?
3. As well as intimidation (4:1–23), and the threatened break in fellowship (5:1–19), Nehemiah himself faced distraction (6:1–14). How did he deal with it? In what ways must we handle the same problem?

☐☐☐ Reading 48 (6:15–9:37)

1. Nehemiah 6:15–7:4 brings this part of the story to a conclusion and then 7:5–73 lists the families that were qualified to be part of the 'new Jerusalem'. It was necessary to guard God's city. The Tobiah-party wanted to compromise with the surrounding pagans because they would make good business associates. What sort of people do these represent in the modern world?
2. It was necessary to fill God's city with willing workers. Gatekeepers, singers and Levites were brought in (7:1). Can we find equivalents in today's world to the willing workers of Nehemiah's times?
3. Life in the 'new Jerusalem' is to be life guided by the written word of God. How does Ezra bring it about?

☐☐☐ **Reading 49 (Nehemiah 9:38–11:36)**

1. Often in the ancient world 'covenants' (that is, promises made more secure by the taking of an oath) would begin with a sketch of the relationship between the two partners in the covenant. The prayer of 9:5–38 is a summary as well as a prayer and tells how Israel and God have related to each other. The essence of the covenant is the oath itself (10:29). How is the new covenant via Jesus different in promises, in relationship to God, in requirements?

2. Nehemiah was avoiding disputes in 11:1–36. How should we do the same?

3. Some Jews had to serve God in a place where they did not want to be. What does this say to us? What was God's purpose?

☐☐☐ **Reading 50 (Nehemiah 12:1–13:31)**

Nehemiah 12 consists of lists of priests of various kinds.

1. What are the differences between Old Covenant and New Covenant that we might consider from this chapter? Who are 'priests' today (judged by the New Testament)? How does one generation of God's servants arise from the previous generation? If not by tribe or physical descent, then how?

2. In God's work it is necessary to protect our distinctive message. How does this principle show itself at the end of the book of Nehemiah?

3. If Ezra-Nehemiah were a novel or a movie it would have ended with Ezra and Nehemiah triumphantly marching round on the tops of the walls and the story would have closed with the implication that the nation would go on triumphantly and the people would live happily ever after. But life is not like that! In what way is Nehemiah 13:1–31 a call to us to be realistic?

Psalms 89:1–102:28

□□□ **Reading 51 (Psalms 89:1–90:17)**

1. God's oath (the central ingredient in a covenant) 'fixes' the divine purpose. Threats may be turned aside by repentance *before* an oath of wrath. Promises may be lost by unbelief unless they are made certain by God's oath. Psalm 89:1–52 reflects on the stability of God's covenant-oath. What was God promising to David? Why could it not be lost? What would happen if David's line sinned?
2. Psalm 89:1–52 seems to contain both great promises and yet severe disappointments and troubles. How do we use God's promises when they seem to be unfulfilled?
3. In Psalm 90:1–17, what is the secure dwelling-place of the believer (90:1–2)? But what threatens the human race in Psalm 90:3–6? And in 90:7–11? Verses 12–17 follow the thought by giving us five or six prayers (12, 13, 14, 15, 16–17). What is the heart of the prayers we should pray for ourselves when we become conscious of how fast time is passing by?

□□□ **Reading 52 (Psalms 91:1–92:15)**

1. Is Psalm 91:1–16 only a generalisation? Or is it true only when life after death is taken into account? Is it a statement of faith or of experience? How can we draw comfort from this psalm?
2. Psalm 91:14–16 describes a very privileged person. What is said to

261

such a person? And what is said about such a person?

3. In Psalm 92:1–15 an individual is praising God (note 'me' and 'my' in 92:4, 10, 11, 15) on the Jewish Sabbath (as the psalm title says). So what should our times of individual prayer be like?

☐☐☐ **Reading 53 (Psalms 93:1–94:23)**
Psalms 93:1–100:5 are all songs about God's king reigning in Jerusalem.

1. In Psalm 93:1–5, God is robed as a king (93:1–2), despite storms that rage against him (93:3–4). Verse 5 deduces two lessons based upon the mighty stability of God. What are they and how should they affect our lives today?

2. God is King over the earth and over his enemies (94:1–3). But what are the difficulties we face? In verse 4? Verses 5–6? Verse 7?

3. Psalm 94:8–23 considers the comforts and strengths that come to us because God is King. What are they in verses 9–11? In verses 12–15? In verses 16–19? In verses 20–23? How then do we cope with life's storms?

☐☐☐ **Reading 54 (Psalms 95:1–96:13)**

1. In Psalm 95:1–11, the theme of kingship continues. God is the King over all gods. First comes a call to joyful praise (95:1–2). God is great in creation (95:3–6) and in his care for his people (95:7a–7c). But God wants a response to his greatness (95:7d–11). What does it mean to 'test' God? What kind of a response does he want from us?

2. In Psalm 96:1–13, we are invited not only to sing to God (96:1–2a, 7–9) but also to tell out to others near and far what we know of God (96:2b–3, 10). Our message is God's supremacy over all rivals (96:4–6), his right to judge all peoples on earth (96:11–13). In these days of pluralism, what should we tell the nations about the God and Father of our Lord Jesus Christ? How do we do it? But is the world so 'pluralist', or is there more tyranny than 'pluralism' suggests?

3. What does the psalmist mean by 'the beauty of holiness'? The phrase alludes to the beauty of the priests' clothing, but is it only clothing that is in mind? What kind of 'beauty' does God want from us? What if we feel unworthy?

☐☐☐ **Reading 55 (Psalms 97:1–100:5)**

1. The king of Psalms 93:1–96:13 is a king who establishes righteousness – as Psalm 97:1–12 emphasises. 'Righteousness and justice are the

foundation of his throne' (97:2). What do we feel, what should we feel, as we consider a God of burning and purifying righteousness? What does God's righteousness mean for the ungodly? What does it mean for the people of God?

2. 'Sing!' says Psalm 98:1–3. 'Shout, make a noise!' says Psalm 98:4–6. 'Let the whole earth join in!' says Psalm 98:7–9. What is biblical worship like, really? Is it quiet, respectable? Is it noisy, exuberant? But, more important: What do we shout about?

3. Psalm 99:1–9 is gripped by the thought of God's holiness. Psalm 99:1–3 ends with 'Holy is he!' Psalm 99:4–5 ends with the same words. Psalm 99:6–9 ends with: 'but the LORD our God is holy'. But is not God's holiness scary (note 99:1a)? So how (according to the psalm) can people like Jacob, Moses, Aaron, Samuel (99:4, 6) – and you and I – be close to such a holy God?

☐☐☐ Reading 56 (Psalms 101:1–102:28)

1. What are the personal standards to which the king of Israel was to be committed (Psalm 101:1–8)? How are they fulfilled in Jesus?

2. Consider the first two verses of Psalm 102. Do we need, in this way, to ask God to hear us? Maybe we do – for our sakes more than for God. How sympathetic is God to our pleas and tears?

3. It seems the psalmist's agonies were caused by his own foolishness (for in 102:10 he refers to God's anger). But in such a state, how do we pray? The psalmist turns his attention away from himself. What does he pray for instead?

Ephesians

The letter to the Ephesians was probably written by Paul when he was in prison in Rome in the early AD 60s. If Romans is his most basic letter, Ephesians is his most mind-expanding letter. It was probably originally a circular letter; it contains no greetings. Its theme is the vastness of God's plan to bring all things into unity under the Lord Jesus Christ. Paul wants his readers to see the exceeding greatness of God's power in creating the Christian church out of both Jewish and gentile peoples (see 1:18–19; 3:8, 18, 19, 20, all of which emphasise the greatness of what God has done for us in Christ).

Recommended reading: M. A. Eaton, *Ephesians* (Preaching Through the Bible, Sovereign World, 2002).

☐☐☐ Reading 57 (Ephesians 1:1–23)

After an introduction (1:1–2), the letter opens with a burst of praise for the marvellous blessings of salvation (1:3–14).

1. What did God do for us before history began? What does he do for us in this age? What is his plan for the future?

2. In Ephesians 1:15, Paul begins to pray. Do people who have already come to salvation still need further enlightenment? What three things (1:18–19a) does Paul pray for and what does each one mean? Should we pray for ourselves and others in this way?

3. How is God's power seen in the resurrection of Christ? What was Christ raised from? What is Christ raised to? What is the connection (according to 1:19) between God's power at work in Christ and God's power at work in us?

□□□ Reading 58 (Ephesians 2:1–22)

In Ephesians 1:19b–2:22, Paul develops the theme of the exceeding great power of God. It is seen in Christ (1:19b–23), in the raising of the Christian to newness of life (2:1–10) and in the creation of the Church as 'one new man' (2:11–22).

1. How is God's great power seen in the lives of individual Christians? What were we like before? What did God do for us? Where are we now?

2. According to 2:8–10 how did the great change from death to life take place in the life of the Christian? Why do we have to give the honour for the change to God alone?

3. How is God's great power seen in the creation of the church, the body of Christ? What was the position of gentiles? What did God do for them? What is the position of gentile Christians now?

□□□ Reading 59 (Ephesians 3:1–21)

1. In Ephesians 3:1–21, Paul starts to resume his prayer (from 1:19a) but then immediately digresses again and does not pick up his prayer until 3:15. In the digression he is explaining his own ministry (3:2–13). What is it that was new and distinctive about the ministry of the apostle Paul?

2. If Christians already have Christ living in them and are sealed by the Holy Spirit, what exactly is Paul praying for in 3:15–19? What would it be like for this prayer to be answered in our own lives?

3. Paul closes this section of his letter with something that is both a prayer and an encouragement. How is 3:20–21 related to the prayer of 1:15–19a; 3:1, 15–19? How is it greatly encouraging?

□□□ Reading 60 (Ephesians 4:1–5:2)

From Ephesians 4:1 onwards Paul calls the Christians to put their knowledge of God into practice in their lives. In agreement with God's mighty plan, the first matter he deals with is the unity of the fellowship in the church (4:1–16). He calls them to holiness in general terms, dealing with what they must not be (4:17–19) and what they should be

(4:20–24). Then he comes to details: truth (4:25), anger (4:26–27), stealing (4:28), talk (4:29–30), kindness (4:31–5:2), common sins (5:3–7).

1. 'I beseech you therefore . . .' (4:1). What is the New Testament way of asking for godly living?
2. What are the reasons why Paul pleads for the *unity* of the Christians in Ephesians 4:1–16? And what are the reasons why he pleads for the *variety* of the Christians?
3. In what ways should the Ephesians break away from what they have been in days gone by (4:17–19)? What are the new ingredients in their lives (4:20–24)?

□□□ Reading 61 (Ephesians 5:3–21)

1. In Ephesians 5:8–14 and 5:15–21, Paul has two more ways of appealing for godly living. What are they?
2. In Ephesians 5:5, is Paul questioning the salvation of his Christian readers? He knows that the true Christian might fall into sins such as these (otherwise why raise the matter at all?). His tenses are present tenses. What is his point?
3. Ephesians 5:7 moves to a warning about the future. In what way can the coming anger of God affect sinning Christians?

□□□ Reading 62 (Ephesians 5:22–6:9)

1. In Ephesians 5:22–6:9, Paul comes to deal with relationships. Christian godliness involves relating skilfully to people who are close to us: husbands, wives, children, parents, workers, employees. What are the special difficulties of these relationships? Paul says one thing to each group. What is it in each case?
2. Paul's instruction in 5:22–6:9 shows that he is concerned about Christian families. Yet Paul had no family himself. Was he qualified to speak on such matters? How much may a preacher's teaching go beyond their own experience? Is there a perfect husband? A perfect wife? A perfect parent? How do we cope with failure in these areas?
3. Of all 'conditions of employment', slaves in the Roman empire had what must be among the worst! How much of Paul's advice may we use today?

□□□ Reading 63 (Ephesians 6:10–24)

Paul cannot end his letter just yet. He has been appealing for the Christians to live godly lives, yet there is a complication – the devil!

1. What is the difference between the call to 'be strong' (6:10) and the call to put on the Christian armour (6:11)? How do we obey the first command? Is the order significant?
2. Does it help us (if so, how?) to know that opposition to the Christian life does not come from 'flesh and blood'?
3. There are six pieces of armour. Three items of equipment are envisaged as already being worn. Three pieces of armour have to be put on in addition to the first three. What do these pieces of armour represent? Is there a reason why when speaking of prayer (6:18–20), Paul does not use a piece of armour (a spear?) as an illustration of prayer?

Psalms 103:1 –109:31

☐☐☐ **Reading 64 (Psalms 103:1–104:35)**

1. Psalm 103:1–5 speaks of the character of God as it has been experienced by the psalmist. The central section is 103:6–18. Psalm 103:19–22 summons the universe (ending with himself) to praise God. What good things does God do for us and to us? How do they reveal his character? Why does David talk to himself?

2. Psalm 104:1–35 could be called a poet's version of Genesis 1:1–31. The psalmist is following the order of items mentioned in Genesis. What does God's love of his own creation (Genesis 1:31) and the psalmist's love of God's creation (Psalm 104:1–35) mean to the modern reader? How should we respond to what God has done for us in creation?

3. What are the purposes of creation as we can see them in Psalm 104:1–35?

☐☐☐ **Reading 65 (105:1–107:43)**

1. Psalm 105:1–45 surveys God's dealings with his people. The psalmist considers the days following Abraham (105:7–11), the time of wandering in Canaan (105:12–15), and so on. What do we learn of the goodness of God from these different times? How are God's people asked to respond to him?

2. Psalm 106:1–48 has similarities to Psalm 105:1–45. It tells of the many wonders God performed in the early history of Israel. But this psalm has greater emphasis on the failures of God's people. What are the results when God's people respond with unbelief and forgetfulness?

3. Psalm 107:1–43 describes the various threats that God's people face and describes their prayers and God's answers. There are four pictures in 107:4–9, 10–16, 17–22, 23–32 describing four typical calamities. How do they picture four problems we all might have? How do God's people reach safety and provision?

☐☐☐ Reading 66 (Psalms 108:1–109:31)

1. The psalmist begins by being determined to praise God (108:1–3). He tells us his reason for his determination (108:4) and prays for God to be exalted (108:5). Why do the psalmists often speak with a note of firm determination ('I will give thanks . . .')? Were they tempted to give up praising God? How much should we decide in advance to praise God whether we are 'in the mood' or not?

2. How should we respond to our enemies according to Psalm 109:4? The psalm is notable for its fierce prayers in verses 6–19. But should we not admire and copy verse 4? So is David really vindictive? Acts 1:20 applies Psalm 109:8 to Judas. So how should we take the psalm? Is it a case of David speaking in the Spirit words which only the pure and holy Lord Jesus Christ could pray?

3. What does the psalmist want most in 109:20–31? How can we be like him when we find ourselves in a situation where we are being badly treated?

Luke's Gospel

Luke, the author of Luke's Gospel, was a friend and colleague of the apostle Paul. Tradition says that he was a Syrian from Antioch, a gentile who remained unmarried and lived to an old age. Luke obviously made use of Mark's Gospel in writing his own Gospel. He nearly always follows the same order of material that is to be found in Mark's Gospel; only he compresses Mark's stories, leaves some out and adds much material of his own. His special interest is the grace of God to the needy, and he takes special note of Jesus' teaching concerning prayer.

Recommended reading: M. A. Eaton, *Luke 1–11*; *Luke 12–24* (Preaching Through the Bible, Sovereign World, 1999, 2000); J. C. Ryle, *Expository Thoughts on the Gospels: Luke* (various reprints are available).

☐☐☐ Reading 67 (Luke 1:1–25)

1. Luke 1:1–4 is Luke's own introduction. What were Luke's sources? What was his method of research? What was his purpose in writing?
2. As Zechariah is about his duties, he receives an unexpected answer to prayer. But how does he respond? And what does God think about his response? Should we ever give up expecting something we are praying for? If so, when? If not, why not?
3. What are the similarities between Elijah and John the Baptist? Is there such a thing as an 'Elijah ministry'? If so, what is it?

☐☐☐ Reading 68 (Luke 1:26–38)

1. Luke 1:26–38 was undoubtedly the greatest moment in the life of Mary, the mother of Jesus. God seems to like to give surprises. In what ways was this event surprising? It was a miracle. What else?

2. Why is Mary afraid? Are we unnecessarily afraid of God?

3. How much suffering was there in the lives of Zechariah and Elizabeth? And in the lives of Joseph and Mary? Why should suffering and privilege be found in the same people?

☐☐☐ Reading 69 (Luke 1:39–56)

1. Mary goes from Nazareth to a city in Judah, about eighty to a hundred miles away (1:39). It is good to have fellowship with a believing friend. But what kind of believing friend should we choose?

2. The meeting between Mary and Elizabeth was a very special occasion. There are more things in heaven and on earth than our philosophy ever dreams of! Can God fill an unborn baby with the Holy Spirit? What is this 'filling' of the Holy Spirit here?

3. There is much music, worship and boldness of speech in this chapter. What causes the singing and what are the people singing about? Is this likely to happen to us?

☐☐☐ Reading 70 (Luke 1:57–80)

1. Zechariah had been severely chastened for his unbelief. For many months he had been unable to speak (1:20, 22) and unable to hear (as 1:62 suggests). He had been living in a world where he was cut off from people and had much time to think over what had happened. What were the lessons he had to learn? But is God's purpose altered? At what point does the 'punishment' end?

2. What should be the themes of our worship of God – judging by the song of 1:68–79?

3. What is so special about 'the oath which he swore to our father Abraham' (1:73)? Why does the song mention this point of Abraham's life? Can we expect God to take any oath about us?

☐☐☐ Reading 71 (Luke 2:1–21)

1. In a few verses we are told of the birth of Jesus. How do we see here Luke's special interest in history? Why is this important to him? Would it make any difference if the Gospels consisted of fictional stories teaching us spiritual lessons?

2. It was Roman rule that brought Mary to Bethlehem in fulfilment of

Micah 5:5. What must have Joseph and Mary have felt – being 'pushed around' by a colonial power? Does God have any purpose in the midst of political oppressions?

3. Jesus was not born in a palace with admiring attendants and servants. There was not the kind of publicity that we might expect. Why does God use such obscure people and places?

□□□ Reading 72 (Luke 2:22–52)

1. We read a lot about angels in this chapter (and elsewhere in the stories of Jesus' birth). What does this tell us about Jesus, and about what is happening here? How is Jesus being described? He is 'the Lord' whose way John the Baptist prepares (1:16, 17, 76). What other titles and descriptions are there?

2. Jesus grew in four ways. What does this tell us about Jesus' real human nature? What did it mean for him to grow spiritually?

3. When we read Luke 2:41–52, might we not sympathise with Mary here? Did the young Jesus experience a clash between his call to be God's servant and his call to obey his parents? How did he solve the problem?

□□□ Reading 73 (Luke 3:1–38)

1. Luke 3:1–2 finds six ways of pin-pointing exactly when it was that the ministry of Jesus began. Can you list them? Luke also has more references to the Holy Spirit in his Gospel than Matthew, Mark or John. What is the point of this double interest in history and the Holy Spirit?

2. In the days of John the Baptist, God acted to restore his people. How did he do it?

3. In John's baptism, the water symbolised the cleansing of sins. Getting oneself baptised expressed the fact that you were believing in John's message. It was an expression of repentance. Why did it create a community of prepared people? Does Christian water-baptism still have this function? What do the two baptisms say to onlookers? What do they say to the believer themself? What do they say to God?

□□□ Reading 74 (Luke 4:1–15)

1. Jesus was quite young – in his early thirties – when he spent time seeking God in the Judean wilderness. His being tested came immediately after his receiving the power of the Holy Spirit. What is the significance of the timing of Satan's attack?

2. Jesus was tempted by the devil for the whole of the period of forty days, but three particular temptations came at the end of his weeks of fasting, at a time when he was exceptionally hungry (4:2). First, there was the temptation to put his material welfare above the will of God (4:3–4). What were the other two?

3. How did Jesus withstand temptation? Are we able to do the same?

□□□ Reading 75 (Luke 4:16–44)

1. Luke 4:23 shows that this story is not the first event in Jesus' Galilean ministry. Luke wants us to know from the start that Jesus was rejected, even in his home town. At first the people were impressed (4:22). Yet Jesus went on to say that they were not really heeding what he was saying. Why is it that people find it difficult to believe God can be using someone they think they know well?

2. What are the people wanting from Jesus? What is Jesus wanting to give them? How often does our expectation disagree with what God wants to give?

3. Jesus stops mid-sentence. Isaiah 61:1–2 spoke of 'the Lord's favour' and 'the day of vengeance of our God'. But Jesus stopped in the middle of a sentence, and quite deliberately 'closed the book'! What is the significance of this?

□□□ Reading 76 (Luke 5:1–26)

1. Shortly after the time of Jesus' baptism, he had met Simon and had given him the name Cephas or Peter (John 1:35–40). Now it is several months later and Jesus has come to preach in Bethsaida where Peter has a fishing business. The incident had many lessons for Peter. What were they? And for us?

2. Peter's future ministry is defined as a new kind of fishing. David went from being a shepherd of sheep to being a shepherd-king of Israel. Peter went from fishing for fish to fishing for people. Does God use our past skills in a different manner when he brings us into his service? In what other ways might he do this?

3. Something happens that makes Jesus turn to prayer (5:16). The prayerfulness of Jesus is one of Luke's persistent themes (see 3:21, 22 already). What kind of incidents would make us want to pray?

☐☐☐ Reading 77 (Luke 5:27–39)

1. The conversion of Levi is one of the great conversion stories of the Bible. How great was his sin? How suddenly did he come to faith? Was there any preparation for it? In what ways is the story a model of conversion?

2. The Pharisees get upset when they see Jesus being so gracious. What is it about the grace of God that offends religious people?

3. The next story (5:33–39) is connected with the amazing grace of God that has just been seen in the life of Levi. Jesus' critics refer to three 'denominations': the disciples of John the Baptist; the Pharisees; and the disciples of Jesus (3:33). Why does Jesus not follow the ways of the other well-known religious movements in Israel? What do we think about new movements in the life of the Church? Should we try to prevent it from happening?

☐☐☐ Reading 78 (Luke 6:1–19)

The first phase of the Galilean ministry came to a climax when Jesus became popular, and yet was in danger of being killed by the Pharisees. About this time a second phase of Jesus' Galilean ministry begins (Luke 6:12–8:56). People came from all over the country to hear Jesus, from as far as Idumea in the south, from as far as Tyre and Sidon in the north (Mark 3:7–12). At this point Jesus chooses a high place among the hills to the north of the sea of Galilee. It is a less populated area and Jesus goes there to pray (6:12), to choose twelve disciples (6:12–16), to heal the sicknesses of his followers (6:17–19) and to teach them (6:20–49). Jesus' ministry to his disciples takes place at a lower part of the mountain where there is a level place. There he preaches the famous 'Sermon on the Mount', perhaps a block of teaching that lasted several days.

1. How much should we expect to pray for lengthy periods of time (note 6:12)?

2. From quite early on in his work, Jesus trained colleagues (6:13–16). What is his vision for the future? How much should modern churches follow Jesus' example here? What kind of training was Jesus providing?

3. Luke records that before the famous 'Sermon on the Mount' Jesus brought his disciples into a state of physical and mental peacefulness. How much should churches follow the example of Jesus in ministering to 'the whole person'? Can it be done?

□□□ Reading 79 (Luke 6:20–50)

The material of Luke 6:20–8:3 has no parallel in Mark's Gospel. The first part tells of the Sermon on the Mount but the extracts are not 100 per cent identical to those in Matthew's report of the same occasion.

1. How does Jesus lead his disciples to be free from snobbishness or class-consciousness?
2. Our attitude to poor people, our experience of need, our attitude to wealth or the lack of it have a lot to do with our experience of the kingdom. What might it mean to 'experience the kingdom'? What will help us or hinder us along the way?
3. There is blessing in the kingdom of God if its members are people of love (6:27–35). Practically, what kind of love is required of us?

□□□ Reading 80 (Luke 7:1–23)

Next Jesus heals a centurion's servant (7:1–10), raises a widow's son from the dead (7:11–17), answers a question from John the Baptist (7:18–35) and is anointed by one of his followers (7:36–50).

1. The story in 7:1–10 is a classic example of great faith. But do some believers have greater faith than others? What are the marks of great faith? How might my faith grow?
2. There are three occasions mentioned in the Gospels when Jesus raises someone from the dead. This one is the first. The other two are the raising of Jairus' daughter and the raising of Lazarus. What is unusual about this one? Did any needy person ask for it (as in 5:12)? Was the widow previously known to Jesus? Who was showing faith? So what do we learn from this unusual miracle?
3. If the miracle stories of Jesus are always (among other things) acted parables, what are the spiritual lessons of this one? Consider it as (i) a parable of revival. Revival is a sovereign act of God in which he restores his Church to life. (ii) Could it be taken as a parable of conversion? The whole human race is like a funeral procession! In what ways does the story illustrate the way Jesus gives life?

□□□ Reading 81 (Luke 7:24–50)

1. Jesus encourages John to go on believing. How does Jesus encourage us to persist in faith?
2. What were the strong points of John's character and ministry? He was notable for his firmness. What else?
3. John was not present on the Day of Pentecost. John was a great man

but anyone who came under the ministry of Jesus, who knew of the atoning death of Jesus and experienced the outpouring of the Holy Spirit by Jesus, would be in an altogether greater position. In what ways?

☐☐☐ Reading 82 (Luke 8:1–21)

1. The group of women in Luke 8:1–3 are not mentioned at this point by the other Gospel-writers. It was quite scandalous for women to leave home and family in order to travel with Jesus. So what must we think of Jesus' willingness to allow these women to serve him as they did? And what must we think of the women themselves? But if he allowed them a place in serving him, what must we think of the fact that he did not appoint one of them as an apostle?

2. What sort of 'soil' is the word of God being sown in? Hard? Rocky? Weedy? Or do we truly hear God as he speaks? What kind of soil are our friends? What kind of soil are we?

3. A sudden request comes to Jesus from Mary his mother, from James and Jude and his other half-brothers. Jesus used the occasion to make a point. Again Jesus is quite shocking (in 8:21). What was the point he wanted everyone to understand? Were his family offended? Maybe, but what do we think of the fact that James and Jude later wrote letters that are in our New Testament?

☐☐☐ Reading 83 (Luke 8:22–56)

1. The kingdom of God comes through persistent faith (8:13, 15). How does the story of the storm on the lake (8:22–25) make the same point?

2. What are we to think of the man who was rescued from evil spirits? What would it be like to stay with Jesus (8:38)? What would it be like to remain in the village after what had happened there? Is the mission Jesus gives him (8:39) the easy one or the hard one?

3. The woman with a discharge of blood touched Jesus (8:45), and Jesus touched the dead girl (8:54). To Jewish ways of thinking, death and emissions of blood spread pollution. If you touched such a person or if he touched you, you 'caught' the pollution. If Jesus wanted contact with sinners so much that he disregarded Jewish taboos, what will his attitude towards us be? What will Jesus do if we reach out to touch him – by faith?

☐☐☐ Reading 84 (Luke 9:1–20)

There is now a another tour of Galilee, like the ones in 4:42–44 and 8:1–3. This third mission (Luke 9:1–6) is undertaken by the apostles alone.

1. The apostles' ministry involved destroying the works of Satan. The disciples are sent out to extend the mission of Jesus. They are given power and authority over demons and over sicknesses, and they are sent out to preach the powerful reign of God and to heal (9:1–2). What is the relevance of such commands today? Does the Christian Church have authority to cast out demons? Do we heal the sick? Modern Christians must not pretend they are experiencing power on a level with what happened in New Testament times, yet could there yet come an age in the Church that is as great as the first generation?

2. What else was involved in the apostolic mission? Preaching (9:6)? What is 'preaching'? Simplicity of life (9:3)? How are these instructions relevant for us?

3. When should Christian workers look for support from others (as is implied in Luke 9:3) and when should they *avoid* looking for support from others (as in 1 Corinthians 9:12b, 18)?

☐☐☐ Reading 85 (Luke 9:21–43)

1. Jesus tells the disciples how to 'come after' him (in the pathway from suffering to glory). 'If anyone wants . . .' Why does he speak so individualistically ('If anyone', not 'If you all'). Under the law, no one had much choice but to obey. But Jesus says, 'If anyone wants . . .' What is Jesus' way of encouraging his disciples to live the life of serving God?

2. What is Jesus' way (in 9:24–27) of motivating his disciples?

3. Peter seems to have wanted to keep Jesus, Moses and Elijah on the mountain-top for a long time (9:33) but he was speaking in ignorance. Why did the cloud obscure the view? Why did the two lesser figures disappear? Why did the event not take a long time? Do we have 'mountain-top' experiences like this – in spiritual experience if not in physical location? If so, in what ways does the story help us to know what to expect?

☐☐☐ Reading 86 (Luke 9:44–62)

1. Jesus is increasingly warning his disciples that his work in this world involves his going to the cross to die. Imagine you were writing a biography of someone who lived until he was about thirty-three years old. Would you be dealing with how he came to die when you

were less than halfway through the biography? Why is the cross of Christ so important?

2. Do you want to be 'great'? What are the marks of greatness in verses 46–48? In verses 49–50?

3. Jesus is ready to die in Jerusalem. He travels there by a twisting and turning route (avoiding Herod). Everything in Luke 9:51–18:14 happened at some stage on the lengthy journey. On the way he enters a Samaritan village but they reject him because they hear he is going to Jerusalem (Luke 9:52–53). The Samaritans hated Jerusalem. What is the disciples' response to rejection? What is Jesus' response to rejection? What is your response to rejection?

☐☐☐ Reading 87 (Luke 10:1–20)

As Jesus travels towards Jerusalem, he appoints seventy-two co-workers to go ahead of him (or perhaps seventy; the manuscripts vary). They will announce Jesus' message and his coming visit to them. There are some things that are unique about the sending out of the seventy-two workers; later on some of his instructions would be changed (see 22:35–38). Yet there is also much that we can learn about our own calling today.

1. Our task in this world involves outreach. What does this mean in practice? If Christians are not to be static, what changes would have to come into our lives?

2. Jesus gives us some practical help in knowing how to extend his reign. The disciples are to go out as thirty-six pairs of workers (10:1). Why is isolation in such work risky?

3. For the moment Jesus' workers must travel light. They carry no spare cash, no spare equipment or provisions. They must trust God for everything. Soon Jesus will be giving them fresh instructions (see Luke 22:35; Acts 1:8). Why were they specially being called to travel with little at this point? When are we in a similar situation?

☐☐☐ Reading 88 (Luke 10:21–42)

1. Jesus makes a statement about himself. Who is Jesus – in himself and in God's plan – according to 10:22?

2. It is important to realise that the question about 'inheriting eternal life' (10:25) is asking about something greater than one's initial experience of salvation. It is a larger matter than being 'justified'. Inheritance is reward. It is fully reaping the benefits of salvation. What is Jesus' first answer (10:26b)? At this point, what is Jesus encouraging us to do?

3. Which part of the law would we quote in answer to the question, 'What must I do to enter into everything God has for me?'? How does love lead to life?

4. What was so good about the good Samaritan? He had no religious qualifications. He had no theological qualifications. He had nothing to commend himself in the eyes of the average Jew. But he did not run away when he came across a situation of need. What else?

□□□ Reading 89 (Luke 11:1–26)

1. Jesus does not say much about the externalities of prayer, the posture or place or the type of language that should be used. He spoke mainly about what we should pray for (11:2–4), the character of true prayer (11:5–10), the willingness of God to hear us (11:11–12) and the greatest gift to pray for (11:13). What was his teaching on these four aspects of prayer?

2. People who say they believe in the miraculous but then are confronted with the miraculous may well attribute the events they see to Satan. How does Jesus respond to the claim that he is demonically empowered (11:17–26)? How do we tell whether something that seems to be miraculous is truly from God or not?

3. Two ingredients are needed if we are to have a close relationship to Jesus. What are they (11:28)? Are they distinct or are they tied together always?

□□□ Reading 90 (Luke 11:27–54)

1. Jesus was not a very 'religious' person. He loved God, but he was not concerned to keep a multiplicity of regulations about how to eat food! In Jesus' times, traditional religion worried more about externalities than the state of the heart, yet it was inner cleanliness that was needed (11:39). What are the marks of 'religion on the outside' today? What are the matters of the heart that really concern Jesus?

2. The Pharisees were actually a very greedy people; it is surprising how often religious people want plenty of money! Do you see signs of greed in your own religious friends? And in yourself? What does Jesus promise if we overcome greed for money and start being generous to the needy?

3. What are the other marks of traditional religion? Over-interest in receiving tithes? Love of praise? What else?

☐☐☐ Reading 91 (Luke 12:1–31)

In the story of Luke's Gospel, thousands of people are now following Jesus eagerly, but the religious leaders are fiercely opposed to him.

1. What gives us strength in a time of controversy or danger? The secrets of the heart will soon be made known (12:2–3). How else does Jesus encourage his disciples? In 12:4–5? In 12:6–7? In 12:8–9? In 12:11–12?

2. Jesus still has the opposition of the Pharisees in mind when he warns that rejection of himself is unforgivable (12:10). Why were so many Pharisees beyond forgiveness at this time of Jesus' ministry?

3. As Jesus is preaching, a man shouts out from the crowd. It leads Jesus to talk about money. The Christian faith is not just a means to prosperity. In what ways do people think that the Christian church is simply a social agency to solve the world's problems? How would Jesus have answered?

4. Jesus is led on to tell the 'parable of the rich fool'. How does the man seem to be very wise? In what way is he in fact a fool?

☐☐☐ Reading 92 (Luke 12:32–59)

1. 'This night your life is required of you', said God to the rich fool. Yet Jesus can visit and summon his people in more than one way. One day Jesus will return to this world bodily. But are there other times when the Christ 'comes'? In what ways are we to be always ready for Christ to come?

2. What sins does Jesus mention that might be suddenly judged? Ill-treatment of others (12:45–46). And what else?

3. There are a number of sayings of Jesus that begin with the words 'I have come . . .' (as in 12:49). These sayings are very helpful because they tell us the purpose of Jesus' coming to this world. But what does this saying mean? What is the fire? What does fire do? What was it that motivated Jesus?

☐☐☐ Reading 93 (Luke 13:1–17)

The Roman governor, Pilate, had killed some men while they were sacrificing at the temple. Then there was another tragedy. A building in Siloam had collapsed, and eighteen people had been killed. Everyone was talking about these events and Jesus referred to them in his teaching.

1. People sometimes like to 'interpret' what is happening in the lives of others. But how good are we at this? Is suffering a sign of special

wickedness? If not, how should we relate to people who have experienced tragedy?

2. God likes fruitfulness (13:6–9). What kind of fruit does God want from us?

3. Can a person be a truly saved person and yet be oppressed by Satan for so long? Why had the woman in this chapter got no help for eighteen years? She needed a liberating word from Jesus (13:12) and liberating touch from Jesus (13:13). How then did she come to get this liberating word and liberating touch from Jesus?

□□□ Reading 94 (Luke 13:18–35)

The 'kingdom of God' is a phrase that speaks of experiencing the power of Jesus as God's King. Jesus is the King. Where Jesus is, there is the kingdom of God. The parables are an invitation to experience the kingdom of God.

1. The kingdom of God may be compared to a mustard seed (13:18–19). God's kingdom has small beginnings but leads to big results. How will this affect the way we live? What small things might seem more important than we thought?

2. The kingdom of God may be compared to the working of yeast (13:20–21). Jesus uses yeast as a picture of the spreading influence of the kingdom of God, with unnoticed beginnings but large results eventually. How successful do we expect the gospel of the Lord Jesus Christ to be? What difference will it make to us whether we do or do not believe in the success of the gospel before the second coming of Jesus?

3. Jesus spoke of entering the kingdom of God by a narrow door (13:24). How did he work out the picture? For example, it is narrow so a lot has to be left behind.

□□□ Reading 95 (Luke 14:1–14)

1. How important is it to have meals with other people? Why did Jesus so often have meals with people, even with those who were very critical of him? On one occasion they were watching him suspiciously, wondering whether Jesus would heal someone on a Sabbath. The suffering man does not seem to be a guest. After he is healed he is sent away. How does Jesus use the occasion?

2. How should we respond to the warning of Luke 14:11? In what way should we humble ourselves? In what way might we expect to be exalted?

3. While talking of feasts, Jesus points to a better way of living, one of humble generosity (14:12–14). The proud Pharisee in his attention-getting, proud, legalistic religion is full of his own self-importance. Better, says Jesus, to learn another way. What is the different way?

☐☐☐ Reading 96 (Luke 14:15–35)

1. Jesus liked to use opportunities for speaking about God's kingdom. Sometimes people would make random comments about some aspect of Jesus' teaching – and then Jesus would use what was said. We have already seen it in connection with Luke 12:13. Now there is another remark from the crowd (14:15) and again Jesus uses it. How should we use unexpected opportunities for God's kingdom? Is there any way of preparing for such occasions?

2. The kingdom of God is like a banquet with invitations which go out to many people (14:16). What is the free food? What is the wine? Who are the people for whom the banquet is intended? Who are the people who are entirely unsuitable! (Luke 14:21–24). And who might be the people today who are entirely unsuitable as guests in God's kingdom? What does God think of them?

3. When large crowds followed Jesus, it would lead Jesus to specially speak about the costliness of discipleship. What does it cost to enter into the full blessings of God's kingdom?

☐☐☐ Reading 97 (Luke 15:1–16)

Jesus tries to help the Pharisees by telling them three parables: one about a lost sheep, one about a lost coin, and one about a lost son.

1. What is the point of the 'lost sheep' parable? Jesus specially goes after people in bad trouble. In what ways is he like a shepherd?

2. To the parable of the lost sheep, Jesus adds the parable of the lost coin (15:8–10). It makes roughly the same point but what is the special point it makes? How is Jesus like a woman searching for hours, looking for a valuable coin?

3. The younger son of the third parable treats his father shamefully. To ask for an inheritance while a father is still alive was itself an insult. How is God like the father of the parable? How much difference does it make to us whether we believe in God's graciousness towards a disgracefully wicked son?

☐☐☐ Reading 98 (Luke 15:17–32)

1. The younger son rehearses what he will say (15:18–19) but the father does not allow him to complete it (15:21). What is it that the father will not allow to be said – and what does it imply for the way we relate to God?

2. The parable has as much to say about the older son as about the younger son. In what ways was the older son as much alienated from the father as the younger son? What kind of people does the older son represent and what does the parable say to them? Is everyone either like the younger son or like the older son?

3. How easy is it to apply Luke 15:11–32 to ourselves? Does the parable make grace too easy? Or is it still difficult to believe in God's graciousness?

☐☐☐ Reading 99 (Luke 16:1–31)

1. 'The master' in Luke 16:8a refers to the rich man (since it is the same word as that used in 16:3, 5). The 'manager' had in the short time left in his stewardship used what money he had to benefit others, so that later others would be grateful to him. Worldly people use their possessions to their own advantage. Why should spiritual people not use their possessions for their eternal advantage? What are the practical implications of the parable?

2. Luke 16:10–13 and Luke 16:14–15 continue the theme of faithfulness in the use of money. God's day of reckoning will deal with other things besides the use of money. What other kinds of faithfulness does Luke mention?

3. In the parable of the rich man and Lazarus, Lazarus represents the poor; the rich man represents all rich people who are careless and self-centred. The descriptions must not be pressed too much. People in Hades do not literally talk to Abraham. The details are part of the picture language. It teaches some lessons about wealth. For example, wealth cannot be taken beyond the grave. What are the other points being made here? How should wealth be used?

☐☐☐ Reading 100 (Luke 17:1–21)

1. Jesus is still travelling towards Jerusalem. Along the way he gives instruction to the crowd and to the disciples. Luke 17:1–3a, 3b–4, 5–6, 7–10 contains four challenges to the disciples. What are they?

2. In Luke 17:11–21, the Gospel goes on to speak of some people who did not regard themselves as duty-bound to serve God. Jesus is still on the last journey towards Jerusalem (17:11). There was a road that ran along the border between Galilee and Samaria. Somewhere along the way Jesus entered a Samaritan village and healed ten lepers (17:12). They must all have been Samaritans. Are these lepers believers in Jesus Christ? Will we meet them in heaven? Jesus speaks of only one of these ten men coming to salvation (10:19). If wanting miracles and wanting salvation are not the same thing, what is the place of miracles in the Christian church?

3. How important is it to be grateful? What makes us neglect showing gratitude?

☐☐☐ Reading 101 (Luke 17:22–37)

As Jesus was on his last journey to Jerusalem, the Pharisees raise a question about the kingdom of God.

1. There is a worldly way of seeking the kingdom of God. How do we see this in the Pharisees? And how is it seen today?

2. The kingdom of God comes in stages. It has come; it is coming; it will come. How resistible is the kingdom of God?

3. 'The time will be coming when you will long to see one of the days of the Son of Man, but you will not see it' (17:22). 'The days of the Son of Man' refers to days when the royal power of God is strong. The disciples will want days of evangelistic success for Israel, but it will be delayed and Israel will go through times of sufferings. Is the kingdom of God slower in coming than we might like? If so, what are the dangers likely to arise in the time of delay?

☐☐☐ Reading 102 (Luke 18:1–17)

1. Luke is still continuing his emphasis on prayer. The main point is put first: people ought always to pray and not lose heart (18:1). Then comes the parable, which makes the point more forcefully. How should we pray? With persistence. What are three more lessons about prayer? Is verse 8b about answers to prayer?

2. In the two stories in Luke 18:9–14, 15–17, we have two things that are necessary if we are to be acceptable to God and experience his kingdom. The first is humility or conviction of our own sinfulness. What is good about the first man? But what was wrong? What was wrong about the second man? But what was good?

3. What is the second need (18:15–17), if we are to experience God's kingdom? What do children represent?

☐☐☐ Reading 103 (Luke 18:18–43)

1. 'Inheriting' eternal life is more than justification by faith. The man of Luke 18:13 was 'justified' (18:14) without being told to do anything about the Mosaic law! The Pharisee spoke of matters mentioned by the law (adultery, tithing –18:11, 12) but was not accepted by God. But 'inheritance' refers to reaping from God everything that he has to give us. The disciples call it being 'saved' (18:26) – but it is reaping salvation that is in view, the occasion when we inherit reward from God. This is clear from the way Jesus answers the disciples' question of 18:26. He goes on to speak of reward. So what does Jesus require here if we are to receive all he wants to give us?

2. In what ways is wealth a hindrance to inheriting God's purposes?

3. Immediately after the statement of the disciples' spiritual blindness (18:34) comes the story of the gift of sight for the blind man. The miracles of Jesus are literal events, but they are also acted parables. What do the disciples need to do to come to clear spiritual vision? What does Jesus want them to see? How can they learn from the blind man?

☐☐☐ Reading 104 (Luke 19:1–27)

1. There were many reasons (what are they?) why Zacchaeus was not likely to have any faith in Jesus. But against all probability he does come to receive Jesus as the Saviour. How do we come to salvation? What follows?

2. Jesus' disciples thought that God's glorious kingdom was very near at hand (19:11), but Jesus told them a parable to persuade them to expect a lengthy period in which we are to serve God. How is the parable an illustration of what happens in the story of Jesus? How does it picture the situation of each Christian?

3. What kind of fruitfulness does God want from us? What loss will lazy Christians suffer?

☐☐☐ Reading 105 (Luke 19:28–48)

1. Jesus comes now to Bethphage and Bethany, two villages side-by-side on the outskirts of Jerusalem (19:29). Three attitudes to Jesus are visible in the story of his entry into Jerusalem. How does God provide for him? What do the disciples think of him? What do his enemies think of him? And now that we look back at the story, what do we think of Jesus?

2. As Jesus approaches Jerusalem he breaks down and begins to weep (19:41). It lets us know Jesus has real emotions. What makes Jesus

weep? He is not fearing for himself (note 9:51). What is the tragedy of Jerusalem at this point that Jesus finds so distressing? Can we find the same tragedy in our own times?

3. The temple had become spiritually dead and traditional. Jesus gave the temple an opportunity to welcome him, but they were forgetful (no longer keeping in mind the purpose of the temple) . . . and what else? It often happens that something that was truly used by God in days gone by gets to be misused. What are modern examples?

☐☐☐ Reading 106 (Luke 20:1–26)

1. The religious leaders are doing their utmost to get Jesus into trouble. Their first question is a question about authority. What kind of authority do the religious organisers of the temple have? What kind of authority does Jesus have? So what does this mean for us? What kind of authority should the churches seek?

2. The religious leaders of Israel hate Jesus; so Jesus now tells a parable that explains what is happening. Seven points in the parable represent what was happening in the last week of Jesus' life. (i) The one who plants and owns the vineyard is God the Father. (ii) The vineyard is . . . ? (iii) The servants are . . . ? (iv) The son represents . . . ? (v) Ill-treatment of the son represents . . . ? (vi) The destruction of the tenants stands for . . . ? (vii) The giving of the vineyard to others represents . . . ?

3. Jesus uses another picture. Some builders go looking for a stone. They want a 'cornerstone', a large stone to be the main stone in the foundation of the building. But these builders could not see a good stone when it was in front of their very eyes! How is Jesus like a foundation-stone? How is Jesus like a stone that causes people to fall over? Do people still stumble over him?

☐☐☐ Reading 107 (Luke 20:27–47)

1. The Sadducees were worldly, sceptical people. They tried to ridicule the idea of resurrection by telling a hypothetical story (20:27–33) designed to make the resurrection look silly. Jesus bluntly tells them they are wrong. But what is his argument? Do the promises given to Abraham imply that Abraham will have to be 'living' in a resurrection body for God to be completely faithful to him?

2. The Jewish leaders have been trying to get Jesus into trouble. Elsewhere Jesus is called 'the faithful witness' (Revelation 1:5). How is Jesus a faithful witness at this point of the story?

3. Jesus' question (Luke 20:44) is not a difficult question for a Christian, but it was a difficult question for the scribes and teachers of the law in the temple at Jerusalem. Who is Jesus? What is he? A prophet? A wise man? God's eternal Son? Why was Jesus' question so difficult for them?

Note Jesus speaks of those who are 'considered worthy of taking part in that age and in the resurrection from the dead' (20:35). No one is saved by being 'worthy'. But this is a reminder that resurrection is the occasion when one reaps the results of what one has done in this life. Resurrection involves reward.

□□□ Reading 108 (Luke 21:1–19)

1. The widow who gave her copper coins to the temple treasury is also in the temple like the religious leaders, but she is a very different kind of person. What are the differences between the religious leaders and the widow? What does it imply for our own relationship to God?

2. When Jesus walked past the temple with his disciples they began to admire the wonderful buildings (21:5). But Jesus is not very impressed with the wonderful buildings. What is it that really matters in the life of a country?

3. The disciples want to know about the timing and the signs of the destruction of Jerusalem. Contrary to what people often think, Luke 21:1–37 (and Matthew 24:1–51 and Mark 13:37) are not giving 'signs of the end'. Jesus is warning that despite great social upheavals the end is not to be as soon as one might think. International conflicts will come (Luke 21:10), plus earthquakes and famines and pestilences (21:11). Even great signs in the skies will appear. The last few words of Luke 21:11 is in Old Testament language, speaking of a great change in events coming through the fall of a city (see Isaiah 13:10; 34:4; Ezekiel 32:7). Sometimes literal signs in the skies appear (as in Luke 23:45), even before the end of the world.

4. What is the significance of the fall of Jerusalem? Is there significance in the sudden destruction of some modern buildings?

□□□ Reading 109 (Luke 21:20–38)

Luke 21:12–24 is dealing with the time before the fall of Jerusalem when the disciples will go through difficult times. There is no reference to the second coming of Jesus before verse 25 and probably not even then. Unlike Matthew 24:1–25:46, and Mark 13:1–37, we do not have here in Luke 21:1–38 any teaching about Jesus' second coming. The two-part book of Luke-Acts is interested in evangelism and in the part Jerusalem will play in the years of outreach after Jesus' death. The gospel goes out from Jerusalem (see Acts 1:8)! But they will have only one generation to get on with the work of preaching the gospel before Roman armies march on the city and Christians have to leave it (as Luke 21:21 says will happen).

1. What is the advice Jesus gives about enduring persecution? There are at least four principles here. Persecution will assist evangelism. What else?

2. What is the advice Jesus gives for times when they escape disaster? Is it always God's will that we stay where we are under persecution? Did they have permission to escape? The 'sign' for escaping Jerusalem would be the sight of Roman soldiers. When the soldiers were seen they would know that the end of Jerusalem had arrived (21:20), and that Jerusalem would not be a centre for evangelism for a long time. When is it right for the Christian to go elsewhere when they are persecuted?

3. Jesus obviously did not expect his disciples to be living lives of ease and luxury. There were dangerous days ahead of them, but Jesus did not tell them how to escape the dangers and live nice easy lives with good employment, plenty of comforts and nice holidays! How should Christians seek to be closer to the New Testament standards in their lifestyle?

Note The phrase 'the times of the gentiles' (21:24) has interested interpreters of prophecy. Gentiles obtained control of Jerusalem in about 600 BC when it was invaded by the Babylonians. Jerusalem stayed under gentile control until AD 1967 when the state of Israel got full control of the walled city of Jerusalem. The idea in Jesus' prediction is that Jerusalem (from the viewpoint of the AD 30s) will not be given peace, and that after its fall it will be dominated by gentiles for a long time. However, the phrase suggests that one day there will be a change and that Jerusalem will again become a centre of spiritual blessing as it was in the days of David. I doubt whether 1967 was the fulfilment of these words. There has not been much peace in Jerusalem since 1967 and it has not become a centre of evangelism! Also it must be remembered that a person 'is not a Jew in a visible manner, nor is the circumcision that he has something in the open, in the flesh' (Romans 2:28).

☐☐☐ Reading 110 (Luke 22:1–30)

1. Judas was never a believer. From the very beginning, Jesus knew he was a betrayer. He was never 'clean' (John 13:10, 11). He was not a 'backslider' (a Christian overtaken by some serious sin); he was rather a person who mixed with the disciples and claimed to be one of them but had no faith. Why do some people find it convenient to pretend to

believe what the Christians believe? What do they hope to gain? What was it in the case of Judas? Are there other reasons for being a pretender? What are the dangers of such pretence?

2. 'I have very much wanted to eat this Passover with you before I suffer', Jesus says (Luke 22:15). Why was this 'last supper' so important to him? What aspects of the Christian faith are so vital?

3. The first cup of Luke 22:17 (before the cup of Luke 22:20, which is different) emphasises that we are on the way to a heavenly banquet. The Lord's Supper is the occasion when we have a foretaste of the heavenly banquet. In what ways is heaven like a banquet? How is the Lord's Supper a foretaste of it?

☐☐☐ Reading 111 (Luke 22:31–46)

1. The disciples are facing the greatest change they are ever going to experience. 'Satan has asked to have all of you to sift you like wheat' (22:31). The word 'you' is plural. But what comforts and encouragements does Jesus share with the disciples?

2. Jesus tells his disciples to pray (22:39–40). What are the lessons about prayer here? How is Jesus himself a model pray-er? Was the prayer that the cup should be taken away answered as Jesus wished? Was it answered in any way at all?

3. The disciples fail in their praying (22:45–46). Are there any steps we can take to make sure we do not fail in prayer?

☐☐☐ Reading 112 (Luke 22:47–71)

1. There are five people or groups of people here. Only Jesus is faithful. He had been faithful in prayer. What is the spiritual condition of the crowd? What was happening in the heart of Judas? What are we to think of the religious officials? What is the great characteristic of the disciples? And what is Jesus doing?

2. Luke 22:54–65 describes some kind of night-time trial. There are at least five trials altogether. (i) Jesus was questioned late at night on Thursday evening in the house that belonged to Annas and his relative Caiaphas. (ii) Then he was tried again on the Friday morning before the Sanhedrin, the Jewish parliament. (iii) He was sent to Pilate. (iv) Pilate sent him to Herod. (v) From Herod he came back to Pilate again. What were the sufferings and burdens of Jesus at this time? From his accusers? From his followers? What led to Peter's fall? Over-confidence. What else?

3. What are Jesus' sufferings in Luke 22:63–71? Violence (22:63). What else in verse 64? What are the marks of the prejudice he faced?

☐☐☐ **Reading 113 (Luke 23:1–25)**

1. Pilate faced the question that everyone has to face: What will you do with Jesus? What stages did Pilate go through as he struggled with a decision he did not want to make? He tried to make a right decision (23:4). Then what? What do we find in Luke 23:5? In 23:6–12? Do we have a similar decision to make about Jesus?

2. There is one thing that is worse than being confronted with a decision and that is not to be confronted with a decision because Jesus will not speak to you. What is the character of Herod? He is interested in the supernatural. What else? What is it that will make Jesus refuse to talk to us?

3. Everyone acknowledges Jesus' innocence. Pilate could find no reason to accuse him of any crime (23:13–14). Herod was hostile but had no charge to make against him (23:15). Peter, who witnessed the early stages of these events, said Jesus 'committed no sin' (1 Peter 2:22). The soldier who observed Jesus said, 'This man was innocent' (Luke 23:47). Why is the sinlessness of Jesus important? Why did the Old Testament sacrificial lamb have to be without blemish?

☐☐☐ **Reading 114 (Luke 23:26–56)**

1. In what way is the story of the thief on the cross (23:39–43) a very clear presentation of the gospel message?

2. Two things happen as Jesus dies. Darkness comes over the whole land, for three hours, as the shining of the sun was miraculously obscured. At the same time the curtain of the temple was torn into two. What is the significance of the very sun refusing to shine on Jesus? Why does what Jesus is doing open the inner temple into view?

3. Immediately there is the feeling among the witnesses that something immense has happened. A soldier is instantly convinced of Jesus' genuineness (23:47). The crowds are instantly convinced that they have assisted something that was deeply wicked and yet deeply meaningful (23:48). The women stay there for a long time, so great is the feeling that something immense has just happened (23:49). Have you ever done something and a few seconds later had a feeling that what has just happened is immensely significant? Why do we have such a feeling *after* the event?

☐☐☐ Reading 115 (Luke 24:1–34)

The women leave their various homes before dawn, and dawn breaks as they are going to the tomb (24:1a). They were planning to anoint the body of Jesus (24:1b), but when they get to the tomb the stone is rolled away (24:2) and the body of the Lord Jesus is not there (24:3; for the first time Jesus is called 'the Lord Jesus').

1. Why did the Jewish authorities never produce the body of Jesus after the Christians claimed Jesus was raised from the dead?
2. Would the disciples have been so willing to suffer terrible persecution when their enemies got angry about the preaching of Jesus' resurrection – if it were not true?
3. On the road to Emmaus, the disciples' hearts burn within them *before* they realise they have been with the risen Jesus. What is the significance of this? What made their hearts burn?

☐☐☐ Reading 116 (Luke 24:35–53)

1. There are at least two kinds of knowledge, and two ways of knowing things. You can know things by observation, and you can know things by faith in what God says. In what way does the Christian Church know about the resurrection? By eye-witness testimony? By spiritual experience? By both eye-witness testimony and spiritual experience? Or what? What kind of knowledge does Jesus expect the disciples to have first?
2. The disciples let Jesus down badly, but how does he relate to them when he returns from the dead? What is the character of Jesus towards wayward disciples – perhaps including us?
3. How did Jesus use his forty-day ministry between the resurrection and his final departure to heaven? What new things were taught in this period?

Philippians

In the spring of AD 50, Paul and Silas went northwards up the Mediterranean coast, encouraging the churches in Syria. Finally they reached Troas (Acts 16:8), which was as far east as they could go if they were to stay within that part of the mainland. It was a port on the Aegean Sea, and was further east than they had been on their previous journey.

They were not sure where to go next but that night God called them in a vision to cross the sea that was between Troas and Europe. Soon after, they left Troas by boat and landed at Samothrace on the other side (Acts 16:11). From there they travelled to Neapolis (Acts 16:11) and then reached Philippi (Acts 16:12). They stayed there 'some days' (Acts 16:12), during which many striking events took place (Acts 16:13–40), and it led to the founding of the Philippian church, to which this 'letter to the Philippians' was written. The story of Acts 16:1–40 tells of the first Christian converts in this city in the province of Macedonia. Some years later, when Paul was in prison, probably in Rome, he had occasion to write this letter to them. Yet he was triumphing in the midst of his difficult circumstances and was still busy serving God.

Paul had been arrested in connection with his preaching of the gospel. But he uses his time well while he is in prison, and writes to the church or to the churches that he had started in Philippi. He has three main things on his mind as he writes. (i) The church tended to have a lot of rivalry and disunity in it and he wants to say something about that. (ii) There were false teachers bringing in a false gospel. (iii) He had also received a gift from the Philippians and he wants to say 'Thank you' to them.

Recommended reading: J. A. Motyer, *Message of Philippians* (IVP, 1984); D. M. Lloyd-Jones, *Life of Peace, Life of Joy* (Hodder, 1989, 1990).

□□□ Reading 117 (Philippians 1:1–26)

Paul follows a pattern of letter-writing that would be easily understood in ancient Philippi. He moves from his opening greetings (1:1–2), to prayer (1:3–11), and then comes to some remarks giving the Philippians reassurance concerning himself (1:12–26).

1. We are struck here by Paul's confidence in a time of trouble. What makes him so confident? What help does he expect?
2. For Paul, to live is Christ. What is life for you? Money? Pleasure? Family? Your work? Your ministry? Your marriage? Your friends? Your church? How did Paul get to be so content with Christ?
3. To die is gain. What did Paul expect to gain if he died?

□□□ Reading 118 (Philippians 1:27–2:30)

Paul calls his friends to work out their salvation. He deals with conflict against enemies (1:27–30) and then with internal conflict (2:1–4). Paul will go on to present to them the supreme example of humility, Jesus (2:5–11), and then will ask them to work out their salvation in the way in which they live (2:12–18).

1. Paul has some instructions concerning the way they face the outside world (1:27–30). What does he ask of us?
2. In 2:1–4 Paul refers to four things that are the basis of Christian love. What are they? Then he proceeds to tell the Philippians of three things he wants from them. One is unity. What else?
3. In the famous passage in Philippians 2:5–11, Paul begins with the advantages that Jesus had (the 'very nature' of God, 'equality with God'). He goes on to deal with an attitude Jesus did *not* display ('He did not consider equality with God a thing to be exploited'). Then he deals with what Jesus did when he came to earth as a man ('He made himself nothing . . .'). Verses 9–11 will go on to speak of what God did for Jesus as a result ('Therefore God highly exalted him . . .'). What advantages did the Son of God have? How did he use them? How did God eventually reward him? So what is his example for us?

☐☐☐ **Reading 119 (Philippians 3:1–21)**

1. In Philippians 3:1–21, Paul comes to speak of a group of people who were constantly a trouble to him: the 'Judaisers', as they are often called. In every age the Christian gospel tends to be counterfeited and replaced by an imitation-Christianity that is a mixture of national religion, ritual and moralism. Where can it be seen today? What does Paul think of it?

2. Philippians 3:4–7 takes up the point that the Christian puts no confidence in the flesh. What are the kinds of earthly advantage that make us feel confident in ourselves? But how can we get to know Christ?

3. Paul spells out in detail how he is seeking to get to this high level of resurrection glory. He begins: 'Not that I have already received this or have already been perfected . . .' What does Paul do to get to a high level of final reward?

☐☐☐ **Reading 120 (Philippians 4:1–23)**

1. Paul offers supernatural peace in Philippians 4:6–7. But how precisely do we obtain it? Is any kind of praying enough?

2. Much of the letter to the Philippians has been concerned with cultivating a Christian mind. How should we feed our minds according to 4:8?

3. Paul shows great care and caution in speaking of material support. He seems to be in difficulty in what he says. What is his difficulty and how does he handle it?

Ezekiel

Ezekiel lived in Babylon in the seventh century BC and preached to exiles from Judah who were in captivity there. He was born in the days of Josiah (641–609 BC), at a time when Judah was given a fresh opportunity to turn from its wicked ways. Josiah renounced the paganism of his grandfather but his influence was not great and Judah's wickedness continued. When it became clear that Judah had no intention of turning from its idolatry, God raised up another military conqueror to invade the land. King Nebuchadnezzar of Babylon began to be ambitious to take over Judah.

In 609 BC, Josiah tried to stop Pharaoh Necho from marching through Israel on the way to bring help to the Assyrians. As a result Josiah died in the battle of Megiddo, while he was resisting the Egyptian forces. His son Jehoahaz became king but the Pharaoh, Necho, removed him and in 609 BC appointed his brother Jehoiakim, another son of Josiah, as king in his place. The idolatry of Judah became as bad as ever. Egyptian pagan religion was popular in Israel as well as Assyrian idolatry.

In 605 BC Nebuchadnezzar defeated the Egyptians and began to control the coastland of Israel. In about 604 BC he attacked Jerusalem. Jehoiakim became subject to the Babylonians. Some of the population were deported to Babylon (including Daniel). For a while Jehoiakim transferred his allegiance to Nebuchadnezzar but when, a few years later (in 60 BC), he tried to rebel against Babylon the Babylonians marched against Jerusalem

(December 598 BC). Shortly before Jerusalem fell, Jehoiakim died (or was murdered), and the Babylonians appointed his son Jehoiachin as king in December 598 BC. His reign in Israel lasted for only three months and ten days. Nebuchadnezzar decided to remove Jehoiachin and take him into exile in Babylon. The young king and his mother were taken into exile and never saw Israel again. There was a second group of people deported at this same time, and among them was Ezekiel.

God sent prophets to interpret the exile. There were three great prophets at this time. While all of this was happening, Jeremiah was the leading prophet in Judah. He had been called to be a prophet during Josiah's days (in 626 BC) and during all of these years he preached against the wickedness and idolatry of the Judeans and warned them that only those who submitted to chastening in Babylon would come through the judgment of God. Another man with a prophetic ministry was Daniel, who was taken to Babylon in 604 BC, and spent his life there. Our special interest is Ezekiel, born in about 622 BC, a few years before Jeremiah's ministry began. He was exiled to Babylon in 597 BC when he was twenty-five years old. Five years later, when he was thirty, he saw a vision of the glory of God and was called to be a prophet.

Ezekiel had a wife but she died the day Nebuchadnezzar invaded Jerusalem (24:1, 2, 15–18). He seems not to have been a very normal person. God gave him strange gifts. He spent the whole of his ministry in Babylon but most of what he had to say was about Jerusalem. He made a lot of use of symbolic actions in his preaching. Some of them, such as cooking on dung, were weird, but he had a passionate love for God.

Recommended reading: C. J. H. Wright, *The Message of Ezekiel* (The Bible Speaks Today, IVP, 2001); P. C. Craigie, *Ezekiel* (Daily Study Bible, St Andrew, 1983).

□□□ **Reading 121 (Ezekiel 1:1–2:10)**
Ezekiel's book is a well-edited report of his life's preaching. The first unit covers the first seven chapters of the book.

- Section 1: Call and preliminary messages of Ezekiel (1:1–7:27)
  A. Title (1:1–3)
  B. Ezekiel's call (1:4–3:22)
    i. The vision (1:4–28)
    ii. The call (2:1–3:15)
    iii. Appointment as watchman (3:16–22)

C. Ezekiel's early messages (3:23–7:27)
  i. The fall of Jerusalem (3:23–5:17)
  ii. The high places (6:1–14)
  iii. The end (7:1–27)

1. What did and what did *not* make Ezekiel a prophet? Was he a prophet because he wanted to be? Because his ancestors were priests? Because of the great need of the exiles? What is a call to Christian ministry?

2. The first part of Ezekiel's call is a vision of the glory of God. In the distance he sees a great storm (1:4a). Then the vision gets nearer and Ezekiel sees more. It is an appearing of the glory of God riding upon an angelic chariot. There are angels at the lower part, then halfway up there is a platform. On the top of the platform is the shining glory of God. In Ezekiel 10:5 the creatures are called 'cherubim'. They are part-human and part-animal-like in appearance. They represent the entire creation. The living creatures follow the Spirit in their movements. They go straight forward directly to wherever they are to go (1:12) and they moved 'whither the Spirit was to go'. This refers to the divine Spirit of God. The Spirit of the One who sits on the throne (in 1:25–28) is directing the angels and giving them commands. Over the angels is a platform (1:22), and above the platform is a vision of the glory of God (1:26–28). The whole appearing of God is a revelation of the sovereignty of God. Is there any special reason why Ezekiel should have been given a vision of the kingship of God at this time? Remember Israel has no reigning king in Jerusalem.

3. The chariot-throne is a whirl of activity, able to move immediately in any direction at any second. What is the symbolism here?

☐☐☐ Reading 122 (Ezekiel 3:1–4:17)

1. What is the work of a 'watchman'? How is it a good picture of the work of a prophet – or of the Christian church?

2. Ezekiel acts out a little drama portraying the besieging of Jerusalem. He also represented (by laying on the ground) the sin of Israel from as far back as the days of Solomon. When we are suffering for past mistakes, do we not need to *know* it? How today might we get to know the significance of what is happening? In our land? In our churches? In our own life?

3. Who is Israel's real enemy, Babylon or God himself? Does it happen in our own lives that we ever face the enmity of God?

□□□ Reading 123 (Ezekiel 5:1–7:27)

1. Ezekiel is called to publicly shave himself with a sword, then to burn his hair in three parts (5:1–4). It symbolises the terrible degradation of Jerusalem. Ezekiel is persuading the exiles to break away completely from the sins that had been common among them when they were back in Judah. How much trouble does God take over his people to persuade them of the sins that they are inclined to deny?

2. Why does God hate idolatry so much (Ezekiel 6:1–14)? In these days when any number of religions are tolerated in many parts of the world, how do we fight idolatry? Not with violence – but how?

3. 'An end has come', says Ezekiel. How does sin tend to bring any situation to an end?

□□□ Reading 124 (Ezekiel 8:1–10:22)

In the second section of Ezekiel, clearly marked by a new date in 8:1, God's visible glory leaves the Holy of Holies. The section unfolds as follows:

- Section 2: The glory departs from the temple (8:1–11:25)
  A. Idolatry in the temple (8:1–18)
  B. Punishment by slaughter (9:1–11)
  C. The glory partially leaves (10:1–22)
  D. The judgment of leaders (11:1–13a)
  E. The message of hope (11:13b–25)

1. The glory of God appears again to Ezekiel. By the power of the Holy Spirit he is able to see events that are happening a thousand miles away in Jerusalem. He sees four scenes of idolatry (8:5–6, 7–13, 14–15, 16); the different forms of idolatry involved sexual sin, political corruption, trusting pagan philosophies for agricultural success and for influence among the nations. What do we trust in to give us success and a meaningful life? What is likely to be the effect upon our land if we look for blessing from sources that are hostile to the God of the Bible?

2. In Ezekiel 9:1–11, angels of judgment appear, but there is one group of people who will be exempt from God's judgment (see 9:7). How can we be kept safe amid the judgments of God upon our own land?

3. The glory of God moves to the threshold of the temple (10:18). Where idols are brought in, the God of holiness departs. Is it possible for us to drive God out of our lives? In what way?

□□□ **Reading 125 (Ezekiel 11:1–13:23)**

Ezekiel 12:1–28 sees the beginning of the third major section of the prophecy. It concerns the nature of prophecy.

* Section 3: Prophecy true and false (12:1–14:23)
  A. True prophecy (12:1–20)
  B. True prophecy despised (12:21–28)
  C. False prophecy (13:1–28)
  D. False prophecy encouraged (14:1–11)
  E. True prophecy reasserted (14:12–23)

1. A group of elders are planning their future. They see themselves as being like high-quality meat protected by an iron cooking pot. Verse 3 is difficult to translate but it obviously implies the elders think all is well in Jerusalem. But God gives a word against them and one of them dies abruptly. What can we learn here about the foolish over-optimism of wicked people? Are sinners foolishly optimistic in their assessment of their own safety? What is the real but altogether different hope for Israel (11:14–21)?

2. In Ezekiel 11:1–11, we have a sample of true prophecy: Judah will be sent to exile. Zedekiah would also try to escape but would fail (12:12–16). Ezekiel is to imitate the person who eats his food with anxiety (12:17–20). But prophecy is not always appreciated (see 12:21–28). How is prophecy despised in the proverbs of 12:22 and 12:27? When God's voice comes to us but is too painful, what are the ways in which it is avoided?

3. Ezekiel 13:1–23 deals with false prophecy. How are false teachers like little foxes and like whitewashed walls?

Note In Jerusalem, Jehoiachin's uncle Zedekiah, another son of Josiah, was made king from March 597 BC onwards. After a few years he made yet another attempt to rebel against Babylon. Nebuchadnezzar again sent an invading force. The city was again besieged in December 589 BC and fell to the Babylonians in July 587 BC. Zedekiah's sons were executed, and Zedekiah himself was deprived of his sight and taken to Babylon. This time Jerusalem was destroyed. Gedeliah was made governor over Judea. There was never again a king in the line of David ruling over Judah in Jerusalem. This time large numbers of the people of Judah were sent to Babylon.

□□□ **Reading 126 (Ezekiel 14:1–15:8)**

Ezekiel 14:1–23 is still considering the matter of true and false prophecy. The elders of the Israelites in Babylon come to Ezekiel seeking advice and

Ezekiel gives them a true word from God. A fourth major section of the prophecy is found in Ezekiel 15:1–19:14, each part of which focusses on one or another aspect of the sins of the people.

- Section 4: Aspects of Israel's sin (15:1–19:14)
  A. Uselessness (15:1–8)
  B. Ingratitude (16:1–63)
  C. Treachery (17:1–24)
  D. Guilt (18:1–32)
  E. The funeral song (19:1–14)

1. The elders have idols in their hearts and yet they seek the advice of God's prophet. Why should we ever refuse the God of the Bible and yet at the same time want his help? What are the modern idols? What kind of answer were the elders hoping for?
2. In what way are the people of God like a vine-tree?
3. The fruit of a vine was valuable; the wood of a vine was useless; burnt wood was even more useless. How does Ezekiel use his illustration? How does sin damage our usefulness?

□□□ Reading 127 (Ezekiel 16:1–17:24)

1. Ezekiel's next picture is of a pitiful girl-child who is rescued, becomes a bride but then turns to extreme and disgusting promiscuity (most English translations tone down the shocking vocabulary). The main point is Israel's extreme ingratitude. In what way are God's people like a rescued child? In what ways does Ezekiel's picture speak of God's generosity towards us?
2. How do modern nations respond to God with ingratitude?
3. In the parables of two eagles and a vine, the eagle represents Nebuchadnezzar, the topmost of the tree is the first exiles, and the second eagle is Egypt. Some Judeans were still hoping Egypt would rescue them from Babylon. When God is chastening us, we tend to look in the wrong place for deliverance. What are the wrong deliverers to which we look today? In what way is it treachery to look to useless rescuers?

□□□ Reading 128 (Ezekiel 18:1–19:14)

1. To what extent can we blame previous generations for our own problems? Do we see any fatalism and blame-shifting in our own society? What is Ezekiel's approach to the matter? When we sin, are we responsible for what we do? Or are we victims of what someone else has done?
2. When we are suffering because of the sins of a previous generation,

what can we do about it, according to Ezekiel?

3. The poetry of Ezekiel 19:1–14 has the atmosphere of a funeral procession. In Ezekiel's picture-language, the lioness is Judah. The first of the cubs is Jehoahaz who was taken captive to Judah. The second is one of the later kings (which one is disputed). Ezekiel 19:10–13 is another parable of Judah's exile. But verse 14 begins 'Now . . .' How can a burned and destroyed vine be replanted? When God's people are severely chastised, what hope is there for a fresh start somewhere else?

☐☐☐ Reading 129 (Ezekiel 20:1–21:32)

Ezekiel's message is slowly developing. He has a call from God to announce the chastening of Judah (1:1–7:27). The glory of God is about to depart (8:1–11:25). Anyone who says anything different is a false prophet (12:1–14:23). The many aspects of Judah's sin will result in the funeral of the nation (15:1–19:14). The next section, announced by a new date (20:1) insists that God judges sin and that his judgment will take place in the real world of Judah's history.

* Section 5: Sin, history and judgment (20:1–24:27)
  A. The Lesson of Israel's history (20:1–44)
  B. Judgment by fire and by sword (20:45–21:32)
  C. A catalogue of sins (22:1–31)
  D. Two adulterous sisters (23:1–49)
  E. The fall of Jerusalem (24:1–27)

1. The elders ask a question. Ezekiel replies by reminding them of Israel's history. God's original redemption was by an oath (20:5, 6). Can redemption ever be reversed if it is accompanied by an oath? But what does God want from people who have been redeemed by a non-reversible salvation?

2. What is the point of verse 9? Does God protect himself when his people sin? If so, how?

3. Ezekiel 20:45–48 describes forest-fire in the Negeb, but the Negeb was desert! 'Is he not a maker of parables?' they said about him (20:49). So Ezekiel says more (21:1–32). How often does God's word come to us in stages, where the first stage is puzzling and we have to ask for more? Why does God often at first speak in puzzling ways?

☐☐☐ Reading 130 (Ezekiel 22:1–23:49)

1. Ezekiel 22:1–31 gives a catalogue of the crimes that had been committed by Jerusalem (what are they?) and yet Jerusalem had once

been famous as 'the faithful city' (Isaiah 1:21). Do societies *always* deteriorate? Is there any case where a land gets purer and greater? If so, what reverses the deterioration?

2. The two wicked sisters of Ezekiel 23:1–49 are northern and southern Israel and their capital cities. Their 'lovers' are pagan nations, such as Assyria and ancient Egypt. A lot of Ezekiel's oracles are about *history*. Samaria was only a memory in Ezekiel's time. In what sense do all the problems of God's people arise from forgetfulness? Do Christians need a sense of history – of their own lives and of their churches?

3. If all nations are to note the terrible consequences of the sins of two nations (see 23:48), what lessons should we learn for our own nation? How may we truly be patriotic?

☐☐☐ Reading 131 (Ezekiel 24:1–26:21)

The next section of Ezekiel turns from Israel to consider the lands that are nearby to Israel. It divides into units as follows:

- Section 6: Judgment upon the Nations (25:1–32:32)
  A. Hostility to Israel (25:1–17)
  B. The pride of Tyre and Sidon (26:1–28:26)
  C. The arrogance of Egypt (29:1–32:32)

1. Supernaturally Ezekiel (who is in Babylon) is able to say, 'Today (the tenth of the month) is the day of the beginning of the siege of Jerusalem' (24:1–2). How often are people given a preview of what is to happen? Does it happen today? If so, what should it mean to us? Should we always take note when someone gives us a prediction and it turns out to be true?

2. What were the sins of the nations towards Israel? In the case of the Ammonites it was malice (25:1–7). What was it in the others? How does God judge different kinds of ill-will towards his people?

3. What were the sins of Tyre (Ezekiel 26:1–21)? How much are the same sins found in modern lands? What are the particular ways in which God punishes them? What happens to commercial centres that get too proud?

☐☐☐ Reading 132 (Ezekiel 27:1–29:21)

1. Ezekiel 27:1–28:26 is still focussing on Tyre and Sidon. They were both famous for the wealth that came to them because of their commercial enterprises, but Ezekiel sees a day when all that will be lost (27:34–36). What caused the great loss according to 28:1–10?

2. Ezekiel 28:1–26 has often been taken as a description of Satan. Although strictly it is about the king of Tyre, is it possible that it is a

shadow of Satan? In the picture-language the king was in Eden but fell because of commercial sins (note 28:16). What are the commercial sins today that are likely to come under God's judgment?

3. Ezekiel 29:1–21 begins to concentrate on Egypt. What was Egypt's sin (29:6, 16)? What was the source of the nation's self-confidence (29:9b)? What are the nations of today most confident about? But is there any security against God?

☐☐☐ Reading 133 (Ezekiel 30:1–32:32)

1. Ezekiel spends much space on Egypt because the exiles were hoping that Egypt would somehow rescue them and the exile would come to an end very shortly. How much 'wishful thinking' comes into our interpretation of the ways of God?

2. The 'day of the Lord' involved military defeat (30:3–4) and abandonment by friends (30:5–9). May we have a taste of the 'end of the world' even before it comes? In which case, how might the 'day of the Lord' be near to some modern nations?

3. How might a nation be like a tree (Ezekiel 31:1–18)? How might it be like a monster in the sea (32:2)? How does Ezekiel use these prophetic pictures?

☐☐☐ Reading 134 (Ezekiel 33:1–34:31)

Ezekiel 33:1–33 summarises the book so far, and prepares the way for the remainder. The next section may be outlined as follows:

- Section 7: The Restoration of Israel (33:1–39:29)
    A. Summary of Ezekiel's message thus far (33:1–33)
    B. Faithless shepherds replaced (34:1–31)
    C. Edom destroyed (35:1–15)
    D. Restoration and regeneration (36:1–38)
    E. Resuscitation (37:1–28)
    F. Gog and Magog (38:1–39:29)

1. In what ways are we to be 'watchmen' to our generation, and to our friends?

2. In the light of Ezekiel 33:12–20, it seems the present state of our lives is more important than what we have been in the past. What will this mean to us in day-to-day living?

3. A 'shepherd' in the Old Testament refers to a 'king' (not a New Testament 'pastor'). What is the ideal political leader to be like according to Ezekiel 34:1–31?

Note The 'life' and 'death' of Ezekiel 33:1–33 are not to be completely equated with 'going to heaven' or 'going to hell'. It is not a reference to what Paul would call 'justification by faith'. It is clear from 33:10 that these terms refer to quality of life in Babylonian exile. 'Life' and 'death' refer to what we reap in this life according to whether we do or do not please God. Do we rot away in exile from God, or do we 'reap' eternal life (see Galatians 6:8)?

☐☐☐ Reading 135 (Ezekiel 35:1–36:38)

1. The chapters about Israel's restoration have to say something about Edom (Ezekiel 36:1–38) since Edom was viewed as one of the most vicious of Israel's enemies, and they would be quick to move into Judah's territory once the Judeans had been exiled. What does God feel about 'perpetual enmity' (35:5) from one people towards another? Are there people against whom we are at 'perpetual enmity'?
2. What exactly were the sins of Israel? What does 'defiling' (36:18) and 'profaning' (36:20) refer to? What will God do about it (36:22–38)? How do you think these promises are fulfilled? In the restoration under Ezra and Nehemiah? In the death and resurrection of Jesus? In the return of modern Israel to its land? In worldwide revival? In the second coming of Jesus? Or does the vision take in more than one of these possibilities? If so, which ones?
3. Is Ezekiel 36:25–27 the background to John 3:5? If so, what exactly is being promised here? Who or what is 'Israel'? Every Jew? Jews who come to faith? Everyone who comes to faith, Jew or gentile? Jews who come to faith, with believing gentiles added to them?

☐☐☐ Reading 136 (Ezekiel 37:1–39:29)

1. Ezekiel 37:1–28 promises some kind of 'restoration' of Israel. Again the same question may be asked as we have asked before. To whom does the promise belong? It seems the unburied 'bones' speak of a terrible battle in which Israel was defeated a long time ago. This must surely – in symbolism – be the Babylonian invasion and Israel's exile. We have already heard of the possibility of recovery (36:25–27). What must the return to life represent? What is the prophesying? What is the coming of the breath into the bones? What New Testament Scriptures throw light on the prediction here? John 20:22? Romans 11:12, 15? Romans 11:25–26?
2. If Ezekiel 37:1–28 refers to some kind of restoration of Israel, Ezekiel 38:1–39:29 refers to a final battle of some kind before the end of the world. 'Gog' is an unidentified enemy. 'Magog' means simply 'the place where Gog is to be found'. Where are the passages in Scripture that

speak of an end-time burst of opposition against God? 2 Thessalonians
2:1–17? Where else?

3. In Satan's last desperate attempt (if we may use New Testament
language) to destroy the Christian church, what hope do the people of
God have of survival and victory?

Note It is certainly a mistake to think that modern nations or cities such as
Russia or Moscow are mentioned here. However difficult the interpretation
may be, the meaning has to be something that Ezekiel's readers could have
at least partially understood.

□□□ Reading 137 (Ezekiel 40:1–42:20)

Ezekiel's message continues to move forward logically. The first twenty-four
chapters made the point that Israel was under severe judgment. Ezekiel
25:1–32:32 insisted that the nations were in no better condition. Yet God
was determined to act. Exile was stage one in Israel's cleansing. Yet further
renewal would follow. The mightiest opposition against God's people would
fail (Ezekiel 33:1–39:29). What we expect now is a description of the final
recovery – and that is what we have in Ezekiel 40:1–48:35.

* Section 8: The Temple and the City (40:1–48:35)
  A. The Temple (40:1–42:20)
  B. Glory (43:1–27)
  C. Regulations (44:1–46:24)
  D. Healing waters (47:1–12)
  E. Division of restored land (47:13–48:35)

There is good reason (which cannot be fully presented here) for thinking
these chapters describe the gospel in the language of Israel's institutions.
Much of it is obviously symbolism. It held out the hope of a 'new Israel'
but the details would become clear only as the day of the coming of Jesus
drew near.

1. The new Jerusalem is all temple. The walls are not for protection (they
are too low) but to mark separation from what is outside the temple. The
rooms were for the workers in the temple. Each of them was square. The
porches were for shelter. Are each of these facts symbolical? If so, what
is the symbolism? What other symbolism may be found?

2. In the porch of Ezekiel's visionary temple, there were eight tables for
sacrifices (40:41). What are the many 'sacrifices' of the gospel?

3. In the temple-vision of Ezekiel 8:1–11:25, there was much that was
chaotic and vile. In the temple-vision of Ezekiel 40:1–48:35, every-

thing is regular and orderly. Is there chaos in idolatry and orderliness in the gospel of the Messiah? What is the orderliness of the gospel?

☐☐☐ Reading 138 (Ezekiel 43:1–44:31)

1. In Ezekiel 43:1–27, the glory of God returns; it is a reversal of what had happened in Ezekiel 10:1–11:25. The 'glory' of God is the out-shining of God's holiness. How is the church of the Lord Jesus Christ the location of the glory of God?
2. Ezekiel 44:1–31 begins to itemise some of the regulations of the visionary temple. When the glory of God enters the gate is shut, not to be opened again. Possibly this means that the glory of God will not be leaving (contrast Ezekiel 10:1–11:25). How is this fulfilled in the New Covenant people of God?
3. In the past the Levitical priests (descended from Zadok, one of the two lines of the tribe of Levi) had been unfaithful. Now in Ezekiel's vision he sees faithful priests. In the New Covenant who are the priests?

☐☐☐ Reading 139 (Ezekiel 45:1–46:23)

1. The people were to be given land in the new Israel, but at the heart of their territory was an area allocated for God (45:1). What is the symbolism here?
2. Israel's new king would uphold righteousness in a way that had failed before the exile (45:7–12). How is the new Israel a kingdom of right-eousness?
3. Numerous sacrifices and festivals were to take place. Ezekiel 45:17 mentions many of them. How does the new covenant fulfil these institutions of Israel?

☐☐☐ Reading 140 (Ezekiel 47:1–48:35)

1. The new Jerusalem is also like the garden of Eden with refreshing rivers in it. What does this 'river of life' represent?
2. The river flows from the temple, the place where God's glory is revealed. As it proceeds it gets deeper and deeper. It flows into the Dead Sea but turns the sea into a fresh-water sea, where there can be living creatures. The banks of the river are lined with trees. What is the symbolism of all of this?
3. Ezekiel's book ends with a description of the City of God (Ezekiel 48:1–35). Its outstanding characteristic is the presence of the Lord (48:35). In the church of God, what are the 'portions' of our 'inheritance'?

1 Chronicles

1–2 Chronicles was originally one lengthy book, written shortly after the return from Babylonian exile. It reviews the history of the Davidic line of kings in the southern kingdom of Judah. The history starts with Adam and goes rapidly through the genealogies of the people of interest from Adam to David.

Recommended reading: M. Wilcock, *The Message of Chronicles* (The Bible Speaks Today, IVP, 1987); J. G. McConville, *Chronicles* (St Andrew, 1984).

□□□ Reading 141 (1 Chronicles 1:1–3:24)
The first nine chapters of 1 Chronicles consists of genealogies. This may not seem a very exciting beginning to the book but it is the writer's way of hurriedly reminding us of the background of the various characters in the story of Judah.

1. Of what importance is the fact that Judah's story (and our story too!) is traced back to Adam? Why should every Judean (and we also) always remember it?

2. The kings of Edom (1:43–54) are of interest. These verses show there was blessing even for the sidelines of the people of God. Of what importance to later Judea was the story of the patriarchs (Abraham and his descendants)?

3. Why are David's family ever to be remembered?

☐☐☐ Reading 142 (1 Chronicles 4:1–6:81)

The next three chapters of 1 Chronicles consider the tribe of Judah (4:1–23), Simeon (4:24–43) and those who lived on the other side of the river Jordan (5:1–26), then the tribe of Levi (6:1–81).

1. What was so foolish in the story of the half-tribe of Manasseh (5:25)? How may the modern believer surrender to an already defeated foe?
2. The tribe of Levi were not expected to fight and had no rural territory allocated to them. The two most famous names in this list are Aaron and Moses. But what can we find out about other names, such as Miriam, Nadab and his brothers, Gershom and his two brothers, and others who may be recognised?
3. Why do singers and musicians come in this genealogy (6:31–48)?

☐☐☐ Reading 143 (1 Chronicles 7:1–9:44)

The remainder of the tribes are considered in 1 Chronicles 7:1–40. 1 Chronicles 8:1–9:44 considers Benjamin (from whom King Saul came).

1. What are special callings of the various tribes? Judah is famous for its kings. Levi is famous for its priests. What is the character of the tribes of 1 Chronicles 7:1–40? There are some famous names in the listing of the people of Benjamin (note 8:33). In what ways are these characteristics – kingship, priesthood and whatever – fulfilled in modern Christians?
2. Jonathan gets special attention here; his descendants are listed for about ten generations. Why is this? What profit did Azrikam (for example) gain from the fact that he descended from Jonathan (8:38)? How important is our ancestry? How much does it affect our lives?
3. 'They lodged around the house of God' (9:27). Is there a modern equivalent to this? Would it be something geographical or spiritual?

☐☐☐ Reading 144 (1 Chronicles 10:1–12:40)

At 1 Chronicles 10:1 we move from genealogy to narrative. The writer shows little interest in the details of the story of Saul. He shows only how the kingdom passed to David.

1. What were Saul's sins? What action did God take? How long does it take before God removes ministry from a wayward servant? Does it always (or often or rarely) involve premature death?

2. The privileges of kingship are seen here (11:1–3). How does David receive honour from his people? How does Christ get honour? How do we get honour when we reign in Christ?

3. In 1 Chronicles 12:1–40 some people are famous (for what?). Others are obscure. All are gathered around David the king. How does David and his people picture Christ and his Church?

☐☐☐ Reading 145 (1 Chronicles 13:1–15:29)

1. The story of the ark is obviously very important to the chronicler. It represented the presence of God. What does the story mean to the Christian? What is seeking to bring back the ark?

2. David had pagan friends (14:1–5) and pagan enemies (14:6–17). We too may expect friends and enemies in the work of God. What are the blessings and temptations of having such people close to us?

3. David was the originator of the musical and choral side of Israel's life, which is very obvious in 1 Chronicles 15:1–29. Why did Michal the daughter of Saul not like the jubilant way David was behaving? Why do some Christians rejoice more than others?

☐☐☐ Reading 146 (1 Chronicles 16:1–18:17)

1. Most of the psalm in 1 Chronicles 16:1–43 is not sung to God but is more an exhortation for the people (16:8–34). Only in 16:35–36 is God addressed directly. What is it David is encouraging us to do?

2. The plans of David and Nathan were redirected (17:1–27). What do we learn about guidance from this chapter?

3. 'The Lord gave victory to David wherever he went' (18:13). What has pleased God so much in the life of David so far? The victory that God gives us today is not so much military – but what is it?

☐☐☐ Reading 147 (1 Chronicles 19:1–21:30)

1. 1 Chronicles 19:1–3 is a classic case of unnecessary suspicion. How can we avoid being gullible and yet at the same time avoid being over-suspicious? What might suspicion lead to (judged by 19:1–19)?

2. David takes the crowns of other rulers and puts them on his own head. His victory comes slowly and giants are among the last to be conquered. Are there spiritual principles here that may be reapplied to the Christian?

3. Numbering the people (21:1–30) might not seem such a bad thing and yet there was obviously something wrong with the way David did it. In what way might our assessing our own strength be a reflection of pride and unbelief?

☐☐☐ **Reading 148 (1 Chronicles 22:1–24:31)**

1. David collected material for the temple to be built in the next generation. Should we ever do this – prepare something for others to do at a
later stage? What projects of this kind might be prepared for?

2. David was not only a military man; he was also an organiser of the
temple-worship. In several ways David changed the Mosaic law
(allowing Levites to start work at twenty years, instead of twenty-five,
23:24; pointing out that some parts of the law were now irrelevant,
23:25–26). Was this not a bold thing to do? May we also change the
law of God?

3. In organising the Levites, David made sure both halves of the Levites
(the descendants of Eleazar and the descendants of Ithamar) were
equally involved. One half was not allowed to be left out. What other
principles of good organisation may be seen here?

☐☐☐ **Reading 149 (1 Chronicles 25:1–27:34)**

1. Again the chronicler lists the musicians (25:1–31). Some of the names
here appear in the titles to the psalms (see Psalms 50:1–23; 73:1–
83:18; 39:1–13; 62:1–12; 89:1–52; 42:1–49:20; 84:1–85:13; 87:1–
88:18). Special musicians never appear in the New Testament as they
do in the Old Testament. Is there any reason for this? Who are 'the
choir' according to the New Testament passages about singing? How
do we apply 1 Chronicles 25:1–31 to the New Testament situation?

2. 1 Chronicles 26:1–19 deals with the gate-keepers. What might be the
job of a 'gate-keeper'? To prevent the temple from being misused? What
else – and how might the equivalent tasks be performed for the people
of God today?

3. 1 Chronicles lists military leaders (27:1–15), tribal leaders (27:16–
24), royal officials (27:25–31). Sometimes we learn from the Old
Testament by *contrasting* it with the New Testament. Can we learn
something here from what we no longer do?

☐☐☐ **Reading 150 (1 Chronicles 28:1–29:30)**

1. David is busy in his old age. What kind of preparations for the future
might we make as we come to the end of a busy ministry or a busy life?

2. David is challenging his people to be as committed to the temple as he
is. How does he do it? Are there lessons here in the art of motivating
others?

3. How might the prayer in 29:10–19 be a model for our own praying?

Colossians

Paul's letter to the Colossians will tell us of the glory of the Lord Jesus Christ, and will help us to live the Christian life. Paul wants us to 'walk in him, having been rooted in him, and now being built up in him' (Colossians 2:6–7). Paul felt responsible for helping this church. It was under Paul's direction and guidance that Epaphras had preached in the cities of the Lycus valley in Phrygia and founded the churches of Colossae, Hierapolis and Laodicea. When he visited Paul during Paul's imprisonment in Rome in the AD 60s, his news of the churches led Paul to write the Epistle to the Colossians. The Colossian church was tempted to look favourably upon a religious philosophy that was popular in their area. We can call it 'the Colossian philosophy'. He refers to it in Colossians 2:8, and mentions some of its particular teachings in Colossians 2:16, 18, 21, and elsewhere. (i) It was Jewish in background and involved such things as circumcision, and Jewish food laws. (ii) It was mystic – that is it depended on religious experiences thought to come directly from God. (iii) It was ascetic – that is, it took to excessive fasting and physical self-humiliation as a source of blessing. Paul points to the fullness of life and power in the person of Christ (needing no philosophy, no tradition, no asceticism) and assures the Colossians that they have come to fullness of life in him. In Colossians 1:1–14 he introduces himself and gives his thanksgiving and prayer for the Colossians. He cites a poem or song describing the fullness of Christ, which he will mention again later (1:15–20). He describes *their* spiritual resurrection in Christ (1:21–23) and *his* ministry (1:24–2:5).

313

The letter then moves to its main content at 2:6. Every blessing is found in Christ (2:6–7). Philosophy is deceitful (2:8). They already have what the philosophy is offering (2:8–15). So they have 'died' to their old life (2:16–23) and have risen to a new life (3:1–4). The rest of the letter works out what Paul has said, practically. How they must not live (3:5–11), how they should live (3:18–4:1). Prayerfulness (4:2–6). Colossians 4:7–18 is his final conclusion.

Recommended reading: William Hendriksen, *Colossians* (Banner of Truth, 1979).

☐☐☐ Reading 151 (Colossians 1:1–29)

1. Colossians 1:1–8 reveals the existence of a powerful spiritual revival in the area of Colossae. What is a spiritual awakening like?
2. There is a kind of logic in Paul's prayers. First we pray for spiritual knowledge. Then what?
3. Colossians 1:15–20 is a kind of hymn or poem, with two 'stanzas' – two sections of poetry – consisting of 1:15–16 and 1:18–20. Colossians 1:17 is a key statement in the middle of the two stanzas. What is Jesus' relationship to God? To creation? To the church? What will it imply for the Colossian Christians (1:21–23), and what will it imply for us?
4. The idea in Colossians 1:24 is that there is a measured and predestined amount of suffering to be endured before the kingdom of God is established as fully as it will be. Paul says, 'I am completing the sufferings of the Messiah' because he knows that there is a certain quantity of suffering that will have to be experienced by the apostles and their churches before a day of success and victory can be reached. What will this imply for Christian ministry today?

☐☐☐ Reading 152 (Colossians 2:1–23)

The heart of what Paul wants to say is in Colossians 2:6–7; it is followed by a warning in 2:8.

1. How does salvation begin? How does salvation continue and develop?
2. The Colossian 'philosophers' said that God's 'fullness' – his entire divine nature – is shared by a series of angelic beings. 'Fullness' of spiritual life is (they said) a matter of receiving special knowledge, which comes through ascending to higher and higher levels of spiritual experience by means of rules about diet (see 2:16), the keeping of holy days (see 2:16) and regulations about what you can touch and what you cannot

touch (see 2:21). But what does Paul say is the truth of the matter?

3. Why must the Christian refuse bondage to petty legalism about small matters?

Note 'Taking delight in false humility' seems to refer to the cult's extreme stress on submission to the system of fasting and discipline and physical severity. 'The angel's worship' probably does not mean worshipping the angels themselves, but to some religious feeling in which the worshipper felt he was having an experience similar to that of Isaiah in Isaiah 6:1–4. The next phrase (probably to be translated 'wanting to enter into the things which he has seen in a vision . . .') suggests that by his severity to the body, the cult member has an ecstatic vision in which they feel they are joining in with angelic worship. Then they try to investigate what they have seen, that is, to 'enter into' the vision to interpret it. It sounds peculiar and yet there are still people who have weird experiences and then try to get special doctrines from their experiences.

□□□ Reading 153 (Colossians 3:1–25)

1. The Christian has died in Christ. The Christian has also risen with Christ. What follows from the Christian's new position in Christ?

2. What is implied by the word 'therefore'? What is Paul's way of preaching holiness?

3. There are things the Colossians must put to death (3:5–11). What are they? And what are the things they must put on (3:12–17)?

□□□ Reading 154 (Colossians 4:1–18)

1. Paul is concerned that they should be faithful in prayer. But what must accompany prayer (4:2–6)?

2. How important was teamwork to the apostle Paul? How did it work out practically?

3. How is Epaphras a model of faithful ministry?

Psalms 110:1–118:29

☐☐☐ **Reading 155 (Psalms 110:1–111:10)**

1. The writer of the letter to the Hebrews built his doctrine of the priestly work of Christ upon Psalm 110:4. How is Jesus like Melchizedek? What are the differences between the priests in the tribe of Levi and Jesus who was born in the tribe of Judah? What does it mean to live daily, relying on Jesus as our great high priest?

2. If the Levites' priesthood could come to an end, can Jesus' priesthood come to an end? If not, why not? (What is the point of Hebrews 7:20?)

3. Psalms 111:1–118:29 form a group of psalms and within that group, Psalms 111:1–112:10 form an opening pair. Both are 'acrostic' (with the first letter of each half-verse proceeding through the Hebrew alphabet). In both, the word 'Hallelujah' ('Praise the Lord') is outside the acrostic sequence. In Psalm 111:1 the psalmist resolves to praise God personally and with God's people. Verses 2–9 give the reasons. God is great (111:2–3). Details are given (111:4–9). Verse 10 calls for obedience and praise. How is this psalm a model of what a time of devotion ought to be? What should be the ingredients of our own times of worship?

☐☐☐ Reading 156 (Psalms 112:1–113:9)

1. Psalm 112:1–10 has five topics. The first is about the individual and the family (112:1–2). The second is about prosperity and misfortune (112:3–4). What are the other topics and what is said about each one (112:5–6; 112:7–8; 112:9–10)?

2. What are the punishments of sin according to Psalm 112:1–10?

3. Psalms 113:1–118:29 are a group of psalms that were sung during the celebration of Passover: 113:1–114:8 before the meal and 115:18–118:29 after the meal. Psalm 113:1–9 looks at the height of God combined with his willingness to come down to meet the lowly. What parts of the psalm show us God's ability to transform impossible situations?

☐☐☐ Reading 157 (Psalms 114:1–115:18)

1. Psalm 114:1–8 continues the theme of the previous one, only in more detail, considering the exodus as the classic case of rescuing the lowly. What are the pictures here? A strange language. An impossible barrier – the sea. An uncrossable river – Jordan. Mountains. Hard, rock-like situations. In each case what did God do?

2. What is the point of 114:8? What does idolatry do to the idolater? What is idolatry?

3. God is worthy of praise (115:1–3); idols are worthy of scorn (115:4–8). So every group of people is to trust in Yahweh (115:9–11) and every group will find that he brings blessing (115:12–13). The psalmist prays for that blessing (115:14–15), and calls upon his people to praise God while they are still alive (115:16–18). Verse 17 is not a statement about life after death. It simply makes the point that dead people do not go to the temple! Why is it important to praise God, according to this psalm?

☐☐☐ Reading 158 (Psalms 116:1–118:29)

1. The writer of Psalm 116:1–19 had been deceived (116:6, 10) and was in danger of losing his life (116:3). What are the lessons we are to learn when we find God to be faithful in time of trouble?

2. Psalm 117:1–2, the shortest chapter of the Bible, gives a reason for calling all nations to worship God. What is the reason? How does Paul use the psalm in Romans 15:11?

3. The writer of Psalm 118:1–29 seems to be a king who has survived a great conflict. How is the psalm fulfilled in the Lord Jesus Christ?

Numbers

At the beginning of the book of Numbers the people are stationary at the foot of Mount Sinai. There is no movement of the people between Exodus 19:1 and Numbers 10:10. The early part of the book is continuing Leviticus and is still describing events that took place at Sinai. Then Numbers describes their travels from Sinai to Kadesh (10:11–12:16), the years spent near Kadesh (13:1–19:22), their journey to the plains of Moab (20:1–22:1), and what took place on the eastern side of the Jordan river (22:2–34:13).

Recommended reading: P. J. Naylor, 'Numbers' in *New Bible Commentary, 21st Century Edition* (ed. D. A. Carson et al., IVP, 1994); G. Wenham, *Numbers* (Tyndale Commentary, IVP, 1981).

☐☐☐ **Reading 159 (Numbers 1:1–2:34)**

1. The census of Israel (1:1–46) was a counting not of every individual but of the men. It was a reminder that entering the 'land of promise' would be a fight of faith. What kind of 'fight' is involved in the Christian life? Who qualify as the 'warriors' today?
2. The Levites were not numbered in the same way (1:47–54) as the other fighting units, for their work was different. What is the equivalent of 'the Levites' in the New Testament churches? 'Full-time' ministers? The more 'spiritually minded' Christian? Or are all Christians the equivalent

of Levites in the New Testament churches? What aspect of Christian faith do the Levites point to and anticipate?

3. Numbers 2:1–34 tells of the arrangement of Israel's tribes in the camp of Israel. It was arranged as a square with the tabernacle in the middle, the Levites around it, and the twelve tribes yet further out in four groups of three tribes at the north, the south, the east and the west. What is the symbolism of the tabernacle being in the midst? What is the symbolism of the Levites being close to it? What are the equivalents of all of this in the Christian Church?

□□□ Reading 160 (Numbers 3:1–4:49)

In Numbers 3:1–4 we have listed the family of Aaron and Moses. The priests were the direct descendants of Aaron. Then we have the description of the functions of the Levites (3:5–10, 11–13) and the census of the Levites (3:14–39). The Levites were assistants to the priests. Then we have the duties of the Levites (4:1–33) and the description of the completion of the census (4:34–49). The tribe of Levi had three clans in it, descending from Kohath, Merari and Gershom.

1. To what extent do the arrangements here resemble New Testament church officials? To what extent are the ministers of the Old Testament and the ministers of the New Testament entirely different?

2. God redeemed the firstborn sons (the representatives of the whole nation) at the time of the exodus from Egypt. So their lives were bought by God. Yet human sacrifice was not God's will and so the firstborn sons did not lay down their lives literally. The Levites gave their lives specially to God as substitutes for the firstborn sons (3:11–13). In what ways should we 'lay down our lives' today?

3. Obviously there were a lot of differences among the priests and Levites. Some had more access to the tabernacle than others. Some clans had privileges others did not have. How might differences in responsibility (then and today) lead to envy? What might be said to a person jealous of the position of someone else?

□□□ Reading 161 (Numbers 5:1–6:27)

Numbers 5:1–4 deals with the need of keeping the camp 'clean'. There were clearly tents outside the central camping area and the 'unclean' were to go there until they were cleansed. The 'cleanliness' was not necessarily moral; it was more a matter of ritual and hygiene. Numbers 5:5–10 deals with offences between the people where restitution was needed. Numbers 5:11–31 describes a ritual for detecting and punishing infidelity.

1. The permanent lessons of Numbers 5:11–31 have to do with human character. Unfaithfulness is still possible. What other characteristics of human nature are found here? The weaknesses of the Mosaic law are also obvious here. What are they, and in what ways might a modern Christian handle this kind of problem in an entirely different manner?
2. The Nazirite was a symbol of special dedication to God. Are all Christians to be *spiritually* Nazirites? What do the regulations mean for the Christian? Obviously we do not understand them literally, but do they have a spiritual fulfilment? What did the Nazirite do if he slipped in his commitment? What does the Christian do?
3. In the Old Testament the priests prayed for the people. But what does the priestly blessing of 6:22–27 mean for the Christian? Is it what we pray for each other? If so, what are the six blessings we seek from God?

☐☐☐ Reading 162 (Numbers 7:1–8:26)

Numbers 7:1 is one month earlier than the date in 1:1. If Numbers 1:1–4:49 dealt with self-assessment, and 5:1–6:27 dealt with separation and holiness, then Numbers 7:1–10:10 is a 'flashback' dealing with the inauguration of the tabernacle worship.

1. The leaders of the tribes give a one-time provision of carts and oxen for the transporting of the tabernacle. How is 7:1–3 an example of spontaneous generosity? How is 7:4–9 an example of care in receiving a gift?
2. Numbers 7:10–88 narrates a twelve-day ceremony. Each tribe gives exactly the same things, so why does the narrator repeat the details twelve times? What point is it making? Why is there such exact equality?
3. The lampstand (8:1–4) had to shine continually. The Levites (8:5–26) were a permanent reminder that all Israel belonged to God. What was needed for their work to commence? What are the Christian equivalents?

☐☐☐ Reading 163 (Numbers 9:1–11:35)

1. Numbers 9:1–14 records the second Passover ever in Israel's history. What are the main points in the symbolism of the Passover? Salvation is by the death of a substitute. What else?
2. What do we learn about guidance in Numbers 9:6–9, 15–23?
3. What are the four uses of trumpets according to 10:1–10? How does this help us interpret such passages as 1 Thessalonians 4:16?

☐☐☐ **Reading 164 (Numbers 12:1–14:45)**

1. What do we learn about jealousy from Numbers 12:1–16? How should we respond when others are jealous of us? What is God likely to do?

2. Whose idea was it to 'spy out the land' (13:1–33)? Was it a good idea? Was it practicality or was it unbelief? Did God originate the scheme? Or did he accommodate himself to what the people wanted to do? What lessons of faith do we learn here?

3. What are the side effects of unbelief as we see them in Numbers 14:1–45?

☐☐☐ **Reading 165 (Numbers 15:1–16:50)**

Numbers 15:1–21 gives some regulations concerning sacrifices. Then 15:22–31 gives laws about intentional and unintentional sins; 15:32–36 deals with one special incident; and 15:37–41 deals with the wearing of tassels.

1. No burnt offering, or sacrifice for a vow, or free-will offering could be offered without a meal offering (15:1–4) and a drink offering (15:5). Numbers 15:1–12 gives the details of the amounts required for each kind of sacrifice. If for a Christian the sacrifices point to the Lord Jesus Christ, it means that Christ not only dies for the sins of his people but also becomes their food. What does it mean for Jesus to be our food?

2. Numbers 15:37–41 refers to something ritualistic, but what is the spiritual equivalent?

3. Numbers 15:32–36 and 16:1–17:13 tell us of incidents in the years when the Israelites wandered in the wilderness. The rebellion against Moses was a serious one. What are the characteristics of the rebels and their rebellion? What is their argument (16:2–3)? How does Moses handle the matter? What kind of rebellions against God's authority do we find today – and how should we view them?

☐☐☐ **Reading 166 (Numbers 17:1–19:22)**

1. Numbers 17:1–13 continues the story of Korah's rebellion. Why was 'Aaron's rod that budded' so important that it was kept in the tabernacle (Hebrews 9:4)? What is its spiritual message?

2. The Levites had to offer sacrifice for their own sins (Leviticus 16:6) and for any kind of defilement of the tabernacle (Leviticus 16:16). Now it is said they 'bear the guilt' (Numbers 18:1–7) of everything that happens at the tabernacle. It means they have responsibility for it, and must offer sacrifices when sins are committed. What are the Christian equivalents to this responsibility? What Christians 'bear the guilt' for what areas of life?

3. The 'ordinance of the red heifer' (Numbers 19:1–22) was a means of removing ceremonial uncleanness. A red cow that was without blemish was killed and burnt to ashes. The ashes were mixed with water to make a paste, and the paste was used to symbolically cleanse from sin. How does Hebrews 9:13 help us as we read this story? What was the symbolism, and how does Christ fulfil the symbolism?

☐☐☐ Reading 167 (Numbers 20:1–22:41)

1. Some terrible crises come upon Moses at this time. What are they (20:1–7)? What was the sin of Moses at this point (20:8–12)? What did he lose as a result? What may the Christian lose as the result of unbelief?

2. What does John 3:14 tell us about the bronze snake (Numbers 21:6–9)? How does it resemble the cross of the Lord Jesus Christ?

3. Balaam seems to have been a prophet of some kind who travelled around cursing military enemies for money. What good characteristics does he show in 22:1–14? What goes wrong in 22:15–19? What are the consequences in 22:20–35? Why does God give him permission to go with the visitors and yet God is angry at the same time? Does God ever give us permission to do what he does not approve of?

☐☐☐ Reading 168 (Numbers 23:1–25:18)

The Balaam story continues in Numbers 23:1–30. Balaam dedicates himself to Yahweh in readiness to receive a revelation from him (23:1–3). God does indeed speak to him, and gives him a message. Balaam speaks of the distinctiveness of Israel and of the vast multitude of people who will come into being as the people of God (23:4–10). King Balak protests and gives Balaam another chance to curse Israel (23:11–17). Again Balaam predicts nothing but good for God's people (23:18–24). A third attempt to curse Israel produces the same result (23:25–24:9). King Balak is angry (24:10–11) but Balaam's final predictions are still full of promises for Israel (24:12–25).

1. Can a servant of God have the right message but the wrong motive? Can God bless someone whose motive is so wrong? How does this fit with (for example) the teaching of 2 Timothy 2:21?

2. A major disaster takes place in the story of Israel at Peor. What exactly was the sin (in 24:1–5) that led to such disaster? What comment can we make on modern 'pluralism' in the light of Numbers 25:1–18? To

what extent is 'pluralism' a mistake? Is there any way in which it is something that should be supported?

3. Obviously no Christian can literally do what Phineas did. But in what way might a modern Christian be a 'Phineas'?

☐☐☐ Reading 169 (Numbers 26:1–27:23)

1. After the plague upon Israel, the number of fighting men in Israel was again counted (Numbers 26:1–65). What effect does sin in God's people have upon their number? How important is the number of people in the kingdom of God? Consider Genesis 13:16; Acts 2:41; Revelation 7:9.

2. Some women thought they were about to lose their inheritance (Numbers 27:1–11). They brought their case to Moses their king and Eleazar their high priest. Can this be taken parabolically? Are we ever in danger of losing our inheritance? What can we do about it?

3. Does the Bible give us any advice in how to pass on the work of God to the next generation? Does Numbers 27:1–23 give us any help?

☐☐☐ Reading 170 (Numbers 28:1–30:16)

1. Numbers 28:1–31 gives instructions about offerings of different kinds. What is the Christian equivalent to daily burnt offerings, daily cereal offerings, daily drink offerings, which were used daily and in connection with the various special days?

2. The New Year (29:1–6), the Day of Atonement (29:7–11) and the Feast of Tabernacles (29:12–38) all required large quantities of animals, grain and wine. The regulations presumed that Israel would one day be in the land of Canaan. Yet the people given the law of Moses had been told they would never enter Canaan. Does this give any message of hope to those who have experienced God's anger?

3. Vows in ancient Israel were taken very seriously, although a woman's vow was subject to the approval of the man in authority over her (30:1–16). Does the Christian gospel at this point agree with the law or contrast with the law?

☐☐☐ Reading 171 (Numbers 31:1–33:56)

1. Israel is to 'take revenge' on Midian because they were the people who led them into sin (see 25:16–18). What kind of 'revenge' against temptation may the Christian take today?

2. 'Be sure your sin will find you out' (Numbers 32:23) is a famous verse.

What sin did Moses have in mind? Why was it possibly sinful not to cross the Jordan? In what way does sin 'find us out'?

3. Moses wanted Israel to remember the stages they passed through in journeying from Egypt to Canaan. Does Israel's journey remind us of any steps and stages in the life of the Christian?

□□□ Reading 172 (Numbers 34:1–36:13)

1. Numbers 34:1–29 describes the extent of Israel's borders. Then twelve men are to be appointed to divine the land. If in the New Testament the 'inheritance' is the kingdom of God (1 Corinthians 6:9), how does Numbers 34:1–29 help us to see how God supervises our lives?

2. The 'cities of refuge' were a part of the law that helped to protect the life of an accused person in a 'borderline case' where it was not clear whether he was guilty or not. In what modern ways should we protect someone in an accusation where we are not sure of the truth?

3. Numbers 36:1–13 takes up the case of the daughters of Zelophehad again. They are not allowed to marry outside of their tribe. This ruling prevents their ancestral land from being taken away from one tribe and given to another tribe (by marriage). What part of this ruling is the opposite of the gospel? What concern of the law is *fulfilled* by the Christian walking in the Holy Spirit?

2 Samuel

In what we call '2 Samuel', David hears the news of Saul's death (2 Samuel 1:1–27) and is made king (2:1–32) but for a few chapters he is still not king of all Israel, and has to learn how to establish a starting point in the work of the Lord. There is civil war between David's supporters and followers of Saul (3:1–4:22). Finally David becomes king of all Israel at Hebron, Jerusalem becomes his capital city, he defeats the Philistines and establishes his empire (5:1–9:13). At that point David almost ruins his life. There is a time of war with Ammon (10:1–19). At such a time David commits adultery but is rebuked by God through Nathan, and (although he is forgiven) terrible problems are predicted for his life (11:1–12:31). 2 Samuel 13:1–20:26 tells of the immense conflicts he had within his own family and nation. 2 Samuel 21:1–24:25 tells of his warriors (21:1–22), his music (22:1–51), his last words (23:39) and his self-confidence in numbering the people (24:25).

Recommended reading: M. A. Eaton, *2 Samuel* (Preaching Through the Bible, Sovereign World, 1996).

☐☐☐ **Reading 173 (2 Samuel 1:1–3:39)**

1. It seems that the Amalekite of 2 Samuel 1:1–27 (who was lying) was not prepared for David's response. What was the difference in character between David and the Amalekite?

2. What were the first steps David took in being king? Are there principles of leadership here, which deserve wider application?

3. No doubt David had been thrilled as a young man when Samuel had told him he would be king. But what were the problems he now faced? David had to show persistent faith and had to refuse to give up. What did God do for him as he continued in faith?

□□□ **Reading 174 (2 Samuel 4:1–5:25)**

1. In 2 Samuel 4:1–5:3, David stands still and does nothing and sees the salvation of God. In what circumstances are we called to do nothing?

2. David is now thirty-seven years old (5:4–5) and king of the whole nation. The next thing is to create a capital. What were the advantages of choosing Jerusalem, not Hebron, in Judah? Why did he not choose a town occupied by one of the other tribes? What can we learn about our own choices?

3. Jerusalem looked impossible to capture but David felt called to take it for God. God has a habit of overthrowing sinful strongholds. What are the 'strongholds' of our own situation? How are we to view them? The world feels entirely confident that it can resist and even overthrow Jesus Christ, but what is the lesson of 2 Samuel?

□□□ **Reading 175 (2 Samuel 6:1–8:18)**

1. What mistakes were made in David's bringing the ark to Jerusalem? What are the dangers of God's presence? What changes did he make in his second attempt?

2. David seems to be free to do what he wishes in the kingdom of God – but then he receives God's overruling (7:1–29). So what do we learn about the balance of freedom and submission?

3. God is more concerned to build David a house than for David to build a house for God's ark. God actually proposes to do something wonderful for David, and he reveals his plans for David here. How does the kingdom of the Lord Jesus Christ appear here?

□□□ **Reading 176 (2 Samuel 9:1–10:19)**

1. How is David a model of forgiveness and generosity?

2. In 2 Samuel 10:1–19, David's generosity is received with suspicion. David's love is rejected. His loving ways get him into trouble. Hanun becomes suspicious of David. Doubts were sown by the Ammonite nobles (10:2b–3). It is always foolish to have a suspicious attitude towards other people, but it is even more foolish to let one's suspicions grow because of the suggestions of other people. How much damage does suspicion do in our lives? How can we avoid it? What other examples of suspicion can you remember from the Bible? And from the life of Jesus?

3. David treats his own ambassadors with kindness and prevents them from being humiliated back in Jerusalem (10:5). They are to stay in Jericho for a while and by the time they return will not be disgraced by their half-beards. How may we show such concern to others around us?

□□□ Reading 177 (2 Samuel 11:1–13:39)

1. What made David vulnerable to sin? How could the temptation have been avoided?

2. God let some time go by, time for David to repent. No repentance showed itself. God decided to act. When God decides the time has come for sin to be found out, what can anyone do about it? How do we try to escape when God is convicting us of sin? Does it succeed?

3. David was guilty of big sin. But then his repentance was equally great. His restoration started at the point where he was convicted of the sinfulness of what he had done and frankly confessed it. When he said, 'I have sinned' (2 Samuel 12:13a), his recovery had started. In what way did he begin to recover?

□□□ Reading 178 (2 Samuel 14:1–15:37)

From this point on in 2 Samuel, the highlights of the story all tell of the troubles David brought into his life by his sin.

1. In 2 Samuel 14:1–33, in what way is David experiencing what he himself did in connection with Uriah? How much does God rebuke us by our experiencing our own sins – from someone else?

2. There was much wickedness in Absalom's life. What encouraged it? What were the techniques of his deceit and ambition? Play-acting and pretentiousness (15:1). What else?

3. Jesus experienced abandonment by his closest friends. In David's case, his being betrayed was part of God's teaching him how wicked he had been to betray Uriah to his death. What was it in Jesus' case?

□□□ Reading 179 (2 Samuel 16:1–18:33)

1. We are still following the way in which the prophecy of Nathan works out in David's life. 'I will raise up calamity against you from your own

household', said God (2 Samuel 12:11). David is exiled from Jerusalem. But why is David not overwhelmed with panic? What keeps us calm even in the midst of the judgment of God?

2. It is only when our position is ambiguous and success uncertain that the true convictions of men and women about us surface. Shimei curses David because he thinks that David's cause is lost. Ittai adheres to David because he is convinced David is God's king. How does the same 'ambiguous' situation appear when we consider our Lord Jesus?

3. David's own son shows immense contempt towards David (16:15–17:29). There are four characters in this story: Hushai, Absalom, Ahithophel and David. What are the characteristics of each one?

□□□ Reading 180 (2 Samuel 19:1–20:26)

1. Sometimes we make a bad mistake and then wish we could change our minds. This was the way it was in Israel immediately after the death of Absalom. Having made a bad mistake, they begin to blame each other. 'Why do you not bring the king back?' But David takes the initiative! How might Jesus take the initiative when we have failed him badly? What reassurance does David (Jesus?) give?

2. Even Shimei, who had cursed David, receives mercy. What encouragement does this give us? Is Jesus less merciful than David?

3. Sometimes when there is a remarkable combination of circumstances we are impressed with the 'providence' of God. But at times the devil seems to have his 'providence' also! How do we see that here? How does David react? 'Sheba . . . will do us more harm than Absalom' (20:6). But what happened? How does God teach us to live without panic?

□□□ Reading 181 (2 Samuel 21:1–22:51)

The last four chapters of 2 Samuel are a series of appendices to the story that has been told so far. There are six sections in it. There is a narrative (21:1–14), a list (21:15–22) and a song (22:1–51), followed in the opposite order by a song (23:1–7), a list (23:8–39) and a narrative (24:1–25).

1. The first narrative records an occasion when a public betrayal of an oath plus a racist desire to exterminate a whole people is punished by God as a serious breach of justice. How much is the providence of God *visible* in such matters? How does the strange story show the importance in every community of satisfying the people's sense of justice?

2. The last battles with the Philistines are mentioned next, plus a list of

David's heroes (21:15–22). How do these heroes make us think of Jesus? What are the similarities and contrasts?

3. Romans 15:8–12 applies David's psalm to Jesus. In 2 Samuel 22:1–51 we have a song of praise in which David worships God for the many victories God has given him (22:1). It begins with praise for the protection of God (22:2–4). What is the point of the various descriptions of God: Rock, Fortress, Shield, Horn, High Tower?

☐☐☐ **Reading 182 (2 Samuel 23:1–24:25)**

1. David's last words (2 Samuel 23:1–7) describe him as 'the man who was raised up on high' (23:1). God had created him. God made him the person that he was in his temperament, his circumstances, his background. Even the fact that he was 'son of Jesse' was part of God's plan. The thing he likes most is that he is the 'sweet psalmist of Israel'. What do you like most about the way God has blessed you? In David's descriptions he is describing an ideal. How are they fulfilled in Jesus?

2. The list of David's mighty men (2 Samuel 23:8–39) is next to the story of how he numbered the fighting men of the nation (2 Samuel 24:1–25). We read of three courageous men, Josheb (23:8), Eleazar (23:9–10) and Shammah (23:11–12). How are they models for us?

3. The warriors of Israel came to a total of 1.3 million men. But when we look at the mighty deeds of 2 Samuel 23:8–39, how many had God needed? Thirty-seven! The story of David counting the fighting men of the nation (2 Samuel 24:1–25) is surprising. Why was it displeasing to God?

4. God sent a prophet to invite David to choose three possible chastening judgments. What was the choice meant to do?

1 Thessalonians

After the 'consultation at Jerusalem' in about AD 49, Paul went back to Antioch to continue his work. Some time later, in the spring of AD 50, he felt that he and Barnabas should go on a second ministry tour, starting with visits to the churches they had founded a year or so previously. Barnabas and Mark went to Cyprus while Paul and Silas went northwards up the Mediterranean coast, encouraging the churches in Syria. Then they reached Troas, which was as far east as they could go, if they were to stay within that part of the mainland. One night God called them in a vision to cross the sea that was between Troas and Europe. They left Troas by boat and landed at Samothrace on the other side. From there they continued eastwards preaching in such places as Philippi and Thessalonica. In Thessalonica Paul went to the synagogue and for three weeks preached to Jews, with some success. But then the Jewish authorities used drifters from the market-place to start a riot against Paul, Silas and Timothy. Paul and Silas had to leave the city. Organised persecution continued after Paul and Silas had left, but the church stood firm and became a centre of further outreach.

Paul went on to Berea and Athens (Acts 17:10, 15). While in Athens he sent Silas and Timothy to Thessalonica to find out how the church was doing. By the time Timothy got back, Paul had gone on to Corinth, where he stayed from the autumn of AD 50 to the spring of AD 52. 1 Thessalonians was written from there probably about late AD 50. 2 Thessalonians was sent shortly after (perhaps early AD 51).

Recommended reading: M. A. Eaton, *1, 2 Thessalonians* (Preaching Through the Bible, Sovereign World, 1997); J. R. W. Stott, *The Message of Thessalonians* (The Bible Speaks Today, IVP, 1991).

☐☐☐ **Reading 183 (1 Thessalonians 1:1–10)**
1. How is Paul a model of prayerfulness in this chapter?
2. What can we learn about Christian ministry from Paul's descriptions in this chapter?
3. What is the *content* of our faith according to 1:9–10? What is it that we believe in?

☐☐☐ **Reading 184 (1 Thessalonians 2:1–20)**
1. Paul is obviously a man of sincerity. What are the marks of his genuineness in this chapter?
2. What do we learn about 'the word' in 1 Thessalonians 2:13–16?
3. What is the preacher's crown? What is the connection between ministry (which all Christians have) and heavenly reward?

☐☐☐ **Reading 185 (1 Thessalonians 3:1–13)**
1. How did Paul watch over new Christians?
2. Faith, love and joy are clearly important matters to Paul. How may we promote them?
3. How should we prepare for Jesus' coming? Why should we prepare for Jesus' coming?

☐☐☐ **Reading 186 (1 Thessalonians 4:1–18)**
1. What is Paul's style of appealing for holiness? Does he threaten? Does he expound the Mosaic law? What is his method of helping his people?
2. 1 Thessalonians 4:4 tells us to know 'how to use his or her body in holiness and honour' (as it is best translated). How do we do this? What does he have in mind?
3. Those who are alive when Jesus returns have no advantages over those who have died. Why is this?

☐☐☐ **Reading 187 (1 Thessalonians 5:1–28)**
1. Paul uses night-time and daytime as a picture of sin and salvation. How does he work out the illustration?

2. Paul gives us a series of assurances and encouragements in 5:9–11. How important is assurance? What encouragements does Paul give?

3. How does Paul encourage the Christians to stay together in Jesus?

Job

The book of Job is a massive, poetic description of a good man who suffered unjustly because of a spiritual battle taking place between God and Satan. The book does not so much explain suffering (except to note that there might be a hidden spiritual conflict raging around the sufferer). Rather it describes how the sufferer might react and how others react to him. No one can be sure of the date of the book of Job. The hero himself seems to have lived in patriarchal times before Israel settled in Canaan.

The book has a clear structure. First we are taken behind the scenes and we learn of the battle taking place between God and Satan (Job 1:1–2:13). Job asks why it is happening (Job 3:1–26) and three rounds of debate take place between him and his three friends (Job 4:1–14:22; 15:1–21:34; 22:1–31:40). Then another character steps into the debate: Elihu (Job 32:1–37:24). He is ignored by everyone, but God finally speaks to Job (Job 38:1–41:34) and the story comes to a conclusion (42:7–17).

Recommended reading: 'Job' in *New Bible Commentary* (IVP, 1994 edition); F. I. Andersen, *Job* (Tyndale Commentary, IVP, 1974).

□□□ Reading 188 (Job 1:1–2:13)

1. What does God think of Job? He loses servants (1:13–15), wealth (1:16–17) and family (1:18–19) at the hands of cruel men (1:15, 17)

and through God's creation (1:16, 19). How does Job respond? Does God want us to be silent when we suffer (see 1:20–22)?

2. What are we to think when a lot of sufferings all come upon us at the same time? Is there any explanation?

3. Both God and Satan seem to be involved in suffering. But what is the difference between what they are doing?

□□□ **Reading 189 (Job 3:1–4:21)**

1. Job's silence does not last for ever! Eventually Job can bear his sufferings no more, and the pain in his heart bursts out through his lips. What is happening now? Is he sinning? Would we have done any better? How do we help such a person? Is it possible?

2. Job curses the very day when he was born (3:1–10). May a Christian believer have suicidal thoughts? Are there other examples of such despair in the Scriptures?

3. The three friends all hold the same doctrine. They all believe that suffering is caused by the sin of each individual. A truly righteous person – they believe – does not suffer. But although the three friends all hold the same doctrine, they each have their own character. Eliphaz's character is marked by gentleness. How does a 'tactful' person counsel others? What are the advantages and disadvantages of gentleness?

□□□ **Reading 190 (Job 5:1–7:21)**

Eliphaz continues his counsel in Job 5:1–27; Job replies in Job 6:1–7:21.

1. We know something of the explanation of Job's suffering (because of Job 1:1–2:13). So what mistakes are being made by Job here?

2. When do people 'bray like a donkey' (6:5). How should we respond to them?

3. Job describes his physical condition (7:1–10). What are the marks of extreme suffering? But Job is determined not to keep quiet and pretend things are other than what they are. 'I will not keep silent . . . I will speak out . . . I will complain' (7:11). Is he right or is he mistaken?

□□□ **Reading 191 (Job 8:1–10:22)**

Bildad speaks in Job 8:1–22. Job replies in Job 9:1–10:22.

1. Eliphaz appealed to charismatic experience (4:12–16); Bildad is characterised by bluntness and severity. Job 8:4 refers to 1:5, 19. Are they not excessively severe? What makes a 'counsellor' talk in such a way?

2. Job replies to Bildad in Job 9:1–10:22. In what way are Job's anxieties destined to be answered in Jesus (see especially Job 9:33)?

3. Eliphaz appealed earlier to charismatic experience (4:12–16); Bildad now appeals to tradition (8:18–19). What is the value of the two ways of finding the truth? What are the limitations of both ways?

☐☐☐ Reading 192 (Job 11:1–13:28)

1. Eliphaz is gentle (see 4:2); Bildad is harsh (see 8:4). What is Zophar's main characteristic (see 11:2; 20:3)?

2. Job 11:13–14 is surely good advice. So why is Zophar a 'miserable comforter' (16:2; see also 42:7)?

3. Job longs to talk things out with God (13:21). Can we give any reasons why God might want to remain silent? What difference would it make if God gave us all the answers we wanted?

☐☐☐ Reading 193 (Job 14:1–16:22)

1. Job's mood is not steady. Nor is there any trend towards faith or towards despair. His feelings go up and down quite violently. In Job 14:1–22, what mood is he in? Is there any way we can help ourselves when our feelings are going up and down?

2. In Job 15:1–35 the debate begins to get more heated! Gentle Eliphaz still speaks of gentleness (see 15:11) but is more severe than before. He argues that Job is not wise (15:11–13), not innocent (15:14–16) and is badly mistaken. How often is gentleness a pretence? Should we ever *pretend* to be gentle? What makes Eliphaz become more harsh towards Job?

3. Job reaches a deeper level of loneliness in 16:1–22 (note 16:2, 7), yet briefly rises to a high level of faith in 16:19. Is there any connection? Is there any blessing in loneliness? Is Job getting a preview of Jesus in 16:19? If so, how did he come to such a viewpoint?

☐☐☐ Reading 194 (Job 17:1–19:29)

1. Is Job's view of righteousness (17:9) an advance upon Job 1:1?

2. Bildad's second speech is a study in savage, harsh traditionalism. He tends to take Job's words and twist them. Job 17:12 and 18:5 are examples. Can other examples be found?

3. Job 19:1–29 describes Job at his worst (see 19:13–19) yet he rises to great heights in 19:25–26. He comes to assurance ('I know'). He glimpses atonement ('my Redeemer'), and even seems to grasp the idea of resurrection. Again we ask: How did the worst experience lead to the best understanding?

☐☐☐ Reading 195 (Job 20:1–21:34)

1. Zophar is the one who loves intellectual arguments (see 20:3). He wants to 'answer' Job. His speech is tidy and logical, moving from the brevity of the joys of the wicked (20:6–11), through the severity of their sufferings (20:12–19) to the certainty of the judgment of God (20:20–27). It is a logical lecture. But what is wrong with its spirit?

2. Job's points are the exact opposite of Zophar's. He asks Zophar to listen (21:2) and to look (21:5). What kind of doctrine do we reach if we fail to listen and look?

3. Is there a cause-and-effect relationship between our godliness and the spirituality of our children? What did Job say about the matter?

☐☐☐ Reading 196 (Job 22:1–24:25)

1. Job 22:1–30 begins the final round of the debate. What leads Eliphaz into the terrible accusations of 22:5–9? Is it possible for a doctrinal theory to lead us into slander?

2. Job is distressed by the *absence* of God. Does God's absence from us always mean he is angry with us? What other possibility does Job consider?

3. The sufferings of the needy (24:1–12) oppress him. He has to believe in the punishment of the wicked (24:18–24). So what is the difference between the three friends and the way in which Job understands the punishment of the wicked?

☐☐☐ Reading 197 (Job 25:1–27:23)

1. Bildad thinks humanity to be 'a maggot' and 'a worm'. Is he right? If not, what is his mistake? What is wrong with viewing men and women in this way?

2. Zophar has no more to say! The friends have run out of ideas and arguments. Job seems to have left behind the problem of his sufferings. He is shocked by Bildad's last words ('You' in 26:2–4 is singular). He is now summarising his feelings and his convictions. He begins with a description of God's power in creation (26:5–14). Is this a good place to begin his conclusions? If so, why?

3. Job's next topic is a restatement of his problem. He insists on God's

involvement in what has happened to him (27:2) and on his own innocence (27:3–6). He affirms his faith in God's justice (27:7–23). But it is precisely this combination of facts that is his problem. How is Job's procedure here a model for us when we meet inexplicable problems in the way God deals with us? What is Job's approach at this point?

□□□ **Reading 198 (Job 28:1–29:25)**

1. Having stated God's power (26:1–14) and the ingredients of his problem with God (27:1–23) what does Job do next? What is the point of Job's poem on the inaccessibility of wisdom (28:28)? How does this thought help Job? How does it help us?
2. Job describes his original happiness, before his great crisis began (29:25). What is he doing at this point? What is the point of his going over his original circumstances? How may we obtain a clear mind when we are trying to think through a problem?
3. How many people get to live the life described in Job 29:1–25? Why is not such a life lived by everyone – not even by everyone who trusts the God of the Bible?

□□□ **Reading 199 (Job 30:1–31:40)**

1. Job turns from his earlier life (29:1–25) to his present experience (30:1–31). The Lord gives; the Lord takes away. Paul suffered the loss of all things. What do we gain when we lose everything that is dear to us?
2. In Job 31:1–40, Job sums up his position. In an incidental manner Job is describing what he considers a godly person should be. What are the points of special interest in this description of godliness?
3. What is Job doing at this point? He has described God's power (26:5–14). He insists on God's involvement in what has happened to him (27:2) and on his own innocence (27:3–6). He affirms his faith in God's justice (27:7–23). Wisdom is inaccessible (28:1–28). He states his original happiness (29:1–25) and his present experience (30:1–31). Now he affirms his righteousness (31:1–34, 38–40) and pleads for someone to listen (31:35–37). So what is Job expecting to happen now? What is the point of his lengthy summary?

□□□ **Reading 200 (Job 32:1–33:33)**

Now there are two reactions to Job's assessment of his situation (26:1–31:40). First there is a human response (Elihu in 32:1–37:24). Elihu 'declares his opinion' (32:17). Then there is God's response (38:1–40:2; 40:6–41:34).

1. Elihu is young and angry with everyone. He speaks very self-confidently. Which of his characteristics might we admire? But is there anything wrong with his attitude?
2. Who does Elihu represent in modern life? Why does everyone – including God – ignore him?
3. Elihu asks Job to listen (33:1–7), summarises Job's complaints (33:8–11) and then starts to reply to the accusation that God is silent (33:12–33). What do you think of Elihu's list of ways in which God speaks? Is he right? Does God speak in these ways today?

□□□ Reading 201 (Job 34:1–35:16)
1. Next Elihu speaks of God's justice (34:10–37). He seems to be simply restating the arguments of the three friends. So why did he think he could do any better in answering Job? In what way is Elihu typical of the youthful or the inexperienced person? Why do young people claim to know so much – and what happens as we get older?
2. Are Elihu's statements about God's justice correct? If they are, then in what way is he mistaken in applying them to Job?
3. In Job 35:1–16, Elihu complains about Job's self-righteousness. What kind of God does he believe in (see 35:6–8)?

□□□ Reading 202 (Job 36:1–37:24)
1. In Job 36:5–12 Elihu says God sends troubles to test and train people. Is this true? Is it the explanation of Job's case? Do troubles train us necessarily? What is needed in us if we are to profit from them?
2. Elihu speaks of the marvels of God's handiwork in creation (36:27–37:13). Does the glory of God in creation help the sufferer?
3. 'The Almighty – we cannot find him' (37:23). Does Elihu have anything comforting to say? Are we to surrender to the thought that God cannot be found?

□□□ Reading 203 (Job 38:1–40:24)
1. When God finally speaks to Job, does Job get the kind of answer that he wants? God does not say anything about Job's sufferings, but points to the mystery of God's creation. What do the wonders of creation have to teach us about suffering?
2. Among the animals there is unpredictability (39:1–4), freedom (39:5–

8), stubbornness (39:9–12), foolishness (39:13–18), courage (39:19–25), wisdom (39:26), perceptiveness (39:27–30). But what is God's point?

3. 'Who am I?' asks God, 'and who are you?' (Job 40:1–24). In what way is God telling Job how to face suffering?

☐☐☐ Reading 204 (Job 41:1–42:17)

1. 'Leviathan' seems to be a mythological name being applied to a crocodile. The point is: If one hardly dares stir a crocodile to action, how much more foolish is it to try to stand before God as Job has done? How bold are we allowed to be in arguing with God?

2. Does Job get any answers to his questions? Does he finally arrive at peace? What conclusions are to be found in 42:1–5?

3. Does it spoil the story that Job has a happy ending? Do all stories of innocent suffering have happy endings? Does the happy ending in Job foreshadow a happy ending that may be beyond the grave?

Amos

Amos preached at a time when two powerful kings were ruling the two nations. Uzziah (779–740) ruled Judah, and Jeroboam II (783–743) was king of northern Israel. Both in the north and the south these were days of economic stability. They were also days of military danger. The Assyrians to the north were ambitious to extend their territory. Both halves of Israel were full of social injustice and religious idolatry. Amos' short period of preaching was at about 760 BC or maybe earlier.

Recommended reading: M. A. Eaton, *Joel and Amos* (Preaching Through the Bible, Sovereign World, 1998); J. A. Motyer, *The Message of Amos* (The Bible Speaks Today, IVP, 1974).

☐☐☐ Reading 205 (Amos 1:1–3:8)
The theme of this section of Amos is in 1:2. God is roaring with anger against the wickedness of the nations. In 1:3–2:16 Amos develops his point, presenting God's message to eight nations.

1. What do the sins of the six pagan nations have in common (1:3–2:3)? What are the basic sins of nations with little knowledge of the God of the Bible?
2. The six nations condemned in 1:3–2:3 were never condemned for disobeying God's law. But Judah had a written revelation of the will of

345

God. What difference does it make whether we do or do not know God's will?

3. Amos 3:1–8 belongs with 1:2–2:16. Amos is pressing upon his readers the message of what was said in Amos 1:1–2:16. The situation is now an open one – but it will soon close down. God is announcing what will happen soon. Israel has committed 'three transgressions' already. What will come next? Will the lion get its prey? Will the trap spring upon the fluttering bird? The situation will soon close down – in judgment or renewal. When God gives a warning, how long does the situation stay open before the warning is implemented?

□□□ **Reading 206 (Amos 3:9–6:14)**

Amos likes the style in which one moves through topics to a central point and then works backwards through the same topics in reverse order. He does it in Amos 5:18–27:

A. Inescapable judgment in the day of Yahweh (5:18–20)
    B. Rejection of worship (5:21–23)
        C. Let justice roll (5:24)
    B. Rejection of idolatry (5:25–26)
A. Inescapable exile (5:27)

1. The nation was full of violence (3:9–12); its religion was powerless (3:13–15); its upper-class citizens were arrogant (4:1–3); its pilgrimages were useless (4:4–5). If this is Amos' analysis of his own society, how should we put forward a similar analysis of our own society?

2. Many calls from God have gone unheeded (4:6–11). God is giving Israel a last call to repentance (4:12–13). Now Amos sings a 'funeral song' (5:1). The death song is to be found in 5:3 and continues in 5:16–17. Seeking God is mentioned in 5:4–5 and 5:14–15. The sin of Israel is explained in 5:7 and 5:10–13. In the heart of the section is a song about the great power of God (5:8–9). This means that the sections of the poetry have an A-B-C-D-C-B-A structure. Actually Israel did die as a nation less than forty years after Amos' ministry. The Assyrians invaded Israel in the late 720s BC, and northern Israel, with its capital city Samaria, was destroyed. Can sin destroy a culture or nationality completely?

3. Amos 6:1–14 brings the middle section to an end by coming back to the cause of everything: Israel's utter complacency and carelessness despite everything that God has done for them in their previous history. There are two small units of analysis in which Amos looks at their complacent pride (6:1–3) and their carelessness amid many privileges

(6:4–6). Then there are two units of final announcements that the end is near. A calamitous punishment (6:7–11) is at hand, based upon the certain principle that God cannot indefinitely ignore the sin of his people (6:12–14). Are there signs of ease and complacency in our national life? What would Amos have said to us if he had viewed our land?

□□□ **Reading 207 (Amos 7:1–9:15)**

The last section of Amos deals with God's sovereign graciousness (7:1–9:15). It unfolds as follows:

* Judgment *without* hope of *present* renewal (7:1–9)
    * The word of God rejected (7:10–8:3)
        * Crime and punishment (8:4–10)
    * The word of God lost (8:11–9:6)
* Judgment – *with* hope of *future* renewal (9:7–15)

1. Amos 7:1–9 brings before us three visions. In the first two Israel is faced with the threat of extermination, first by locusts and then by divine fire. In both of the visions, the threat of extermination is turned aside by Amos' intercession. But why is there no intercession the third time? Is intercession ever to be abandoned?

2. What are the marks of a call to the ministry of the word of God? Does Amos' call give us any help in this matter?

3. The question at end of Amos' book is: Is Israel to be exterminated altogether? The nation will not be allowed to continue as it has been for centuries. 'I will destroy it from the face of the earth.' Yet God judges his people with a discriminating, purifying judgment. The hope for northern Israel was to be found in the south (9:11). What is involved in the promises of 9:11–15?

Psalm 119:1–176

☐☐☐ **Reading 208 (Psalm 119:1–88)**

Psalm 119 is an alphabetic psalm, with each line of each section of eight verses beginning with the same letter of the Hebrew alphabet. Verses 1–8 each begin with 'aleph' (a letter not found in the English alphabet). Verses 9–16 begin with the letter 'b', and so on. The psalm is a sustained meditation on the Word of God, mentioned in almost every verse.

1. How should we handle the word of God, according to Psalm 119:1–88? We walk in it (119:1); we keep it (119:2). What else?

2. What will the word of God do for us, according to Psalm 119:1–88? It will bring blessing (119:1), boldness (119:6), purity (119:9). What more will it do for us?

3. In Psalm 119:1–88, what prayers does the psalmist present to God concerning his word?

☐☐☐ **Reading 209 (Psalm 119:89–176)**

1. How may the Christian become like the writer of Psalm 119:97?

2. The psalmist often refers to his enemies (verses 95, 98, 110, 115, 121, and so on). How are we to relate to our enemies?

3. What does verse 148 suggest to us about times for meditating on God's word?

2 Thessalonians

One gets the impression in 1 Thessalonians that the Christians had recently come to salvation, but in 2 Thessalonians one gets the impression that various developments have gone a stage further. 2 Thessalonians 2:15 refers to a previous letter. So it is likely that 2 Thessalonians was written not long after 1 Thessalonians. Paul is still in Corinth and still with Silas and Timothy. The gospel has spread further than Thessalonica. Persecution has got worse. The teaching concerning the second coming was being misunderstood and matters were made worse because of a false letter that had reached the Thessalonians (2 Thessalonians 2:2). The 'disorderly' or 'unruly' people were as much a problem as ever. Paul writes to give them the positive teaching that is needed by the different sections of the fellowship.

Recommended reading: M. A. Eaton, *1, 2 Thessalonians* (Preaching Through the Bible, Sovereign World, 1997); J. R. W. Stott, *The Message of Thessalonians* (The Bible Speaks Today, IVP, 1991).

□□□ Reading 210 (2 Thessalonians 1:1–16)

1. How does Paul describe the Church? What are the marks of a 'growing' faith? Growing love?
2. The main idea of verses 5–12 is that when Jesus comes again it will be a day when all injustices are rectified, and people receive back from

God judgments and rewards according to the way they have treated the people of God. If we really believe such things what difference will it make to us in day-to-day living?

3. How is Paul motivated to pray according to 2 Thessalonians 1:11–12? What is it that he prays for?

□□□ **Reading 211 (2 Thessalonians 2:1–17)**

1. Is it possible to be overexcited about the doctrine of the second coming? How does Paul remedy this overexcitement?

2. 'That day will not arrive unless the rebellion comes first, and the Man of Lawlessness is revealed, the son of perdition, who opposes and exalts himself over against everything called god and against every object of worship, so that he takes his seat in the temple of God, proclaiming himself to be God.' What can we say about the future 'Man of Sin' on the basis of these words?

3. What restrains Satan from causing great apostasy even now? What might verses 6–7 refer to? (i) Is it the Roman empire or civil government? (ii) Some have said the restrainer is the Holy Spirit. Is this what Paul has in mind? (iii) Could the restrainer be an angelic power? (iv) Is it Paul himself and the preaching of the gospel?

Note The 'Anti-Christ' theme in the Bible. The law of Moses warned against times of falling away from godliness (Exodus 20:3–4). So did Moses in his preaching (Deuteronomy 6:14; 11:16). Such times of 'falling away' have often occurred in the story of God's people. We may think of northern Israel during the days of King Ahab and Queen Jezebel. Then there was a rebellion in the second century BC, predicted by Daniel 8:27. Sometimes in these spiritual rebellions there is one particular man who rises up in opposition against God. The prophecy of Daniel predicted that there would be such a person in Israel. Daniel 8:5–8 undoubtedly refers to Alexander the Great. It was in the time of the Greek empire that there came 'a little horn which grew exceedingly'. Daniel 8:9–14 refers to Antiochus the Great who was the 'antichrist' of the Old Testament period. Then in about 63 BC when the Roman emperor Pompei invaded Israel, many at that time also fell away from faith in the God of Israel. Also about twelve years before Paul wrote 2 Thessalonians, there had been a mad emperor, Caligula, who had tried to set up his own statue in the temple in Jerusalem. Jesus predicted that before the fall of Jerusalem there would be a similar period in which the love of many would grow cold. Then there would be an 'abomination of desolation', defiling the temple before it was destroyed.

Led by the Holy Spirit, Paul predicts that there will be a similar figure in the story of the Church before the second coming of Jesus. It is not exactly identical to other passages and we must pay attention to Paul's words, rather than read them in the light of other events and predictions.

□□□ Reading 212 (2 Thessalonians 3:1–18)

1. How confident is Paul in the power of prayer? How does it influence him here? And how should our view of prayer affect us? What should we pray for, according to Paul?

2. Paul is very realistic when he says, 'not all people have faith'. What are the implications of his realism?

3. Paul is confident in God's faithfulness. 'But the Lord is faithful . . .' In what ways should we expect God to be faithful despite difficult times ahead of us?

Obadiah

Obadiah is a small-scale version of many of the themes found elsewhere in the prophets: the judgment of wicked nations, the Day of the Lord, kingdom, appropriateness in judgment, the importance of the land. We do not know much about Obadiah the prophet himself. Since Obadiah is undated it would be unwise to base too much interpretation on its date. Its theme is clear. The book of Obadiah is a prophecy of judgment against the nation of Edom. In verse 1 there is a title. In verses 1b–4 we have an announcement of judgment, and the reason for God's judgment is given. In verses 5–9 the prophet deals with the completeness of judgment. In verses 10–14 the reason for judgment is told in fuller detail. Then in verses 15–21 the principles are widened; Obadiah applies what he has said to all the nations.

Recommended reading: D. W. Baker, 'Obadiah' in *Obadiah, Jonah and Micah* (ed. D. W. Baker, Tyndale Commentary, IVP, 1985).

☐☐☐ **Reading 213 (Obadiah)**
1. In what ways are the judgments of God appropriate? How do sinners (and we ourselves?) get back our own sins as judgments?
2. Edom and Israel were related nations (see verse 10). One sin God hates is the betrayal of those who are close to us. In what ways (judging by Edom's bad example) may we be guilty of betrayal?

3. In verses 15–21 Obadiah takes his message and applies it to the entire world. How can it be said that 'the day of Yahweh is near against all the nations'?

1 Kings

Kingship or kingdom is an important theme in the Bible, and 1–2 Kings will help us understand it. 'Kings' is the story of how God was looking for a perfect king. David was God's king, the man after God's own heart. Could there be another king like David? Not until Jesus! Only Jesus is the perfect Son of David! The main point of the book is that the kings of Israel failed because of idolatry; idolatry is fatal! 1–2 Kings presses home the teaching of Deuteronomy, with its warnings against false gods.

Recommended reading: M. A. Eaton, *1 Kings* (Preaching Through the Bible, Sovereign World, 1996).

☐☐☐ Reading 214 (1 Kings 1:1–2:46)

1. In the first chapters of 1 Kings, Solomon is being called to rise up to kingship. In what ways are all Christians called to rise up to kingship? How does Solomon have to learn to rise to kingship despite opposition?
2. Consider Adonijah. Ambition is not wrong in itself, is it? But what mistakes did Adonijah make? How does our ambition need to be refined and purified?
3. In 1 Kings 2:1–46, David is concerned for the future of the kingdom of God. In what ways does he act on behalf of God's kingdom? How much of David's character may we follow?

☐☐☐ **Reading 215 (1 Kings 3:1–5:18)**

1. Solomon was from the earliest beginnings of his reign a mixture of silliness and wisdom. What were his mistakes? What were his strongest points?

2. Solomon sought and received a miraculous gift of wisdom. What is wisdom? How do we get it (remember Proverbs 1:7)? What aspects of wisdom are found in 1 Kings 4:1–34? What did it lead to in the life of the nation?

3. 1 Kings 5:1–9:14 is concerned with the two major building projects of Solomon, which took twenty years to complete. The section begins and ends with mention of Hiram (5:1–12; 9:10–14). What do you think of Solomon's making use of the skills of the world (Hiram)? Was it wise? May we do the same? Josephus the Jewish historian tells us that Solomon married Hiram's daughter. It is probably true.

☐☐☐ **Reading 216 (1 Kings 6:1–7:51)**

1. God planned to put his name or 'glory' in the temple. He said, 'I will put my name there' (1 Kings 3:2; 8:16–20, 29; 9:23). There are three things that are mentioned as being God's temple in the New Testament: (i) the body of Jesus (John 2:21), (ii) the Church, the fellowship of believers (1 Corinthians 3:16; Ephesians 2:22; Hebrews 3:6; 1 Peter 2:5; 2 Corinthians 6:16), and (iii) individual believers are God's temples (1 Corinthians 6:19). What does the temple tell us about these things? Our need of the presence of God. What else?

2. The windows of the temple spoke of freshness, freedom from stuffiness. Where the presence of God is experienced, there is freedom. What is the New Testament equivalent of all of this?

3. Near to the temple were some other houses, a court for Solomon to do the work of a king, a private apartment for himself, and something similar for his wife (7:1–12). These places reveal his secondary concerns. He was concerned about justice and built a 'hall of pillars' (7:7) as a central court where he might sit in judgment to deal with difficult cases. What other concerns of Solomon are visible here? Should they be our concerns also?

☐☐☐ **Reading 217 (1 Kings 8:1–9:28)**

1. God honoured Solomon by the coming down of his glory. What is the equivalent of this in the Christian life? How important is it to be honoured by God?

2. God honoured Solomon despite his imperfections. Solomon had married pagan women (3:1). He had tolerated high places (3:3). The law of Moses had forbidden intermarriage with pagans (Deuteronomy 7:3), had forbidden the multiplication of horses, and had specially forbidden that trade in horses should lead to renewed contact with Egypt (Deuteronomy 17:16). The king was forbidden to take many wives (Deuteronomy 17:17), especially ones who would take him into idolatry. He was told not to accumulate gold or silver (Deuteronomy 17:18). Solomon was doing all of these things. What impact does this kind of compromise have on our lives? Immediately? Eventually? Why did God still honour him?

3. Solomon both instructed the people and followed his instruction with intercession. Where else is this pattern to be found? What is its importance?

☐☐☐ **Reading 218 (1 Kings 10:1–12:33)**

1. Solomon became famous throughout the territories surrounding Israel, but he was drawing close to disaster. On the other hand, the queen of Sheba was showing great eagerness to know about the God of Israel. What was it that roused her interest in the name of the Lord? How may people baffled by the perplexities of life come to Jesus, who is 'greater than Solomon' (Matthew 12:42)?

2. Solomon himself was slipping into complacency. What was it that was leading to his spiritual ruin? What were the consequences? What are the consequences of sin in a believer?

3. After the reign of Solomon, the land of Israel divided into two countries. It was a major tragedy. Why did it happen? What were the stages in which it happened? How could it have been averted? How does the judgment of God damage our own concerns when we are out of his will?

☐☐☐ **Reading 219 (1 Kings 13:1–14:31)**

1. What do we learn about prophecy from the story in 1 Kings 13:1–34? How do we handle prophecies today (keeping in mind the warning of 1 Thessalonians 5:20)?

2. Why was the Judean prophet dealt with more severely than the older backslidden prophet? Why does God sometimes deal with sin severely, but at other times seem not to do so?

3. Jeroboam wanted miraculous help, but he did not want personally to submit his life to God. Jeroboam was to consult Ahijah without anyone knowing. In what way does this resemble much popular religion? What does God do about it?

□□□ **Reading 220 (1 Kings 15:1–16:34)**

1. The lesson of Abijam's reign is that no spiritual advance can come unless favourite sins are repudiated (15:1–8). What is the lesson of Asa's reign (15:9–24)?

2. In 15:25 the writer of 1 Kings turns from Judah to the story of the northern kingdom. The central lesson of 1 Kings 15:25–16:28 is that idolatry has a corrupting effect in society. There are five kings mentioned here. Nadab of Israel (15:25–31) was assassinated. From him we learn that God's word is fulfilled, for he fulfilled the prophecy of Ahijah. Baasha of Israel (15:33–16:7) had the opportunity of reversing Jeroboam's sins. But what do we learn from his reign?

3. Elah of Israel (16:8–14) had a short reign that achieved nothing. Why not? The new king, Zimri, did to his family exactly what he and his father had done to Jeroboam's family. Why did he not learn from history? History repeated itself. Omri emerged at a time of chaos. He was famous among ancient kings but had no significance in the progress of God's kingdom. Why do none of these kings of Israel make any real progress? What causes stagnation and decline in the story of the nations?

□□□ **Reading 221 (1 Kings 17:1–18:46)**

1. Elijah is a man with great courage and boldness. What makes him so bold? His temperament? His knowledge of God's will? His family background? His call? Which? How does he know it will not rain for three years? If Elijah is a human being just like us (remember James 5:17!) may we be just like him?

2. A sudden change in God's will for Elijah's life appears. For some time he dwelt near Kerith while the drought was taking place. Then the brook dries up; he must leave Kerith (17:7). How do we cope with sudden change? How does Elijah face the matter?

3. Elijah is called by the Lord to swing around the entire nation for God. How does he begin? In what ways might we try to dramatically change the people for whom we are responsible, or who are close to us?

□□□ **Reading 222 (1 Kings 19:1–20:43)**

1. Elijah suddenly falls into depression and self-pity. What is the cause of his problem? Is it physical? Spiritual? Psychological? Demonic? How did God set about restoring him? What should we do when we feel the same as Elijah did?

2. Elisha's call comes as Elijah throws his mantle over him. It is a *subtle*

call. In what ways does it put a lot of responsibility upon Elisha? Does God often call us to his service in this way?

3. Does it come as a surprise that God is willing to help Ahab at all? He is a wicked king, no better than Ben-Hadad. Why should God be willing to help Ahab? What encouragement can we take from the fact that he helps such a person?

□□□ **Reading 223 (1 Kings 21:1–22:53)**

1. What are the characteristics of the Mosaic law in the story of Naboth's vineyard? Was there any advantage in the illegality of selling family land? Are we under the law? Are we free from it? Need we look to it for wisdom?

2. How did Jezebel relate to the Mosaic law? So what is the advantage of Israel's having its legislation?

3. In 1 Kings 22:1–52 we have a weak king and a bold prophet. What are the weak points of Jehoshaphat in 1 Kings 22:1–52? How does he compare with the prophet Micaiah? Who is really a good witness for the God of Judah – and why? Who is vindicated in the end?

Jonah

Jonah is one of the more surprising books of the Bible. It is included among the prophets but it is unlike any of the other prophets. Jonah himself lived about 760 BC. The date of his book is unknown. What is its purpose in the Bible? Many answers to that question have been given, but two of them seem more convincing than the others. (i) The book of Jonah is the story of a man who was a rebel. We learn about God from the experiences of the prophet himself. (ii) The book of Jonah is also an account of God's concern for the nations. As soon as we read its opening lines, we find that God has an interest in the gentile nations as well as in Israel. Jonah did not like it. He did not want to preach mercy and compassion to the savage wicked Ninevites who were famous for their hateful ways. The two major themes of the book of Jonah are God's care for the individual, and God's care for the nations.

Recommended reading: R. T. Kendall, *Jonah* (Hodder, 1978).

□□□ **Reading 224 (Jonah 1:1–4:11)**

1. God has a will for our lives. In Jonah's case it was: 'Arise and preach . . .' but Jonah did not want Nineveh to be spared. How easy was it to become a rebel? At first? Eventually? Why does God let it be so easy to become a rebel? How did God deal with Jonah?
2. Jonah is called to prayer by pagan sailors. Is there ever a time when the

world calls upon us to do what we ought to be doing? In what way is Jonah 1:1–17 a picture of the Church and the world? Why does the storm continue even after Jonah has confessed his sin? What is Jonah learning about prayer?

3. God disciplines those whom he loves. In what way is it good news when we find ourselves being chastised by God? Note Jonah 2:8–9. What are the three things that Jonah was made to learn? What is it like to be given a second chance to live for God, after a period of rebelliousness?

4. Repentance is being made to think again. How does God get Jonah to rethink his attitudes?

Psalms 120:1–131:3

□□□ **Reading 225 (Psalms 120:1–123:4)**

Psalms 120:1–134:3 are a group of fifteen psalms that are often called the 'Songs of Degrees'. It is likely that they were psalms sung by pilgrims going to Jerusalem.

1. Psalm 120:1–7 is the song of a man with fearful enemies. How should we handle slander?
2. Where in fact do people look, when they are in trouble (Psalm 121:1–8)? To the experts? To their own ingenuity? To their friends? How much should we look to God? How much should we take practical steps for our own protection?
3. What does God to do for our protection?
4. How are we to apply Psalm 122:1–9 to our own lives? Obviously David was thinking of the actual city of Jerusalem, but Jerusalem has since that time fallen away from significance in the kingdom of God (Matthew 21:43) and the tribes of verse 4 no longer exist. So what is the Christian application of the psalm? Is the Christian politically pro-Israeli, and anti-Palestinian?
5. Is there any progress in the 'psalms of degrees'? Psalm 120:1–7 spoke of troublesome surroundings. Psalm 121:1–8 persuades us to look to God for our safety. Psalm 122:1–9 approaches the house of God in Jerusalem. What is the fourth step in Psalm 123:1–4?

□□□ **Reading 226 (Psalms 124:1–127:5)**

1. Do all Christians go through times when they say, 'If the Lord had not been on our side . . . they would have swallowed us up alive'? What happens? How should we respond? What lesson should we learn (124:8)?

2. In what situations do we need to show special faith so that we 'cannot be moved' (125:1)? Danger? Delay? What else might be mentioned?

3. The man of Psalm 126:1–6 had clearly gone through some terrible nightmare of suffering. What hope is there for such a person?

4. Psalm 127:1–5 lists several kinds of building: building a city as David did, building a temple as Solomon did, building a family. What is needed to successfully build anything that will last?

□□□ **Reading 227 (Psalms 128:1–131:3)**

1. The psalmist describes a happy home (128:1–4) and then makes it a matter of prayer (128:5–6). Is it an absolute rule? Are godly homes always so prosperous? Is it then a generalisation? When it is not fulfilled literally, is God able to fulfil the vision in another way?

2. The song-writer (Psalm 129:1–8) is conscious that Israel has suffered many hurts in earlier stages of the nation's story. How does he handle the hurts of the past? How can we be among those who say, 'But they did not get the victory'?

3. The writer in Psalm 130:1–8 is conscious of his need of mercy, and conscious of his sins (130:1, 2). What does he do after he has prayed?

4. Is Psalm 131:1 humility or pride? How can one ever get to say such a thing about oneself? What are the marks and the fruits of humility – judged by Psalm 131:1–3?

1 Timothy

The 'pastoral epistles' (as 1 Timothy, 2 Timothy and Titus are often called) were written by the apostle late in his life. Some scholars have thought that Paul did not write them and that they are 'pseudonymous' (that is, written by someone else using Paul's name). But that is not likely. There are very personal references in these letters (such as Paul's speaking of his plans to visit Timothy, mentioned in 1 Timothy 3:14 and 4:13). Are these personal references totally artificial and fraudulent? It is quite possible that Paul used secretarial help and that not every word of the letter is Paul's. We might ask: When did the various events mentioned in these letters take place? Probably after the time mentioned in Acts 28:30–31. It is difficult to fit these three letters into the time recorded by the book of Acts. The pastoral epistles are evidence that he must have done some later travelling. As Eusebius the first church historian tells us, after his first Roman imprisonment he 'again journeyed on the ministry of preaching'.

In 1 Timothy 1:3–4, Paul lets us know exactly why he was writing this letter. There was a false teaching that was causing problems in Ephesus. Exactly what the teaching was is uncertain, but clearly it *pretended* to make use of the Old Testament. It invented 'myths' by rewriting the stories of the Old Testament for their own purposes. The teachers used very obscure parts of the Old Testament (the genealogies) to get across their teaching. One might compare this with the way in which some cults in our day love to make use of the book of Revelation. As is clear from 1 Timothy, it was ascetic (that is, it encouraged harsh and legalistic abstention from marriage, and had strict regulations about foods, and so on). In some way it made use of the Mosaic law. Paul had once given warning (see Acts 20:17–35) that the elders in the church of Ephesus would one day go astray and now it had happened. There were elders in the church who were influenced by some current philosophy and they were teaching some kind of weird nonsense to the Christians. As we read 1 Timothy 2:9–15; 5:11–15; 2 Timothy 3:6–7, it is clear that the false teachers were having a lot of influence upon the women of the church.

So Paul writes a public letter. Timothy must bring an end to the corruption of the church, and undo the damage done by these influential teachers.

Recommended reading: J. R. W. Stott, *The Message of 1 Timothy and Titus* (The Bible Speaks Today, IVP, 1996).

□□□ Reading 228 (1 Timothy 1:1–20)

1. In 1 Timothy 1:3–4 it is clear that there was a false teaching that was causing problems in Ephesus. How are we to protect the gospel message without seeming to have a negative and heresy-hunting mentality?

2. Paul talks of the 'outcome of our instruction'. What are the implications of what he says for Christian ministry?

3. For Paul the Mosaic law was always temporary. Abraham did not need it or make any use of it. He lived hundreds of years before the Mosaic law (see Galatians 4:17). He was righteous before God without ever knowing the Mosaic law. One has to die to the law in order to bear fruit for God (Romans 7:5–6). People found this – and still do find it – very difficult to understand. Who was the law intended for? The individual believer? Israel as an entire nation? It was given 'on account of trespasses' (Galatians 3:19) in Israel. Was it for good people or lawless people? How do we use the law 'lawfully'?

□□□ Reading 229 (1 Timothy 2:1–15)

1. Christians are to pray for everyone (2:1–2), expressing a concern for the whole of society. 'Kings' is in the plural; it must include not only the Roman emperor (Nero!) but many lesser rulers. Their prayers must not be confined to the needs of Ephesus. It specially has in mind non-Christian rulers – for at the time when Paul wrote there were no Christian rulers anywhere in the world! How might we put Paul's command into practice today?

2. How do we apply today Paul's instructions concerning the Christian women in Ephesus? Consider first what he says. He asks the women to accept the men's leadership (2:12). Paul wants the women to learn. He is willing to be quite unconventional and go against the ancient (and in many parts of the world, modern) culture, which holds women down to a very lowly position. But at the same time he asks for their willingness to stay within a God-given order. He has to ask Timothy to correct what was happening in Ephesus. What sort of teaching is being forbidden here? And for how long does the command apply? Paul certainly does not permanently forbid a woman from every kind of teaching. There is abundant evidence in the New Testament that women were colleagues of men in the early churches. Given the situation in Ephesus, I suggest that the 'teaching' is the authoritative teaching needed to steer the entire direction of the churches in Ephesus. It was that teaching that was going astray. It is that teaching which Paul wants to get right. It is that sort of teaching that is being forbidden to the women.

There are three ways in which we might try to apply this passage. (i) Could it be that everything in this passage is permanent in the life of the Church? (ii) Could it be that the specific instructions here are for one reason or another not normative in the life of the Church today? (iii) Could it be that in some aspects it is permanent and in other aspects it is temporary?

3. What would women think of male leadership if it was mainly a matter of lifting up holy hands and being without anger? Are there men who like the idea of male leadership but haven't noticed what Paul says?

▢▢▢ Reading 230 (1 Timothy 3:1–16)

1. Paul now tells Timothy about the need for good elders. It is likely that new elders have to be chosen to replace some who have become false teachers. We know that the church of Ephesus had elders even many years before this time (see Acts 20:17, 28). 'If anyone desires the work of overseeing he desires a noble work' (3:1). How much do our own wishes play a part in the call of God?

2. Paul himself was not married and did not have a model family life. Both in Scripture and out of Scripture there have been men who were used as servants of God yet who were never married (notably Jesus), or whose marriages had gone sour (Hosea, perhaps Paul), or who were widowers (Ezekiel in the latter stage of his ministry), or whose marriage had dubious origins (David and Bathsheba), or whose children were rebellious (Samuel). So what kind of advice or instruction is being given here?

3. Is every elder to have teaching as his special gift?

☐☐☐ Reading 231 (1 Timothy 4:1–16)

1. Are Christians sufficiently persuaded of the goodness of God's creation (note 4:3–5)? What difference does it make how we think of God's creation?

2. This chapter mentions a food that is needed, and poison to be rejected. What kind of teaching comes in each category?

3. Next we have mentioned exercise to be taken. Just as a person needs good food, they need good exercise. You cannot get strong by sleeping on a bed every day! What are the Christian's daily 'exercises' in the things of God?

☐☐☐ Reading 232 (1 Timothy 5:1–25)

1. Paul wants to give positive instruction concerning the life of the Church. His way of doing it is to give instructions concerning the different groups in the Church. A lengthy section is concerned with Christian widows. He distinguishes between different kinds of widow. What are the different kinds of 'widow' that he mentions? The 'qualifications' of a widow may be compared with the 'qualifications' of the elders and deacons. At some points they are similar. What are they? This kind of widow is totally without family responsibilities and therefore gets no support from any family (3:5). What else?

2. Paul is emphatic that the Church's first concern is that widows should be supported by their families. He takes it for granted that everyone has a sense of obligation to their own families. What does this imply for modern Christians in the society in which we live?

3. What would it do for the churches if (following Paul) we had a recognised group of women, who were over sixty, widowed, free from family responsibilities, and had status in the churches as dedicated woman workers?

☐☐☐ Reading 233 (1 Timothy 6:1–21)

1. Much employment throughout the world rather resembles ancient slavery! There are plenty of places in the world where people are so poor and are so desperate for any kind of employment that they often have to become servants working in conditions which are not so

different from ancient slavery. So are Paul's instructions relevant today? In what way?

2. What is Paul's teaching about money here? He does not say, 'Money is the root of all evil'. He says love of money is a source of all kind of evil. What is the difference?

3. Paul's words concern fleeing, following, fighting, fulfilling. There is something to be got away from (fleeing), something to be gone after (following), something to be grappled with (fighting), and there is also something to be grasped hold of! What does he say about each?

Micah

The opening verse of Micah gives us the setting of his work. He lived in Judah and preached his message in about 740–687 BC at roughly the same time as Isaiah (who ministered during 740–700 BC). Jotham was one of the five 'good' kings of Judah, who did not build the kingdom on idolatry (1 Kings 15:32–35). But apart from building the upper gate of the temple, he did not do much for God, and the threat of Assyrian invasion was growing while Jotham was tinkering with the temple (2 Kings 15:32–38).

Micah lived also in the days of Ahaz, an unbelieving man who abandoned the faith of his father and of his grandfather and went back to Canaanite idolatry and the ways of northern Israel. In 715 BC Ahaz died and Hezekiah took over the kingdom. Soon Assyria wanted to take over Judea. Hezekiah was the greatest king that Judah had had since David. He began to rule with his father in 729 BC, became sole ruler in 715 BC, and died in 687/6 BC. He was one of the three kings of Judah who did right 'according to all that his father David had done' (2 Kings 18:1–3). He removed the 'idolatrous' high places and broke down the utensils that had been used in pagan worship. But even he on one occasion turned to worldly help when he asked Shebiktu, the Pharaoh of Egypt, for protection against the Assyrians.

So these days were marked by political danger, religious idolatry and social decay. Micah's message at such a time seems to fall into three sections, marked by the word 'Hear . . .' or 'Listen'. Each time he calls upon people to listen to what God says, he starts with a severe message but then ends with a promise of salvation:

- A title (1:1)
  - Hear, O peoples, all of you . . . (1:2–2:11)
    - A promise (2:12–13)
  - Listen, you rulers of Jacob (3:1–12)
    - A promise (4:1–5:15)
  - Listen to what Yahweh says (6:1–7:7)
    - A promise (7:8–20)

Recommended reading: B. K. Waltke, 'Micah', in *Obadiah, Jonah and Micah* (D. W. Baker, ed., Tyndale Commentary, IVP, 1988).

□□□ Reading 234 (Micah 1:1–2:13)

1. What does Micah have to say about cities? About idolatry? About misused privileges?

   In Micah 1:10–15 the prophet plays with the names of the towns he mentions. The various towns (Gath, Acco, Beth-Ophrah, Shaphir, Zaanan, Beth-ezel, Maroth, Lacish, Moresheth-gath, Achzib, Mareshah, Adullam) are mainly in Judah. The names of the towns often sound (in Hebrew) like various nouns or phrases with a meaning. Micah plays upon the similarity to meaningful words. 'Gath' sounds like a town meaning 'tell'. In English we could call it 'Tell-Town' – and so on.

   > Tell it not in Tell-Town (Gath),
   > In Weepy-City (Acco), do not weep at all.
   > In the Dust-House [Beth-Ophrah], roll in the dust (1:10).

2. In Micah 2:1–5, the prophet identifies some of the sins that are arousing God's anger in this way. Some of the people protest against Micah's preaching (2:6) but Micah insists on his message and reaffirms it (2:7–11). Only in Micah 2:12–13 does he introduce any note of hope and at that point he is looking through and beyond the judgment of God to the ultimate hope of God's promised salvation. How is sin punished? By shame ('Pass on your way . . . in nakedness and shame'). By loss of courage ('The inhabitants of Come-Out-Town [Zaanan] do not come out'). How else? What were the sins that brought judgment?

3. Micah 2:12–13 comes into the book of Micah quite abruptly. It is prophetic picture language. (i) There is a ruined people, scattered far and wide like lost sheep. (ii) Then – as Micah visualizes it – they are brought together like sheep who have been found. (iii) Although they are only a 'remnant' of what they once were they are now, when

brought together, a numerous people. (iv) They are however still enclosed in a small enclosure, like people locked inside a city (the picture is changing from sheep in a sheep-fold to citizens in a city!). (v) 'Someone' breaks out through the locked gates of the city and leads the people out as a mighty army. (vi) The one who broke open the gates marches at their head as a king. How is this fulfilled in Jesus?

☐☐☐ Reading 235 (Micah 3:1–5:15)

1. The basic accusation of Micah against the rulers is that they know nothing of 'justice' – the basic goodness and fairness they ought to show in their treatment of others. What is 'justice'? Did the prophets have anything to say about it in Micah's day? How should Christians deal with injustice in society?

2. The severest passage speaking of the doom of Jerusalem (3:12) is immediately followed by a glorious prediction for the people of God. Micah is given a vision, which makes the point that the people of God are to be gloriously exalted at some future time (4:1–5). How successful do we expect the Church of the Lord Jesus Christ to be?

3. Micah says there will be a new Jerusalem, which will be a place of great safety for the people of God (4:6–8). The believers in Israel must not despair (4:9). After exile to Babylon they will be rescued (4:10). A new age will begin (4:11–13). The Messiah will be born in Bethlehem, and raised to power (5:1–6). The remnant will rule the nations (5:7–9). The Lord will protect his purified kingdom (5:10–15). Worldly arrogance will be conquered by a humble Saviour born in a humble town. How does the birth of Jesus put human arrogance to shame?

☐☐☐ Reading 236 (Micah 6:1–7:20)

1. In Micah 6:1–16, Micah comes back to speak once again of Israel's sin. God speaks like a judge in a court case. Everyone is to listen to the charges against the accused (6:1). The planet earth is to be the witness (6:2). What are God's charges? How does the case proceed? What sentence does the judge pass against the special sins of the capital city?

2. Micah feels very involved with his nation and its sins ('What misery there is for me!). He feels like a poor person looking for some fruit. How should we identify with our own people? Was Jesus like Micah in this? In what way?

3. Each of the sections of Micah (Micah 1:1–2:13; 3:1–5:15; 6:1–7:20) ends with the hope of salvation. So once again Micah turns to the far-ahead future and to the hope of salvation. He knows of 'Someone'

who 'will break open the way' (2:13), and of a ruler who will be born in Bethlehem who will act on behalf of God in bringing salvation to the world (5:2). Micah writes a prayer that he can himself pray. Yet it is a prayer that any one of the godly could pray. It has four sections (verses 8–10, 11–13, 14–17, 18–20). He sees first how God shows everlasting love (7:8–10). Second, God uses his people to bring worldwide blessing (7:11–13). What are the main points of the next two units? How does Micah view the greatness of God's love?

Nahum, Habakkuk

The subject of Nahum's prophecy is the judgment of God upon Nineveh, a persistent enemy of the people of God. The city fell to the Babylonians, Medes and Scythians in August 612 BC. The city was the capital of one of the cruellest empires that ever existed. Nahum called it 'the city of blood' (3:1). Nahum's prophecy was put into writing somewhere between 663 and 612 BC, more likely at the earlier part of that period.

Recommended reading: D. W. Baker, *Nahum, Habbakuk, Zephaniah* (Tyndale Commentary, IVP, 1988).

□□□ **Reading 237 (Nahum 1:1–3:19)**
1. What should the thought of the wrath of God against cruel empires mean to us today?
2. Why is judgment of wickedness certain, according to Nahum?
3. What were the reasons for the judgment of Nineveh, according to Nahum 3:1–19?

□□□ **Reading 238 (Habakkuk 1:1–3:19)**
Among the last kings of Judah were Manasseh and his son Amon (687–642 and 642 BC) – both wicked kings. Then there was Josiah who tried to remove idolatry from the land. He was partially successful but when he died in 609 BC, his successors went back to their old sinful ways. Jehoahaz

had a short reign in 609 BC. Then Jehoiakim came on to the throne (609–597), and it was probably during the early stages of his reign that Habakkuk lived and worked, somewhere between 609 and 605 BC. Judah was going back to its old wickedness. Habakkuk's book is not very long – fifty-six verses. It is fairly easy to understand. It records the dialogue between God and the prophet.

After the title, it has five sections:

1. Habakkuk 1:2–4 Habakkuk talks to God. His first complaint.
2. Habakkuk 1:5–11 God talks to Habakkuk. God's first answer.
3. Habakkuk 1:12–2:1 Habakkuk talks to God. His second complaint.
4. Habakkuk 2:2–20 God talks to Habakkuk. God's second answer.
5. Habakkuk 3:1–19 Habakkuk talks to God. His psalm.

Recommended reading: D. M. Lloyd-Jones, *From Fear to Faith* (IVP, various editions).

1. Are we allowed to complain to God? When does he allow it? When does it make God angry?
2. Can God punish one group of sinners by sending another group of sinners? Are there more biblical examples? Are there modern examples?
3. In Habakkuk 2:2–20, the prophet received a revelation that would be important for the rest of the history of the world! God told Habakkuk that the answer he was about to receive should be shared with others and would be a message for all time, to be proclaimed everywhere. What is this message that has worldwide importance?
4. How are we to think of God (Habakkuk 3:1–19)? How do we respond to what we know of God?

Psalms 132:1–139:24

□□□ **Reading 239 (Psalms 132:1–134:3)**
1. Psalm 132:1–5 is David's oath that he will bring the ark to Jerusalem. It had been almost forgotten (note verse 6 and 1 Chronicles 13:3). Now the king says, 'We heard . . . we found . . . we will go . . . we will worship.' How much determination does it take to continue the life of worshipping God in his presence?
2. Two pictures of unity are found in Psalm 133:2, 3 (the anointing of the high priest and the heavy refreshing dew of the northern hills of Hermon). What are the points of the two illustrations?
3. What difference does it make that the One who blesses us is the Creator? What does it mean that he blesses us from Zion – the places where sacrifices were offered every day?

□□□ **Reading 240 (Psalms 135:1–137:9)**
1. Psalm 135:1–21 calls upon many groups of people to praise God (see verses 19–21). It gives reasons why we should praise the Lord ('for . . . For . . . For . . .' verses 3, 4, 5). What are the reasons?
2. Psalm 136:1–26 is known to Jewish people as 'the great Hallel'. It contains nothing but praise. How is God described? What is his character? What are the great things he has done? The Bible so often moves from creation (136:4–9) to redemption (136:10–24).

Are our praises to follow the same procedure?

3. Psalm 137:1–9 was obviously written at the time of the Babylonian exile. It considers the facts of the case (verses 1–4), determines not to forget Jerusalem (verses 5–6), and prays against the people of Edom (who exploited Jerusalem's weakness at the time of the Babylonian invasion). The Christian takes none of this literally! Do we have to single out Jerusalem in our prayers? Should we not pray for other capital cities just as much? We do not pray in the style of verse 9. Edom no longer exists. So what are the principles that must be applied in reading the Old Testament – and that are specially relevant here?

Note The 'Cursing' Psalms. Psalm 137 contains (in verse 9) one of the severest of the 'curses' in the psalms. This is a good point at which to remember how these psalms should be interpreted. The following points should be kept in mind: (i) They are realistic. They consider what is actually likely to happen if (for example) Edom is overthrown. We might have prayed for the downfall of Edom without being realistic. (ii) They are prophetic. The writers do not indulge in personal vindictiveness, but they speak on behalf of God. (iii) They are written upon the assumption of the holiness of God and the rightness of his sending or controlling events that punish sin.

☐☐☐ Reading 241 (Psalms 138:1–139:24)

1. Psalm 138:1–8 begins with a call for gratitude towards God. It is good to be grateful, but in addition to its own importance, what effect will gratitude have upon our own lives? Can any other 'spirits' ('gods', verse 1) help us?

2. What is the Christian equivalent of praying towards the temple (where God's presence was specially revealed and where sacrifice for sin was offered)?

3. Psalm 139:1–24 has four sections, which focus upon God's knowledge (verses 1–6), God's presence (7–12), God's creation of our personality (13–18) and God's holiness (19–24). If we are gripped with awareness of what God is like, how will it make a difference to us?

Deuteronomy

Deuteronomy presents itself to us as a series of addresses that Moses gave to the people of Israel just before they crossed over Jordan into the promised land. It reviews their history, reminds them of the Ten Commandments, and of their implications and details.

Recommended reading: R. Brown, *The Message of Deuteronomy* (IVP, 1993); C. Wright, *Deuteronomy* (New International Biblical Commentary, Paternoster, 1996).

☐☐☐ Reading 242 (Deuteronomy 1:1–3:29)

1. Deuteronomy begins with a historical review (1:1–4:49). Do you keep a journal of what God has done? Why is it good to recall what God has done? But should a journal be used to keep records of supposed wrongs against us? What is the purpose of the records in Deuteronomy? What should we remember and what should we forget? What should we record and what should be buried in forgetfulness?

2. What do the records of Israel past tell them about (i) what delays the purpose of God, (ii) how brother-nations should be treated, (iii) how God gives us new beginnings?

3. When one victory has been won (see Deuteronomy 3:1–28) in the life of faith, how should it be used as a pattern for future victories?

☐☐☐ **Reading 243 (Deuteronomy 4:1–5:33)**

1. Keeping the law will lead to 'life'. What kind of 'life' does Moses have in mind? Is he referring to the 'eternal life' mentioned in the New Testament? Is it hypothetical? Does it refer to national life rather than spiritual life?

2. Consider the Ten Commandments as a whole. Three are about God (5:7–11). One is about the Sabbath (5:12–16). Five are about society (5:17–20) focussing upon family, the sanctity of life, purity, theft, truth. One is about the heart (5:18–21). Why did Paul regard the last one as rather special (Romans 7:7)?

3. Is it possible to improve on the Ten Commandments? If we were giving ten principles to help young Christians grow, what would they be? How different would they be from the Ten Commandments? Why the difference?

☐☐☐ **Reading 244 (Deuteronomy 6:1–8:20)**

1. The law in Exodus-to-Numbers does not refer to the heart very much (not at all in the legislation itself), but Moses preaching forty years later constantly mentions the 'heart'. What makes Moses bring in this extra point?

2. The people of Israel are to slaughter the Canaanites. They were a people who had become exceedingly depraved and had been tolerated for over four centuries (note Genesis 15:13, 16). It was a unique ruling, a foretaste of final judgment. At this point it would be sin to follow the law! So how does the Christian learn from the law at this point? Do the Christian's standards *contrast* with the Mosaic law?

3. The Israelites are promised multiplication (8:1). Is the promise of multiplication given to the Christian Church also? What other promises in Deuteronomy 8:1–20 have their equivalent in the life of the Christian?

☐☐☐ **Reading 245 (Deuteronomy 9:1–10:22)**

1. In Deuteronomy 9:1–29, the Israelites are just about to cross over the River Jordan and *dispossess* the Canaanites of their land. Is there any equivalent to this in the Christian life? What do Christians 'dispossess'? Sinful habits? Wickedness in the world? How is possession and dispossession a good picture of the Christian life?

2. Deuteronomy 10:1–16 emphasises that Israel is being taken back to where they went wrong, and is being given a new opportunity ('like the first . . . as at the first time', verses 1, 10). What is necessary if they are to make good use of the new opportunity?

3. Deuteronomy 10:1–22 demands that we 'circumcise our hearts' to live in a way that suits the character of God. What aspects of the character of God does he mention? How does it affect the way we live? What does it mean to 'circumcise the heart'?

☐☐☐ Reading 246 (Deuteronomy 11:1–13:18)

1. The generation who were about to cross Jordan had actually seen the miracles of the exodus at the time when they themselves had been children (11:2–7). But the next generation had not seen the original events. So what provision was made for the next generation (11:19–21)? How do the different generations of God's people relate to each other?

2. A major change comes in Deuteronomy 12:1–32. Deuteronomy 1: 1–4:49 dealt with the history of Israel. Deuteronomy 5:1–11:32 dealt with the general principles of God's law. Deuteronomy 12:1–32 begins to deal with smaller details. First is the rule that only the worship of one God was allowed in Israel. What does this mean for the Christian? Does this law demand an 'establishment' of one religion in a country? Does it demand purity in the Church? Does it point to what will be true in the new heaven and new earth? What is the significance of such a law for the Christian?

3. What is the connection between 'signs and wonders' and the word of God according to this passage? What will this mean for the Christian Church today?

☐☐☐ Reading 247 (Deuteronomy 14:1–15:23)

1. Deuteronomy 14:1–21 deals with clean and unclean foods. It is clear that unclean foods symbolised pagan peoples (note the connection between food and people in Acts 10:9–48). Rules about food kept Israel separate from paganism. What kind of 'separation' is to be practised by the Christian?

2. Deuteronomy 14:22–29 adds fresh rulings to the laws concerning tithes. How was the tithe given? Who was it given to? Is the Christian exactly under the tithe? If not, what is its equivalent?

3. What principles of mercy in society are to be found in the seventh year? Is there anything in it that might be worth reapplying in today's national legislation?

☐☐☐ Reading 248 (Deuteronomy 16:1–18:22)

1. What are the spiritual lessons that were taught by Passover, the Feast of Weeks, and the Feast of Booths? How does the Christian celebrate the same principles?
2. What was to be the difference between Israel's kings and the pagan kings of the ancient world? What can we learn about the dangers and privileges of leadership?
3. In what way should we seek to know the will of God (see Deuteronomy 18:15–22; remember Acts 3:22)?

☐☐☐ Reading 249 (Deuteronomy 19:1–20:20)

1. The cities of refuge gave protection in a situation where it was uncertain whether someone had or had not committed a crime. How do we handle situations where we have to make a judgment but the position is full of uncertainty?
2. Israel's law protected the ownership of land (although its ultimate owner was God). Does this have implications for modern societies?
3. Deuteronomy 20:1–20 gives laws concerning warfare. Are these laws totally out of date or do we need something similar today? Is God identified with any nation in the way in which he identified with ancient Israel? If not, how does the Christian read this chapter?

☐☐☐ Reading 250 (Deuteronomy 21:1–23:25)

1. What are we to think of the legislation in Deuteronomy 21:10–14? It is surely of no *direct* relevance to the Christian. But does it teach us anything indirectly? Is it compassionate? It is a case of the 'lesser of two evils'?
2. Why did God allow Jesus to be crucified (note 21:22–23)?
3. How does Deuteronomy 22:5 relate to Galatians 3:28? Does the gospel cancel out the difference between the sexes altogether? Is the Christian obliged to obey Deuteronomy 22:5? Does it still apply as a matter of wisdom? How does the leading of the Holy Spirit come into this kind of topic?

☐☐☐ Reading 251 (Deuteronomy 24:1–25:19)

1. Deuteronomy 24:1–4 is the main passage in the Mosaic law concerning divorce. How does it differ from the teaching of Jesus (see Matthew 5:31; 19:7)?
2. The main theme in the many and varied laws of Deuteronomy 24:1–

22 is that of compassion. How does the law encourage compassion?
How might we be ready to go beyond the Mosaic law?

3. Deuteronomy 25:17–17 is surprisingly severe. Can we find any reason
for its severity? Why do some parts of the Bible emphasise forgiveness
but other parts emphasise justice?

□□□ Reading 252 (Deuteronomy 26:1–28:68)

1. 'A wandering Aramean was my father' (Deuteronomy 26:5). How
much does God like to lift people up from humble origins?

2. Nowadays people are very interested in 'curses' stemming from the
past. What kind of 'curse' is of interest in the Mosaic law? How does
the Christian relate to it?

3. What are we to think of these promises and threats about 'curses' and
blessings? How do they relate to the book of Job (Job was righteous but
not blessed!)? How do they relate to problems that biblical writers have
with the prosperity of the wicked (e.g. Psalm 73:1–28)?

□□□ Reading 253 (Deuteronomy 29:1–31:30)

1. In Deuteronomy 29:1–29, Moses calls the people to be ready to take
an oath of allegiance to God. What arguments does he use to persuade
the people? Can we use Christian equivalents? But is it right to take an
oath at all?

2. Deuteronomy 30:1–20 promises that Israel will be restored after
experiencing God's 'covenant curse'. Is the promise unconditional?
What do we learn about the security of God's purposes?

3. What arrangements may we make for the future of God's Church? Does
Moses help us here? Does singing come into it?

□□□ Reading 254 (Deuteronomy 32:1–34:12)

1. Deuteronomy 32:1–52 contains the famous song of Moses. It calls
upon the witnesses to listen (32:1–2). It praises the character of God
(32:3–6) and tells of the things God has done for his people (32:7–
14). The song goes on to tell of Israel's ingratitude (32:15–18), which
God is likely to punish (32:19–25). But the final promise is that God
will judge Israel's enemies and save his people. What is the application
of all of this to us? What should be the main themes of Christian
singing?

2. In Deuteronomy 32:48–33:29, Moses gives his last blessing as Israel's
spiritual father. His words contain prayers, doxologies, commands
and promises. How much power does a spiritual leader have in their

prayers? Do they have more power in prayer than the ordinary Christian?

3. In Deuteronomy 34:1–12, Moses saw the promised land but did not enter it. Does a believer ever see something but not obtain it? Did Moses lose his position as a child of God? If not, what did he lose? May we lose something of the promises of God? How and why?

Acts

The book of Acts is the only book of the New Testament to deal with the history of the earliest church. The two-part work, Luke-Acts, is strictly anonymous, although there is plenty of evidence to show that it was written by Luke, the travelling companion of Paul. Luke wrote initially for 'Theophilus', a high-born Christian wanting to know more of the origins of the Christian Church. Actually Acts has no account of any of the apostles except Peter and Paul. John is noticed only three times; and all that is recorded of James, the son of Zebedee, is his execution by Herod. It could better be called 'The Acts of the Glorified Lord Jesus Christ'. Luke the author nowhere mentions his own name, but he appears in the word 'we' from 16:11, and occasionally later on in the book.

All the way through the story, the ever-present rule of the Lord Jesus Christ is visible to the eye of faith, as he works through the power of the Holy Spirit. The book may be divided into these three parts. Acts 1:1–12:25 describes the early years of the Christian Church, focussing on the extension of the Church among the Jews, mainly by the ministry of Peter. Acts 13:1–21:40 gives the story of the extension of the Church among gentiles. Then Acts 21:1–28:31 tells of the events that led to Paul's being taken to Rome.

Recommended reading: J. R. W. Stott, *Acts* (The Bible Speaks Today, IVP, 1990).

☐☐☐ **Reading 255 (Acts 1:1–26)**

1. As with his first book (the Gospel of Luke), Luke begins his book with a preface. There are two parts to Jesus leading his Church (Jesus began . . .; Jesus continues). What does this imply about the present rule of Jesus over his Church?
2. Luke wants us to know about the period from Easter Sunday to the Thursday, forty days later, when Jesus ascended into heaven. What happened in this period? Why is it important?
3. The question of Acts 1:6 seems to be a very confused question. What were its assumptions? How does Jesus answer it?
4. It has often been discussed whether the early Church was truly guided by God in choosing Matthias as a replacement-apostle. Was Luke just recording something without meaning to recommend it? If not, how may we justify what he did?

☐☐☐ **Reading 256 (Acts 2:1–21)**

1. What was the Day of Pentecost? The beginning of God's people? The day when the Church began? How is it described in Acts 1:5, 8? What was the result of the 'receiving of power'? Boldness. What else?
2. How do the accompanying phenomena (wind, fire, languages) help us to understand the Spirit's work? The disciples were 'filled' with the Spirit. It was a decisive event in their lives. To what extent was this unique? To what extent is it a model for us?
3. The book of Acts is the book of the Bible that more than any other gives us a living and practical description of the nature of the Church. So what is the Christian Church?

☐☐☐ **Reading 257 (Acts 2:22–47)**

1. Peter preaches a sermon from Joel 2:1–32, but what is the difference between this kind of preaching and 'Bible exposition'?
2. The central message of Peter's preaching is Jesus himself. What does Peter say about him?
3. Here we have a model of bold preaching. Peter's message contains biblical exposition yet it is not *mere* biblical exposition. It leads the people themselves to ask what they should do. Peter is ready with an answer (2:38). They have already come to faith. He does not need to tell them to believe on the Lord Jesus Christ. The question is: As believing people, what should they now do? There are two things they must do, and two things they may expect to happen. What are they?

☐☐☐ Reading 258 (Acts 3:1–26)

1. Luke tells us of one of the 'signs and wonders' (2:43). They have seen the crippled man many times before, since the cripple is laid there daily (3:2) and they go to the temple daily (2:46). But this time something unusual happens. Is this story a model for miracles today? If so, what do we learn from it?

2. As soon as possible Peter begins to speak about Jesus (more than about the miracle!). What does he say about Jesus? About their sin and wickedness? About the offer of salvation?

3. Peter says: 'Repent therefore and turn around . . .' What is the difference between the two words? If they take notice, what does he promise them?

☐☐☐ Reading 259 (Acts 4:1–37)

1. Must the gospel inevitably arouse opposition? How are we to face opposition? We notice Peter does not apologise. He does not modify his message. He makes no attempt to avoid mentioning Jesus. What do they do?

2. The Christians prayed. It was loud praying. What other characteristics of their praying can we discover? How may our prayers become like their prayers?

3. How does the church's prayer meeting use the Bible? The prayer has only one request. Why is that?

☐☐☐ Reading 260 (Acts 5:1–20)

1. The church felt led to do something exceptional for God. What are the principles here? Must we always share all our possessions? May God tell us to do something that is never to be done again? It worked well in the case of Barnabas (4:36–37). It led to something terrible in the case of Ananias and Sapphira (5:1–11). So how do we use principles such as 'having all things in common' as a model for ourselves?

2. The money was laid 'at the apostles' feet' (4:35). This also was entirely voluntary. To do something 'at someone's feet' means 'led by them, guided by them'. It does not mean that they gave the money *to* the apostles. Paul studied 'at the feet of Gamaliel'; it means that Gamaliel was his guide and supervisor. So these generous church members were being led and counselled by the apostles as they showed this great generosity. We notice also that the word is plural ('apostles') not singular ('apostle'). In Acts 11:30 we shall see another case where two

people are involved in the handling of money. In modern times, who do we give our money to? How do we do it wisely?

3. What leads us into hypocrisy? There have been many people in the Church who have sinned in the same way but they have not died. So why did God judge Ananias and Sapphira so severely?

☐☐☐ Reading 261 (Acts 5:21–42)

1. The Church must obey God rather than people. What are the practicalities of this?
2. The Church must proclaim its central message. What is it?
3. Three groups of people are found here: the angry Jewish opponents of the gospel, the 'nice' man Gamaliel, and the apostles. But there are only two groups – those who are for or against the gospel. Is Gamaliel really a friend of the gospel? What is the difference between him and the apostles?

☐☐☐ Reading 262 (Acts 6:1–15)

1. The Jerusalem church had two kinds of Jewish believer in it: Greek-speaking Jews who were at home in the wider world, and Aramaic speakers who were less familiar with what went on outside Israel. What did the first church do about cultural tensions? How may the principles found here be applied in today's multicultural churches?
2. How did 'church government' develop in the first church? What was required of leaders? What different kinds of leader were to be found? How were they appointed?
3. What leads to persecution? Is it ever possible for powerful revival to occur without persecution?

☐☐☐ Reading 263 (Acts 7:1–16)

1. Stephen reviews Israel's history. What are the lessons he discovers in the life of Abraham? Was Abraham justified before God by good works? By circumcision? What do we learn from his life?
2. What does Stephen suggest about jealousy, as he surveys Joseph's life?
3. As Stephen preaches, what is on offer for the nation of Israel?

☐☐☐ Reading 264 (Acts 7:17–34)

1. How does Stephen find the theme of a rejected Saviour in Israel's history? In what way are some of Israel's leaders like Jesus?
2. What fresh opportunities did God give Israel? Was there any possibility

of the nation entering into blessing after the crucifixion of Jesus?

3. In what way does God's surprising grace appear in the story of Moses? How does God like to surprise us?

□□□ Reading 265 (Acts 7:35-60)

1. The Jewish leaders took it that Moses was God's last word to the nation. But how does Moses himself show that this is not true? Who does Moses say is God's last word?

2. Israel is often thought to have a genius for religion. Is it true? If not, what is the significance of God using Israel?

3. Why was the end of Stephen's sermon so blunt? Should we speak in the way he did? Is he a model preacher?

□□□ Reading 266 (Acts 8:1-24)

1. What is the difference between Simon and Philip – or between magic and faith?

2. What is the difference between the Samaritans' response to the gospel and Simon's response to the gospel?

3. Was the gift of the Spirit delayed? Can the gift of the Spirit be delayed in the same way today or not? How do you know?

□□□ Reading 267 (Acts 8:25-40)

1. Wealth and influence had not satisfied the Ethiopian eunuch. What trouble did he take to find satisfaction? What had to happen before he found it?

2. Why had the Ethiopian eunuch not already found peace with God in Jerusalem? What is the difference between what Philip offered him and what Jerusalem could have offered him?

3. Is Acts 8:29 a model for us today? It was not a verse of Scripture that came to Philip but the voice of the Holy Spirit. What do you think about such impulses of the Holy Spirit?

□□□ Reading 268 (Acts 9:1-22)

1. What made Saul of Tarsus reject the gospel for so long? Was it his intellectual ability? Why are people so slow to consider the gospel message?

2. How much of his later message could Paul have learned at the time of his call to salvation and apostleship?

3. Saul of Tarsus was not allowed to come to full conversion totally

without help. Why did God send Ananias? Can anyone come to Christian salvation totally on their own?

□□□ Reading 269 (Acts 9:23–43)

1. A murder plot, a healing, a resurrection (Acts 9:23–31, 32–35, 36–43). The early Church lived in exciting days! But would we have liked it so much? How would Saul the ex-rabbi have felt about escaping through a wall in a basket? Would he be having regrets about his conversion?

2. What is the ideal character of the Church according to Acts 9:31? How are we able to maintain it?

3. How should we view the miracle of Peter in Acts 9:32–43? How much may we expect such things today? Never? Constantly? As God wills? Occasionally? Why did they send for Peter? What was the purpose of the miracles (see verses 35, 42)?

□□□ Reading 270 (Acts 10:1–22)

1. Acts 10:1–48 brings us to the point where the gospel is about to reach gentiles. It takes place only slowly. First a gentile believer in the God of Israel is brought to full Christian faith. Why does God sometimes move slowly and prepare the way for what he does?

2. Acts 10:1–43 is an example of God's working at both ends of a situation at the same time, preparing Peter for Cornelius, and Cornelius for Peter.

3. Peter saw all kinds of animals both clean and unclean (see Leviticus 11:1–47) and was commanded to kill and eat. Peter starts arguing with God. Was this so wrong? Does God mind if we question him? What was the connection between animal-symbolism and people?

□□□ Reading 271 (Acts 10:23–48)

1. Peter was very slow to preach to gentiles, even to one who already believed in the faith of Israel and was accepted by God (note 10:35). What made him so reluctant? What might make us reluctant to reach out to others who are different from us?

2. At this stage in Acts, Peter is fading out of the scene and Paul is about to become prominent. How are we to feel when one person's ministry is coming to an end and another's is becoming more prominent? What if we are one of them?

3. In Acts 2:1–47, the Jews believed, and were told to be baptised and were promised the same outpouring of the Spirit that the apostles had

experienced. In Acts 8:1–40, the Samaritans believed and were baptised, and then received the Spirit by the laying on of the apostles' hands. Here in Acts 10:1–48, the gentiles believed the gospel, received the Spirit and then were baptised. What do we learn from these differences? Notice that faith comes first every time. What kind of 'receiving of the Spirit' do we have here?

☐☐☐ Reading 272 (Acts 11:1–30)

1. Acts 11:1 says, 'The gentiles had received the word of God.' How much should we expect to see entire communities coming to faith at the same time? Why do we not see it so much?

2. The Jerusalem Christians seemed quite angry that Peter should minister to gentiles. What does this tell us about the Jerusalem church at this time? A church that received such blessing as the Jerusalem church later became conservative. Why does this happen?

3. Peter experienced a vision in a trance. What made him know that this was truly from God? We are told to test our spiritual experiences (1 John 4:1). How might we do that?

☐☐☐ Reading 273 (Acts 12:1–25)

1. James was killed; Peter was rescued by an angel. Why were their experiences so different? What does it teach us about suffering for the sake of Christ?

2. Herod wanted to please the Jewish leaders (12:3) and the people wanted Peter executed like Jesus and James. So what do we learn about the opponents of the gospel? What should we expect from 'the world' in our own day?

3. The church prayed; Peter was rescued; Herod was suddenly punished. Yet not all persecutors are suddenly punished. Was there any reason why Herod should be so unexpectedly judged by God? Is there any sin that prompts God to act speedily?

☐☐☐ Reading 274 (Acts 13:1–25)

1. How much evangelistic planning (or any other planning) should arise from special guidance? How do guidance and planning fit together?

2. What does it mean that Paul was filled with the Holy Spirit (13:9)? What is the difference between this and what happened to him in 9:17?

3. In his evangelistic travelling, Paul began his preaching in the synagogues when it was possible. His preaching surveyed Israel's history to the point of the promises to David (13:17–22) and then said Jesus was

the fulfilment of the promise (13:23–25). In what way is this a model of what preaching ought to be?

□□□ Reading 275 (Acts 13:26–52)

1. Paul's preaching focusses on events that have happened (13:26–31). How important are the historical events of the Christian faith? Would it matter if they had not happened?
2. Next Paul's preaching focusses on the interpretation of the Old Testament (13:32–41). He jumps from passage to passage (Psalms 2:1–12; 16:1–11; Habakkuk 1:1–17). Why does he not simply expound one passage? What kind of preaching is this and how is it a model for today?
3. 'As many as were ordained to eternal life believed.' It does not say: 'As many as believed were ordained to eternal life.' But could it have been put the other way around? Why is it a comment on the sermon but not in the sermon itself?

□□□ Reading 276 (Acts 14:1–28)

1. 'The residents of the city were divided' (14:4). What does this tell us about early Christian evangelism? The apostles tried to reach whole towns. What else? And what more can we find out about the way the gospel proceeds in the world?
2. The style of Paul's preaching in 14:15–18 is rather different from what we have had before in the book of Acts. What are the differences? When should we use this style of speaking without quoting the Bible?
3. The experience of the apostles in this chapter varies from being worshipped (14:18) to being almost killed (14:19). What does this tell us about the goodwill of the world? What does it imply for the way we should live from day to day?

□□□ Reading 277 (Acts 15:1–21)

1. The people from Judea thought it was vital that gentile Christians become Jewish-Christians in culture (15:1). When we help someone come to faith in Jesus, must they accept our culture or is faith in Jesus enough? What does this imply about (i) the way of salvation and (ii) the way we have fellowship with different kinds of people? Why are these questions so controversial (15:2)?
2. What is the essence of the gospel according to Peter (15:7–11)? And according to James (15:13–17)?
3. The requests made to gentiles seem to have been that: (i) they should

not eat food that had previously been offered in sacrifice to idols;
(ii) they should not marry people forbidden as partners according to
the Mosaic law; (iii) they should not eat food that was not 'kosher'
(cleansed from blood in the Jewish manner). Were the regulations
permanent? If not, what is the place for *temporary* rulings in the
Church?

□□□ Reading 278 (Acts 15:22–41)

1. 'Then the apostles and the elders, with the consent of the whole
   church, decided . . .' (15:22). How is this a model of how the Church
   should make decisions?
2. What kind of authority did the church of Jerusalem have over the
   church of Antioch, if any? Are they writing as a superior church? As a
   church with well-known men of wisdom? As a 'mother church'? Are
   they commanding? Advising? Suggesting? How should churches work
   together? Are there any special biblical principles about how churches
   relate?
3. 'It has seemed good to the Holy Spirit and to us . . .' What does this
   mean? How do we know what is good to the Holy Spirit?

□□□ Reading 279 (Acts 16:1–24)

1. After many battles to be free from circumcision (Acts 15:1–41), why
   did Paul circumcise Timothy? When should we compromise and when
   should we not compromise?
2. What does the 'forbidding of the Spirit' feel like? Does the Holy Spirit
   forbid even something that is good? What part does the *direct* voice of
   the Spirit have in the modern Christian life?
3. Acts 16:10 records the first time a preacher went to Europe. What led
   the preachers to go to a new place? How did they start? What meetings
   did they hold? How might their new venture be a model for modern
   Christians? What are the 'new frontiers' for the modern Christian?

□□□ Reading 280 (Acts 16:25–40)

1. Who would ever have imagined that someone like the gaoler would
   come to salvation? But God has ways of reaching his elect when they
   are stubborn and resistant. What were the steps (if any) that were
   involved in the gaoler's coming to faith? Does pioneer evangelism often
   get unexpected help from God?
2. Can a pagan man be transferred from death to life in a few moments?
   It seems so. How can such a great change take place so speedily?

3. There is only one answer to the question: What must I do to be saved? 'Believe on the Lord Jesus Christ and you will be saved – and the same thing is true of your household.' We come to our first experience of salvation by faith alone. But what does faith lead to?

☐☐☐ Reading 281 (Acts 17:1–34)

1. The congregation at Thessalonica was founded with incredible speed. The church is born amid a burst of spiritual power. But what 'methods' did God honour in bringing this church into being so quickly?
2. At Beroea Paul found an exceptionally responsive people. What can we learn from Acts 17:11? 'Nobility' is a matter of openness to God's word. What else?
3. Acts 17:16–34 tells us of the first contacts between the gospel of the Lord Jesus Christ and pagan philosophy. Does Paul have a different way of relating to philosophers? If so, what is different? Or, what is not different?

☐☐☐ Reading 282 (Acts 18:1–28)

1. At this point of the book of Acts, Paul is far away from any place that he might call home (Antioch? Tarsus?). What are Paul's attitudes towards money and financial support (18:3)?
2. What is Paul's attitude towards Israel? How does Paul's experience in Corinth illustrate his point in Romans 11:12 and 11:15?
3. Acts 18:23–28 emphasises how much one may have progressed in knowledge and ministry *without* knowing the full gift of the Spirit. Is there any special lesson for us in this?

☐☐☐ Reading 283 (Acts 19:1–20)

1. Paul comes to Ephesus and meets some 'disciples'. Anyone who has closely read Acts and noticed the twenty-seven times the word 'disciple' has been used should have no doubt that 'disciple' means 'Christian' (although obviously these people are somewhat defective as 'Christians'). The linguistic usage is strict and clear. Obviously these men were an exception to normal Christian experience. But if there could be an exception then, may there be exceptions now? Why so or why not?
2. It becomes obvious in the events of Acts 19:1–41 that the spiritual world is real. How is the devil's power overcome?
3. In Acts 19:13–16 we learn the folly of being unreal with God. Why do people get involved in playing spiritual games? What are the dangers?

☐☐☐ **Reading 284 (Acts 19:21–41)**

1. In Acts 19:1–41 we have a classic glimpse of the true nature of men and women. Two of the things that characterise the vast majority of men and women are love of money and love of religion – in that order! What do we learn here about each? What are the connections between the two?

2. What must Paul have thought of what happened here – in connection with his teaching about the sinful nature of men and women? What passages of his letters could have arisen from what he saw here?

3. What must Paul have thought of what happened here – in connection with his teaching about the Church and the state (see Romans 13:1–7)?

☐☐☐ **Reading 285 (Acts 20:1–21)**

1. What is the difference between 'repentance towards God and faith towards our Lord Jesus Christ' (20:21) and 'the whole counsel of God' (20:27)? What different kinds of preaching are needed in the Christian Church? And what about 'exhortation' (20:2)?

2. In what ways does Paul strengthen and encourage young churches? Do you need this kind of encouragement? What does this imply for your involvement with a congregation?

3. Why is 'repentance' often mentioned before 'faith'? What should we learn from this?

☐☐☐ **Reading 286 (Acts 20:22–38)**

1. Paul says he knows that he must go to Jerusalem (see 19:21), and that the Holy Spirit has told him he must go; he goes 'bound in the Spirit'. Yet people keep speaking to him 'in the Spirit' warning him about what will happen in Jerusalem. How much notice should we take of what we think is the Holy Spirit? How much notice should we take of what other people think is the Holy Spirit?

2. Paul mentions his clear conscience (20:26). Like Ezekiel (in Ezekiel 3:15–21; 33:4) he has been a faithful 'watchman' who has told them everything he ought to have told them. How are we to have a clear conscience in this matter?

3. 'Keep watch over yourselves . . .' The Christian worker's first 'congregation' is themself. How do we watch over ourselves?

☐☐☐ **Reading 287 (Acts 21:1–19)**

1. What do we learn about hospitality from Acts 21:4, 7, 8, 16?

2. Acts 21:5 is a moving scene. It resembles 20:38. They would see each other one day but not just yet. From now on they would read Paul's letters but not see him as much as they had seen him before. What is the relationship that should exist between preachers and people?

3. 'Your sons and your daughters shall prophesy', said Joel 2:28. Philip had experienced the fulfilment of the prophecy. How does it happen that the daughters of one family all have the same gift? What is happening here?

☐☐☐ Reading 288 (Acts 21:20–40)

1. Acts 21:16 is important for us if we are to note what is happening in this part of Acts. Did the fears and conservatism of the Jerusalem Christians damage their spiritual liveliness? If so, could the same thing happen to us?

2. Were James and his friends somewhat deceitful in their scheme? Outside of Israel, Paul often lived like a Christian gentile (as 1 Corinthians 9:21 makes clear). Paul was under pressure to pretend something that was not really true. Did the plan succeed? The very act of going to the temple was the thing that led to Paul's being imprisoned for the next few years. What should James and his friends have done in this situation? Would we have done any better?

3. In AD 62, five years after the events of Acts 21:1–40 (which is to be dated AD 57), the high priest in Jerusalem plotted against James. James was stoned to death 'on a charge of having broken the law' (Josephus, *Antiquities* 20:200). After that time there is evidence in early church history that the Jerusalem church became more proud of itself than ever. In the late AD 60s, Roman armies began to march on Jerusalem, and the Christians fled the city as Jesus had told them to (see Matthew 24:1–2, 16). They had to leave their 'holy city' after all! They had to get used to Greek culture whether they liked it or not! Jerusalem was destroyed in AD 70. The Christians had already left. In AD 70 the temple in which some ultra-conservative Christians had wanted to give a 'hair offering' thirteen years previously was burned to the ground. What are we to learn from this history?

☐☐☐ Reading 289 (Acts 22:1–30)

1. How much 'explaining' does Paul do before he starts speaking of the gospel? Is there a reason for this? Is it something we should do?

2. 'What shall I do, Lord?' he asked. From that point onward he was living step-by-step upon the guidance of God. The first step was for him to go to Damascus. When he has done that, the next step will be shown him (22:10). Is this typical of the way in which the Christian life is to be lived? How much guidance may we expect?

3. It would be wonderful if the book of Acts had gone on to say, 'Now when they heard this they were cut to the heart and they cried out and said to Paul, "What shall we do?" ' (as happened on the Day of Pentecost – see Acts 2:37). Why is their response so different?

□□□ Reading 290 (Acts 23:1–15)

1. Paul now has the great privilege of speaking to the Jewish parliament. He claims *always* (even before his conversion) to have lived a conscientious life (23:1). How did Saul of Tarsus have a good conscience even when he was a persecutor of the Christians? How is our conscience to function?

2. The high priest, Ananias, was in office during AD 47 to about AD 58. He was known for his greed. Paul's apology is cleverly worded. 'I am sorry', he says. 'I really did not know that a man who speaks like that could possibly be the high priest!' Paul must in fact have known that Ananias was the high priest! It is an apology and a rebuke at the same time! Actually God did strike Ananias. After a wicked life he was murdered in AD 66. What do we learn about the Mosaic law here? It was quite illegal for an uncondemned man to be beaten. Paul's apology refers to Exodus 22:28. At the moment he is being more law-abiding than the high priest. These Jewish leaders claim that they keep the Jewish law, but do they? What do we learn about the law and the gospel here?

3. Paul found a way of compelling the meeting to focus immediately upon the heart of what he wants to say. He forcibly raises the issue of resurrection. Paul sees a way of bringing this matter to the centre of attention. What do we learn here about Paul's concerns? What should be our concerns when we are in trouble with others, or even in danger?

□□□ Reading 291 (Acts 23:16–35)

1. We do not read, 'And the church at Jerusalem were gathered together and were praying for Paul . . .' – as they prayed in an earlier stage of the church's history when Peter was in prison (see Acts 12:12). What can we learn from the Jerusalem church at this point?

2. These men of the law say, 'This is the man who preaches . . . against . . . the law' (Acts 21:28), but they seem not to notice that the law is against deceit and conspiracy and murder! What must we say about

the power of law? If it is too weak, then what can be done? What must we say about the idea that 'the law' convicts of sin?

3. How does God give us protection when we are in danger?

☐☐☐ **Reading 292 (Acts 24:1–27)**

1. Tertullus and Paul are both people who spend their lives in public speaking. But what kind of 'public speaker' is the preacher? How is he different from Tertullus?

2. The Christian gospel is a pathway. Paul says, 'According to the Way, which they call a sect . . .' (24:14). What puts us on to the road? What kind of road is it thereafter?

3. In what other ways is the gospel described here? The Christian gospel is a choice (24:14). What else?

Note Acts 24:6b–8a are not found in the best Greek manuscripts of the New Testament.

☐☐☐ **Reading 293 (Acts 25:1–27)**

1. There is certainly no slackness or laziness in Paul's enemies. Festus has only been in office for three days when Paul's enemies are pressing to have Paul back in Jerusalem. They are still hoping to assassinate him (25:3b). What is the secret of motivation? In the Christian? In others?

2. Paul has only one choice. He appeals to a higher court. Any Roman citizen had the right to appeal to trial before the Roman emperor, Caesar. So Paul makes use of his legal status as a Roman citizen. Pagan Romans were fairer to Paul than those professing faith in the God of Israel. So what may we learn from this?

3. Paul came very close to losing his life. But to the extent that Roman law was upheld Paul was safe. How useful is civic law? How much should Christians be concerned with the law of their nation, and with international law? What are its limitations?

☐☐☐ **Reading 294 (Acts 26:1–18)**

1. Paul is standing in front of very worldly people. Here is the greatest figure of the Christian church (after Jesus) standing before an assembly of worldly rulers. Why should they not receive the Lord Jesus Christ? Why is the gospel often rejected? Sometimes it is simply too painful to admit its truth. With all this display of pomp and pride, will Agrippa and his 'wife' admit that actually their inner lives are very different from what appearances might make us think? What other reasons for rejecting the gospel are found here?

2. The heart of Paul's message is the resurrection of Jesus. What do we learn about the resurrection here? What is the actual answer to Paul's question in 26:8?

3. Who is more genuine, pompous Agrippa or Paul the prisoner? Who is facing facts the most? Who has truth on his side? How much are men and women really open to spiritual challenges?

□□□ Reading 295 (Acts 26:19–32)

1. People give 'psychological' reasons for rejecting the Christian faith. 'He has a religious complex. He has become unbalanced!' 'Paul, you are out of your mind. Too much study has driven you crazy!' (26:24). But who has the greater intellect, Festus or Paul? Who knows more about life? What do you think of 'psychological' reasons for rejecting Jesus?

2. How does Paul reply to Festus' theory? How does he preach the gospel to such people?

3. Agrippa never did believe. He had had his last opportunity, for he would never hear Paul again. If not many high-born and powerful people come to faith in Jesus, should we bother? What would Paul say to this?

□□□ Reading 296 (Acts 27:1–20)

1. Are things going well for Paul or badly? Paul must now appear before the emperor himself. It was as if he was on one of his evangelistic tours, although he had never had a Roman escort before! Does Romans 8:28 mean that when things are going badly they are going well?

2. Are we imagining things to feel that this journey is being fiercely opposed even by the winds and the waves? After all the abundance of wonders in Acts, with its healings, its angels, its resurrections, its life-giving shadows (5:15) and life-giving handkerchiefs (19:11–12), we half-expect there to be a few miracles to assist Paul at this time of great danger. Why does nothing like that happen?

3. If God does not give Paul the comfort of miracles, what other comforts does Paul get?

□□□ Reading 297 (Acts 27:21–44)

1. Luke's story here is extremely detailed. What might be the reasons why what is happening here is so important?

2. Paul liked to use the picture-language of being shipwrecked. What are the spiritual lessons that Paul might have remembered in his

experience of being shipwrecked? (i) They were brought to much danger because they would not listen to God's apostle. (ii) They were over-optimistic about their own ideas. Anything else?

3. 'You should have listened to me in the first place . . . But now . . .' What new opportunities do the travellers have? How do they picture the new opportunities God sends us?

☐☐☐ Reading 298 (Acts 28:1–16)

1. Paul could have done with a few miracles when he was lost at sea! Now that they are safe on land, Paul is miraculously protected when bitten by a poisonous snake. Then Publius' father was healed (28:8). Then other sick people came and further healings took place (28:9). Why is the giving of miracles so erratic?

2. 'They honoured us in many ways and when we were ready to sail, they furnished us with the supplies we needed.' After the scarcities of the sea-trip Paul is given abundance. How did Paul learn to say what he said in Philippians 4:11–13?

3. Paul is given a holiday in Malta for three months, until early spring (28:11). Finally Luke says, 'and so we came to Rome'. It had been several tough years since Paul had said, 'I must also see Rome' (Acts 19:21). Rome was full of criminals and the vilest kinds of wickedness. Why did he so much want to go there? How must preachers of the gospel follow Paul's example?

☐☐☐ Reading 299 (Acts 28:1–31)

1. Paul's ministry at Rome begins with those who previously had been the people of God – the Jews. In Paul's day the bulk of the nation was becoming hardened to the gospel of the Lord Jesus Christ. Why did he begin with them?

2. Paul succeeded in getting in touch with Jewish leaders in the city. A day is arranged for Paul to explain the gospel to them (28:23). Some Jewish people believed, but the majority did not (28:24). What would Paul have thought about this?

3. Paul quotes Isaiah 6:9–10. God warned Isaiah right at the beginning of his ministry that he was not about to be a prophet that everyone would heed. Paul quotes these words and says what happened in Isaiah's day is being fulfilled in Paul's day (Acts 28:25–27). Yet the Jews must realise that if this gospel is rejected by them, it will go all the more quickly to the gentiles (28:28). Does the rejection of the gospel by Israel lead to anything good?

2 Kings

Recommended reading: M. A. Eaton, *2 Kings* (Preaching Through the Bible, Sovereign World, 2000).

☐☐☐ **Reading 300 (2 Kings 1:1–2:25)**

1. Amaziah of Israel has some questions, and God has some answers. Where should we take our questions? What should we do with God's answers?
2. Elisha knew he was called to be Elijah's successor. What was necessary if he was actually to receive the call he had been promised?
3. What challenges faced Elijah at his call? He does not pray, 'Where is Elijah?' but, 'Where is the Lord God of Elijah?' How should we face the challenges to God's will?

Note The word 'children' in some translations of 2 Kings 2:23–25 is misleading. It can refer to young adults. They are deliberately ridiculing the call of God's prophet.

☐☐☐ **Reading 301 (2 Kings 3:1–5:27)**

1. Jehoshaphat was a godly man but he was a man who compromised too easily. What results of compromise do we see in 2 Kings 3:1–27?
2. What is the point of each of the miracle stories in 2 Kings 4:1–44? The first speaks of God's promise of endless supply (4:1–7). And the other three (4:8–37, 38–41, 42–44)?

3. How does the story of 2 Kings 5:1–27 illustrate the simplicity of God's grace? Here is a great man with a great problem, and a little girl with a great God who knows how to help him. The great man has some great ideas about himself and about religion. But what did he (and what do we) have to learn?

☐☐☐ Reading 302 (2 Kings 6:1–8:24)

1. How might we take encouragement from a miracle that points to God's ability to recover what is lost (6:1–7)?

2. Elisha was a man with a gift of supernatural knowledge. He was often given revelations that helped the king of Israel. So steps were taken to get rid of Elisha (6:13–14) and Elisha found himself in a town that was well fortified but surrounded by Aramean soldiers (6:15). In what ways does he – and in what ways may we – experience God's protection?

3. The story of 2 Kings 7:1–20 becomes a remarkable foreshadowing of the gospel. A Christian reading it sees something of their own experience in it. (i) The background to good news is a situation of great need. (ii) When the needy men venture out in instinctive faith, they experience gifts and plenty, more than they could have imagined. In what other ways does the story remind us of the abundance of the gospel?

Note The 'sons of the prophets' were 'prophets-in-training' under Elisha, and acted as his assistants (2 Kings 2:16; 4:1; 6:1–3; 9:1–4). At times they would come together as a group (4:38–44; 6:1) and Elisha would give them advice and teaching (4:38). They delivered Elisha's messages (9:1–4) or were given messages of their own (1 Kings 20:35). They did not have much wealth but they were serving God by bringing his word to northern Israel despite the paganism that was to be found everywhere.

☐☐☐ Reading 303 (2 Kings 8:25–10:36)

Jehoshaphat's son Jehoram married a daughter of Ahab, and so introduced a daughter of Ahab and Jezebel into the rule of the house of David, in Judah.

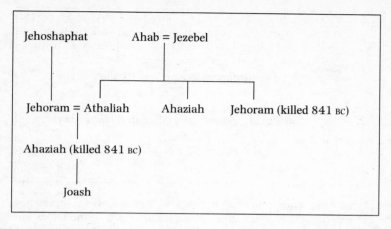

1. In 2 Kings 9:1–13, Jehu is anointed by God. But does this mean that Jehu is a godly man? Can God appoint an unholy person to be the leader of a country? If so, how does he use them?

2. What is the difference between a Hazael, a Jehu and an Elisha? All three were used by God to get rid of Baal-worship. But what about Hazael and Jehu?

3. As Jehu travels towards Samaria he meets Jehonadab, the founder of the 'Rechabites', who were strict observers of the law of Moses, followed a simple lifestyle in the rural areas and avoided the use of alcohol. Why do Jehu and Jehonadab support each other? Do people sometimes associate together for dubious reasons? What other examples are there?

□□□ Reading 304 (2 Kings 11:1–12:21)

1. Between 841 and 835 BC when Athaliah reigned, the promise of God to David was severely threatened. God had promised that the house of David would last indefinitely. But God has ways of preserving his promise. Ahaziah had a half-sister, Jehosheba, a daughter of Jehoram by another wife. She was married to Jehoida the high priest of the priests of Jerusalem (2 Chronicles 22:11).

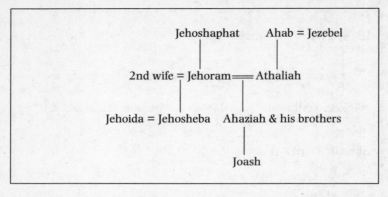

1. What do we learn from these stories? The Church is always threatened by extermination. What other examples are there in the Bible? But what are the ways God uses to rescue his people?
2. How is the description in 11:17–21 a picture of spiritual revival?
3. Joash of Judah reigned from 835–796 BC. In what way was it a time of small progress? Why was the progress so little? Nothing and no one stands still in the kingdom of God. How can we avoid the sluggishness of the days of Joash?

□□□ **Reading 305 (2 Kings 13:1–14:29)**

1. The story of 2 Kings now moves to the north again and focusses on Jehoahaz and Jehoash, both kings of northern Israel, and upon Elisha. How are the ways of the prophets superior to the ways of the kings? What are the characteristics of Elisha here? He is now old. But in what ways are we to serve God to the very end?
2. Amaziah of Judah (796–767 BC, including a twenty-four-year co-regency with his son) is a classic example of 'hotheadedness'. How does his reign illustrate Proverbs 26:21 ('As charcoal to hot embers and wood to fire, so is a quarrelsome man for kindling strife')?
3. Jeroboam's reign over Israel (co-regent with his father in 793 BC; died in 753 BC) was long and significant. Through the long days of Jeroboam, the Lord was giving them a last chance. The nation had one generation left before the volcano would erupt. But how was it badly used?

☐☐☐ **Reading 306 (2 Kings 15:1–17:41)**

1. Azariah of Judah, also known as Uzziah (as in 15:13), began to reign as co-regent with his father in 791 BC, took the throne as sole ruler in 767 BC and died in 739 BC. His days were days of easy prosperity and formal inherited religion. The first chapter of Isaiah's book is an analysis of the state of the nation at the end of Uzziah's long years. But how can easy success be misleading? How can we 'learn to do good' (Isaiah 1:17) at such times?

2. Very few kings were faithful to the end. Azariah was godly because he followed his father. What is the difference between true godliness and following good tradition? What happens at the end?

3. Northern Israel never could form a stable line of kings. Ten dynasties started but failed. Then the Assyrians brought the northern kingdom of Israel to an end. What was it that prevented there ever being stability in northern Israel? Does God hate any sin more than another? But why did northern Israel last so long?

☐☐☐ **Reading 307 (2 Kings 18:1–20:21)**

1. Hezekiah (co-regent from 729 BC; died 687/6 BC) was one of the three kings of Judah who did right 'according to all that his father David had done' (2 Kings 18:1–3). What were the marks of his greatness? Do we expect to be 'great'?

2. One might think after the bold actions of Hezekiah at the beginning of his reign (18:1–8) that he would live happily ever after! But what are the possible ways of responding when we find ourselves in a threatening situation?

3. Hezekiah became badly ill, but is not ready to die. What arguments does he use in his prayer? Are we allowed to argue with God? Does it do any good?

☐☐☐ **Reading 308 (2 Kings 21:1–22:20)**

1. After the greatest king of Judah since David we have the worst king ever in the story of Judah – Manasseh. You would think that Israel might now be a godly people, but why did it not happen? Are there equivalents to this in our own nation? Sometimes God has no choice but to put his people into exile. What is 'exile' for the Christian? Does the church get 'exiled' if it conforms to the world's ways?

2. Manasseh was followed by Amon, who became king in 643/2 BC as a young man of twenty-two years (21:19). He reigned for two years but

they were two years of continued wickedness. Manasseh had been through a period of intense suffering (see 2 Chronicles 33:11) and in that time he had come to regret his depravity. But which bit of Manasseh's life did Amon follow? What is the significance of Amon's reign?

3. Josiah came to the throne in 641/640 BC when he was a young boy of eight years (22:1). He began to seek the Lord and the story of 2 Kings goes straight to something that happened when he was twenty-six years old (623/22 BC). How did it happen that the Scriptures were 'lost'? In what ways does it happen today?

☐☐☐ Reading 309 (2 Kings 23:1–25:30)

1. By the year 609 BC, Josiah had died and Jehoahaz had become king (23:31). There had been a prediction that Judah would be punished for its sins not by the Assyrians but by the Babylonians (2 Kings 20:12–20), for God's anger against idolatry would not be quenched (22:16–17). Why did Josiah's reform not turn aside God's anger concerning Judah's idolatry? Is repentance ever too late?

2. God's chastening was obviously drawing near. But still there was no spiritual change. Jehoiakim reigned for about eleven years (609–598 BC), but during that time there was no turning to God; the warnings were not taken. In what ways might we see warnings but not heed them?

3. The judgments of God may come slowly but when they finally arrive they advance rapidly. How did this happen at the end of Judah's story? How may it happen to us?

4. God's chastenings hold out hope. The book ends sharply, as though it were ending with a string of dots. 'The king was doing well and . . .' How do God's chastenings hold out hope?

2 Timothy

2 Timothy seems to have been the last letter Paul ever wrote. When he wrote it he was in prison (1:8; 2:9) and he expected to die shortly – only he did not put it that way! He says he expected 'to receive the crown of righteousness' (4:6–8). Some years before, Paul had been taken to Rome under arrest. He had been imprisoned in Rome for at least two years and wrote at least four letters while he was there (Ephesians, Philippians, Colossians, Philemon). Then he was released. After that he must have continued his ministry tours. We have no precise details, but he must have visited places such as Crete and Ephesus to consolidate the work of God there. Timothy was given responsibility for the work in Ephesus. Then Paul was arrested again. This time he knows he is not likely to be released. Now Paul is handing over the leadership of his work – at least in the Ephesus area.

Recommended reading: M. A. Eaton, *2 Timothy* (Preaching Through the Bible, Sovereign World, 1999); J. R. W. Stott, *The Message of 2 Timothy* (The Bible Speaks Today, IVP, 1986).

☐☐☐ Reading 310 (2 Timothy 1:1–18)

1. 2 Timothy is a letter preparing Timothy for Christian leadership. Often-times when we think of leadership we think of techniques, how to preach, how to chair committees, how to set goals and objectives. But

Paul has different concerns. What kind of concerns for a future leader does Paul show in 2 Timothy 1:1–18?

2. In 1:9 Paul reminds Timothy of what the message of the gospel is all about. What in fact are the main ingredients of the Christian gospel as we have it here?

3. It seems that Onesiphorus is someone who has deserted Paul but served him well in the past (if verse 16 continues the theme of verse 15). So how does Paul deal with a person who has disappointed him?

☐☐☐ Reading 311 (2 Timothy 2:1–26)

1. What should be done (and by whom?) to promote the future well-being of God's gospel?

2. Paul uses pictures of the soldier, the athlete, the farmer. What should we learn from each of these illustrations?

3. God's firm foundation stands having this seal: 'The Lord knows those who are his' and 'Let everyone who names the name of the Lord depart from iniquity' (2:19). A 'seal' is something that keeps something else safe. It might be a document or a tomb or a box. Here Paul is speaking of the church. It is like a building. It has a foundation – the person of Jesus as he comes to us in the teaching of prophets and apostles – and that foundation has a 'seal' (something that makes it unshakeably sure). What is it that makes the church safe – from God's side and from the side of men and women?

☐☐☐ Reading 312 (2 Timothy 3:1–17)

1. 'In the last days difficult seasons will come' (3:1). The 'last days' is the period between the first coming and the second coming of Jesus. What are we to expect for the future of the church? Success? Failure? Hardship? A mixture of circumstances? Or what?

2. Why are some people 'always learning but never able to come to the knowledge of the truth' (3:7). What is the problem that blocks progress?

3. What is Paul's teaching about the Bible? Its inspiration? Its sufficiency? Its usage? And so on.

☐☐☐ Reading 313 (2 Timothy 4:1–22)

1. Paul now gives his last solemn charge to Timothy. He is anticipating the judgment hall of the final judgment. There are five aspects: 'preach the word; be steadfast when the time is right and when the time is not so right! Reprove, rebuke, exhort, with great patience and great instruction' (4:2). What does each one mean?

2. How much should the Christian be controlled by the thought of heavenly reward?

3. Paul pictures his life as a sacrifice, as a journey, as a fight, as a race, as a period of duty as a guard. What are the lessons of each picture?

Zephaniah

Zephaniah was the great-great-grandson of Hezekiah, the king of Judah. He came from the upper classes of Judah and says more in his prophecy about princes and judges than he does about the ordinary people of Israel. He lived in the seventh century BC, at the time of Josiah the king (640–609 BC). He has one central message: the approaching end of the world.

Recommended reading: J. A. Motyer, 'Zephaniah', in *The Minor Prophets*, vol. 3 (ed. T. E. McComiskey, Baker, 1992).

☐☐☐ **Reading 314 (Zephaniah 1:1–3:20)**

1. In 1:2–2:3, Zephaniah's message is that sin will be punished by bringing down upon itself the end of the world. What particular sins does Zephaniah mention and where may they be found in our society?
2. In 2:4–3:8, he develops the theme further but finally brings in a note of hope for the people of God. What does it mean to 'wait' for God (3:8)?
3. In 3:9–20, the note of hope in 3:8 is expanded. How is the story of Babel reversed (3:9–10)? What happens to Jerusalem (3:11–13)? What is it like in the new Jerusalem (3:14–20)? How are these predictions fulfilled?

Haggai

The prophecy of Haggai consists of oracles preached by the prophet at a time when the exiles who returned from Babylon to Jerusalem were flagging in zeal. It calls the people to get involved in the work of rebuilding the temple at Jerusalem.

Recommended reading: J. A. Motyer, 'Haggai', in *The Minor Prophets*, vol. 3 (ed. T. E. McComiskey, Baker, 1992).

□□□ Reading 315 (Haggai 1:1–2:23)

1. Was the slackness of the Judeans in building the temple justified? Do we sometimes give up God's work too easily? What does Haggai have to say about the matter?
2. When Haggai calls the people to be strong and take action (Haggai 2:1–23), what encouragements does he give them? What is the New Testament equivalent to Haggai's appeal?
3. A 'shaking' of the universe began in Haggai's day, and is still continuing. What does the 'shaking' include and involve?

Titus

The letter to Titus is concerned with putting down a false teaching that was becoming influential on the island of Crete. Titus is to appoint or reorganise an eldership to lead the church. He is to show how false is the heresy that is becoming popular. The letter to Titus is mainly a straightforward call to a life of godliness. After introducing himself (1:1–4) and calling for the appointment of elders (1:5–9), Paul warns the people against a cult that is damaging the churches (1:10–16). Then he asks for the different groups in the churches to re-establish the life of godliness (2:1–10). The grace of God has appeared for their salvation (2:11–15). Then he reminds them of their social responsibility (3:1–2). Their sinful past (3:3) may be left aside now that the grace of God has appeared for their salvation (3:4–8a). Titus must see that the believers work out their salvation in godly living (3:8b). He must avoid useless controversies (3:9) and repudiate those who will not submit to his call for godliness (3:10–11). In Titus 3:12–15, Paul gives his instructions about his colleagues (3:12–13) and their message (3:14), and gives the final greetings of the letter (3:15).

Recommended reading: J. R. W. Stott, *The Message of 1 Timothy and Titus* (The Bible Speaks Today, IVP, 1996).

☐☐☐ Reading 316 (Titus 1:1–16)

1. Titus 1:1–4 contains a compressed description of Paul's work. What are the purposes of the preaching ministry? What are the ingredients of the gospel we are to proclaim? What is the kind of life it leads to?

2. What are the differences between the characteristics of an 'ordinary' Christian and the characteristics of an elder? Is there any requirement other than Christian godliness? Why does Paul think that elders are needed?

3. Is Paul being racist in Titus 1:12–13? Or do we have to note the weaknesses of different nationalities – including our own?

☐☐☐ Reading 317 (Titus 2:1–15)

1. What are the particular spiritual requirements that are asked of the six groups of people mentioned in Titus 2:1–10?

2. 'The grace of God has appeared . . .' Paul is thinking of the coming of Jesus into the world. In what ways can the graciousness of God be seen in the life and work of the Lord Jesus Christ? How did God's grace 'appear' more visibly than before?

3. What other reasons for godly living may be found in Titus 2:11–15? How does each one have an impact upon our lives?

☐☐☐ Reading 318 (Titus 3:1–15)

1. What is the difference between what a Christian *was* and what a Christian *becomes* – in Titus 3:3–8a? What then is our view of the spiritual state of the people around us? What difference does it make to the way in which we relate to them?

2. All the early church 'fathers' took Titus 3:5 to refer to water baptism, but they took Isaiah 1:16 ('Wash, make yourselves clean . . .'), Psalm 1:5–6 (a tree 'planted by the entry through into the waters') and Isaiah 33:16 ('his water is sure') in the same way! Did the early church 'fathers' not make some big mistakes here? What is your view of the 'washing of regeneration-and-renewal by the Holy Spirit' (it can be read in that way)? What are your reasons for thinking that salvation is or is not by water baptism? Which approach fits your experience? What difference will it make if a person thinks that their baptism brings salvation?

3. How might Titus 3:10 be put into practice in modern times?

Zechariah

In January 588 BC the city of Jerusalem was attacked by the Babylonians. It was a time that Judah would never forget. The city was besieged for eighteen months until the middle of 587 BC, and most of the population were exiled to Babylon. Then about fifty years later, at the point where the story of Ezra-Nehemiah opens in 538 BC, the Babylonian empire had just come to an end, and Cyrus the Persian issued a decree allowing the Jews to go back home. But there was a lot of opposition towards the newly returned Israelites, and because of this the work of rebuilding the temple stopped in 536 BC, and from about 535 to about 520 BC the people were discouraged and gave themselves to their own pursuits. 'It is not the right time for building God's house', they said (see Haggai 1:1). But Ezra 5:1 says, 'Haggai . . . and Zechariah . . . prophesied . . .' The first six chapters of the book of Zechariah refer to his preaching in 520 BC. Then Zechariah 7:1 refers to a time in December 518 BC when some men came from Bethel to ask a question about fasting. It is the last date in the book, for there are no dates given in Zechariah 9:1–14:21.

The book of Zechariah falls into four sections. In Zechariah 1:1–6:15, after an opening prophetic message (1:1–6) we have eight visions (1:7–17, 18–21; 2:1–13; 3:1–10; 4:1–14; 5:1–4, 5–11; 6:1–8) and a closing oracle in 6:9–15 balancing the one in 1:1–6. A second section comes in Zechariah 7:1–8:23, and another in Zechariah 9:1–11:17. Then a final section comes in Zechariah 12:1–14:21. That it is a distinct section is suggested by the title in 12:1.

Zechariah 1:1–6	An opening message.	Interpreting the past.
Zechariah 1:7–17	Riders in the valley.	God's love of Jerusalem.
Zechariah 1:18–21	The horns and the craftsmen.	Enemies overthrown.
Zechariah 2:1–13	The man with a measure.	Plans for new Jerusalem.
Zechariah 3:1–10	Clothing for the high priest.	Cleansing and renewal.
Zechariah 4:1–7	Two trees and a lampstand.	The power of the Spirit.
Zechariah 5:1–4	The flying scroll.	The curse of the law.
Zechariah 5:5–11	The woman in a basket.	Inevitable exile.
Zechariah 6:1–8	The four chariots.	The Lord of the nations.
Zechariah 6:9–15	A closing message.	Crowning the King.

Recommended reading: T. V. Moore, *Haggai, Zechariah, Malachi* (Banner of Truth, 1960).

□□□ **Reading 319 (Zechariah 1:1–4:14)**

1. Why is it necessary to view the past rightly before we can press on into the future with God's blessing (1:1–6)?
2. There are times when nothing much seems to be happening (1:7–17). How do we interpret such times?
3. God plans to rebuild his people (2:1–13), but what is needed first, according to 3:1–10 and 4:1–7? If spiritual renewal is to come today, is anything needed first?

□□□ **Reading 320 (Zechariah 5:1–8:23)**

1. The flying scroll (5:1–4) and the woman in a basket (5:5–11) speak of the curse of the law and inevitable exile. The eighth vision (6:1–8) is a vision of God's heavenly home. The chariots come out from between two mountains. The region among two mountains is a way of picturing the dwelling-place of God. The end of the chapter contains a section in which the Messiah (or his representative) is crowned king and priest. How is God steering and shaping his kingdom amid all that is happening in the world? What difference does it make what view of history we hold?
2. Zechariah 7:1–8:23 tells of an incident that led Zechariah to give another word of guidance to the people. In the town of Bethel, nineteen kilometres from Jerusalem, a discussion had arisen about a day of fasting. 'Religiosity' is the habit that some have of enjoying religion for

its own sake without much reference to God! 'You fasted', says God, 'but was it for me?' How might we be guilty of 'religiosity' today?

3. The temple that Zechariah is seeing built is but the shadow of a much greater thing that God was doing – and is still doing – in the history of the world. The promises in Zechariah 8:20–23 (and in many other Old Testament Scriptures) are fulfilled in the gospel of the Lord Jesus Christ. In what ways are God's people like a temple?

□□□ Reading 321 (Zechariah 9:1–11:17)

It is difficult to find any logical structure in Zechariah 9:1–14:21. There is general agreement that 9:1–8, 9–10; 12:1–9 are distinct units. But at other points it is difficult to define the smaller units. What seems certain is that we have in these chapters a few themes presented in a way that jumps from vision to vision without logical order. There are at least three themes interwoven: (i) the nations are to be conquered, despised for their great hostility to the people of God. (ii) God himself is to come personally to take part in the achievement of salvation. (iii) God's people will suffer because of poor leadership but God will train them under good leadership and they will take part in conquering the nations.

These themes are put side-by-side like a string of unconnected photographs. Why are they not put in a more logical order? Because chronological sequence is deliberately not being given to us. It is not for us to know the times and the seasons. The whole patchwork of predictions will come about in God's way and in God's order. The repeated title in 9:1 and 12:1 suggests that Zechariah is perhaps going over the same ground twice. When we look at the contents of these chapters in detail we discover that Zechariah roughly puts a series of themes before us, ending up (in 11:1–17) with a picture of calamitous defeat. Then he gives the same heading again, and goes roughly over the same ground but this time giving some answers and ending up with a picture of glorious victory.

9:1–8	Conquering Nations. The nations being defeated. God has a plan to conquer the nations.	12:1–9	Conquering Nations. The nations being defeated; Israel rescued.
9:9–10	The King's Arrival. God's plan to conquer the nations involves the sending of his king.	12:10–13:1	The Spirit's Arrival. The people come to repentance.
9:11–10:1	Imprisoned People are Released (9:11), used in battle (9:13), Yahweh the warrior with them saving them (9:14–17), prayer (10:1). When God sends his king, his people are to be used as his warriors.	13:2–6	Unclean People are Cleansed. A cleansed people; false leaders despised (13:1–6)

10:2–12	Bad Leaders are Replaced by Good Leaders. People without a shepherd (10:2), God's concern (10:3) and creation of good leaders (10:4). They tread down their enemies (10:5). God restores them to become warriors (10:6–8). Though scattered they return (10:9–10) and are rescued from every distress (10:11–12).	13:7–9	A Good Shepherd. A good shepherd who is smitten for the people (13:7–9). The people are scattered but purified.
11:1–17	An Overview of Terrible Defeat. Israel has bad leaders before it ever has good leaders. Facing a difficult situation (11:1–3). The nation abandoned, God and his prophet despised (11:4–14). Abandoned to the worthless shepherd (11:15–17). This is terrible defeat.	14:1–21	An Overview of Glorious Victory. Conflict against Jerusalem (14:1–4a), rescue by earthquake (14:4b–5a), God comes (14:5b). Jerusalem exalted even physically (14:6–11). All nations incorporated into Jerusalem (14:12–21).

1. The great theme of the Old Testament is 'the King's arrival'. Is Zechariah 9:9–10 completely fulfilled in the events of Palm Sunday or is there more than one way in which the king can arrive? What is the point of riding on an ass instead of a war-horse?

2. The nations will be defeated (9:1–8). God will visit his people (9:9–10). He will bring them to triumph and fruitfulness (9:11–10:1). The main point of Zechariah 10:2–12 is that despite poor leadership in the land, God has plans to bring his 'Israel' into power and influence. He will rescue them from a sea of troubles. How are our troubles like a stormy sea? How does God rescue us?

3. The next unit could be called 'The foolish shepherds and the Good Shepherd (11:1–17). Zechariah is told to act a part. He says: 'So I became the shepherd of the flock that was about to be slaughtered truly those who were the poor ones of the flock. I took two wooden rods. One of them I gave the name "Graciousness". The other I named "Unity", and I cared for the sheep' (11:7). Zechariah begins to act the part of a shepherd who cares especially for poor and needy people (as Jesus would later care for the needy people of Israel). What are the characteristics of a 'good shepherd'?

☐☐☐ **Reading 322 (Zechariah 12:1–14:21)**

1. Zechariah predicts that the surrounding nations will attack Jerusalem, but without success. The questions must be asked: When does the prophet envisage this situation, and what kind of 'Jerusalem' does he envisage? For some interpreters a passage like Zechariah 12:1–9 is all about antichrist marshalling forces of the world to gather against Jerusalem at a 'tribulation period' for Israel after the rapture (an event that they think is not the same as Jesus' final 'second coming'). Such interpreters believe that this is to interpret 'literally', and that it is the only way to interpret such Scriptures as these.

Yet there is great difficulty in this style of interpreting. To read prophetic theories back into Zechariah is a dubious procedure. The interpretation is not as 'literal' as it may appear. For example, is the future warfare to be conducted by horses and chariots? If not, then the interpretation is not literal!

What is taught here is that despite the terrible sufferings that will come on Jerusalem, God's 'Jerusalem' will be indestructible. What kind of Jerusalem is this? How can all of this ever take place? The first answer is: Israel will have to reach a day of national repentance, a repentance that is so deep and sweeping that the entire nation comes to repentance, family by family. What other answers are given?

2. What are the marks of spiritual revival?

3. In Zechariah 13:7–9, someone is struck with God's sword of judgment. He is a shepherd looking after the sheep belonging to God. Yet he is a close associate of God himself. It is at God's command that he is smitten. Who is this?

4. It is typical of Zechariah that he jumps from one scene to another with abrupt transitions. The last twenty-one verses of Zechariah seem to fall into an A-B-C-B-A pattern:

A. The day coming for the Lord (14:1–3)
   B. Geographical symbolism (14:4–5)
      C. The final glory (14:6–9)
   B. Geographical symbolism (14:10–11)
A. The day coming for God (14:12–21)

How do we interpret the geographical symbolism here? The language here is picturesque. Although it refers to real events in future history, yet much picture-language is being used. Cutting mountains into halves would hardly make any difference in modern warfare and we must not read this with too modern a viewpoint. We have to put ourselves in the mind of Zechariah and realise that he is using a highly symbolical prophetic vision. Although the second coming of Jesus obviously fulfils parts of what we have in Zechariah 14:1–21, yet this is not to be viewed as a kind of TV documentary giving us a photographic preview of the second coming.

God is pictured as being like a giant standing upon the mountains. It is a picture that we have elsewhere. In Micah also we have a similar giant figure. 'Yahweh is coming out of his dwelling-place', said Micah. 'He will come down and tread upon the high places of the earth . . . The mountains will melt under him . . . the valleys will burst open . . .' (Micah 1:2–4). Here we have something similar. In Zechariah's picture, God's people are trapped in Jerusalem. Their enemies are threatening to wipe them out altogether. Suddenly God appears! Like a giant he treads upon the mountains. As he does so Mount Olive divides into two! The people escape and run to Azal (which seems to be the name of a village not far from Jerusalem, the same as Beth-ezel mentioned elsewhere). The enemies are being shaken by an earthquake, and the people of Jerusalem run from the scene (just as the people did in a famous earthquake earlier in Israel's history). How does this kind of language picture the mighty occasions when God rescues his people?

Malachi

The difficulty with the people of Israel in Malachi's day was that they were struggling with the feeling that God did not love them after all. Malachi ministered at a comparatively late stage in Israel's history, a century or so after the return from Babylonian exile. By Malachi's time (450–430 BC, so far as we can tell), the temple had been built for half a century; Jerusalem had been re-established. Yet despite all of this 'restoration', all was not well with the newly constituted Israel. The people felt that they had not really been 'restored' at all. The royal line of David had not been restored. The people had no Judean king, and they were under the rule of a governor, a Persian appointee. They faced opposition from people in Judea who had no interest in Israel's historic faith. The rebuilt temple was tiny compared to the glory of the old temple of Solomon. The people still felt that the 'good old days' had gone for ever. God did not love them – they thought. There was no real justice for them. The pagans got on as well as the people of Israel. So the people lapsed into deeper and deeper cynicism. The book of Malachi is structured around six sceptical questions that the people were asking:

1. In what way have you loved us? (1:2)
2. In what way have we despised your name? (1:6)
3. How have we defiled you? (1:7)
4. In what way have we wearied him? (2:17)
5. In what way shall we return? (3:7)
6. In what way have we robbed you? (3:8)

In Malachi 1:2–3:15, six sections revolve around these six questions:
1. The love of God (1:2–5)
2. The name of God (1:6–2:9)
3. Faithfulness (2:10–16)
4. The justice of God (2:17–3:6)
5. Returning to God (3:7–12)
6. The service of God (3:13–15)

Recommended reading: W. C. Kaiser, *Malachi: God's Unchanging Love* (Baker, 1984).

☐☐☐ Reading 323 (Malachi 1:1–4:6)

1. The first question to be tackled is: 'In what way have you loved us?' This question is taken up first because it has claims of priority over all other questions. If God does not love us, to answer any other question would be a waste of time. But God does love his people. How do we know God loves us as his people? How does Malachi prove it?
2. The longest section of Malachi is 1:6–2:9. It deals with the spiritual carelessness in the priests. What are the marks of spiritual carelessness and what does God say about it?
3. In Malachi 3:16 we have the people's response to Malachi's message. 'Then those who feared Yahweh spoke to one another . . .' This verse is the narration of a decisive event. It refers to the way in which godly people in Judah responded to Malachi's preaching. They discussed with each other what Malachi had been saying about these six topics. As they were responding to Malachi, God was listening. 'A book of remembrance was written before Yahweh . . .' (3:16). Malachi 3:17–4:6 is God's encouragement and wisdom for those who have responded to him:
   * God delights in his people (3:17–18)
   * Evil annihilated; righteousness honoured (4:1–3)
   * Honouring the law (4:4)
   * The ministry of Elijah (4:5–6)

How do the people respond and how does God respond to their response? What notice does God take of the way we hear his Word?

Philemon

The beautiful little letter to Philemon is a study in persuading a Christian to be a Christian! It also gives us an answer to the question: How does Paul tackle social problems? Slavery – the ownership of some people by others – was well established in the first century AD. Kidnapping was forbidden for Christians (see 1 Timothy 1:10) but people could become slaves as the result of war, and as a result of debt. Sometimes people would sell themselves into slavery as a means of escaping poverty or with the hope of eventually becoming Roman citizens. Parents could sell their children into slavery. In the large cities of the Roman empire as much as a third of the city might consist of the slaves. Slaves were often set free when they reached the age of thirty, and it was not quite as cruel a practice as one might imagine. But obviously the slaves were a downtrodden and much abused part of society.

There are plenty of places in our modern world where house-servants are in exactly the same sort of situation as the house-slaves of the ancient Roman empire, and for much the same reasons. They get virtually no salary. They are very much tied to the home where they live, unless they run away. They work long hours and have no free days. They get enough food to survive and they have a place to sleep at night – but that is about all they have. Not every country in the world has a legal 'minimum wage', and even in countries where there is a legal minimum wage it is not a very easy matter to enforce it. In many parts of the world 'servants' are cousins or relatives. They earn no salary back home in their village, and so they are brought to live with a slightly more wealthy relative. In some places even the house-servants have house-servants! When you are desperately poor, what can you do to survive? All you can do is sell yourself and your willingness to work! Perhaps you will not be paid at all, but at least your 'owner' will keep you alive and well. Better to be a slave and alive, than 'free' but starving. The 'Atlantic slave trade' of the nineteenth century was of course wicked, and many Christians fought to get it declared illegal. But there have always been other kinds of slavery. Philemon was not a slave-owner of the 'Atlantic slave trade' variety. Nor was he a 'man-stealer', a kidnapper for the purposes of slavery (which, according to the Bible, is worthy of the death sentence). But he did participate in the social structure of the ancient world and since he was able to afford it he had a slave named Onesimus.

The letter to Philemon gives us some glimpses of the social problems of Paul's day. Paul himself was unjustly in prison, 'a prisoner of Christ Jesus'. He writes to his friend who had owned a slave. All of this makes Philemon a very interesting social document. How do Christians behave in such a situation?

Recommended reading: D. E. Hiebert, *Titus and Philemon* (Moody, 1957).

☐☐☐ Reading 324 (Philemon 1–25)

1. If Paul had called upon his people to rise up in rebellion and protest against slavery, what would have happened?

2. What then is Paul's way of handling a social problem? He is working within the situation. How should we handle social problems today? Racism? Exploitation of the poor? International capitalism's exploitation of poorer nations? Dangers on our streets and corrupt politicians who misuse their powers? Land-grabbing and the devastation of the world's forests? Economic systems that in the name of freedom boost the profits of the business community but lead the poor into powerlessness and desperation and greater poverty than ever? What did the apostles do directly? What did they do indirectly?

3. The central section of the letter (verses 8–20) may be viewed in several ways. We can see that Paul moves from an emphasis on the past (verses 8–12), to an emphasis on the present (13–16) and on to an exclusive concern for the future (17–20). What are the great changes that are brought about in our lives by new birth by the Holy Spirit of God?

2 Chronicles

2 Chronicles is part of the one lengthy book which we call 1–2 Chronicles, written shortly after the return from Babylonian exile. It reviews the history of the Davidic line of kings in the southern kingdom of Judah. The history starts with Adam and goes rapidly through the genealogies of the people of interest from Adam to David.

Recommended reading: M. Wilcock, *The Message of Chronicles* (The Bible Speaks Today, IVP, 1987); J. G. McConville, *Chronicles* (St Andrew, 1984).

☐☐☐ **Reading 325 (2 Chronicles 1:1–2:18)**
1. Was not God taking a big risk in 2 Chronicles 1:7? What would we ask for if God gave us the opportunity to ask for anything we wanted? Is God likely to make the same offer to us?
2. The chronicler (as we call the author of this book) emphasises Solomon's trade with other nations. What is the point of this? Why might there be emphasis on the *international* links of God's king?
3. The chronicler emphasises the lavishness of the treasures of the temple more than its architecture. Why should there be this 'pride' in the glory of the temple? It was much smaller in the chronicler's day! In what way is the glory of the temple prophetic of something else?

□□□ **Reading 326 (2 Chronicles 3:1–4:22)**

1. Are we to be concerned about 'holy buildings' today? Or is the temple only prophetic of spiritual experience? Should we say perhaps that the whole of life is one gigantic Holy of Holies?

2. The largest items in the temple grounds were the bronze altar and 'the sea' – a gigantic bowl for the priests to wash in, called 'the sea' because it was so large. What was the symbolism of these two items outside the building? Why were they *outside* the temple building? What is needed to enter the presence of God?

3. The temple was very ornate; the tabernacle was much simpler. Is the church of Jesus Christ to be more like the temple or like the tabernacle?

□□□ **Reading 327 (2 Chronicles 5:1–6:42)**

1. After the temple, Solomon attended to the ark. What does it represent? What does bringing the ark to the temple represent for the Christian?

2. There is no equivalent to 2 Chronicles 5:11–14 in 1 Kings. Interest in music grew over the course of Israel's history. Why is it important to have music in the church?

3. David was not allowed to build the temple. Is there anything in our age that we have to leave to the future? But David prepared the way for his son. Do we have to prepare anything for the future servants of God?

□□□ **Reading 328 (2 Chronicles 7:1–8:18)**

1. Fire fell from heaven after the building of the temple (7:1–3). In what way would we like God to acknowledge that what we have done is honoured by God?

2. It was taken for granted that the temple would be a place of prayer (7:11–22). The prayer would be 'made in this place'. What is the 'temple' through which the modern Christian prays?

3. Is it not strange that Solomon took a wife who was not allowed to enter a holy building in Jerusalem (8:11)? So why did Solomon take her as a wife? In what ways do we take things into our lives that cannot be allowed to enter into our relationship with God?

□□□ **Reading 329 (2 Chronicles 9:1–10:19)**

1. The queen of Sheba recognised that God had been at work in Solomon's life (9:8). What is the difference between someone admiring us and someone admiring God's work in us? Is it possible to want one but not the other?

2. What Solomon was given (9:10) he used for God (9:11). Would we be

allowed to be richer if God knew we would be the same? What is the connection, if any, between generosity towards God and wealth?

3. The chronicler is only interested in the kings of Judah. He says little about the kings of northern Israel. The next Judean king, Rehoboam, rejected the advice of older people. As a general rule what is the advice of older people like? And what kind of advice do younger people give? Should we listen to one? To the other? To both? To neither? To one at one moment and another at another moment? Does the principle of Romans 12:6 apply ('Having gifts that differ . . .')?

☐☐☐ Reading 330 (2 Chronicles 11:1–13:22)

1. Rehoboam was about to act against a split that never should have happened, but God stopped him. 'The Lord says you must not go . . . I made all these things happen.' Is something that seems to be bad ever brought about by God? The cross is an example. But in our own lives does the same thing happen?

2. If success spoils us as it spoiled Rehoboam (note 12:1), how should we handle success?

3. Abijah ruled in Jerusalem for three years. The Judeans were victorious in battle because they trusted in the Lord (13:18). What is it like to depend on God? What is involved? Do we do nothing? Do we pray hard? What does it mean practically?

☐☐☐ Reading 331 (2 Chronicles 14:1–16:14)

1. The fifth king in the line of David was Asa. It was said to him: 'The Lord is with you, while you are with him. If you seek him, he will be found by you, but if you abandon him, he will abandon you.' What does it mean to 'seek God' – a theme mentioned nine times in the chapters about Asa?

2. Asa was intensely loyal to God at one stage (15:16) but then looked for help in the wrong place (16:7). In what ways may we also fail to persist in confident trust of God alone? Is it possible to trust in God and trust in something else at the same time?

3. Asa responded badly to a prophetic message (16:10). The one who had sought God so much eventually failed to seek him. What does this mean in practice? What are the signs that we are failing to seek God?

☐☐☐ Reading 332 (2 Chronicles 17:1–19:11)

1. The sixth king in the line of David was Jehoshaphat. He also sought God (17:4) and he grew steadily greater (17:12). But almost every king

seemed to make some bad mistake. What led to Jehoshaphat's making a marriage alliance with Ahab (18:1)? What did that lead to? What sort of 'alliances' should we avoid today?

2. Jehoshaphat seemed to want to be loyal to the Lord – Yahweh – and also to the rulers of idolatrous northern Israel. Again this is a false alliance. Are some people specially inclined to make wrong alliances? What sort of people make this mistake?

3. What are the marks of true prophecy as we have them in these chapters? What kind of 'prophecy' may we expect today?

□□□ Reading 333 (2 Chronicles 20:1–22:12)

1. In what ways does Jehoshaphat's prayer make a good example for our own praying? The situation was desperate. 'We are powerless against this great multitude that is coming against us. We do not know what to do . . .' What kind of arguments did he put before God?

2. 'As they began to sing and praise, the LORD set an ambush . . .' What is the connection between worship and God's action on our behalf?

3. Jehoram succeeded Jehoshaphat (21:1) but murdered his rivals (21:4). 'Yet the LORD would not destroy the house of David because of the covenant that he had made with David . . .' God will not break a covenant even if Jehoram is a multiple murderer. What covenant does God make with us? Will anything make him break it?

□□□ Reading 334 (2 Chronicles 23:1–24:27)

1. Joash was crowned king at a young age, through the courage of Jehoiada the priest. His scheme took seven years to bring to pass. What does this imply about Jehoiada's patience and his planning? How much should we look to the long distant future in making plans for the gospel of the Lord Jesus Christ?

2. What other aspects of Jehoiada's faithfulness to God can be found in these chapters? Yet his loyalty was to a king, not to himself. What can we learn from this about our loyalty to the Lord Jesus Christ?

3. Joash seems to have needed to lean on Jehoiada, or on other people. His zeal for God only dealt with small matters. What happened when his support was taken away? How should we handle ourselves if we find we have similar weaknesses?

□□□ Reading 335 (2 Chronicles 25:1–26:23)

1. The tenth king in the line of David was Amaziah. 'He did what was right in the sight of the LORD, yet not with a true heart' (25:2). What

does this mean? What did he do that was right? What was wrong with his 'heart'?

2. Why did God hand Amaziah over to his own foolishness? What made God so angry? How may the same thing happen today?

3. Uzziah was the next king. He had a good beginning but a bad end. What matters most, the character of the whole of our life, or how our life turns out at the end? What do the biblical writers regard as important?

☐☐☐ Reading 336 (2 Chronicles 27:1–29:36)

1. Jotham 'became strong because he ordered his ways before the LORD his God' (27:6). What does it mean today to 'order our ways before God'?

2. Ahaz copied the ways of the kings of Israel, and looked to Assyria for guidance. Why do people who grow up within the people of God like to copy those who are so ungodly?

3. What does trouble do for us? Does it drive us close to God or away from God? Or may it do either?

☐☐☐ Reading 337 (2 Chronicles 30:1–32:33)

1. Spiritual renewal in the Old Testament often involves a return to the celebration of the Passover. How enthusiastically was it kept in Hezekiah's time? The people remembered the origin of the nation in their rescue by the blood of the Passover lamb. What is the spiritual equivalent of this? What blessing is promised if we return to the 'blood of the lamb' (30:6–9)?

2. What do we learn about the nature of Mosaic law from 30:17–20?

3. How is Hezekiah a model for us in his zeal, his approach to opponents, his concern for the blood of the Passover lamb? What else can we find in his life that commends itself to us?

☐☐☐ Reading 338 (2 Chronicles 33:1–34:33)

1. Manasseh was the fourteenth king in the line of David. After a life of wickedness he came late to repentance. Why was such a good king followed by such a wicked king? What did his late repentance do for himself? What did it do for his country and his work as the king?

2. 'Judah and . . . Jerusalem did more evil than the nations whom the LORD had destroyed before the people of Israel' (33:9). Can God's people be worse than those who are not God's people? If so, what does God do about it?

3. Which part of Manasseh's life did his son Amon follow? How do we pass on godliness and faith to the next generation? Can it always be done?

□□□ Reading 339 (2 Chronicles 35:1–36:23)

1. Again spiritual renewal involved going back to the principles of the Passover. What are they? What happened in the original Passover that is never to be forgotten? Remember also that the Lord's Supper is a transformed Passover service.

2. 'Act according to the word of the LORD by Moses . . .' (35:6). Josiah was deliberately following the Scriptures. How close do we need to keep to the written word of God? Must we do everything in it? The law is abolished. Is anything else abolished from the New Testament? May we do things not mentioned in Scripture? How closely must our worship be shaped by the Scriptures?

3. The people fed on the Passover lamb (35:13). We 'feed' on Jesus. What does this mean practically?

Psalms 140:1–150:6

□□□ Reading 340 (Psalms 140:1–142:7)

1. In Psalm 140:1–13, as so often, David is in trouble with enemies. What kind of schemes do they follow? What does David pray? How confident is he? Does the Christian really expect to have many enemies? Is it a good sign if we have no enemies?

2. Psalm 141:1–10 deals with the temptations that come from the 'company of men who work iniquity'. What are the psalmist's concerns as he is invited to 'eat of their delicacies'? How must we watch for pleasant enemies (Psalm 141:1–10) as well as violent enemies (Psalm 140:1–13)?

3. Psalm 142:1–7 is a mixture of cries of distress (verses 1–2, 4, 6) and expressions of confidence about his way (verse 3), his inheritance (verse 5), his expectation (verse 7). How often do we find ourselves in the same mixture of alternating despair and confidence? What is the remedy? What did David do?

□□□ Reading 341 (Psalms 143:1–145:21)

1. In deep distress David prays for mercy. He knows that he himself is not sinless (143:2) and he finds help in prayer, in psalm-writing, in meditation on the works of God (143:5). How much help can we get by simply pondering what God has done in the past?

2. Psalm 144:1–15 first meditates on God's strength and faithfulness

(144:1–3), alongside human weakness (144:4). Verses 5–11 call upon God to send rescue from heaven for his people (144:5–8, 11) and promises praise for the rescue that is expected (144:9–10). Verses 12–15 pray for the peace and prosperity that is expected after the divine rescue. How can we get to know God as rock, trainer, steadfast lover, fortress, shield (144:1–3)? Is it a matter of Bible-reading? Experience? Or what? What leads us to be like the psalmist?

3. Psalm 145:1–21 (an alphabetic psalm) gives us an A-to-Z analysis of why we should praise the Lord. The psalmist calls upon himself ('I') and all peoples everywhere ('one generation . . . to another', verse 4) to worship God. Along the way he mentions the items that call forth our praise: God's works and God's character. What in fact does God do that is worthy of our praise? What in fact is he like? What difference would it make to us if we regularly praised God in the way that the writer of Psalm 145:1–21 did?

☐☐☐ Reading 342 (Psalms 146:1–148:14)

1. The psalmist has learned to trust in God, but he has also learned not to trust too much in 'princes' (146:3). What is it that God can do that 'princes' normally care nothing about?

2. The book of Psalms builds up to a final crescendo of praise. What aspect of God's character and activities make the psalmist think 'it is good to sing praise to our God' (Psalm 147:1).

3. The creation is to praise God (Psalm 148:1–10) as also are the people in it (Psalm 148:11–14). It takes delight in God's glory, seen in his world and the people in it. Many of the psalms (and our prayers also) are dominated by the problems that people face. But should there not be songs that are full of praise and where the problems of life are left aside? What should be the balance of praying for ourselves and forgetting ourselves?

☐☐☐ Reading 343 (Psalms 149:1–150:6)

1. Some people seem to have high praises in their mouths (149:6) but no swords in their hands. Others seem to have swords in their hands but no high praises in their mouths. In what way is the Christian to be a person of spiritual warfare and spiritual praise at the same time?

2. The worship of Psalm 150:1–6 is obviously very noisy (see 150:3–6). The wonders of Psalm 150:1–2 are worthy of exuberance. Should our worship be noisy? Dignified? Or what?

3. Now that we have read so many psalms, what place should they have in our lives? They put doctrine to us gently in the form of songs and testimonies. They encourage us because the psalmists seem to have even more problems than we do! Yet sometimes they seem to be rather fierce in the way they pray. What are the main lessons we should learn from the book of Psalms?

Revelation

From the second century BC onwards, various books in the ancient world claimed to be 'revelations' or 'apocalypses'. They modelled themselves on the characteristics of the book of Daniel, using a lot of symbolism and focussing their attention on the end of the world. The book of Revelation is one of them. It is a mysterious prophecy written to encourage persecuted Christians. Although it is a controversial book, it should never be the ground of division or conflict or hostility among fellow Christians. We must approach it with great humility. It claims to be 'a revelation of Jesus Christ' (1:1). In Revelation 1:1–3:22 Jesus is seen as the glorified Saviour in the midst of his churches. In Revelation 4:1–8:1 Jesus is the Lord of history, the one who opens the seven scrolls. In Revelation 8:2–11:18 Jesus reigns amid the judgments coming on the world, being announced by the trumpets of judgment. In Revelation 11:19–15:4 Jesus is victorious over the dragon. In Revelation 15:5–16:21 Jesus is the one who expresses the anger of God against the unrepentant and he pours out bowls of wrath upon them. In Revelation 17:1–19:10 Jesus is the destroyer of godless Babylon. In Revelation 19:11–22:21 Jesus is Victor over sin and Satan, and the One who brings the new heaven and new earth.

This 'revelation' makes use of a lot of symbolism. The word 'signified' (1:2, literally) is deliberately chosen. This book is packed tight with signs of various kinds. The key to the symbolism is generally to be found in the Old Testament. The entire book of Revelation is saturated in the language of the Old Testament. Most of the numbers are symbolical in the book of

439

Revelation. Consider the symbolism in Revelation 1:1–20. The number seven is symbolical (even in 1:4). The 'seven spirits' is a piece of symbolism. 'Signs' are used when Jesus is called 'the alpha and the omega'. The candlestick, the robe, the sash, the white hair, the bronze feet, the stars, the sword, the sun, the keys, are all pieces of picturesque language. We must be ready to find symbolism everywhere. The 144,000 of Revelation 7:4–8 is not literal (especially since it is 'a multitude that no one can number').

Early Christian tradition claims to know that the apostle John spent his later years in Ephesus, and from there he was exiled to Patmos. Yet the style of Greek is rather different from the Greek of John's Gospel and John's letters. It is written as if John were thinking in Hebrew but writing in Greek. The precise reason for this is uncertain; it may have something to do with his expressing in Greek words that were given to him in Hebrew or Aramaic and that he wished to portray as literally as possible in another language. Certainly John's characteristic language is found in Revelation ('witness', 'glory', 'lamb', and other typical vocabulary of John).

Recommended reading: M. Wilcock, *The Message of Revelation* (The Bible Speaks Today, IVP, 1984).

□□□ Reading 344 (Revelation 1:1–20)

1. What is the special blessing attached to this book (1:3)? What will it mean to us practically?

2. John speaks of 'what must soon take place'. 'The time is near' (1:3). It is always possible for God's final day of judgment to break through into the present and we have a foretaste now of God's final judgment, a foretaste of the second coming of Jesus. In what other ways is the second coming always near?

3. The white hair in the vision of Revelation 1:14 speaks of Jesus as the everlasting king. What other symbolism can be found in the vision of Christ's glory?

□□□ Reading 345 (Revelation 2:1–29)

1. Jesus is to send seven letters to seven churches. What were the good points and the points of weakness in the churches of Ephesus, Smyrna, Pergamum and Thyatira?

2. How does Jesus mix encouragement and the sharpness of a two-edged sword with which to pierce our sinfulness or our compromise? How may we be like Jesus in this respect?

3. What are the rewards for 'overcomers'?

☐☐☐ Reading 346 (Revelation 3:1–22)

1. Every congregation needs a different word from the Lord Jesus Christ. What is the distinctive problem of the congregation at Sardis? What is a 'dead' church? How may we be sure that we stay alive? Yet the situation in Sardis was not utterly hopeless. What hope was there for it?
2. What are the five things Sardis must do?
3. The 'book of life' is the list of the citizens of the kingdom of God (see Exodus 32:32–33; Psalm 69:28; Daniel 12:1; Malachi 3:16; Luke 10:20; Philippians 4:3). It is therefore a list of those who potentially qualify for reward. A good illustration of this point is to be found in Esther 2:21–23; 6:1–11. The Christian is in the book of life because he qualifies for reward (remember Colossians 1:12). What are the rewards of heaven?

☐☐☐ Reading 347 (Revelation 4:1–11)

The next section of Revelation runs from 4:1 to 8:1. 'After these things' refers to a new phase of the vision. It does not mean that the events referred to are after the events of Revelation 1:1–3:22.

1. What difference will it make to us if we look at earth from the viewpoint of heaven?
2. The elders represent the entire people of God. The twenty-four is a symbolic twelve plus twelve, speaking of the twelve tribes from twelve brothers who were the origin of Israel, and the twelve apostles who were the origin of the new covenant Church. The vision pictures the entire people of God gathered around the throne of God. What else does John tell us about heaven?
3. The inhabitants of heaven worship God for his creation. What should God's creation mean to us?

☐☐☐ Reading 348 (Revelation 5:1–14)

1. We must remember that Revelation 4:1–8:1 is all one section of 'the Revelation' being given to John. The scroll and the seals are a symbolic way of speaking of the future plans and purposes of God. John weeps at the thought that the purposes of God might be unfulfilled. What difference would it make if God's plan of history did not come to pass?
2. Why is Jesus able to fulfil the purposes of God?
3. In what ways is Christ, the Son of God in the flesh, both a Lion and a Lamb?

□□□ **Reading 349 (Revelation 6:1–17)**

1. Opening the seals is a way of saying 'carry forwards God's purposes in history'. The first horse seems to be a vision of the Lord Jesus Christ. The word 'conquer' has been used frequently by John. Constantly he says the believer may conquer (Revelation 2:7, 11, 17, 26; 3:5, 12, 21) and he explicitly says that the believer conquers as Jesus has conquered (Revelation 3:21). Revelation 5:5 has told us how he conquers – by his death and resurrection. So at this point of the book there is only one person we would think of who is going out 'conquering and to conquer' – the Lord Jesus Christ. If the first horse represents the triumphant preaching of the Lord Jesus Christ, what are the three things that follow the preaching of the gospel (6:3–4; 6:5–6; 6:7–8)?

2. How are we to think about persecution? The book of Revelation is full of this theme (see 1:9; 2:9, 10, 13; 3:10). All who are godly will suffer persecution (2 Timothy 3:12). So what if we are not persecuted?

3. Does the Christian suffer economically because of their faith?

Note The fifth seal (6:9–11) shows the purpose of the Lord Jesus Christ to use martyrs in the progress of his kingdom. The sixth seal (6:12–17) is the end of the world and the final preparation for judgment.

□□□ **Reading 350 (Revelation 7:1–8:1)**

1. We are now expecting the opening of the seventh seal, and it will soon come (in 8:1). But before the end of final judgment and whatever may come with it in the seventh seal, there is another vision. Before John goes on to the last seal (in 8:1) the vision jumps back a stage to let us know that God's elect were not involved in the judgment of the sixth seal. God's people are safe in judgment. But what are the characteristics of God's people? They are God's true Israel (7:4–8).

2. The people of God are 'a great multitude, that no one was able to count' (9:9a). The 144,000 people are a symbolic representation of the whole people of God. It certainly is not a number that is meant to be taken with strict literalness. Scarcely any number in the book of Revelation is literal. By what method can God's judgment totally by-pass God's people?

3. The redeemed 'have come out of great distress'. In the book of Revelation all Christians are people who experience tribulation. Every Christian has to 'overcome' and only 'overcomers' get to the fullness of their final reward. How do we identify with the people of God who are more severely persecuted than we ourselves?

Note Revelation 8:1 closes this section of the book of Revelation. Our chapter divisions give the impression that the trumpets of 8:2–9:21 and 11:15–19 arise as the seventh seal is opened. This is a false impression. Revelation 8:1 closes the section. Revelation 8:2 starts something new. The entire universe reacts with stunned silence for half an hour when the final vision of the last stage of world history is revealed. The Lord is in his holy temple, acting in judgment. Let all the earth keep silence before him! (see Habakkuk 2:20).

□□□ **Reading 351 (Revelation 8:2–13)**

Revelation 8:2–13 is not speaking of something that follows the events of Revelation 1:1–7:17. It is going back and considering them again from another angle. It is not a history of the Church in chronological order. It goes round and round the entire period of the history of the Church from the first to the second coming of the Lord Jesus Christ.

In Revelation 8:2–6, seven angels are given seven trumpets (8:2). Trumpets are used to warn, to sound an alarm. Another angel offers incense upon the incense-altar (8:3–4). Something is about to happen, which is the result of the praying of God's people. Burning coals are thrown upon the earth (8:5). This is a picture of the holiness of God acting in judgment. The angels get ready to blast a warning upon the trumpets (8:6). Then there come four trumpets of warning (8:7, 8–9, 10–11, 12). The seven trumpets fall into a group of four and a group of three. This is emphasised in 8:13. In Revelation 9:1–21 there are two more trumpets (9:1–12, 13–21). Then there comes an interlude in Revelation 10:1–11:14. At this point we read about the seven thunders (10:1–7), the little scroll (10:8–11) and the two witnesses (11:1–14). Then in 11:15–18 we have the seventh trumpet.

1. In the symbolism of the Old Testament incense was something that makes prayer acceptable. How is the symbolism fulfilled?
2. Trumpets are often used for warning, for sounding an alarm. How do the calamities that fall upon the world constitute a warning to us?
3. The story of our world is a story of endless judgments. Embassies are destroyed by bomb attacks. Planes crash. Economies are ruined. Agriculture is ruined. Deserts overtake green pastures. Animals get diseases. Mysterious diseases appear in the human race that have never been known before. Never is there a time when there is not some war being fought somewhere or other. Treaty organisations fail. Peace organisations fail. AIDS and global warming increase. Rivers and seas are polluted. Our book of Revelation gives us pictures of various kinds of judgment – on land, at sea, in rivers, in the sky. Each one comes as a trumpet blast of warning. What is the Christian message? Is it about

social welfare? About political action? Will our world ever function properly? Will these judgments ever cease in our age? What hope is there?

□□□ Reading 352 (Revelation 9:1–21)

1. The fifth judgment is an invasion by evil spirits. Smoke speaks of obscurity, inability to see. Is Satanic attack a judgment of God? 'Five months' (9:6) is a limited period of time. 'Five' is often used to mean 'a few'. In 1 Corinthians 14:19, 'five words' means short limited talk. In Isaiah 30:17 ('five of you will chase a hundred'), 'five' means 'a few'.

2. The sixth trumpet is clearly worse than the first five and yet it is something that takes place before the end and is less than the final judgment. It is a favourite passage for people who think they can tell us exactly what is going to happen in the future. But we cannot totally write the story of history before it happens! Perhaps the sixth trumpet refers to a climax of troubles that come upon the world at some time before the second coming of the Lord Jesus Christ. The River Euphrates was the border of the ideal nation of Israel, which was to stretch from the Nile to the Euphrates (Genesis 15:18). The Euphrates was a barrier between Babylon and Israel. The picture here is of wicked angels wishing to attack the people of God but being held back at the border and unable to fulfil their wishes until a certain time. Then (by God's permission) they are released and are given permission to attack the people of God. When the Babylonians invaded Israel they came from across the River Euphrates. The sixth seal refers to the time when God's people are violently attacked by a mighty evil power.

3. How are we to face the future? If there are fearful events in the story of the world, and (as in the picture-language here) wicked angels have an army of two hundred million fire-breathing, snake-tailed, lion-headed horses, protected by blazingly bright breastplates as armour, how shall we find any sense of peace and security? This is not a photographic preview of modern warfare. The entire picture is symbolic. We are not to think of nuclear warfare, nor of locust-shaped helicopters! Without being too dogmatic (for the ultimate interpretation of prophecy is the fulfilment!) we must say that there will be a latter-day Babylon that is allowed to cross the Euphrates (symbolically) so as to attack the people of God. But will it last long? How will it end? According to 2 Thessalonians 2:1–17 such a time will come to an end as Jesus intervenes by the breath of his mouth (first!) and then (next!) by the brightness of his coming. So how are we to face the prospect of increasing opposition to the gospel?

□□□ **Reading 353 (Revelation 10:1–11)**

In Revelation 4:1–8:1 we had six seals (6:1–17), followed by an interval (7:1–17), followed by the seventh seal (8:1). Here we have six trumpets (8:7–9:21), followed by an interval (10:1–11:13), followed by the seventh seal (11:14–18). In both places the interval is connected with the protection of God's people. In Revelation 10:1–11:13 there are four incidents before the seventh trumpet sounds. There are the seven thunders (10:1–4), the scroll which is both sweet and bitter (10:5–11), the measuring of the temple (11:1–2) and the two witnesses (11:3–13). Then the seventh trumpet is sounded (11:14–18).

1. The 'seven thunders' (10:1–4) are a reminder that some important matters concerning the future are not revealed to us. How does it affect us when we are asked to be willing not to know everything or have all the answers?
2. What encouragement is given to us in 10:6–7?
3. How is the experience of the gospel a mixture of sweetness and bitterness?

□□□ **Reading 354 (Revelation 11:1–18)**

1. Despite world-shaking troubles, God has plans to build his church. The temple represents the people of God. The measuring rod is a sign that God has plans to do some building. What encouragement are we to find in the knowledge that Jesus is the builder of his church?
2. The courtyard outside the temple would generally have religious people in it, but it was the temple itself that was the dwelling-place of God and therefore the symbol of fellowship with God. The point of the symbolism is that God will abandon any Christian 'religion' that has abandoned its genuineness and sincerity (as suggested by Revelation 2:6, 14–16, 20–23; 3:1–3, 16). 'Dead ex-Christianity' is part of the world, not part of the church. What is the difference between the Christian faith and 'ex-Christianity'?
3. In the midst of persecutions, the Christian church will maintain a powerful witness. The two witnesses are a piece of symbolism referring to the whole church as the witness to God's gospel. The 1,260 days are another way of referring to the 3½ years. We do not have to interpret the two witnesses as literally two figures raised from the dead, such as Moses and Elijah. The two witnesses are a symbol of the Church becoming like Moses and Elijah. The Church will have the power of the Holy Spirit. The symbolism of 11:4 comes from Zechariah 4:14. The olive trees are the source of the oil, which supplies bright burning

power to the lamps on the lampstand. What does it mean in practice for the Church to witness in the power of the Holy Spirit?

Note The church has supernatural protection (11:5), and has prayer-power at its disposal (11:6). Yet often after a time of success will come a time of persecution. Revelation 11:7–10 seems to refer to a latter-day persecution that will bring great distress to the church and also to the world itself. But the persecution will not succeed for very long (11:11–13). The ultimate end is the total victory of God (11:14–18).

□□□ Reading 355 (Revelation 11:19–12:17)

In the next section (11:19–15:4) Jesus is victorious over the dragon. The words 'I saw' (or something similar) come in 13:1, 11; 14:1, 6, 14; 15:1, 2. So there are seven small visions with some preliminaries in 11:19–12:17 to prepare us for the visions. There are also seven key figures in this section: (i) the woman (12:1–6); (ii) the dragon (12:3), (iii) the Male Child, (iv) Michael and his angels, (v) the beast from the sea, (vi) the beast from the land and (vii) the lamb.

1. In Revelation 11:19 the scene opens with John seeing again into the throne-room of heaven (11:19). The woman clothed with the sun (12:1) represents the people of God both in their pre-Christian form as Israel and their after-Jesus form as the Christian church. She is about to give birth (12:2). That is, Israel was destined to bring forth the Messiah. The dragon, Satan, fell from heaven, taking many of the angels of heaven with him (12:3). He is ready to destroy the child the moment he is born (12:4). But Jesus was raised from the dead to become God's King (12:5). Now the dragon turns his hatred upon the church (12:6). Like Israel when redeemed by the blood of the Passover lamb, God's people find this world to be a wilderness yet God provides for them. The 1,260 days (sometimes called 'a time, times and half a time', sometimes $3\frac{1}{2}$ years or forty-two ($3\frac{1}{2}$ x 12) months was a symbolic way of speaking of a period of persecution (Ahab persecuted the people of God for about $3\frac{1}{2}$ years; so did Antiochus in the second century BC). Revelation 12:7–17 goes on to tell us of what happens as a result. What happens in the spiritual world as the result of the exaltation of Jesus?

2. What difference will it make to us day-by-day if we take seriously the reality of a spiritual battle taking place between Jesus and Satan, behind the scenes of the ordinary events of life?

3. How powerful is Satan, 'the dragon'? How much has he succeeded or failed in his attempts to destroy 'the child', God's Messiah?

☐☐☐ Reading 356 (Revelation 13:1–18)

1. The dragon looks for help from a beast arising from the sea. 'And the dragon stood on the shore of the sea' (12:18 in some translations; 13:1a in other translations. The translations that have 'And I stood' use inferior manuscripts). The beast from the sea represents worldly governments opposed to God. Verse 3 alludes to Nero. There was a time when he became a fierce persecutor, but then suddenly in AD 68 he committed suicide and Roman persecutions ceased for a short period. For a while people treated the Roman emperor almost as divine (13:4). How does Revelation 13:1–18 relate to Romans 13:1–7?
2. In what ways are the many peoples of the world like the tossing and turning of the sea? Out of this restlessness human kingdoms arise.
3. The beast from the land (13:11–18) is false 'Christian' religion. How does imitation Christianity persecute the people of God?

Note The book of Revelation is largely symbolical and visionary. The kind of interpretation that looks for a literal identification mark (a credit card, a computer, even a car licence number or 666 in one's telephone number!) is forgetting that John's original readers were also meant to be helped by the book of Revelation as well as the modern reader – and in a few years' time today's utilities will be replaced by something else! 'The number of the beast; for it is the number of a man: and his number is six hundred and sixty six' (13:18). What is this '666'? The number is a symbol, not a calculation. It stands for human wickedness raised to its highest power. We remember that man was made on the sixth day of creation. This is 'the number of man' (not 'a' man) – says our text. It represents human-ness gone wrong. It is what men and women become when left to themselves. When pagan government is allied to fake Christianity the worst kind of human beastliness arises. Only the Lord Jesus Christ can conquer it.

☐☐☐ Reading 357 (Revelation 14:1–15:4)

John is presenting to us seven visions of victory. John sees seven visions concerning the conflict between the dragon and the people of God. (i) The dragon receives help from a beast from the sea (12:18–13:10). (ii) Further help for the dragon comes from a beast from the land (13:11–18). (iii) The children of God are pictured as people who are in the company of the Lamb of God, upon Mount Zion (14:1–5). (iv) A fourth vision tells of the coming judgment of God and the fall of a third friend of the dragon, Babylon (14:6–13). (v) The judgment of God is pictured as a time of harvest (14:14–20). (vi) The last plagues bring God's anger to completion (15:1). Then (vii) a seventh vision shows us the entire people of God in their victory over Satan (15:2–4). In the third and fourth visions of this section (14:1–5, 6–13) we are given an assurance that God's people are safe and Babylon is destined to fall.

1. What is the worship of God's people like? What are the people themselves like?
2. What might 'Babylon' represent? What is its equivalent in our world?
3. What exactly is the punishment of Babylon?
4. When does judgment fall? What are the implications of the 'harvest' picture?

□□□ **Reading 358 (Revelation 15:5–16:7)**
In Revelation 15:5–16:21 we have another section of the book. The pattern of a section with seven-of-something continues. We now have seven bowls of God's anger. The trumpets of Revelation 8:2–11:18 gave a warning that wrath is coming. Now the bowls of wrath are a symbolic way of speaking of the actual occasions when God pours out his anger against sin.

1. The gospel is first and foremost a message about salvation from the anger of God against sin. How will this affect our attitude towards much popular religion?
2. In 15:8 the language echoes Isaiah 6:1–13. Judgment proceeds from God's holiness. The visible glory of God – the shining of God's holy character – is present in the vision but it is obscured by the smoke. Why is no one allowed to see the glory of God?
3. Sin is punished within the history of the human race. Does this help us understand some of the calamities in the world? What are the punishments John mentions?

□□□ **Reading 359 (Revelation 16:8–21)**
1. In the case of the fourth trumpet, the sky was affected; something similar happens with the fourth bowl of God's anger (8:12; 16:8–9). In this case a judgment takes place in our world, which affects the sun. Does this make us think of the 'global warming' that is affecting our planet? Could it get worse? John no doubt could not precisely have imagined our 'global warming' but it was revealed to him that God's judgments could affect the very sun that shines upon us.
2. In the case of the fifth trumpet the human race is tormented (9:1–12). Now again in the fifth bowl of God's anger something similar happens (16:10–11). The trumpets and the bowls are running along parallel lines. As a result of the fifth bowl of God's anger, the human race is

attacked not via their environment but directly. It ought to remind us that our safety is found in the Lord Jesus Christ alone. Anything else?

3. Revelation 16:12–16 brings us to the sixth bowl of God's anger. God's judgments will intensify as the end of the world draws near. 'Crossing the Euphrates' is a symbolic way of speaking of attacking the church. When the Euphrates dries up it is easy to cross into Israel. This pictures a time when the church is violently attacked and the entire world is caught up in some great conflict. The 'kings of the east' refers to the enemies of God. Invaders of Israel and its neighbours were thought of as coming from the east (see, for example, Isaiah 41:2). The prophecy sees the church's protection taken away (Euphrates dried up) and all the possible invaders coming to destroy God's people. It is picture-language. There are no longer 'kings' in the old way; Israel's border no longer reaches the Euphrates. God's restructured 'Israel' now has gentiles in it and is now the international people of the Lord Jesus Christ. The Bible speaks of a day when the Church of the Lord Jesus Christ will face massive opposition. How do we face the future? Blessed are they who stay awake! Blessed is the person who 'keeps his clothes with him'. What does this mean in practice?

Note The battle at 'Armageddon'. This is John's way – and Jesus' way – of picturing a time when there will be very fierce conflict between the world and the Church. All sorts of strange ideas are around about 'Armageddon'. The word 'Ar' or 'Har' is Hebrew for 'mountain' or 'hill'. 'Mageddon' is the town Megiddo, a town in the south-west part of the valley of Jezreel. There have been some famous battles there.

Some believe that the Lord Jesus Christ will return to earth in two stages with a seven-year gap between the two stages. The idea comes from an unlikely interpretation of Daniel 9:24–27. Then the theory is that the 'battle of Armageddon' comes into human history towards the end of the seven years. But the seven-year theory is based on one of the most difficult passages of the Bible, and one should surely not base an entire system of interpretation on one verse that is difficult to interpret! What we have here is symbolism and picture-language. There are in fact no mountains in the valley of Jezreel. But in picture-language taken from Ezekiel 38:1–39:29 a great battle against the people of God takes place in 'the mountains of Israel' (see Ezekiel 38:8, 21; 39:2, 4, 17). We have here a picture put together from the many famous battles at Megiddo combined with the idea of a battle being fought on a large area of high ground. Actually the valley of Jezreel is not high ground, but this ought to confirm that what we have here is picture-language and symbolism.

'Armageddon' is a picture of a worldwide conflict between sin and righteousness, between Jesus and his church (on the one side) and Satan and the forces of wickedness (on the other side). The church does not use literal weapons. The weapons of our warfare are spiritual. Elsewhere the picture-language is different and the battle takes place not at Megiddo but at Jerusalem. That is picture-language as well! If you take the pictures literally you have a lot of contradictions! The 'mountains' of Megiddo have never existed! Satan is always wanting to destroy the church. One day God will allow Satan a time to oppress the church. It will not last very long and it will not succeed. Jesus goes on reigning. Satan will have his 'little season' (Revelation 20:3). A day of triumph has to come first. The nations of the world must be reached.

Revelation 16:17–21 is describing in picture-language the 'bottom of the cup'. Finally the world must drink the cup of God's anger to the very bottom.

☐☐☐ Reading 360 (Revelation 17:1–18)

In the last sections of the book of Revelation (Revelation 17:1–19:10; 19:11–21:8; 21:9–22:21), the question is being asked more than ever: Who is going to win this mighty spiritual battle, the dragon or the child, the devil or the Lord Jesus Christ? Christ has had five enemies according to Revelation 1:1–16:21: (i) the dragon (Satan), (ii) the beast from the sea (pagan government), (iii) the beast from the land (false religion), also called the false prophet, (iv) Babylon (worldly indulgence) and (v) men and women bearing the mark of the beast (the world in its hatred of God). The minor units of this section are marked by new topics, new voices, new angels, new sights.

1. The prostitute or 'the great harlot' (see 17:5, 15, 16; 19:2) is a symbol of the world in its love of fleshly indulgence. Why is the world described in this way?
2. What are the characteristics of the world (pictured in this way)? The great harlot (worldly indulgence) is influential. Anything else?
3. Fleshly indulgence and pagan government go together. Worldly greed is pictured first as a drunken woman riding on an animal (17:3b–6a), and then as a woman sitting on seven hills (17:6b–18). The beast has seven heads. The seven heads stand for the famous seven hills on which is built the city of Rome. In John's day, pagan government meant the government of the Roman empire. (The seven heads do not stand for seven modern kings! People who try to identify them with modern rulers contradict each other and are soon proved mistaken.) The beast has ten horns. They stand for political and military power. (We remember that the 'ten horns' of Daniel 7:7 stand for 'ten kings', according to Daniel 7:24.) The entire vision speaks of paganism, military power, persecution, and control of the economy in the interests of wickedness.

'The beast was . . .' John is thinking of Nero and the great persecutions that had troubled the church at that time. 'The beast . . . is not.'

Nero died. 'The beast . . . is about to come up out of the abyss.' John expects state persecution to return. The beast will come up out of the abyss to persecute God's people.

What is the final end of 'the beast'? The 'seventh king' is John's way of speaking of 'antichrist' – or whatever name one wants to give to a powerful enemy of God and his people who arises in the last days. The vision predicts the intensification of persecuting paganism (17:12). Yet the vision also predicts the victory of God's people (17:14a). Verse 17 looks back over the previous sixteen verses and explains why it is that this mighty rebellion against God should ever be allowed: 'For God has put a plan into their minds, a plan that will carry out his purposes' (17:17a). How does wickedness ever achieve God's will? What is the threefold secret of victory, according to John?

☐☐☐ Reading 361 (Revelation 18:1–19:10)

1. John sees the fall of Babylon (18:1–3). Then he hears a voice calling for separation from Babylon (18:4–24). It does not mean that the Christians are to be superior or pharisaical in their attitudes, or that they must withdraw from contact with people, or that they must treat worldly people as enemies in a personal manner. But what does it mean?

2. Not only are rulers caught up in Babylon's judgment. Business people and 'the merchants of the earth' are involved too (18:11–13). Seven groups of articles are involved: treasures (gold, silver, precious stones, pearls), fabrics (linen, purple, silk, scarlet cloth), materials for furnishing houses (scented wood, ivory, expensive wooden utensils, bronze, iron, marble), sweet-smelling herbs or oils (cinnamon, spice, incense, ointment, frankincense), foods (wine, oil, fine flour, wheat), domestic animals (cattle, sheep, horses for chariots) and human beings (slaves, human lives). What does this tell us about righteousness in business?

3. God's people will be happy to see Babylon disappear (19:1–10). Is it ever right to rejoice in God's judgment of others?

☐☐☐ Reading 362 (Revelation 19:11–20:6)

At the end of Revelation 19:10 we have been brought (once again) to the end of the world, and the final judgment of sin. Then 'the curtain opens' on a new scene. 'I then saw heaven opened . . .' says John. After this 'raising of the curtain' we again find seven visions. When we get to Revelation 21:9 there is again a new angel and a major transfer to a new scene. We may call the section 'Visions of Victory' and divide it as follows:

- The glorious Lord Jesus Christ (19:11–16)
- The supper of God (19:17–18)
- Beast, kings and false prophet – all destroyed (19:19–21)
- Satan bound (20:1–3)
- Martyrs raised; Satan conquered (20:4–10)
- The final judgment (20:11–15)
- The new creation (21:1–8)

This section is not to be thought of as following historically what has happened in the previous vision. There is no need to think that Babylon was destroyed and then later some of the other enemies of God were destroyed. Nor does the binding of Satan have to be a *later* event. The visions come one after another, but the visions are not necessarily fulfilled in historical sequence, one after the other in history. Rather what we have here is that in one vision after another the allies of Satan and then Satan himself are being conquered. The book of Revelation is spiral or 'parallelist' in structure. It goes round and round like a spiral staircase. The curtain opens and closes and opens again to give us revelations about the same gospel-age of the human history.

In Revelation 19:11–16, John again sees a vision of the glorious Lord Jesus Christ. In another small vision, an angel is calling the vultures to come to the supper of God where the food will be corpses for the vultures (19:17–18). In a third vision, the beast and the kings of the earth are wanting to make war against Jesus, the rider of the white horse (19:19) but the beast and his ally the false prophet are both thrown into the lake of fire for punishment and destruction (19:20). The rest of the enemies of God are killed by the rider on the white horse (19:21).

Then there is a fourth vision and the story goes on (or jumps back) to start considering how Satan is progressively destroyed. Before the time when Satan is thrown into the lake of fire where the beast and false prophet are to be found, there is an earlier stage when Satan is bound for a thousand years (20:1–3).

In a fifth vision, martyrs are seen raised from the dead (20:4–6). Then after the thousand years Satan goes out to make war against the saints (20:7–9a), but Satan is defeated and thrown into the lake of fire also (20:9b–10). If the war against Jesus in 19:19 and the war against Jesus in 20:7–9 is the same war, then 20:1–6 has jumped back to give a run-up to the same point when beast-and-prophet-and-Satan are destroyed.

Then in 20:11–15 we have the sixth vision, revealing the last judgment and the extermination of Death and Hades and of the wicked. It is followed by the seventh vision, the introduction of the new universe (21:1–8). The entire section is intensely rich and controversial. Yet one thing is sure: in all of it Jesus is the great Overcomer.

1. Our Lord Jesus Christ rides out like a military conqueror to defeat all enemies. This passage is sometimes thought to be a symbolic representation of the second coming of our Lord Jesus Christ. Yet there are reasons for thinking that it rather represents what Jesus does in history before his second coming. This is a picture of Jesus leading his Church in defeating his enemies, by means of the 'sharp sword' of the gospel. If there is to be a 'marriage supper of the lamb', there is also to be a 'supper of God' – a day when sin is defeated. How triumphant are we expecting the gospel of the Lord Jesus Christ to be before his second coming?

2. A question we might ask ourselves is: What are the implications of the different views of the millennium? Which is pessimistic? Which is motivating? Which fits with the rest of the book of Revelation?

3. What encouragement does Revelation 20:4–6 give to those who suffer for the sake of the gospel?

Note The Millennium of Revelation 20:1–3. There is a third enemy of God to be defeated, the greatest of all, Satan. Revelation 20:1–3 is of course immensely controversial. (i) Some believe that Jesus' second coming comes before this 'binding' of Satan. They are called 'premillennialists' because they believe the second coming will be before ('pre') the event of Revelation 20:1–3. The 'millennium' commences (they believe) at the end of this gospel-age when Jesus comes. These interpreters reckon that the second coming is referred to in Revelation 19:1–21 and so (taking the visions as fulfilled in chronological order in history) they take 20:1–3 to refer to a period of history *after* the second coming but before the final glory mentioned in Revelation 22:1–21. (ii) Some believe that the binding of Satan is the same as the binding that took place in Jesus' death and resurrection. They are called 'amillennialists' because they believe there is no ('a-' means 'no') special 'golden age' either before or after the second coming of Jesus. These people ought to be called 'gospel-age millennialists'. They believe the gospel-age – the time between the first and second comings of Jesus – is the millennium. This means that they understand Revelation 12:1–17 and 20:1–15 to be exactly parallel. Satan is bound now (not in every respect but in his ability to deceive the nations). This 'gospel-age millennialism' believes that the age for the preaching of the gospel is the millennium of Revelation 20:1–3. (iii) In connection with Revelation 20:4–6 there is also an interpretation (which is often combined with 'gospel-age millennialism' in 20:1–3) that I could call 'heaven-millennialism'. The millennium (it is said) is heaven. The Christian who dies for his faith is 'resurrected' to glory. His soul is raised to heaven and Satan cannot touch him. This view of the matter is somewhat easier to hold if one believes that there is a preliminary resurrection at death. (iv) Some interpreters believe that the casting of Satan into the abyss is to take place at some stage in church history but before the second coming of Jesus. They are 'post-millennialists' because they believe that the second coming is to be after ('post-') the event of Revelation 20:1–3. On this view, Revelation 20:1–3 refers to a period of eventual success in the preaching of the gospel in this gospel-age. It could be called 'victory-of-the-gospel millennialism' or 'latter-day-glory millennialism'. At some stage in the gospel-age, before the coming of Jesus, Satan is defeated more than he has ever been defeated before, and the gospel triumphs among the nations. The main argument for this view is that it fits with much that has already been said in the book of Revelation. Revelation 20:1–3 refers to an intensification within the gospel-age of the defeat of the devil that has already taken place at the cross. It is a further reduction in Satan's power that comes about by the preaching of the gospel. We may expect a 'golden age' within the gospel-age. Satan is 'thrown to the abyss' when the power of the blood of Christ is pressed against him. They overcame him – threw him to the abyss, one might say – by the blood of the Lamb . . . On this view the victory of Revelation 20:1–3 is greater than the victory of 12:1–17. (v) If one looks only at Revelation 20:1–6 one might be tempted to think that the millennium and the judgment day are identical. A few writers have held this view.

In Revelation 20:4–6 the phrase 'Then I saw' does not demand that, in the historical fulfilment of the vision, 20:4–6 takes place after 20:1–3. On the contrary it is likely that 20:1–3 and 20:4–6 are two units both describing the same period. Revelation 20:4 picks up from the distressing scene in Revelation 6:1–17. The martyrs are asking for vindication. The people in Revelation 20:4–6 are the entire triumphant and victorious Church that has moved on to heaven – pictured as a martyr-Church. There seem to be two categories: (i) those who were faithful to the point of death and are now reigning with Christ – but were not actually killed and (ii) those who were actually killed in one way or another, for the Lord Jesus Christ. We will be able to follow Revelation 20:4–6 if we realise that it answers a question arising out of 20:1–3. The first three verses of the chapter present a picture of the Church reaching wonderful success in overcoming the forces of evil. But there is an obvious question in this: What do we feel about those who laid down their lives to contribute to this success of the gospel? It is wonderful that Satan gets to be thrown into the abyss! But how terrible that it should be at so great a cost of the lives of thousands of Christians. John says: I did not only see the triumph of the Church (20:1–3). I saw also the triumph of the martyrs (20:4–6)! 'They came alive and reigned with Christ a thousand years.' So what kind of resurrection is in view here? (i) If the millennium and the judgment day were the same thing, it would mean that the martyrs are raised early in 'the judgment day' and take part in God's judgment of the rest of humanity. (ii) If we hold to the amillennialist viewpoint it might refer to 'going to heaven' or the new birth or 'being united with Christ in his resurrection'. (iii) If we are premillennialists it will refer to a literal millennium ahead of the final judgment day – with much more to happen in the history of the world, before the end of the world. (iv) Most 'golden age of the gospel' millennialists think that this resurrection is a spiritual matter (as in Romans 11:15 where 'life from the dead' almost certainly refers to worldwide revival). Such interpreters think that the 'first resurrection' is a resurrection of the influence of the martyrs. The Holy Spirit honours their teaching, and so on. A more convincing option for post-millennialists is to take the 'first resurrection' to mean that the martyr-Church of the book of Revelation gets raised from the dead, as soon as they die, before the unsaved, and before the backslidden Christians. The people mentioned here are 'overcomers'. They are given glorious resurrection bodies before anyone else, as in Revelation 6:9–12. The 'rest of the dead' is everyone else. It will involve the lost, and it will include the rebellious Christian. The reward for the martyrs is companionship with and involvement with the Lord Jesus Christ.

□□□ Reading 363 (Revelation 20:7–21:8)

1. Revelation 20:7–10, we have a vision of something that happens after the symbolic thousand years. Satan is allowed to be a deceiver again. There are various passages of Scripture that seem to teach that towards the end of the gospel-age there will come a mighty resistance to the Church. That resistance is present even now. 'The mystery of lawlessness is already operating', said Paul (2 Thessalonians 2:7). Many antichrists are already here, according to 1 John (see 1 John 2:18). How are we to interpret (i) optimistic and (ii) sobering prophecies within Scripture? Should we try to reconcile them?
2. What is the nature of the final judgment? Everyone is present at it. What else can we say?
3. Revelation 21:1–8 is the last sub-unit of this section. What is the ultimate hope of the Christian?

□□□ Reading 364 (Revelation 21:9–26)

Again (as in 21:1–8) the people of God are at the same time a bride and a city. The one picture speaks of purity and beauty and preparedness. The other speaks of closeness among people and the authority of God as king of his city. But now the vision is described more fully. It is a vision of the people of God as they approach their final glory. Questions that must be asked are: Is this a description of the people of God as they are now? Is it a picture of the way they will be in the day of gospel-success? Or is it a picture of the people of God as they will be for ever and ever in their final situation? I answer: it is all three! In Revelation 21:1–8 the old world has passed away (21:1). All wickedness and suffering – everything that makes one cry – is abolished (21:3, 4). 'The first things are passed away' altogether. God makes all things new (21:4). Revelation 21:5 speaks of the faithfulness of God, and his determination to see that this takes place. It is as good as done (21:6). But in Revelation 21:9–22:5 we see a fuller version of the same vision. In Revelation 21:1–8 the starting-point of the final glory was available even at that moment (21:6). The promise was being held out (21:7). Now in 21:9–22:5 we have a fuller picture of what is involved. It is a glimpse of all that is to happen as the final glory is introduced, and so it includes some stages along the way. Between the opening word (21:9) and the closing remark (22:20–21) there are seven revelations of final glory.

1. In what way is the Church like a bride and like a city?
2. 'The leaves of the tree are for the healing of the nations' (22:2). At what stage of history is this? The city exists now; what happens in John's vision is that it comes down upon earth but it existed even before it came down! Hebrews 12:22 says, 'You have come to the heavenly Jerusalem – already!' The Church is already the fiancée of the Lord Jesus Christ, getting ready for the marriage supper. Do we have here both the success of the gospel and what will happen as the final glory of the Church is introduced, and God 'makes all things new'? In what way does the Church heal the nations?
3. What is the character of the city? Brightness. It has a wall, speaking of distinctiveness, separation, protection. It has gates. It is for the entire people of God (as its edges of twelve thousand 'stadia' and the total of 144,000 emphasise). It is measured and cubical. The gates are precious; the streets are precious. What do each of these characteristics (and others) represent?

□□□ **Reading 365 (Revelation 22:1–21)**
1. God's kingdom is like a flowing river of life. What is the value of a river? What is the special blessing of the kingdom of God? What is this river like? Where does this river come from? Where does it flow to?
2. Nowadays many people are interested in curses inherited from ancestors, but the Bible has more to say about the curse of God against planet Earth because of human sin. What is the good news at the end of Revelation – about the end of curses?
3. The book of Revelation ends with a celebration of God's faithfulness. In what ways is God faithful in the final story of the Church?

APPENDIX: THE TRANSLATION OF HOSEA

Often it is thought that the text of Hosea is more corrupt than many books of the Old Testament, but this is too superficial, and modern discoveries have taught us things about biblical Hebrew that were unappreciated a hundred years ago. There is probably only one place in Hosea where it is certain the Hebrew text should be emended (7:14b). But there are about fifteen verses where it is likely some vowel-pointing should be read in a way that differs from the traditional Hebrew text. (One must remember that the vowel-pointing is not original but stems from the ninth century.) This is a very conservative decision. The *New English Bible* alters the Hebrew text in about ninety places, half of which and emended without any definite evidence at all but only on the basis of intelligent guesswork. A better procedure (followed by F. I. Andersen, in *Hosea* [Doubleday, 1980], and by myself, in *Hosea* [Christian Focus, 1980]) is to leave the text alone as much as possible, but reconsider the vowel-points in difficult passages. The following points will assist in a close reading of the text.

A vowel-point emendation in 1:4 is so tiny it would be noticed only by experts; it scarcely affects translations.

Most translations of 1:7 have something like 'I will not yet again pity the house of Israel . . . Yet I will show love to the house of Judah . . .'. Commentators have noted that this is out of harmony with Hosea's message. The difficulties are overcome if it is realised that the phrase 'not yet again' extends over four verbs, and the Hebrew preposition 'b' may mean 'from' with verbs of departure or verbs of rescue. The Hebrew may be over-literally translated:

> Call her name Lo-Ruhammah for I will not yet again pity the house of Israel, for I will surely [not yet again] forgive them. And the house of Judah I will [not yet again] pity, and I will [not yet again] save them as Yahweh their God. And I will not save them from the bow or from the sword or from war, from horses or horsemen.

Most translations sense that the negative force has to extend over two verbs, but actually the 'never again' may continue over the next two verbs also. There is nowhere in Hosea where God treats Israel one way and Judah another way. 'The Israelites stumble . . . Judah also stumbles with them' (5:5). God is a lion to Israel, and a lion to Judah alike (5:14) and asks, 'What can I do?' about both nations equally (6:4; see also 5:12, 13; 6:10–11; 8:14; 10:11).

In 4:4 the following translation involves no consonantal emendation.

> Surely God has a controversy with a certain person.
> And there is a person God reproves.
> With you surely is my controversy O priest!

In 4:7 also:

> As they became great, so they sinned against me.
> Their glory they changed into their shame.

In 4:10–12:

> They have forsaken Yahweh to keep harlotry.
> Harlotry, wine and new wine take away the heart of my people.
> He makes enquiry from his wood; and his staff reports to him.
> For by a spirit of promiscuity he has led people astray.
> And they act promiscuously in defiance of their God.

In 4:14:

> I will surely send punishment upon your daughters because they are
>   promiscuous,
> and I will send punishment upon your daughters-in-law because they
>   commit adultery.
> The men actually couple themselves with harlots

and they offer sacrifices with 'sacred' prostitutes.
A people without understanding will surely come to ruin.

In 4:15 a likely translation (without emendation) is:

Israel, you are surely not to be a harlot.
Let not Judah be guilty.
And do not come to Gilgal.
And do not go up to Beth-Aven.
And do not swear 'As Yahweh lives'.

In 5:13, 'he sent to the great king' is the best translation (not 'king Jareb' or 'a king who will contend').

The last line of 6:5 (with some re-pointing) is best translated: 'And my judgment is like the light when it emerges.'

Hosea 7:4 may (with some repointing) be read:

All of them are adulterers,
they are like a burning oven.

Most scholars agree that 7:14b should read (with a small emendation):

For the sake of grain and new wine
they slash themselves.

With a tiny change in the vowel-point Hosea 8:2 reads:

They cry out to me,
'God of Israel, we know you!'

As in 5:13 we should read 10:6 as follows.

Also, he will be carried to Assyria
as a gift to the great king.

Hosea 10:11 is best translated:

And Ephraim – whom I love –
is a heifer, trained to thresh the grain.
I have put a yoke upon her fair neck.
I harnessed Ephraim; Judah may cultivate the ground.
Let Jacob break up the ground for himself.

Leaving the Hebrew text alone except for a minor change in a vowel-point, the text of 11:2–5, 7 may be translated:

Others also called to them;
in this way they departed from me.
They offered sacrifices to Baal,
and to images they burn incense.
Yet it was I who was a guide for Ephraim,
taking them by the arms.
They did not acknowledge that it was I who healed them.
I used to pull them with cords of human kindness;
with ties of love
I was to them like those who take the yoke off of the jaws;
I heard their plea and strengthened them.
He shall surely return to the land of Egypt,
and Assyria will be his king,
for they have refused to turn around.
My people are determined to turn from me,
and to their 'High God' they call,
but their god cannot lift them up at all.